Crisis

ALSO AVAILABLE FROM BLOOMSBURY:

Lacan, Miguel de Beistegui
The New Heidegger, Miguel de Beistegui

Crisis

A Critique

Miguel de Beistegui

BLOOMSBURY ACADEMIC
LONDON · NEW YORK · OXFORD · NEW DELHI · SYDNEY

BLOOMSBURY ACADEMIC
Bloomsbury Publishing Plc, 50 Bedford Square, London, WC1B 3DP, UK
Bloomsbury Publishing Inc, 1359 Broadway, New York, NY 10018, USA
Bloomsbury Publishing Ireland, 29 Earlsfort Terrace, Dublin 2, D02 AY28, Ireland

BLOOMSBURY, BLOOMSBURY ACADEMIC and the Diana logo are trademarks of
Bloomsbury Publishing Plc

First published in Great Britain 2026

Copyright © Miguel de Beistegui, 2026

Miguel de Beistegui has asserted his right under the Copyright, Designs and Patents Act, 1988, to be identified as Author of this work.

For legal purposes the Acknowledgements on p. ix constitute an extension of this copyright page.

Cover image by DeAgostini via Getty Images

All rights reserved. No part of this publication may be: i) reproduced or transmitted in any form, electronic or mechanical, including photocopying, recording or by means of any information storage or retrieval system without prior permission in writing from the publishers; or ii) used or reproduced in any way for the training, development or operation of artificial intelligence (AI) technologies, including generative AI technologies. The rights holders expressly reserve this publication from the text and data mining exception as per Article 4(3) of the Digital Single Market Directive (EU) 2019/790.

Bloomsbury Publishing Plc does not have any control over, or responsibility for, any third-party websites referred to or in this book. All internet addresses given in this book were correct at the time of going to press. The author and publisher regret any inconvenience caused if addresses have changed or sites have ceased to exist, but can accept no responsibility for any such changes.

A catalogue record for this book is available from the British Library.

A catalog record for this book is available from the Library of Congress.

ISBN: HB: 978-1-3505-8882-0
PB: 978-1-3505-8886-8
ePDF: 978-1-3505-8883-7
eBook: 978-1-3505-8884-4

Typeset by Deanta Global Publishing Services, Chennai, India
Printed and bound in Great Britain

For product safety related questions contact productsafety@bloomsbury.com.

To find out more about our authors and books visit www.bloomsbury.com and sign up for our newsletters.

Contents

Preface to Crisis: A Critique vi
Acknowledgments ix

Introduction 1
1   Crisis: A Brief Critical History 19
2   Crises of Exception 73
3   Crises of Contradiction 99
4   Deconstructing Crisis? 157
5   Crises of Extinction, or Gaia in Peril 183
Conclusion 247

Notes 255
Index 322

Preface to Crisis: A Critique

Every book has its dominant mood. This one was born of a state of existential and historical *angst*. It is shared by many across the world; and it is experienced in ways that are far more acute by many more. Not a day goes by when I do not feel a profound unease, a combination of frustration, despair, and anger, when reading or turning on the news: yet another climate tipping point has been crossed and yet another fire has ravaged the earth; yet another makeshift boat full of migrants fleeing zones of conflict and hardship has sunk in the Mediterranean or the Atlantic; yet another social movement, indicative of the ravages of globalisation and the limits of the model of growth, largely based on the systematic extraction of fossil fuels, has been ignored; yet another blow has been dealt to the social-democratic model; yet another act of unspeakable violence, often of a racist nature, has torn through our social fabric; yet another far or ultra-right party has won an election. Things seem to go from bad to worse at an alarming speed; and they have done so since I completed this book. War crimes, genocides and the persecution of minorities are carried out by supposedly democratic governments. The rule of law is under attack, whether through the systematic recourse to (spurious) emergency measures, the threat of annexation, or the "war" declared against migrants, political opponents, the intellectual class, science (climate and medical science especially), journalists, or marginalised communities. Authoritarianism, constitutional dictatorships and new forms of fascism are on the rise. Largely facilitated by the algorithms of social media, fear, suspicion and even hatred increasingly dominate our lives. The absurd and deeply troubling Orwellian world, in which black is white, up is down, and true is false, has become *our* world. Again.

The daily spectacle of this depressing situation is hard, almost impossible, to watch. Yet, like so many, I can't help watching; and like so many, I feel at once took close to it, and too distant from it—nervous and numb at the same time, hypervigilant and almost catatonic. A few years ago, I decided to face the music: could I describe the reality behind the mixed, painful emotions so many of us experience daily? Could the word "crisis" capture both the complex situation we face and the emotions it generates? Our time, I realised, is one of deep, multiple and mutually reinforcing crises. Our economies, democracies, social relations, labour relations, constitutions, cultures, identities, physical bodies are subjected to repeated and increasingly severe shocks. How did those crises come about? Are they the manifestation of one monumental crisis, or are they different crises, tied into a very tight knot? Today, the vocabulary of crisis is ubiquitous. It has become common, almost ordinary, whether in political discourse, the media, or scientific journals and books. This should give us pause for thought. For there is no doubt that crisis is easily instrumentalised, even weaponized. Especially today. All the more reasons to try and understand what we mean and say when we speak of crisis. Can all crises be said to be crises *in the same sense*? Or is crisis one of those loose terms that designates events and situations which are in fact very different? The time was ripe, I felt, for a new philosophy, and specifically a *critique*, of crisis.

Have I taken on too momentous a task? For how can I claim to speak convincingly of the ecological catastrophe, the legal mechanism of the state of exception, financial crashes and economic downturns, the general strike and street riots, as well as genocides? How, as a philosopher, can I draw on climate science and the life sciences, legal theory, political economy and economics, as well as the history of philosophy, without running the risk of peddling in generalities and spreading myself thin? I regularly shared those doubts. Ultimately, though, I felt that the work of philosophy was precisely that of identifying and questioning the threads which, held together tightly, shape our lives and define our current predicament. Instead of being overwhelmed by the mixed and often contradictory emotions so many of us feel in these troubled times—agitation and apathy; a readiness to act, however brashly, and utter paralysis; loss and grief, but of an undefined nature—I felt it was imperative to develop the conceptual tools that will enable us to analyse, question, criticise and hopefully overcome the crises that define our historical horizon and individual lives. For ultimately, the question is not simply that of knowing how we got to this point. It is also to ask how we can extricate ourselves from this state of chronic crisis, imagine a better future, and yes, lift our mood.

Acknowledgments

I am fortunate to have benefited from conversations and exchanges with colleagues and friends whilst writing this book. I am especially grateful to former colleagues at the Centre for Research in Philosophy, Literature, and the Arts at the University of Warwick (UK); at the Research Forum of the Department of Political and Social Sciences at the University of Pompeu Fabra (Barcelona); at the Department of Aesthetics at the University of Tokyo; at the Department of Philosophy at the University of Ca'Foscari in Venice. Special thanks to Victoria Rimmell, Camil Ungureanu, Veronica Benet-Martinez, Tanehisa Otabe, and Emmanuele Lepore. An equal debt is owed to the postgraduate students from my students at Universitat Pompeu Fabra who listened to early versions of this book and responded to some of its theses. I am also grateful to the anonymous reviewers of the manuscript for their generous comments and helpful suggestions. Finally, I owe an immense debt of gratitude to Liza Thompson, my editor, whose support and enthusiasm for this project have been nothing short of extraordinary.

Introduction

I belong to what could be called the '89 generation—the generation that, following the collapse of the Berlin Wall, saw the emergence of the narrative of the triumph of liberal and free market economies. Francis Fukuyama was arguably this narrative's most enthusiastic advocate: freedom, he remarked at the time, is finally spreading across the globe, and is unstoppable. Because the *ideal* of liberal democracy cannot be improved on, the new eschatology claimed, liberalism is "the final form of human government," the "end" or unsurpassable "horizon" of History.[1] For Fukuyama, the arrow of history seemed to point in one direction, and one direction only. This meant that while the path toward that end could very well be circuitous and arduous, the principles of equality, liberty, and mutual recognition on which it rests would ultimately triumph across the globe. Unsurprisingly, the word "crisis" does not appear in Fukuyama's book: the end of history is also the end of crisis, and the collapse of the Soviet world only the latest stage in the completion of a historical process.[2] The new iteration of this old (for deeply Christian) eschatology promised the end of the divisions, struggles, and wars that had plagued the twentieth century. A couple of centuries before, the Swiss philosopher of history and politics Isaak Iselin had formulated a similar theory of history as accelerated, cumulative progress. In the fifth edition of his *History of Humanity*, Iselin inserted a discussion of crisis, but he emptied the word of its usual connotations. He describes events such as the division of Poland and the American War of Independence as "moral thunderstorms that will finally clear the air and create joy and tranquillity." These events, he adds, "seem to justify the supposition that Europe is in the midst of a crisis far more serious and dangerous than any since it began to be civilized. While we fearful observers should view this crisis, though distant, as a danger, it offers us rather comforting and hopeful visions of the future."[3]

My generation should have known better. The '89 narrative was just another iteration of the historicism that had dominated European thought in the nineteenth century and been dealt a severe blow after the catastrophe of the Great War. Had we bothered to open other books, such as Guattari's *The Three Ecologies*, published the same year as Fukuyama's influential article, we would have heard a different, less optimistic tune.[4] In his book, Guattari diagnoses a deep, threefold ecological crisis, involving the environment, social relations, and the human mind.[5] Far from signaling a new dawn, Guattari claims, the disappearance of the East-West antagonism and the triumph of liberal democracy will progressively reveal, and most likely reinforce, the environmental crisis, the deterioration of social (including labor) relations, and the narrowing of the existential sphere and human creativity. In his book, Guattari foresees the triumph of a limited subjectivity defined by mass consumption, the homogenization of habits and ways of thinking, the internalization of neoliberal norms of behavior such as productivity, profitability, and flexibility, and the infiltration of "the most unconscious strata" of the human mind by new technologies of surveillance and control. The latter phenomenon has become particularly palpable in the age of social media, data mining, artificial intelligence, and "algorithmic governmentality."[6] New forms of subjectivation and regimes of power have emerged. Through their algorithms, those regimes produce virtual bodies, or bodies at the intersection of the organic and the numerical, which move between pre-identified spaces and categories. The social, economic, political, and aesthetic existence of those bodies is entirely mediated by, or filtered through, numerical programs that reward the recognition, reproduction, and reinforcement of identical patterns, especially those that breed division and hatred.

Guattari supplements his diagnosis with a word of warning: for want of a necessary "ecosophical revival" and a rearticulation of the three fundamental types of ecology—environmental, social, and mental—we can "unfortunately predict the rise of all kinds of danger: racism, religious fanaticism, nationality schisms that suddenly flip into reactionary closure, the exploitation of child labor, the oppression of women. . . ."[7] Those words were prescient: in recent decades, the world saw the invention or expansion of technologies of control and programming, of information gathering and tracking, of manipulation of behaviors and granular targeting of profiles, of social media addiction, and of ideological polarization, as well as the return of disturbing modes of fixation on the past, such as nationalism, religious fanaticism, and even fascism.[8] Labor relations were also transformed. The neoliberal revolution, which began in the early 1980s, coincided with the restoration of cheap labor through wage repression and stagnation; the deindustrialization of key sectors in the North and the rapid industrialization of the global South; the rise of the "flexible" two-income household and the combination of (poorly) paid and unpaid (domestic) work for women; the emergence of the gig economy and the creation of a new, self-employed and atomized proletariat, which struggles to make their countries' minimum wage and lacks the protection and benefits associated with employment. In truth, the collapse of the molar opposition between East and West was quickly replaced by other, equally molar machines—the Facebook, Google, or Amazon machine; the military machine, now unhindered; the religious fundamentalist machine; the paranoid conspiracy-theory machine; and, of course, the techno-capitalistic, growth-addicted, resource-plundering, biosphere-destroying machine.

The Trump phenomenon, which Guattari dissected as early as 1989, is perhaps the most acute symptom of those three interconnected crises:

> Just as monstrous and mutant algae invade the lagoon of Venice, so our television screens are populated, saturated, by "degenerate" images and statements. In the field of social ecology, men like Donald Trump are permitted to proliferate freely, like another species of algae, taking over entire districts of New York and Atlantic City [and Gaza?]; he "redevelops" by raising rents, thereby driving out tens of thousands of poor families, most of whom are condemned to homelessness, becoming the equivalent of the dead fish of environmental ecology.[9]

Even at his most pessimistic, Guattari (who died in 1992) could not have predicted the political rise and triumph of Donald Trump, and the antidemocratic, fascistic forces that swept across America and much of Europe immediately after the height of the narrative of the end of history and the explicit, disastrous attempt, by the likes of Donald Rumsfeld and Dick Cheney, to spread them across the world through military intervention.

Fast forward thirty years. The end of history in the form of the triumph of liberalism has given way to a proliferation of crises internal to liberal, and especially *neoliberal* democracies. Iselin's "comforting and hopeful visions of the future" seem like a distant dream, if not a delusion. I write these lines as the war in Ukraine is entering its fourth year, destruction and killing on a massive scale is happening in Gaza, and the world experienced its first global pandemic. Not a day goes by that we do not hear of a crisis, declared or looming: the energy crisis, the humanitarian crisis, the national health service crisis, the mental health crisis, the housing crisis, the prison crisis, the police crisis, the race crisis, the identity crisis, the migration crisis, the education crisis, the constitutional crisis, the economic crisis. The list seems endless. Barack Obama spoke of an "epistemological crisis" to describe the way many democratic societies, including his own, increasingly blur the lines between what is true and what is false and subordinate truth to political ends, thus marking the beginning of the "post-truth" era; others have also used such terminology.[10] His words rang true then. They ring even truer now, after a Trump-supporting mob assaulted Capitol Hill in January 2021, the launch of Trump's social media platform—called simply *Truth*—following his ban from Facebook, and his reelection as president of the United States of America, which was itself largely facilitated by Elon Musk's social media platform. Plutocracy in America has never been more patent or uninhibited. Soon after his election, President Biden referred to "the climate crisis" as "the existential crisis of our times."[11] And under his presidency, as if to counter one crisis narrative with another, Republicans in the United States spoke of "an economic crisis, with rising prices and overly generous employment benefits; a national security crisis; a border security crisis, with its attendant homeland security crisis, humanitarian crisis, and public health crisis; and a separate energy crisis."[12] To this long list of crises, the No. 2 Republican in the House, Representative Steve Scalise of Louisiana, added "yet another crisis," anti-Semitism in the ranks of the Democratic Party, and a labor shortage crisis—all of which he alleged were "caused by President Biden's actions." We have entered the age of chronic or "polycrisis"; crisis has become the new "normal."[13] Unsurprisingly, a wind of discontent is blowing across every corner of the world. Migrants and/or decadent—"woke"—values are singled out as the main culprits. Everywhere in the world—in the United States, India, Brazil, Russia, Turkey, Argentina, Hungary, Israel—illiberal democracy and constitutional dictatorships are one the rise.[14] We need to learn to live and think in dark times. Does this mean that we should replace the eschatology and narrative of the end of crisis of the 1980s and 1990s with something like a crisology fit for our time? Should the historicist faith in the meaning and coherence of human history, in progress and culture, give way, once again, to crisis-thinking?[15] And what, exactly, should we understand by *our* time, *our* crisis?

A few words of caution before I begin to answer these questions. To even suggest that crisis is the new "normal," or that we have entered the (paradoxical) age of *chronic* crisis, raises immediate questions. To begin with, crisis is usually thought of in opposition to a "normal" situation of whatever kind. In fact, not being normal is a good provisional definition of crisis. But how are we to understand "normal" and "not normal"? And how, by whom, and under what procedures is the norm—the specific norm as well as the very concept of norm—established in the first place? Instinctively, yet in a way that, I will argue, is both historically determined and insufficient, we tend to think of what is not normal as a deviation from the norm, or as "abnormal." But are deviations, even important ones, the only way of thinking about crisis? Or are there crises of a different kind, other ways in which a system—whether social, political, cultural, economic, existential, or ecological—can be in crisis, and its norms affected? These questions will lead me to distinguish between, and explore, what I call regimes of crisis (and therefore of norms), the economy, *modus operandi*, and temporality of which differ quite significantly from one regime to the next.

We should also be cautious about, and even critical of, our use of the word "crisis" for a second reason: the talk of crisis, especially if it is constant, can lead to two opposed traps: that of inaction, and that of extreme (or rash) action. If everything is a crisis, or in crisis, it becomes difficult to distinguish between what is urgent and what isn't, what to act on now and what to act on later. In other words, crisis can easily lead to paralysis. Many choose that option in order not to make the wrong (or unpopular) decision. As early as 1976, Edgar Morin criticized the abusive manipulation of a notion that was no longer related to its initial meaning:

> In the 20th century, the term crisis spread to virtually every aspect of contemporary consciousness. . . . However, by becoming so general it so to speak emptied itself from within. Originally, *krisis* means decision: it signals the decisive moment in the evolution of an uncertain process, which makes the diagnosis possible. Today, crisis is synonymous with indecision: it signals the moment in which uncertainties emerge alongside a given disruption.[16]

On the other hand, the diagnosis of crisis can lead to precipitate, extreme, and questionable action. Crisis is easily instrumentalized, and the proliferation of the *rhetoric* of crisis should raise suspicion. Speaking of the response to 9/11 by the Bush administration, Roitman writes: "The invocation of crisis served to legitimate the abridgement of constitutional rights and the institutionalization of extra-juridical executive powers."[17] Too often, crisis is "an observation that produces meaning" rather than "a condition to be observed."[18] I will return to this opportunistic use of crisis in Chapter 2, when I discuss the decision regarding the state of exception or emergency as a legitimate and adequate response to existential threats facing a nation or state, and therefore as a solution to crises of sovereignty: it was as a response to a situation presented by Hitler as one of total crisis that, in 1933, Article 48 of the constitution of the Weimar Republic, which suspended the rule of law, was invoked, and the fusion of the exception and the norm maintained until the end of the Reich in 1945. Crisis, I argue, is not a neutral or objective term describing a state of affairs, but a hermeneutic construction through which we understand, experience, and order the world; it is also a discursive, performative event, which produces a range of effects.

Unsurprisingly, social scientists and philosophers of various kinds have grown skeptical of the notion of crisis, as Rodrigo Cordero reminds us:[19] they have criticized it as an inadequate concept because it is unable to account for the new realities of a "global risk society";[20] because it operates like a cultural device in the "simulacrum" of capitalist self-destruction;[21] or because it disguises the lack of a proper, system-based theory of society.[22] The few times Michel Foucault refers directly to the concept of crisis, Cordero notes, are mostly in a sardonic tone, often describing the term as a "magical" device in the language of the human sciences, and in Marxist discourse in particular.[23] Derrida, whose position I will discuss in Chapter 4, is also critical of that concept: crisis, he claims, is not the only, or indeed the most useful and urgent concept to use in thinking what is "happening" or "coming" (*ce qui arrive, ce qui vient, ce qui advient*). The event exceeds and undermines the figure of crisis itself; and it is best understood as aporia—that is, as a form of decision against the backdrop of a radical undecidability. More recently still, Bruno Latour declared the concept of crisis no longer relevant to consideration of what he calls the ecological "mutation." Koselleck himself concludes his long article on crisis by saying that crisis has become a media "catchword," often lacking "in either clarity or precision," and "used rigorously in only a few scholarly or scientific contexts."[24] It "is often used interchangeably with 'unrest,' 'conflict,' 'revolution,' and to describe vaguely disturbing moods or situations.... Such a tendency towards imprecision and vagueness, however, may itself be viewed as the symptom of a historical crisis that cannot as yet be fully gauged."[25]

There is, I believe, a final reason to be skeptical of the vocabulary of crisis. If there is a common trope these days, one that moves freely in crisis and leadership circles, entrepreneurship studies, as well as in the culture industry, it is that of the "productive crisis." Crises, whether personal or collective, existential or economic, are seen as opportunities and should ultimately reinforce one's "resilience," ability to "bounce back," and "move forward." "Icons" from the world of business and finance encourage us to imitate them and "try and turn every disaster into an opportunity."[26] The idea of "creative destruction," which Schumpeter formulated in the early parts of the twentieth century, has been very popular in the last few decades. According to Schumpeter, the driver of economic progress is the sum of the technological innovations of pioneering entrepreneurs, backed by bank credit. Disturbances to a static system in a state of economic equilibrium are key to economic development and account for the transformation of that system into a dynamic one, which will eventually reach its own state of equilibrium. Inevitably, crises—breakdowns—occur in that intermediary, chaotic period. But they need to be seen as the consequence of the disruptive power of innovation and the necessary by-product of the economic cycle. The Schumpeterian pioneer is a "leader" equipped with "*Wille zur Macht*" and "*Herrenwille*," whose success inspires company managers and, subsequently, the masses.[27]

A version of this view is also present in the culture industry. A common and, Barthes argues, romantic conception of art claims that crises—anecdotal, sentimental, historical, political, or spiritual—are necessary for the process of creation.[28] Barthes has in mind not the crisis of creativity, or the lack of inspiration, which many artists experience in the course of their careers, but the crisis that provokes them to create: a moment of great physical or emotional suffering, a remarkable encounter, an event that upsets an otherwise tranquil life, an illumination. This "myth" of the founding, "fecund," or "creative" crisis, Barthes claims, turns crisis into a "value" capable of transforming or regenerating a writer's *œuvre*. In the contemporary context, it seems that this value has taken on an additional, "therapeutic" role, which connects artistic production with the ancient—and until the eighteenth century dominant—medicine of crisis: art is (increasingly) recognized and valued as a way of overcoming personal crises and healing emotional wounds, whether for the artists or their audience.[29] Although crisis is not seen as intrinsically positive, the creative process to which it leads is. As such, it is imbued with a creative potential analogous to, but not identical with, the physiological normativity of the human body, which can restore health by introducing new norms.[30] This positive view of crisis can also be found in the literature on self-knowledge and self-help, for which crisis, we are told, leads to self-discovery, self-awareness, self-understanding, and, circling back to the entrepreneurial paradigm, self-management.

So, the question I want to ask is simple: should we "put less faith in crisis," as Roitman suggests, and even avoid the notion and schema of crisis altogether?[31] Should we instead speak of epistemic ruptures, aporias, or mutations? Or, bearing in mind the warnings and criticisms to which it has been subjected, should crisis be analyzed, questioned, and criticized—deconstructed, if you will—not as a catchword or mere warning, but as a historical-hermeneutic schema, bound up with discursive practices, institutions, and techniques of government; and, at the same time and in response, constructed as a philosophical concept fit to describe what is happening today, our age, our own "time out of joint?" In other words, can crisis be subjected to critique and, at the same time (but in a different sense), become a useful and rigorously defined philosophical, indeed critical, *concept*? Similarly, can critique be problematized in this age of *chronic* crisis, can its diagnostic assurance and clinical distance be questioned, and at the same time reaffirmed and reinvented?

In this book, I make a case for this double demand, or those two levels of philosophical analysis.

One is oriented toward an archaeology of crisis as a way of understanding and processing challenges to the norm, and thus as a mechanism internal to the age of normativity: as a discourse of truth, or authority, *and* a technique of government. This means that the historical-critical work I am engaged in does not focus on crisis as an *idea*, and should therefore not be mistaken for a contribution to the history of ideas, or what the Germans call *Begriffsgeschichte*. This, as I already suggested, is because "crisis" is a multidimensional and historically differentiated interpretive schema through which we experience, make sense of, and respond to certain kinds of events. The schema or dispositive of crisis makes an event or situation visible and intelligible. As such, it is phenomenological. But it also produces effects of problematization and subjectivation. And it is the work of critique to reveal and question them—that is, to ask: what kind of crisis are we dealing with? What grid of intelligibility, what practices, what institutions, and what kinds of subjects are mobilized when a given power recognizes a situation as critical? To what extent does the diagnosis of crisis lend itself to disagreement? And can crisis be both the object and the subject of critique, something that critique questions *and* affirms?

The other is oriented toward the conceptual plasticity of crisis. Crisis is a useful concept so long as we make it a polysemic one, and so long as we allow it to operate alongside other concepts, which gravitate around it, in what amounts to a specific *modus operandi*, or regime. This polysemy, I will also argue, is not infinite and can therefore lend itself to a typology rooted in historical as well as analytic work. This, in turn, means that the concept of crisis cannot be constructed once and for all: we cannot tell in advance the kind of situations and pressures we will be confronted with. Crisis is not a transcendental but an empirical concept, destined to evolve. The concept of crisis is therefore open-ended, and its meaning may need to be revised or complemented in light of new events. As I'll try to show in some detail, the event of the Technocene (a term I will favor over such other recent coinages as the Anthropocene and the Capitalocene), which I hold responsible for the ecological "emergency" or "mutation" in which we find ourselves, requires that we understand crisis in a hitherto unsuspected sense, and one that has a retroactive effect on all the other regimes. But, as we'll also see in relation to examples borrowed from law, economics, politics, and science, the concept of crisis, in addition to being descriptive and analytic, is prescriptive and practical. It does not tell us what to do, but it does tell us that something needs to be done.[32] It describes a present situation while intimating the possibility of a different future. So, I will distinguish between *regimes* of crisis and show how each involves a certain relation to the norm and normality. But I will also show how, on the basis of that specific relation (which is also a tension of some kind), the different regimes of crisis require different kinds of responses. The key distinction to be made here is not between the descriptive and the prescriptive—"crisis," I argue, is necessarily both—but between prescriptive frameworks, which depend on the circumstances and are always (in principle at least) an object of debate, if not dispute. In some instances, a purely managerial or techno-bureaucratic response is called for. In others, one might argue for an "exceptionalist" solution, which involves the suspension of the normal legal order. But in the same circumstances, or different ones, a more radical, "revolutionary" response might be desirable. In the case of the ecological crisis—which, I will argue, presents us with a unique (and uniquely grave) situation—the question of what needs to be done is more complex and open. My particular view is that it calls for a revolution of a specific kind, which I define as an "ontological conversion."

At this early stage, and by way of anticipation, let me introduce the four regimes of crisis on which I will be focusing. I should make clear that although I will occasionally refer to crises in a personal—that is, moral, existential, or psychological—sense, as well as crises in certain fields of human thought and activity such as medicine, science, or art, my main goal in this book is to address collective, and specifically social, economic, political, and ecological forms of crisis. In doing so, I will draw on and engage with the discourses and disciplines that, directly or indirectly, analyze, scrutinize, and criticize those various types of crises. They include philosophy, political economy, law and legal theory, sociology, and the earth and life sciences.

Chapter 1 provides a brief history of the notion of crisis, in and outside philosophy. It traces the emergence of the schema or matrix of crisis back to Greek and Roman antiquity, and especially to law, tragedy, and medicine. But it also introduces the modern kind of crisis we are most used to, and I believe have in mind whenever we speak of or think about crisis. That is because they are the most common. I define them as crises of deviation. Crises of deviation presuppose the existence of a system defined and governed by norms, which define its "normal" state. The system can be social, economic, physical, physiological, aesthetic, or technocratic. Its norms define its ordinary behavior, or its state of (relative) equilibrium. The "normal" state of a system does not identify a rigid or fixed set of points, but an amplitude or range, from which an average measure is extracted.[33] We can speak of a crisis of deviation when a system begins significantly to move away from its "normal" range, thereby endangering its own stability. It is a crisis, since the deviation brings about new constraints and translates into unforeseen pressures. Those, in turn, can be interpreted as merely temporary, and expected to be followed by a return to normality, without requiring any *exceptional* intervention on the part of those affected by, or in charge of running, the system in question. Thus, a road system can experience a crisis of deviation following a larger than usual amount of traffic coupled, perhaps, with an otherwise insignificant traffic light failure or minor accident: long delays, frustrated and angry motorists, greater traffic on secondary roads, or technocratic. Health services and hospitals may face a similar situation, for example when they are confronted with a particularly severe flu season, or a rare combination of unfortunate medical events. And flu itself can be interpreted in those terms: although it *can* lead to significant complications, and even death, especially among the very young and the very old, it normally doesn't: rest and a regular intake of fluid will allow the body eventually to recover. Similarly, financial markets undergo regular "corrections" or even move into "bear" territory without requiring the intervention of central banks or states. Crises of deviation, then, need not translate into a review or overhaul of the system in question, or even part of it. Sometimes, though, the crisis is thought to be temporary but only on the condition that something be done about it: intervention is required to stabilize the system and avoid greater, possibly life-threatening complications. This is what we call crisis *management*. Whatever the nature of the crisis, the assumption is that the measures introduced will be sufficient to bring the system back to its normal range. The response to crises of deviation, also known as anomalies, is intrinsically *conservative*: the aim of those in charge is not to create new norms and systems, but to restore the old one. At the collective level, this regime of crisis corresponds to that of liberalism, and neoliberalism in particular. As Rodrigo Cordero puts it, neoliberalism is a political rationality "for which crisis is a vital source of knowledge and focal point of experience of governmental interventions and management of social problems."[34] In other words, crisis operates within neoliberalism as what Foucault also calls a "discursive event," one that produces a certain form of intelligibility, organizes experience, and determines a range of political responses. It is a problematizing element, rather than a mere signifier. It is found not in texts, but in an intricate web of discourses of truth, institutions, laws, conducts, and counter-conducts.[35] It does not exist as such, but only as an effect of a discursive practice—that is, of a social, economic, and administrative construct that defines and hierarchizes problems, and introduces managerial techniques of government.

Chapter 2 deals with crises of sovereignty that lead to the decision regarding the state of exception. In the face of a real or perceived threat, sovereign power, independent of its form of government (democratic, aristocratic, plutocratic, autocratic, or technocratic), suspends the legal *nomos* with a view to saving and restoring it. When subjected to such a procedure, we are targeted as citizens. The situation is an abnormal one, but in a very specific sense, often referred to as one of anomie. I analyze the historical roots of the state of exception; discuss its theoretical justification, champions, and critics; and refer to examples from our relatively and very recent history, including the war waged on terror by the United States following the attacks of 9/11, on Palestinians by Israel following the attacks of October 7, 2023, and the responses to the Covid-19 pandemic. I argue that the state of exception is justifiable under very specific circumstances but that, in our age of chronic and polycrisis, it is increasingly used as a normal technique of government and amounts to a securitization and militarization of crisis.

By contrast with crises of deviation and exception, which are addressed through techniques of either suspension or management and are intrinsically conservative, crises of contradiction, which I analyze in Chapter 3, present us with *antinomies*. They are more severe and indicate a structural problem. For contradictions to be lifted or resolved, one cannot simply tweak a system or introduce minor changes. If a system is such that the coexistence of x and y, or at least the state in which x and y exist within the system, is a threat to both x and y, then the system is thought to be unsustainable. This means that, in the long run, crisis will become its norm and thus call into question the system as a whole. And it can do that in two ways: either by bringing about the slow and painful death of the system (if nothing is done) or by bringing about another system, by creating a new set of norms. If there is such a thing as a crisis of contradiction, the only adequate response is creative, or *revolutionary*. This situation, I will argue, applies to systems as different as the capitalist mode of production, scientific paradigms, and aesthetic regimes.[36] In the face of crises of contradiction, the temptation to fall back on orthopedic techniques of management or more authoritarian techniques of exception is great. But such responses will fail because they will not resolve the contradictions in question. They might attenuate their effect or even suspend them temporarily. But they will not eradicate them.

In Chapter 4, I introduce a momentary pause in my crisology in order to engage critically with Jacques Derrida, whom I take to be the most serious critic of crisis as a philosophical concept. Where a certain philosophical tradition thinks of the event as philosophically relevant in terms of crisis, Derrida prefers to speak of aporia; and where the former identifies crisis with a moment of decision, Derrida sees the aporetic as the site of an irreducible and constitutive undecidability. In the end, however, I see Derrida as rejecting a certain view and concept of crisis—crisis as contradiction and antinomy, crisis as exception and suspension—but only to deploy it in a new direction and context, to displace it and give it a new meaning: crisis as aporia, as an inescapable structure or quasi-transcendental schema within which all the other senses and regimes of crisis unfold. Crisis is *original*: what he calls "supplement" and "*différance*" signal the constitutive crisis of origin and identity. Far from merely rejecting crisis, then, Derrida turns it into a condition of possibility of history, responsibility, and action. Against Derrida, I argue that some crises do confront us with an either/or, which defines praxis. The ecological crisis is one such defining moment.

The ecological emergency, I claim in Chapter 5, is a crisis of the most severe kind. To be sure, it is existential, in that it threatens the existence of living species, including humans, and (to a lesser extent) of the biosphere itself; and it is not the only one of its kind (a deep and chronic state of depression can be seen as a mental crisis of collapse; a genocide and/or ecocide can be seen as a political and military tactic to bring a regime or entire people to a state of total collapse). But the way in which the ecological crisis operates and affects us is, I claim, different from crises of deviation, exception, or even contradiction. And its structure is not aporetic in the Derridean sense. The reason for that lies in the fact that what is being affected in the ecological crisis, which is a crisis of collapse or extinction, is the biosphere's ability to produce norms.

In the case of crises of contradiction, no matter how grave, new norms are called for, and the ability on our part to generate them, whether in the social, scientific, or aesthetic fields, is not in question. In crises of collapse, however, it is precisely this ability that is under threat: not a specific set of norms, but normativity as such. This is why I take the ecological crisis to be the most severe and urgent one of the crises currently being discussed. It is the crisis that takes precedence over all others, the crisis that affects the conditions of possibility of life in general (at least as we currently know it), and of human life in particular. It is the first human-made crisis of the transcendental-physical ground of life itself, the human sin toward the normativity of the biosphere. As such, it is the mother of all crises, the crisis that affects and disrupts all the other regimes of crisis, the crisis of crisis itself. It is through ecological collapse that crisis becomes chronic, by which I mean not only constant and permanent, but disrupting the order of *chronos* itself, or *chronos* as order. As Guattari put it in a manuscript from the early 1990s, and as if in response to Fukuyama's thesis, what was really at stake in this post-East-West world was "the end of history as the collapse [*collapsus*] of the human species and the biosphere."[37] This collapse is a momentous event of a different kind, one that happens over decades, if not centuries, and in silence, until it hits you with a violence and a sense of helplessness never before experienced. Guattari ends his essay with a call to arms, which I want fully to embrace: only through the articulation of a different kind of subjectivity, a constantly mutating socius, and a new relation to the environment "will we escape from the major crises of our era."[38]

What do all those regimes of crisis have in common? I have already alluded to the fact that they presuppose a set of norms, which are tested, eroded, or threatened, whether superficially or fundamentally, temporarily or permanently, externally or internally. I also claimed that the *concept* of crisis is at once descriptive and prescriptive, theoretical and practical. Were one of those two aspects not to be present at all—were the nature of the situation at hand to be entirely confusing, or were we to conclude that nothing can be done about it—we might speak of a disaster, a tragedy, or a catastrophe, but not of a crisis. However grave or severe, a diagnosis of crisis presupposes a certain clarity of understanding as well as the possibility, however faint, of overcoming it. Crisis is not and cannot be purely passive.

There is yet another dimension of crisis, which I have not discussed. I made it clear that, except for the occasional foray into other domains and aspects of human life, I will be focusing on collective crises, by which I mean crises that affect us as citizens, economic agents, members of a society or group, and even, in relation to the ecological crisis, as inhabitants and/or exploiters of the earth. Yet it would be illusory to believe that a situation can be recognized as critical if it is not felt or experienced as such, if it does not affect us at a personal, existential level. So long as the situation does not speak to us directly, to our nervous system as well as our mind (or even our conscience), it is a crisis in name only. As we will see, the ecological crisis is a good example. For a long time, and for the populations of richer countries, it remained a distant reality. The distance was a geographical one—it happened in other parts of the world—as well as a temporal one—it was assumed that it would not affect *me* in my lifetime. But things began to change and the crisis became real for the global North when everyone started to experience severe droughts and devastating wildfires, storms, and floods of biblical proportions. To the analytic and pragmatic dimensions of crisis, then, we should add its affective, emotional, or pathological dimension.[39] This claim does not say anything about the sort of affects associated with crisis. This is because they vary according to the crises, or at least the regimes of crisis, in question. Still, we can make the following two general remarks. First, for obvious reasons, and even if joyful passions such as hope or solidarity can occasionally emerge from their depths, they are mostly sad passions, such as fear, anxiety, panic, depression, frustration, anger, hatred, indignation, or technocratic. Second, those affects often (but not always, nor necessarily) provide the missing link or mediation between the theoretical and the practical: they act as a bridge between a critical diagnosis and the sense of urgency required to act on it. Sometimes, though, affects precede and make possible the analytic moment: my sense of indignation or anger, for example, can lead me to ask about its origin, analyze its causes, and eventually call into question the system of which it is an expression, and which I might now see as unjust or unsustainable. We are therefore dealing with a triangular relation, in which thought (as critique), desire (as the faculty of action), and affectivity (as our ability to feel) play equally significant yet very different parts. This economy of crisis, and the various human faculties it involves, is to be distinguished from the regimes of crisis of which I have spoken, and to which I will devote individual chapters. Naturally, it is also possible to ask about potential crises within this economy, or even within other, larger economies, which might involve our faculties of imagination or memory in addition to those I have already mentioned. We would then ask about the conflict of faculties, and the various ways in which, beyond this moment of conflict, they can regain a harmony or peaceful coexistence. But this (Kantian) form of critique is not the one I pursue in this book, despite emphasizing the significance of the play of some of our faculties in the overall economy of crisis. The sense of critique I *am* concerned about, and explore in detail in Chapter 1, is the critique of our present, of who we are today, of the historical formations of discourses, institutions, social relations, and practices that shape or normalize our subjectivity, and the critical points at which they begin to give, weaken, disintegrate, or collapse. At the same time, the situation of critique today is perhaps far less secure, if not fundamentally threatened by the chronic and all-encompassing nature of *today's* crises, and by the ecological crisis first and foremost. We are all in it together, deeply affected by it, in such a way that it has become difficult if not impossible to stand at a diagnostic distance, identify turning points, and recommend a cure. Our time of crisis, I fear, is also a crisis of critique itself. The clinician herself is infected, her world shaken to the core, her time out of joint, her concepts tentative. Even critique is unhinged. For what is left of critique when tipping points have already been reached, when the (worst) future is already behind us, and when the ability to perform the right action at the right time—the *kairos*—is under threat? And yet, I see no alternative but to persevere in critique, to stay in and with the trouble, in what amounts to a constantly renewed examination of one's place in crisis, a cultivation of affects conducive to the attitude of critique, and the construction of conceptual, aesthetic, imaginary, and social bonds. The "ecosophical revival" requires it.

A typology of crisis, aimed at distinguishing between its various regimes, objects, forms of violence, responses, types of power, and dominant affects, looks something like Table 1.

Table 1

Crises of:	Deviation	Exception	Contradiction	Extinction/ Collapse
Violence to Norms:	Anomaly	Anomy	Antinomy	Paranomy (=violence to normativity)
Responses:	Management	Suspension of (legal) norms	Uprising / creation of norms	Erosion of normativity
Regimes of Power:	Biopower	Sovereign power	Popular power	Technics
Systems/ Objects:	Population/ Labor/Markets	Legal order	Socius/ Science/ The Arts	Biosphere/Life
Affects:	Fright/Relief	Terror/Shock/Awe	Indignation/hope/ joy	Despair/anxiety/ boredom/shame/ ethical fear/Care

1

Crisis

A Brief Critical History

Let me begin by analyzing the ways, contexts, and disciplines in which the notion of crisis has been used throughout history. As my primary aim is not to reconstruct in detail and as faithfully as possible the history of an idea, or a paradigm, but to write a critique of crisis, by which I mean to construct a philosophical *concept* of crisis, distinguish between various types or regimes of crisis, and focus on specific examples to illustrate them, this chapter is only a rough sketch and something like a propaedeutic. To this day, the most systematic history of the concept of crisis, rooted in the German tradition of *Begriffsgeschichte*, can be found in Koselleck's 1959 doctoral dissertation and 1982 article on "Crisis."[1] My account overlaps with, but also differs from, that of Koselleck on several methodological counts. Unlike Koselleck, I do not assume that the *notion* of crisis is the same as the *concept* of crisis, and that its constant use today is a function of its "metaphorical flexibility" or broad semantic range.[2] Furthermore, my claim is that the *concept* of crisis must emerge from within, and be the result of, the work of critique, which includes the critique of the rhetoric and instrumentalization of crisis. Finally, while no doubt illuminating, a history of the manifold *meaning* of the concept of crisis will never be sufficient properly to understand and engage with the *modus operandi* of crisis, which involves different regimes of power, institutions, and techniques of government. In other words, the history that is at issue here is not purely semantic, and its analysis cannot be limited to a hermeneutics. A critique of the operativity of crisis requires an archaeology of its epistemes, or interpretive schemas, and a typology of its regimes, including in their overlap. Another—this time substantial—point of divergence from Koselleck concerns the role and place of the tragic paradigm in the formation of the philosophy of history as a philosophy of crisis, especially in the post-Kantian context, which Koselleck does not mention.

As we'll see, and despite their significant differences, the more technical uses of the notion and grammar of crisis resonate, at times strongly, with the ways in which we tend to use the word crisis today, in what we could call our average, pre-theoretical understanding of it. One thing is certain: initially, and for a very long time, crisis was not part of the philosophical lexicon. Starting in Greek and Roman antiquity, it operated as an organizing or structuring notion in various discourses—medicine, tragedy, and law—before migrating to the social sciences, political economy, and eventually philosophy. At various crucial points, as we shall see, philosophy turned to the medical or tragic model to think the nature of social and political crises, if not the movement of history itself, even when it did not explicitly embrace the notion of crisis. Whether implicitly or explicitly, those models operated as schemas through which philosophy attempted to think the nature of the event, the mechanics of history, and its own present.

Origins (Law, Tragedy, and Medicine)

Etymologically, *krisis* comes from *krino*, *krinein*, to separate or distinguish. It has several meanings. It can refer to the power of judgment, the judgment at the end of a trial, a decision, a choice or election, a trial of skill or strength, a dispute, a court.[3] In Matthew 10:15, *krisis* refers to the Day of Judgment, to the sentencing or justice of God. In the juridical vocabulary, *krisis* designated the judgment or decision that did not result automatically from the accumulation of evidence, thus pointing to the specificity of judgment as a human faculty. The strong connection between law and decision remained central to legal and political theory in modern Europe, and to the question of sovereignty in particular, to which I will return in Chapter 2. From Jean Bodin's *Republic* to Gabriel Naudé's *Considérations politiques sur les coups d'État*, and many seventeenth-century authors of natural law (such as Samuel von Pufendorf), the question of sovereignty revolved around the *decision* on the exception to the legal norm.[4] This question became the focal point of Carl Schmitt's theory of the state of exception (*Ausnahmezustand*). If the state of exception comes to occupy such an important place in legal thought, it is because, by suspending the legal norm (the constitution), the state of exception, which is the prerogative of the sovereign, "reveals with absolute purity a specifically juridical element: the decision."[5] Law, therefore, is defined not only by the clear distinction between what is permitted and what is prohibited, but also by the decision, revealed most clearly by the sovereign.[6] Exception, I will argue in Chapter 2, was and continues to be a key meaning or, better said perhaps, regime of crisis.

Crisis also plays an important role in Greek tragedy.[7] The meaning of crisis in Greek tragedy depends largely on how we understand tragedy and the tragic. Following the Aristotelian line in the *Poetics*, with its emphasis on plot (*muthos*) and character (*ta ethè*; 1450a37), we could say that crisis signals the conflict of characters and the point when this conflict comes to a head. But following another, growing trend, we can emphasize the role and function of pollution (*miasma*) in tragedy; we can point to the impure acts and states that make up the fabric of tragedy, and to the question of purification (including through punishment) that follows.[8] Whenever there is pollution, there is crisis.[9] In Greek tragedy, pollution designates the act of having voluntarily or involuntarily ignored the *nomos*—the rule or right order of things, the principle of distribution and justice—or having provoked the gods' jealousy. To be *anomos* is to be blind to the order of the city and nature, ignorant of a law that is manifest to all. Pollution, especially in the form of bloodshed (or incest), brings about madness (Orestes as a result of having murdered his mother Clytemnestra), plague (Oedipus upon Thebes, as a result of his murder of Laius), or loss of what is dearest (Medea's sacrifice of her two sons to punish her husband's decision to take another wife). The murderer is *miaros*, that is, marked with an indelible stain which establishes a break between the perpetrator and what is *hieros*, sacred. To approach the sacred one must become *katharos*, pure.¹⁰ Conversely, purity is the condition for accessing the law, for seeing the order of things and being able to utter the *nomos*. Crisis is therefore synonymous with impurity and lawlessness. As such, it is often and rightly punished by exile. In that respect, it is more than what Meinel describes as a "difficult situation."¹¹ It is a discriminating, critical point, one that divides and demarcates two sequences of events, two chronological orders. *Krisis* distributes and excludes. It draws a line between the pure and the impure, the sacred and the profane, order and chaos—but also between persons, families, or city-states. As such, it designates an *event* in the strong sense of the term, one that implies the past as a whole, as well as future actions. It signals a moment of interruption or caesura, which changes the course of time and breaks the protagonists' world.¹²

Modern tragedy too is a site of crisis in which pollution and corruption figure prominently. When a most unnatural deed or series of deeds afflicts the integrity of the social order—the Family, the Crown, the Church—tragedy looms large. Consider *Hamlet*. As a result of his murder of his brother, the king of Denmark, and his marriage to the queen, Claudius plunges the state of Denmark in a state of deep crisis. Claudius is a murderer, a usurper, and an "incestuous," "adulterous beast" (I, 5). His crime is monstrous, as is Gertrude's complicity. What is truly tragic is how this crime infects the kingdom as a whole: "Something is rotten in the state of Denmark" (I, 4). As a result of this unspeakable deed, the kingdom has become an "ulcerous place" in which "rank corruption, mining all within, / Infects unseen" (III, 3). *Hamlet* is a tale of physical and mental pollution, which affects the body politic as a whole. Hamlet foresees it in Act I: "foul deeds will rise / Though all the earth overwhelm them, to men's eyes" (I, 2). And Claudius recognizes it: "my foul murder," he admits, and "those effects for which I did the murder, / my crown, my own ambition, and my queen," are the cause of "the corrupted currents of the world" (III, 3). Sadness, madness, and destruction take over the world. "The time is out of joint"—unhinged, dislocated—and needs to be "set right" (I, 5). Have we ever come across a better image of crisis, and a clearer indication of the manner in which tragedy performs it?

It falls on Hamlet to avenge his father and, most importantly, restore the natural and political order (the *naturally political* or *politically natural* order), without which there is no civilization to speak of: "Let not the royal bed of Denmark be / a couch for luxury and damned incest" (I, 5). Unlike the "foul and most unnatural murder" (I, 5) of his father, and the equally unnatural marriage that followed it, Hamlet's revenge is itself natural. About to confront his mother, he says to himself:

> O heart, lose not thy nature; let not ever
> The soul of Nero enter this firm bosom:
> Let me be cruel, not unnatural:
> I will speak daggers to her, but use none . . .
> (III, 2)

Hamlet's harsh words enter his mother's ears like "daggers" (III, 2). They are cruel, but not unnatural. To use actual daggers against her would be unnatural. His resolute and rightful revengefulness is also cruel, but it is not unnatural. Revenge is the way to cleanse the pollution afflicting the body politic and restore it to its state of purity. Hamlet is the physician upon whom fate calls to purge the body politic of its impure fluids and restore its natural equilibrium.[13] As one commentator puts it, "taking revenge—far from being the severing of communal or familial bonds—is an attempt to reestablish them where they are in crisis."[14] At the same time, this purge ends not in the restoration of the *nomos*, but in total destruction: the play, which begins with the murder of Old Hamlet, ends with the death of virtually all the protagonists—Polonius, Claudius, Gertrude, Ophelia, Laertes, Rosencrantz and Guildenstern, and Hamlet himself. Only Horatio survives to tell the tale.[15]

The most enduring and crucial area of deployment of the notion of crisis, however, was medicine. As we just saw in the case of *Hamlet*, the crisis and its possible resolution were themselves largely defined by the medical vocabulary of the Elizabethan era, which was itself mostly shaped by Greek medicine. It would not be an exaggeration to say that the whole of classical medicine, by which we need to understand the medicine that originated in the Hippocratic corpus (from the fifth century BC)[16] and Galen (AD 129–ca. 216)[17] and extended well into the eighteenth century,[18] revolved around the notion and moment of crisis. Unsurprisingly, the medical schema of crisis spilled into other discourses, including poetics and philosophy.

Hippocrates provides us with a useful definition of *krisis* in *Affections*: crisis, we read, is "the determination of the disease as it were by a judicial verdict."[19] Here we see how the medical schema of crisis is itself informed by the juridical form. In classical medicine, a disease was supposed to occur when the equilibrium of the four humors (blood, yellow bile, black bile, phlegm), or their just proportion, known as *krasis*, was disturbed by an "exciting cause" (*prophasis*). Too much phlegm, for example, caused epilepsy; too much black bile, melancholy.[20] The theory of humors was itself rooted in the theory of the four elements (fire, water, air, and earth) that made up matter. Through "coction," the natural constitution of the individual made every effort to restore the necessary *krasis*, or the relation of equality and symmetry between the humors, which defines health. The battle between nature and the disease was decided on the day that coction took place or failed to take place. The result was recovery (partial or complete), aggravation of the disease, or death. The most relevant text, in that context, is arguably Galen's *On Crises*.[21] Galen observed that certain illnesses—malaria and the plague were prime examples—exhibit periodicities, with symptoms oscillating between valleys and peaks of intensity, or paroxysms. Crises, he observes, tend to occur on specific and "critical" days, which punctuate the evolution of the disease.[22] Occasionally, one of these paroxysms strikes with exceptional intensity, corresponding to the decisive moment in the illness, or the point at which one of two things happens: either the symptoms worsen, the illness begins to triumph and the patient eventually dies; or, through the healing power of nature, fine adjustments to patient's diet or exercise, or more radical measures such as purging or fasting, the patient slowly recovers.[23] In that respect, crisis designates, quite literally, the point on which the illness turns. It signals a moment of truth, and reveals truth as a moment, or an *event* (rather than an eternal or atemporal essence). This will turn out to be decisive for philosophy itself, which raises the question of whether there can be a genuine science of accidents and events.

In relation to such a cycle, and this view of illness as crisis, Hippocratic therapy was a matter of observation and, at times, gentle intervention.[24] It focused on facilitating the natural process of healing and preparing the patient to be strong enough to withstand the crisis when it occurred. The physician was expected to give a prognosis (*On Prognosis*), which was closely related to crisis: he could determine when a case was likely to lead to recovery, and when it was hopeless, in which case he refused to treat the patient and thereby avoided damaging his reputation. Since pathologies corresponded to either an excess or want of the humors in their natural equilibrium, treatment consisted in either adding or subtracting the relevant qualities (heat, cold, humidity, dryness), for example through diet, exercise, or bleeding. In a society where exploratory surgery was prohibited,[25] the physician was expected to infer the present and prior condition of the patient simply by observing him or her and relying on external indicators such as urine, excrement, perspiration, or technocratic, without being *told* anything. Through a comprehensive prognosis, he could gain the confidence of the patient. Prognosis involved reading signs in the patient and comparing them with a prognostic theme or theory, such as that of critical days. By themselves, the quality of the patient's bodily effusions were simple facts, devoid of implications for the outcome of the illness. But these facts became prognostic indicators when read through the theory of critical days.[26] Crisis and interpretation were therefore intimately linked in classical (and medieval) medicine; the clinic of the ancients was a semiotics. Thus, Avicenna notes how, by reading the signs of the disease, the physician can anticipate either the death or the recovery of the patient. The knowledge of the rhythms and accidents of the pathology was known as the *scientia temporibus morborum*.[27] It mapped the different stages of the evolution of a pathology and allowed the physician to formulate his judgment. Crisis designated the event that determined the passage from one stage of the illness to another. It signaled the sudden mutation that could transform the evolution of the pathology and propel the patient toward health or death. Knowing the crises—the days when they happen, the changes in the pathological sequence they determine—and being able to interpret them correctly were key elements of the physician's expertise. But the signs could also be slow and weak, or contradictory. In that case, Avicenna claims categorically, the physician should not intervene but should suspend his judgment and wait for the illness to manifest itself.[28]

Mutations

Crisis in Political Economy

In the seventeenth and especially the eighteenth century the notion of crisis began its migration from the field of medicine to other domains, and to the analysis of social movements in particular. Koselleck notes how, in 1627, Sir Benjamin Rudyerd, a poet and politician who sat in the House of Commons, used the term during the battle between parliament and the crown.[29] The Marquis d'Argenson's journal also contains various references to "crises" affecting the economy, the church, or the relation between the king and parliament.[30] In Germany, Frederick the Great applies the term to foreign policy and military affairs in his political correspondence, *Histoire de mon temps*, and in conversation.[31] However, the discourse in which the notion of crisis flourished, from its inception and until today, is that of political economy and economics. Economists, whatever their affiliation, have all recognized something that they call "crisis" as a recurrent feature of economic systems, and of the market economy in particular. But they are far from agreeing on the status or nature of crises in that economy.

For classical, Keynesian, or neo-classical economists, the tendency to crisis is not inherent in the capitalist mode of production. The economist John Hicks summarized this position in his review of Keynes's *General Theory of Employment*: "Ordinary (static) economic theory explains to us the working of the economic system in 'normal' conditions. Booms and slumps, however, are deviations from this norm, and are thus to be explained by some disturbing cause."[32] This is perhaps the clearest expression of what I call crises of deviation. Most often, Simon Clarke argues, economists attribute such crises to "the inadequacy of institutional arrangements and policy responses. As such, they can be overcome by appropriate institutional and policy reforms," for example of the monetary or credit system, taxation, labor or competition laws, or technocratic.[33] In short, the tendency to crisis can be *delayed* and *managed*. It is a technocratic rather than political matter. The economic dogma, therefore, is that the cyclical alternation of boom and bust (which, in Gordon Brown's famous words, was going to be a thing of the past with the advent of New

Labour's "responsible" policies), which has marked the history of capitalism, is an exogenous phenomenon. Crises, economists have claimed since Jean-Baptiste Say, Adam Smith, and Ricardo, are *de facto* exceptional disturbances, like floods and earthquakes. As such, they don't call into question the *de jure* self-regulating mechanism of the free market, which automatically adapts supply and demand to meet and tends toward equilibrium. As one commentator puts it,

> the assumption of a certain kind of stability over time is hardwired into many of the kinds of economic models used today. That even if the economy is temporarily knocked off-balance, it will swing, eventually, back to its steady growth path, plodding on into the future. "Shocks" such as sudden spikes in the price of oil, or wars in eastern Europe, may happen, but, like a roly-poly toy, the economy springs back to where it was before.[34]

The same models assume the deviations from this stable, long-run growth path to be temporary and to not affect the deep structures of the economy. More importantly, because crises are externalized, or excluded from the scientific models of complexity economics, they can be treated—that is, managed—as mere deviations.

The new school of economic theory, known as "complexity economics" and represented by the likes of Eric Beinhocker from the Institute for New Economic Thinking at Oxford, develops a similar line of argument. Its basic idea, according to one commentator, is that "an economy, like nature, is a complex adaptive system whose large-scale patterns emerge from autonomous agents following simple, internally coded rules." Following complexity theory, it also stipulates that "if a complex system is to remain near equilibrium, its positive and negative feedbacks must be roughly in balance."[35] As we'll see, this is a massive double assumption, which the reality of our current economic system contradicts.

However, not all economists agree with the equilibrium view of economic systems and the deviationist model of crisis I have just sketched.

Hyman Minsky, whose work from the 1960s and 1970s as a post-Keynesian economist was largely ignored by mainstream economists in the last decades of the last century, underwent something of a revival after the dot-com bubble and the subprime crisis.[36] Classical economic theory assumes that open, free market economies are fundamentally stable and seek equilibrium. As excesses occur, rational market actors see the excesses and act to make money or avoid losing it, thereby moving the economy back to equilibrium. This means that bubbles and crashes can only be caused by external shocks to the economy, such as diseases, wars, technological discoveries, or events such as the OPEC oil embargo of the 1970s. Minsky's view, by contrast, is that financial markets are intrinsically unstable.[37] His financial instability hypothesis (FIH) is that speculative bubbles are endogenous to financial markets, the cycle of which is one of speculative euphoria, followed by instability and fragility related to excessive borrowing, followed by crisis and the contraction or even suspension of credit on the part of banks, even to healthy companies and institutions. In other words, boom and bust are the natural states of economic cycles. Stable economies sow the seeds of their own instability and destruction by encouraging excessive risk, creating panic, and eventually causing recessions and crashes:

Marx goes one step further. The task, from a Marxist point of view and in relation to the economic dogma to which I was referring, is to explain "the regular recurrence of economic crises as a *normal*," indeed necessary part of "the developmental tendencies of the capitalist mode of production," and as the most dramatic expression of the inherently contradictory foundations of accumulation.[38] Marxism overturns the economic dogma and says: in the capitalist mode of production, crisis is the norm, not the exception. And this overturning coincides with the moment of critique, with the construction of philosophy *as* critique. This view is perhaps best summarized by Horkheimer in his 1937 article "Traditional and Critical Theory":

> To put it in broad terms, the [critical theory of society] says that the basic form of the historically given commodity economy on which modern history rests contains in itself the internal and external tensions of the modern era; it generates these tensions over and over again in an increasingly heightened form; and after a period of progress, development of human powers, and emancipation for the individual, after an enormous extension of human control over nature, it finally hinders further development and drives humanity into a new barbarism.[39]

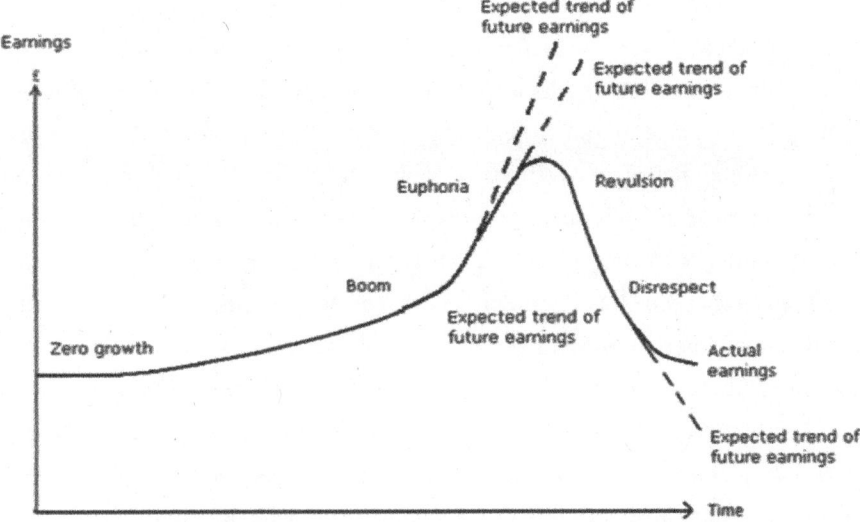

Figure 1.1 *Actual profitability across a business cycle showing expected trends at particular points in the cycle as extrapolations of linear growth at those points in time.* Source: Paul Barnes, "Minsky's financial instability hypothesis, accounting information and the 2007–9 financial crisis in the UK and US," Accounting History 16(4) (nov. 21, 2011): 423-437. Doi:10.1177/1032373211417991.

It's precisely by insisting on the *normal* and *necessary* dimension of crisis, by claiming that crisis is not tantamount to a mere deviation from a norm that will be followed by a moment of normalization, and not merely due to contingent factors that can all in principle be avoided, that discourse becomes *critique*: the "normal" state of the capitalist economy is not equilibrium, but crisis; this is the state toward which it tends spontaneously. This tendency is also what makes socialism *objectively necessary*, and marks the dividing line between social democracy and socialism, between "reform" and "revolution." We could say that with Marx begins the era of *scientific* criticism, based on a scientific theory of crisis as contradiction, and a revolutionary horizon. Without a *science* of crisis, or a crisology, socialism is nothing more than a worldview, an ethical ideal, which can be shared, and indeed implemented, by social democracies or other capitalist forms of social and political organization. I will explore the Marxist and post-Marxist view of crisis as a constitutive feature of capitalism, and of its various phases, in greater detail in Chapter 3.

This is the general context in which we need to understand the title of Wilhelm Röpke's *The Social Crisis of Our Time*, originally published—the date matters—in 1942 and as a response to the Keynesian-inspired planned economies in place at the time.[40] Röpke was a famous political economist and a seminal figure of German ordoliberalism, which, like Austrian and North American neoliberalism, opposed the very idea of a planned economy. Foucault describes Röpke's book as "a kind of bible of neoliberalism."[41] Röpke's argument is that the Great Depression was a profound crisis and extraordinary challenge for liberal democracy. The solution, however, is not less liberalism, but more liberalism, or at least a liberalism of a different kind, which he calls "constructive" or "revisionist."[42] It is, he argues, the only means capable of avoiding the "sterile alternative" between the *laissez-faire* of nineteenth-century liberalism on the one hand, and collectivism on the other. Röpke's vocabulary is largely medical. He compares society to a sick patient, and the political economist to a physician: "This book is the result of reflections of an economist on the sickness of our civilization and on the manner of its cure."[43] The figure of the political economist has replaced that of the philosopher as the technocrat and healer of the body politic; and the discourse of political economy is now imbued with a universal authority, if not an aura, that it still has today.

Röpke's medical metaphor is also consistent with what, implicitly and over a long period, Foucault says about the shift that took place in the late eighteenth and early nineteenth century, one that saw the vocabulary of crisis move from medical knowledge and power to the economic and political rationality of liberal governmentality. Two events need to be mentioned in this context. First, the emergence of a new object of government, namely, the population as a *living* entity, with its characteristics, its patterns of behavior, and its needs, along with the desire to understand it, monitor it, and control it, gave birth to a range of disciplines, including political economy, geography, biology, statistics, and a new form of power, which Foucault calls biopower. With the advent of biopower, the population, which hitherto had been entirely bound up with the problem of sovereign power and viewed as a quantity that can be used to increase the power of the sovereign by providing troops and resources, and by extending its territory, is now defined by a wide range of natural processes and variables, which need to be recognized, analyzed, and integrated.[44] At the same time, the birth of pathological anatomy and the introduction of dead bodies in hospitals transformed medicine entirely, and sounded the death knell of the medicine of crisis, now replaced by a technology of observation and demonstration and a modern, scientific concept of truth as *discoverable*. Regarding the latter development, Foucault writes:

> The appearance of pathological anatomy made it possible to bring to light the reality of the disease in a localized lesion within the organism and identifiable in the body. Then, on the other hand, starting with these different lesions that individualized diseases, this same pathological anatomy made it possible to constitute clusters of signs from which the differential diagnosis of diseases could be established. . . . Under these conditions—ascription of the disease to the body and the possibility of a differential diagnosis— the crisis, as the test in which the disease produced its own truth, became pointless.[45]

The body ceases to be a source of truth and becomes "an object of calculation" and a domain of "administrative control."[46]

However, the disappearance of the discourse of crisis from medical diagnosis did not translate in the disappearance of the vocabulary of crisis *tout court*. On the contrary, the vocabulary of crisis migrated to the new disciplines to which I was referring earlier, as well as to philosophy. But it also became commonplace in everyday discourse. It is as if the classical clinical paradigm, and the idea of crisis in particular, had migrated from the medical body to the social body as a whole. *Prima facie*, this phenomenon might strike one as odd. The concern for, and control of, the health, longevity, and wealth of the population as a living entity, and of a newly ascribed political role to medicine, coincides with a profound transformation of medical knowledge, of its move away from the clinic of crisis, and toward pathological anatomy, demographics, and statistics, all of which are sciences of the norm and deviations from the norm, which give rise to the ideas of the pathological, the abnormal, the unusual, or technocratic. In other words, medicine is transformed by virtue of its integration within the new biopolitical paradigm. But if that is the case, why is the critical paradigm not only retained, but reinforced and extended to all spheres of life? Why and how does the birth of normative power sit alongside the vocabulary of crisis? My hypothesis is that crisis itself is normalized in the process, at least in part. By that, I mean the following: as I have already indicated in passing, for example in relation to political economy, crises are inserted within the theoretical *and* practical apparatus of the norm, of its statistical deviations *and* the need to *manage* them—that is, to allow them to regain their place within the statistically approved or tolerable range. Crisis is now associated, if not identified, with a greater than usual yet still measurable deviation from the norm, where the norm or what is normal refers not to a fixed point, but to a statistical range of values (thus, financial markets are subject to corrections, recessions, and depressions, with a fall value ascribed to each threshold; and the same goes for natality, morbidity, or mortality rates). It is not a coincidence that contemporary crises are managed, or mismanaged. Management is the default, ordinary way of addressing crises, one that reveals its deep connection with the normativity of biopower. Management, and crisis management in particular, are ways of exercising power, or fundamental ways in which power is exercised today. The discourse of political economy and the figure of the economist, now seen as the diagnostician of the ills of society as well as the physician who can administer remedies, are at the heart of this new dispositive.

Foucault makes a very similar point, albeit in passing, in the context of his analysis of "security" as a central concern of biopower and of the emergence of vaccines and vaccination programs in particular. In *Security, Territory, Population*, he analyzes the medical innovation that, in fighting the spread of smallpox and preventing other possible attacks of the disease, consisted in inoculating individuals with a small amount of the virus.[47] He mentions four elements constitutive of security as a dimension of biopower, the final one being *crisis*. The other three are case, risk, and danger. Regarding case, Foucault's claim is that the disease is no longer apprehended as a "prevailing" or "common" disease (*maladie régnante*)—that is, as a "substantial" disease, united with a country, a town, a climate, a group of people, a region, a way of life—as it was in seventeenth- and even eighteenth-century medicine. The disease "no longer appears in this solid relationship of the prevailing disease to its place or milieu, but as a distribution of cases in a population circumscribed in time or place."[48] This is when the notion of case appears. It designates "not the individual case, but a way of individualizing the collective phenomenon of the disease, or of collectivizing the phenomena, integrating individual phenomena within a collective field, but in the form of quantification and of the rational and identifiable."[49] Second, to the extent that the disease is now accessible in this way at the level of the group and the individual, it becomes possible to identify for each the *risk* of catching the disease, of dying from it or being cured, and to establish risk profiles: "for each individual, given his age and where he lives, and for each group, town or profession, we will be able to establish the risk of morbidity and the risk of mortality."[50] Furthermore, this calculation of risk shows that the risks are not the same for all individuals, for all ages, or in every social condition, place, or milieu. Risk is differentiated. The risk of smallpox, for instance, is much greater (more *dangerous*) for those who are less than three years old or who live in town rather than in the country. Finally, the securitization of society, which is also to say its normalization (or, better said perhaps, normativization), recognizes moments or points of crisis. In the case of a disease, it coincides precisely with the shift from an epidemic to a pandemic:

> Phenomena of sudden worsening, acceleration, and increase of the disease can be identified that do not fall within the general category of epidemic, but are such that its spread at a particular time and place carries the risk, through contagion obviously, of multiplying cases that multiply other cases in an unstoppable tendency or gradient until the phenomenon is effectively checked by either an artificial or an enigmatic natural mechanism.[51]

The crisis is precisely this phenomenon of sudden, circular bolting. As such, and while it occurs in the medical context, it is not to be confused with crisis as it was understood in classical medicine. As we saw, it also occurs in other contexts, such as economics or demographics. This is why, as I indicated in my introduction, crisis is best described as a "discursive event" or regime, rather than a purely descriptive signifier. In the modern era, by which I mean the era in which different forms of power—sovereign power, disciplinary power, and biopower in particular—overlap, crisis designates a kind of situation that can be recognized, accounted for, and dealt with (or *managed*) through a range of disciplines, instruments, and strategies, at the heart of which figure the population and its statistical representation. Cordero summarizes Foucault's position nicely:

> To the extent that the phenomenon of crisis faces us with the question of what is to be done in those situations when life is threatening (e.g., a body, a city, a market, a society), the notion of crisis makes its political appearance, more than in the form of failure, in the form of a productive moment of governmentality through the invention, operation, opposition and application of practices of knowledge and strategies of power . . . oriented to the management of populations and their problems. In other words, the constitution of social therapeutics, or therapeutic rationality, traverses different domains of collective life and operates through two interrelated claims: the claim to know society and the constitutive fragility of its processes and the claim to secure society's ideal state and establish the nomos that organizes and regulates relations. Thus, for the liberal art of government crisis becomes a novel mechanism of formation of truth as well as an innovative means of regulation and reprogramming of social life.[52]

This liberal tendency is exacerbated in neoliberal governmentality, which elevates economic knowledge to the level of a new *scientia universalis*, and the economist to the status of a new physician with a normative-therapeutic power on society.[53] This shift comes across most clearly in the Draft Statement of Aims of the first meeting of the Mont Pèlerin Society, named after the place in Switzerland, at which the founding fathers of neoliberalism gathered in 1947 to define a "system of individual freedom."[54] The first article of the Draft states that

1. Individual freedom can be preserved only in a society in which an effective competitive market is the main agency for the direction of economic activity. Only the decentralization of control through private property in the means of production can prevent those concentrations of power which threaten individual freedom.[55]

The second article reads:

2. The freedom of the consumer in choosing what he shall make, and the freedom of the worker in choosing his occupation and his place

of employment, are essential not merely for the sake of freedom itself, but for *efficiency in production*. Such a *system of freedom* is essential if we are to maximize output in terms of *individual satisfactions*.[56]

According to the neoliberal view, freedom is as much an end as a means, as much a natural aspiration as a technique aimed at maximizing utility. Individual satisfaction itself *requires* free, competitive markets. While neoliberals champion freedom as the highest value, they define it in a very specific sense: it is not "the realization of any political, human, or cultural *telos*," but "the positing of autonomous self-governed individuals, all coming naturally equipped with a neoclassical conception of rationality and motives of ineffable self-interest, striving to improve their lot in life by engaging in market exchange."[57] The most radical definition of freedom thus understood is perhaps that of the Chicago School, for which, according to Rob Van Horn and Philip Mirowski, freedom means only "the capacity for *self-realization attained through individual striving for a set of necessarily unexplained (and usually interpersonally ineffable) prior wants and desires.*"[58] The reference to desires, and to desires as wants, is both crucial and unsurprising. For the wants in question designate something we desire, but also, and primarily, something we lack. And freedom is defined not as the ultimate desire, but as the necessary condition for the satisfaction of those desires—a condition that can be realized only in and through the market as a place of truth, yet one that, at the same time, can never be entirely achieved. Risk is therefore a key feature of this system of freedom, and crisis is one of its inevitable consequences.

Crisis in Philosophical Discourse

It is not a coincidence that, for much of its history, philosophy remained unconcerned with crisis. So long as it focused on eternal problems and transhistorical truths, metaphysical questions of first principles and causes, essences and Ideas, or human nature, the notion of crisis had no place within it. So long as it placed itself under the auspices of an analytic of truth and thought of itself as a universal, *a priori* science, critique was possible, at least in the Kantian sense, but crisis was not. This means that *historical* critique was not possible. "Mankind," Hume writes, "are so much the same in all times and places that history informs us of nothing new or strange."[59] Only when philosophy turns to history, when it begins to ask about its own present *and* its own history, when it becomes philosophy of history *and* history of philosophy, when it asks: "who are we *today*?" and constitutes itself as historical critique—only then does the notion of crisis appear.[60] But this inner transformation of philosophy, from an analytic of truth or science of the universal to historical critique, concerned with accidents, contingencies, and singular events, did not happen overnight, or simply internally. As we'll see, the medical and poetic discourses, which I introduced earlier, proved decisive: they provided philosophy with not only (or primarily) the lexicon of crisis, but also a different way of apprehending time, a paradigm to interpret *historical* time. Crisis is therefore not an original philosophical concept, but a schema, inherited from Greek and Roman antiquity, which philosophy deploys (explicitly or implicitly), reworks, and transforms to apprehend its own turbulent present and, more generally, the upheavals, conflicts, and revolutions of history.

In his lectures at the Collège de France on psychiatric power, Foucault sketches a "short history of truth," in which he distinguishes between two types of truth.[61] In an implicit reference to Aristotle's *Peri Hermeneia*, he defines the first as "apophantic." It is the discourse that, saying that something is the case, it happens either that it is indeed the case, in which case it is true, or isn't the case, in which case it is false; or again, saying that a thing is not the case, either it is (in which case the statement is false) or it is not (in which case it is true).[62] Whilst perhaps buried or hidden, and thus difficult to ascertain, the truth in question is thought to be accessible in principle and by anyone, so long as he or she has the right instruments and method, which we are capable of developing. It is thought to be there from the start, waiting to be discovered. It is the truth of what is, from all eternity as it were. It is the object of a demonstration. To this "demonstration-truth," or this "discovery-truth," Foucault opposes the sort of archaic truth he had already analyzed in his first lecture course at the Collège de France, and which he now refers to as the "event-truth." This is the sort of truth that belongs to a specific time and place, the truth that happens (*qui arrive*), as opposed to the truth that is always already there. It involves a shock, rather than an inclination. It is the truth that is spoken by the oracle in Delphi, or Tiresias, or the truth of the god that heals in Epidaurus. But it is also the truth that speaks in and through the moment of crisis in Greek, Latin, or medieval medicine—a critical moment indeed, in that it designates the point at which life can take a turn for the better, or the worse, and requires the intervention of the doctor. It is a fleeting, flashing truth, a "lightning-truth," which Foucault opposes to the truth of the sky above the clouds. As a result, it is a truth that needs to be grasped at the right time or in the opportune moment (*kairos*)—a conjunctural truth that can only be the object of conjectures. It requires a certain eye, a certain training, or the mediation of those whom truth has decided to strike: the prophet, the priest, the soothsayer, the physician, and, I would argue, the philosopher.

For crisis to become a phenomenon in the eyes of philosophy, and a philosophical concept, this shift in the essence or meaning of truth was required. But unlike the other figures I mentioned, the philosopher believes that access to truth as event—to the event of truth and the truth of the event—requires a range of epistemic and methodological procedures, the construction of a conceptual apparatus or grid. That truth is not simply, immediately, or miraculously given. It needs to be extracted from the intricate and often obscure fabric of history. Critique is the name we can give to such an operation.

Although the concepts of crisis and critique do not appear as such in Greek philosophy, Foucault claims that something like a critical attitude began to emerge in Greek philosophy, precisely at moments of social and political crisis. It is an attitude that involves truth in the sense I have just mentioned—that is, as revealing something about the present, and therefore as event. But it involves truth in yet a different sense, one that implicates the very life of those who utter it. This type of truth, which implicates the subject of truth as an ethical and political form of existence, was embodied and played out in what the Greeks referred to as *parrhēsía*. This can be translated as "frank" or "true" speech, as the ability and courage to tell the truth. Before analyzing the nature of *parrhēsía* and its connection with crisis, let me venture two observations. First, Foucault grounds his lectures from the early 1980s on the practice of *parrhēsía* in a reading of Mendelssohn's and Kant's 1784 responses to the question "What is Enlightenment?"[63] Enlightenment is precisely defined as a critical attitude toward one's present, and as the freedom to speak freely in that regard. Second,

Foucault's lectures on the government of the self and others follow those on neoliberal governmentality, which had precisely presented neoliberalism as a technology of the self and of others, constructed around an economic, market-based rationality, and the norms of self-interest, utility, competition, flexibility, and resilience. At stake, then, for Foucault is the possibility of asking about alternative practices of the self and discourses of truth, other ways of relating to oneself and others as a subject of truth.

In a series of readings of the philosophical and literary corpus—of Plato, Plutarch, and Euripides in particular—Foucault notes that the question of frank speech, of saying everything or "telling all" (*pan rēma*), was bound up with, if not motivated by, "the functioning of Athenian democracy and its crises,"[64] and "the great crisis in Athens provoked by the second part of the Peloponnesian war."[65] The object of parrhesiastic truth-telling, he observes, is not knowledge or science, but *ēthos* (i.e., character) and *bios* (i.e., life in the sense of a philosophical style of existence). They converge in courage as a specific virtue, that of speaking truth to power, especially in moments of crisis. Thus, the parrhesiast is concerned less with "the being of nature and things" than he is with recognizing what he is and what others are—with truth in an ethical sense.[66] And whether in the Greek or the Roman context, *parrhēsía* was instrumental in defining a line between individual guidance and the political field, especially around the question of how to govern the Prince's soul (a question that will of course resonate throughout the centuries). The question, then, becomes one of knowing how one can "govern the Prince in such a way that he can govern himself and others,"[67] how one can speak truth to power, without detour or rhetorical tricks.[68] How, Foucault asks, "should one form the Prince's soul so that it may be open to the true discourse that must be delivered to him constantly while he is exercising power?"[69] This problem comes across particularly clearly in Plato's parrhesiastic confrontation with Dionysus the Younger, the son of Dionysus the Elder and the heir to power, who, unhappy with what his counsel has to say, drives Plato out of Syracuse, threatens to kill him, and actually plots his assassination. In that context, Foucault reads the Seventh Letter as an account of Plato's career as a political advisor to Dionysus and a conception of philosophy as political advice "when things are going wrong, when there is illness."[70] If this advice takes the form of *parrhēsía*, it is,

Foucault insists, now only as philosophical truth-telling—that is, as a discourse rooted in *logos*, but also oriented toward actions (*ergon*).[71]

This is precisely the point at which the schema of medicine, and of crisis in particular, reemerges: "Is it not the duty of someone advising a sick man who is following a bad regime to get that man to change his way of life? If the sick man wishes to obey, he will give him new prescriptions. If he refuses, I hold that an upright man and real physician should not agree to further consultations."[72] This medical metaphor, Foucault admits, seems rather "banal."[73] It is much less banal, however, if we emphasize the distinctive features of medicine according to Plato and, more generally, of Greek texts of the fourth century BC. Those features will also turn out to be at work in Renaissance political philosophy, and in Machiavelli in particular (to whom I will turn next). First, Foucault notes, "medicine is an art of the conjuncture, of the opportune moment, and also conjecture, since, through the signs one is given, one must recognize the illness, foresee its evolution, and thus choose the appropriate therapy."[74] Second, medicine is also always characterized as "an art of persuasion," especially among free men: good (that is to say, free) medicine is "an art of dialogue and persuasion."[75] Finally, good medicine is concerned with the patient's whole life, and not just this or that illness. This is why, beyond the treatment required for the pathology in question, medicine establishes a whole regime of life: "for the patient really to be cured, and for him to be able to avoid further illness in the future, he must agree to change everything, his drink, his food, his sexual relations, his exercise, his whole way of life."[76] Now if we take these three features into consideration and "relate them to the task of the political counsellor who, according to the text of the Letter VII, must conduct himself like a doctor, then we see that the role of the political counsellor will not be to exercise the office of a ruler who has to take decisions on a *normal* day to day basis," but "to intervene only when things are going wrong, when there is illness."[77] In other words, the philosopher as parrhesiast intervenes in times of crisis and exceptional circumstances, when a historical-political critical diagnosis and a proper remedy are required. Then, and only then, will "time be set right" and the order of things be restored. It is precisely in critical times that a certain kind of philosophical attitude—a certain kind of truth-telling and a certain virtue (namely, courage, or political prudence)—is required.

> The Philosopher has, if you like, a critical role in the sense of a role performed in the realm of crisis, or at any rate of trouble and illness, and of the patient's, in this case the city's and citizen's awareness that something is wrong. Second, the role of philosophy and the philosopher will not be like that of slave physicians who are satisfied with saying: Do this, don't do that, take this, and don't take that. The philosopher's role must be like that of free physicians who address themselves to people who are free, that is to say, *who persuade at the same time as they prescribe.* . . . Finally, third, the philosopher will not simply have to give advice and opinions regarding this or that trouble affecting the city. He will also have to rethink entirely the city's regime. . . . So, the object of the philosopher's intervention must be the entire regime of the city, its *politeia*.[78]

What matters here is the manner in which, however obliquely, Foucault seeks to respond to the liberal and neoliberal normalizing discourse, its economic-therapeutic paradigm of management, and its practices of the self, which we saw embodied in Röpke's *Social Crisis of Our Time*, with a different kind of truth, a different practice of power, and a different process of subjectivation. Philosophy, he claims—and his claim includes a line of thought that runs from Greek *parrhēsía* to Kant's critical attitude, understood as "the ethics of truth-telling as an action which is risky and free"[79]—differs from other discourses of authority, based on truth and normative power. For philosophy, truth-telling is not a matter of prescribing a norm, or bringing a situation back to its normal state; rather, it is one of "scrutinizing the perplexities and problems of human life," of modifying "the conditions of a problematic situation with a single curative intent."[80] This attitude, Foucault recognizes, is also that of the militant and the revolutionary, who seek radically to transform the relation between truth and power, or who understand, and bear witness to, the changing character of the relationship between them.[81] If it is therapeutic, it is therefore not in the modern, normative sense of bringing a system back to its normal state by allowing "rational" economic agents to express their interest freely, but in the classical sense of uttering a truth through the manifestation of crisis, prescribing a remedy, and establishing a new regime.[82] Crises of this kind, I will argue in Chapter 3, are best understood as crises of *contradiction*, and require profound transformations.

Machiavelli: The Medical Schema of Crisis

This connection between philosophy as *parrhesia*, especially in the form of advice to the Prince, the medicine of crisis, and historical diagnosis, will extend into the medieval period and the Renaissance. In *Critique and Crisis*, Koselleck notes that whereas "criticism" is an eighteenth-century catchword, the term "'crisis' was rarely used in the eighteenth century and certainly cannot be considered a central concept."[83] However, the fact that the notion of crisis was rarely used by philosophers before the nineteenth century does not mean that the *schema* of crisis was not influential. I have already begun to show that it is through classical medicine, with its emphasis on crisis, that history enters the philosophical discourse and allows it to construct itself as a discourse on, or science of, history. I now want to nuance further, if not dispute, Koselleck's claim, and extend Foucault's, by arguing that philosophers of the late Middle Ages and the Renaissance drew heavily on the medical language of the Hippocratic and Galenian corpus to articulate their own views on history and, more specifically, on the emergence, evolution, and transformation of political events and "maladies."

The philosopher, theologian, and physician Marsilius of Padua (ca. 1280–1343), author of the influential political treatise and polemic *Defensor Pacis* (*Defender of the Peace*), written between 1320 and 1324 in Paris, but not known until 1326, would be a case in point.[84] But let me focus on a better-known and still more influential thinker: Machiavelli.[85] As Laurent Gerbier shows in his unpublished thesis, the medical dispositive of crisis provides Machiavelli with an essential tool to think the figures of historical time and the political crises he witnessed during his lifetime. If some of the lexical, syntactic, and conceptual structures of his texts can be traced back to the medical schema, it is because the phenomenon of crisis marks a crucial stage in the development of the broader phenomenon with which medicine is concerned. Crisis is the nodal point of the process that defines pathologies. As such, it forces the physician to insert himself within the flow of time and identify within it regular patterns and "normal" causal sequences. At the same time, those observations, and the discourse of the physician more broadly, make sense only to the extent that they can be related to specific and concrete experiences. What Machiavelli values in the medical discourse, then, is its ability to embrace the duration of a phenomenon, with its events, accidents, or crises, and subsequently to distinguish between the time to act and the time not to act. For that reason, his use of its lexicon by far exceeds the realm of useful metaphors or the simple transposition of readily available notions.

Whether in *The Prince*,[86] the *Discourses*,[87] or the *Florentine Histories*,[88] Machiavelli presents the body politic as a living and mortal body, prone to diseases and crises of various kinds and eminently corruptible. In a further reference to the medical paradigm, Machiavelli describes the city as a mixed or complex body (*corpo misto*)—that is, a combination or "composition" of simple and contrary elements, the "humors."[89] In The Prince and the Discourses, Machiavelli identifies two such humors (and not four, as in medicine): that of the people (*popolo*), rooted in their "desire neither to be commanded nor oppressed," and that of the great (*grandi*), rooted in their "desire to command and oppress the people."[90] As for the mixed bodies, they include principalities, armies, and religions. They are regulated by general rules or norms (the "orders"), which allow them to release (*sfogare*) their powers. The *ordini* of the city are the equivalent of the diet in medicine, in that they guarantee a certain balance and stability and operate in the long term. Laws, by contrast, are punctual remedies, more variable and adaptable than the *ordini*. They can be introduced or modified to correct a sudden imbalance in the body politic.

Unsurprisingly, then, Machiavelli conceives of the *ragionare dello stato* as a medicine of humors aimed at diagnosing, preventing, and wherever possible curing the maladies of the time. In Machiavelli's vocabulary, a malady (*malattia*) designates a state of imbalance between the internal forces of the body politic, which inevitably weakens the city. "Tumults" and "troubles" are the result of a conflict between humors which, by virtue of the constraints of the order in which they find themselves, cannot be released along their habitual or natural lines. When this ordinary effusion or outpouring is inhibited, the literally pathological potential of the trouble can no longer spread evenly and progressively. Concentrated and under pressure in a closed environment, it turns into an uncontrollable force, the sudden explosion of which is analogous to a crisis in medicine.

Like pathologies of the body, those affecting the city have a specific duration: they emerge, develop, peak, and eventually find a moment of resolution, for better or worse. The primary task of the science and art of government, then, is to identify the heterogenous elements—the humors—that "compose" the body politic. For it is that heterogeneity that contains the seeds of "dissension" and "discord," which weaken and threaten the body politic. Since the *corpi misti* are composed, they can always be decomposed. "Resolution" is the word Machiavelli uses to name the process of separation of the composed parts. And he calls the early stages of this process "corruption" (*corruzione*). In the *Discourses*, he takes the example of the corruption of the kings of Rome, which nonetheless managed to bring this process to an end by not allowing it to spread to the entire body politic.[91] Generally, Machiavelli sees in ancient Rome the embodiment of the ideal of the mixed constitution, a perfect state, which reached its perfection "through the disunion between the plebs and the Senate."[92] Roman institutions, he claims in *Discourses*, chapter 1, 2–5, were the result of a compromise between the two basic antagonistic desires: neither humor dominated the other entirely. Still in the *Discourses*, and as Del Lucchese remarks, Machiavelli considers a turmoil that assumed "a more violent and extreme form," namely, "the rioting connected with the agrarian law at the time of the Gracchi," which led to the ruin of the republic and the tyranny of Caesar.[93] Rome's is a history of virtue and power, but one that ultimately experiences decline and crisis. Good government, then, is a matter of the right *mix*. But that mix is always unstable and prone to corruption.

Machiavelli is insistent that the political maladies that affect a city vary considerably in degree and intensity. There are degrees of corruption, which require that we distinguish between situations in order to determine the relevant remedies. In a totally corrupt city, for example, laws are insufficient, since they can resolve a punctual disorder but cannot modify the general fabric of the city or rearrange the orders that compose it. In the case of profound crises, the order itself needs to be changed. Initially, the *ordini* that hold together or compose the *corpo misto* of the city play a positive role, since they regulate the mix of political materiality. Laws are introduced only punctually, to rectify or remedy a nascent imbalance. This, I would argue, corresponds to a crisis of deviation, with which we are today quite familiar. But should this materiality enter a process of corruption, or decomposition, the laws are no longer sufficient to the task of correcting it. At a certain degree of corruption the continuity ensured by the orders becomes a continuity for the worse, not the better. In the event of a graver form of corruption, the *ordini* continue to carry out their function of conservation, but this time by maintaining the imbalance and canceling out the positive effects of the legislative remedies. They retain their status as a principle of duration, but the principle has become harmful. A more radical remedy is thus called for, one that reforms the *ordini* themselves. This corresponds precisely to a dietary or regime change—that is, a transformation of the ordinary rule of composition of the city. In a more contemporary language, which I have already introduced but will expand on, I would say that the degree of corruption or crisis Machiavelli describes here calls for the introduction of new norms and the constitution of a new normality: a revolution. This is because the crisis is no longer one of deviation, but of decomposition.

We are now in the realm of "extraordinary remedies."[94] Such a remedy, Machiavelli argues, cannot come from within the body politic: the people itself, as the matter of the city, cannot spontaneously overturn the process of corruption. The cure must therefore come from without, and specifically from a single man.[95] Now to carry out such a forced cure, the prince needs to choose between a renovation "*poco a poco*" and a renovation "*a un tratto*." The first is theoretically preferable, but requires a prudent prince, able to discern the early signs of the disease. Assuming that such a prince exists, he will still need to persuade the rest of the population to accept the need for radical (or regime) change: one cannot underestimate the weight of habit and the fact that the multitude changes only when faced with the catastrophe. The multitude is essentially reactive. The physician-prince, on the other hand, can calculate in advance the temporal configurations and engage in preventive action. His *ragionare* is the source of his *agire*.

Since it is difficult to convince the multitude of the benefits of progressive reform, a reform *a un tratto* of the deficient *ordini* is preferable. However, this course is not without its own set of problems. To introduce a sudden and violent reform, the prince needs to abandon the ordinary modes of action and "*venire allo straordinario*." This is precisely what surgery does: given the failure of the regular diet, which relies on a "soft" regulation of the movements of the body, to maintain its health, the physician must bring himself to impose a violent form of action on it. Dictatorship, Machiavelli implies, is the political equivalent to the aggressive and invasive methods of surgery. It is right and proper in the case of maladies that are sudden, rather than chronic.

In his illuminating article devoted to Machiavelli's mature political thought, Filippo Del Lucchese shows how the *Florentine Histories* present crisis as "the interpretive paradigm" of the history of Florence, as the "motor" or "spring" without which Florence would not have developed into what Machiavelli described as a "wonderful" equality. In his early work (*The Prince* and the *Discourses*), Machiavelli argues that crises—"division," "dissension," "discord," "disorder," and "tumult"—diminish virtue and cancel power. In the later work, by contrast, Machiavelli intuits "the concept of crisis as a paradigm of possible development, of maturity and power." Crisis, Del Lucchese concludes, does not exclude power (as *potentia*), but contains it. And although the term "is never used directly, it may be supposed that Machiavelli has in mind something analogous to the medical concept of crisis, understood as the nodal and decisive point in the progress of an illness."[96] It should by now be clear that Machiavelli's text provides ample evidence to support this claim. What is really at stake, in the *Florentine Histories*, is the more obviously positive or productive nature of crisis and conflict.

Unlike the history of Rome, that of Florence is one of perpetual conflicts and "dissensions." For Florence, Del Lucchese writes, "crisis is the very substance of history. There is not a moment of this history which is not at the same time a moment of crisis."[97] Its norm is not "tranquillity," as Marsilius's Aristotelian and therefore teleological view of the body politic claimed, but tumult and discord. A state of permanent crisis, not unlike our own, seemed to plague the republic, and in such a way that it becomes impossible to distinguish the "humors," or the physiological elements constitutive of any republic (the desires and appetites of individuals and groups), from the "parties," or the pathological element of Florentine politics.[98] Prior to the moment of crisis, the humors already existed (they always do), but were of no real consequence. Following often minor incidents, they grow in intensity, become inflamed, and eventually overflow, thus "contaminating" the entire city.[99] All the parties involved in Florence—the Guelf and the Ghibelline; the white and the black Guelf; the *grandi* (once the warrior class and now the class of merchants, bankers, and financiers), representing the seven major guilds, and the *popolo*, representing the fourteen minor guilds; the *popolo grasso* and the *popolo minuto*, or *sottoposti*, who, as they were non-guilded, were also, according to the constitution of 1293, barred from being citizens—were in a state of chronic conflict and perpetual violence. An extreme example is that of the uprising of the woolworkers or "Ciompi" in the summer of 1378, to which Machiavelli devotes most of book 3 of the *Histories*. Among the poor, the Ciompi were the closest thing late medieval Europe had to an industrial proletariat. The "tumult of the Ciompi," as it is known, overthrew the governing elites and instituted a short-lived revolutionary regime, before being brutally crushed. Machiavelli's account includes a passionate speech by a fictitious Ciompo.[100]

The major and surprising difference between Florence and Rome, however, is that in Florence crisis translates not into ruin, but into power and virtue—at least for the *popolo*.[101] This is the lesson Machiavelli wants to draw for his own present: the spring or engine of history itself boils down to a conflict between two heterogeneous forms of desire and groups: the desire, on the part of the Great or the powerful, to increase their power and continue to dominate the people; and the desire, on the part of the people, no longer to be dominated, and become free. What is surprising, however—and what anticipates a more dialectical conception of crisis, which the Marxist tradition will equate with the concept of contradiction—is that in the case of Florence the laws that favor liberty are born of the tumult itself. Freedom was made possible by the conflicts internal to the order of the body politic. Crisis, as defined by the opposition between humors or desires, is not an entirely negative phenomenon. Rather, its negativity can be productive, and can produce positive outcomes. The desire of the people is a desire for laws and a common order—for a new regime or balance between the humors.

This, once again, does not mean that Machiavelli favors crisis as a default mechanism of history. The physician-prince needs to educate himself in the art of discerning harm when it first occurs, before it has become fully visible.[102] For when its signs are fully visible, the crisis is already there, and only "extraordinary remedies" can be applied. The prince will therefore seek to arrange the regime of the city by allowing the humors to be released before they reach a crisis point and overflow.[103] Crisis is not inevitable. Prudent and preventive medicine is the key to good government.

The Tragic Schema of Crisis (Schelling, Hölderlin, and Hegel)

Although the medical paradigm of crisis continued to shape the philosophical interpretation of historical time in the eighteenth century—Koselleck mentions the examples of Diderot in pre-revolutionary France, Burke on the French Revolution, and Burckhardt on a range of events, from the English and French revolutions to the Seven Weeks War of 1866 (between Prussia and Austria)[104]—the tragic paradigm underwent something of a revival and transformation in post-Kantian German philosophy. At the very end of the eighteenth century, a generation of German thinkers and writers (Schiller, Hölderlin, Schelling, and Hegel) turned to Greek antiquity, and Greek tragedy in particular, as a model of unity and reconciliation (*Versöhnung*), which they opposed to their own historical present.[105] Modernity, they thought, was a site of tension, conflict, and contradiction (*Widerspruch*), defined in part by the French Revolution and the wars that followed; and art, especially tragedy, appeared "to offer some kind of solution, a way of finding meaning in the apparent chaos of history."[106] By emphasizing reconciliation—a fundamentally Christian and therefore problematic notion in the context of Greek tragedy— as the natural outcome of tragedy, the authors I mentioned turned tragedy into "a uniquely privileged form of historical thought," one that offered "the possibility of finding meaning in events that seem irreducibly chaotic."[107] The German fascination for tragedy, especially Greek tragedy, lasted through the nineteenth and twentieth centuries. In each case, it was a matter of coming to grips with the present, the mechanics of history, and the essence of ethical life.[108] But the German turn to tragedy also took place against the backdrop of the Kantian critical edifice, which elevated metaphysics to the level of a rigorous science by delimiting once and for all the field of philosophical speculation and the role of the faculties corresponding to it. This critical turn, however, came at the cost of introducing what seemed to be unsurmountable divisions—between the theoretical and the practical, nature and morality, mechanical and free causality, the finite and the infinite, subject and object. Thus if the critical philosopher is, in the words of the first *Critique*, a "lawgiver of human reason," his legislative sphere—namely, philosophy itself—must itself be divided into two distinct systems comprising "one single philosophical system": the philosophy of nature, which deals with "whatever is"; and the philosophy of morals, which concerns itself with "whatever ought to be."[109] From then onward, the central task, which defined the very project of German idealism, was that of reconciliation (*Versöhnung*).

The turn to tragedy was to address the question of a possible schematization of, and even solution to, the crisis internal to the critical philosophy and, by the same token, of a possible or even necessary overcoming of the critical horizon. To be sure, one could point to Kant's third *Critique* (and to the role of both aesthetic and teleological judgment) as an attempt to bridge the divide between the philosophy of nature and that of morals. But, for reasons the explanation of which would be too long for this context, those thinking in the immediate aftermath of Kant's Copernican turn viewed that attempt as inadequate. Art, they felt, and tragedy in particular, had the capacity to present the unpresentable (or schematize the intelligible) by situating itself at the juncture of two disjointed orders and effecting the passage through which nothing, of itself, can pass. This poetic turn was eventually to turn back on philosophy itself, and transform it radically: speculation, as the *visio Dei*, the vision of the supersensible, or what Kant calls "intellectual intuition"—an intuition which, he believes, is refused to finite beings—is in fact accessible to human *thought* (and not simply practical reason).[110] As such, tragedy can be seen as the schema that allowed German philosophy to shift from critique to speculation. It is the missing link in the transition from Kantian dualisms to the unity of speculative dialectic. But it is also the schema through which history comes to be understood differently, as a process driven by conflict and contradiction. Contradiction ceases to be a mere fault in logical reasoning, and becomes the very engine of history. If judgment is to be subjected to critique, it is now in a sense fundamentally different from that of Kant: no longer as a reflection on the specific power of a human faculty, but as the diagnosis concerning a historical malaise and a call to transcend it.

Taking the word "metaphor" in its literal sense, as transposition or translation, Hölderlin claims that the tragic poem is the "metaphor of an intellectual intuition," whereas the lyric is the transposition of a feeling, and the epic is the transposition of great aspirations.[111] Thus Hölderlin finds the possibility of intellectual intuition not, as did Fichte, in the practical realm, but in the realm of the aesthetic, as Schiller did in the *Letter on the Aesthetic Education of Mankind*.[112] However, Hölderlin is not actually the first to develop a speculative theory of tragedy. In his *Philosophical Letters on Dogmaticism and Criticism* of 1795–1796, and in spite of his Fichtean position, the young Schelling presents Greek tragedy as a model, which figures the "reconciliation" of necessity and freedom.[113] In his *Lectures on the Philosophy of Art* (Jena, 1802–1803, Würzburg, 1803–1804), Schelling still hails tragedy as the highest manifestation of art, and sees in the tragic hero the one who represents "the unconditioned and absolute itself in his person . . . the symbol of the infinite, of that which transcends all suffering."[114] In this respect, Oedipus is the tragic hero *par excellence*. Who is Oedipus? A mortal destined to become a criminal, who seeks in vain to escape the fate revealed to him by the oracle. In the end, he is punished for a crime he did not intend to commit. How, Schelling wonders in the last of the *Letters*, could Greek reason bear such a contradiction? By accepting voluntarily to be punished for a crime he did not intend to commit, Oedipus pays homage to human freedom. The tragic hero refuses to see his actions as the effects of destiny alone and is ready to die to proclaim the freedom of the will. He gains absolute freedom by choosing to be responsible for *all* that he has done and identifying with his *fatum*. But he can do this only by dying, and thereby simultaneously gaining and losing his freedom. Through this identification "with fate, with the All, the tragic hero achieves the intellectual intuition or *visio Dei* which allows the reconciliation of the subject and the object," even if, in return, "he must lose his life, sacrifice his own finitude."[115] As Billings notes, Schelling sees reconciliation "simultaneously as an affective state," which leads to *catharsis*, "and a philosophical insight."[116]

The same idea can be found in Hölderlin. The tragic poem transposes and transports, it presents, makes sensible, and quite literally stages an intellectual intuition of unity, or of what is originally one: not a unity pure and simple (*Einheit*), but the unity (*Einigkeit*) of intimacy (*Innigkeit*) that holds together and reconciles everything with everything else. It is the unity of the absolute, which precedes and underpins *krisis*, understood as the moment of separation and judgment (*Urtheil*) that divides (*teilt*) the whole into parts (*Theile*),[117] the "arche-separation" or "originary partition" (*Ur-theil*) of "being" (*Seyn*) into Subject and Object. Two passages from "Judgment and Being" (1795) are directly relevant.[118] The first identifies the structural unity of being and intellectual intuition; the second affirms the unity of subject and object in intellectual intuition:

> Being [Seyn]—expresses the connection between subject and object. Where subject and object are united altogether and not only in part, that is, united in such a manner that no partition can be performed without violating the essence of what is to be separated, there and nowhere else can Being pure and simple be spoken of, as is the case with intellectual intuition.
>
> Judgment [*Ur-theil*], in the highest and strictest sense, is the original separation of object and subject which are most deeply united in intellectual intuition, that separation through which alone subject and object become possible, the arche-separation.

The truly modern crisis, then, is that of the division of Being in subject and object, as well as in the divisions inherited from Kantian critique. That crisis, in turn, determines the project of speculative philosophy, which is to reunite them in intellectual intuition and to understand being as "harmonious opposition."[119] Tragedy, for a period at least, provided that generation with a matrix to think the drama (and trauma) of separation, and the promise of reconciliation. The price of tragedy, and of the life of the totality, we saw, is the death of the hero. But, as Hölderlin shows in the "Remarks on Antigone," there are two different kinds of death, the Greek and the Hesperian: a death which is a farewell to the world (Empedocles) and a death which is a living death (Oedipus), the endurance of separation.[120] It is the latter that Hegel eventually retained in his own interpretation of tragedy and, of course, his own conception of the absolute.

Towards the end of his 1802–1803 article on natural law, Hegel presents the tragic as the model for the absolute, or "life."[121] Tragedy, he writes, "is nothing else but the performance, on the ethical plane, of the tragedy which the Absolute eternally enacts with itself, by eternally giving birth to itself into objectivity, submitting in this objective form to suffering and death, and rising from its ashes into glory."[122] Here, one clearly sees how the tragic defines the very unfolding of the absolute, and how, because of this, it is wrested from the mere theory of tragedy and understood according to its philosophical essence and destination. If the tragic provides a privileged point of access to Hegelian speculative dialectics, it is because of its emphasis on conflict (understood as contradiction) and reconciliation. This emphasis is clearly visible in the *Lectures on Aesthetics*.[123] "Above mere fear and tragic sympathy," Hegel writes in response to Aristotle's *Poetics*, "there stands the feeling of reconciliation" that tragedy generates by affording "the glimpse of eternal justice," beyond "the conflict and contradiction of ethical powers."[124] To the cathartic Aristotelian framework, then, Hegel adds a third feeling, one that reveals the true destination of tragedy. For him, the purpose of tragedy is to awaken in us the truly speculative feeling of reconciliation, especially in relation to the powers of ethical life.

In the article on natural law, the problem takes the following form: how can the modern state reconcile two ethical powers that oppose and mutually exclude each other—namely, the absolute ethical life on the one hand, and the relative ethical life on the other? Whereas the first characterizes the truly political moment, the organic nature of the state, which includes those for whom the universal is the whole (the soldiers and the philosophers), the second characterizes the economical-juridical moment of the state, its inorganic nature, which includes the sphere of needs and of rights, the bourgeois state and the peasant state, for whom private interest is everything. Whereas the first state defines the state in all its purity, whether it be for the soldier sacrificing his life to the survival of the universal, or for the philosopher-statesman whose efforts are directed toward the ethical totality, the second remains immersed in the sphere of particularity and, *de facto*, places the authentically political moment of the state in danger. The ethical reconciliation of these two antithetical moments is read through the structure of the absolute Hegel sees at work in Aeschylus' *Oresteia*. Once again, then, tragedy provides the formal schema through which the state of division, separation, or crisis—in this case of the modern state—is envisaged, and the feeling and aspiration, without which reconciliation cannot take place, is apprehended. The tragedy of ethical life (*die Tragödie im Sittlichen*) thus coincides with the emergence of the absolute, or the life of spirit reconciled with itself. It is not a matter, therefore, of a nostalgic attitude toward ancient Greece, nor of privileging an aesthetic genre over others. Rather, it is a matter of recognizing the speculative power of an aesthetic schema, the philosophical translation of which will be the elaboration of the system.

How, exactly, does Aeschylus' trilogy allow the ethical life to be thought of as absolute? By carrying out the orders of Apollo, god of the spiritual or truly political life, Orestes kills his mother, who has herself killed his father, and thus reestablishes the tarnished power of ethical life. But at the same time, Orestes unleashes the wrath of the Furies, goddesses of the natural ethical life and possessors of the powers of right which he violated. The conflict is brought for judgment before the Athenian people, through the mediation of the Athenian judicial council, or Aeropagus. The council decides equally in favor of the two powers, thereby recognizing the powers' equal right of existence but also signaling their own inability to rule on the conflict, and intensifying the crisis. The task of resolving this conflict will fall to Athena, goddess of the people itself. Restoring Orestes to the political or Apollonian life he had himself chosen, on the one hand, and incorporating the Furies within the City as benevolent divine powers (the Eumenides), on the other, Athena in her wisdom reconciles the people with itself. At the same time, she lays out a new mode of political organization. To be sure, she grants a divine and unalienable existence to the powers of private right. But this remains subordinate to the absolute ethical life. Equally, in order to remain within its absolute ethical life, the state must recognize the private sphere of right, of property, and of enjoyment, all the while remaining free from their hold. In other words, in order to remain faithful to its spiritual or divine reality, the state must sacrifice a part of itself and refuse to be only absolute ethical life.[125] This schema, which emerges toward the end of the article, defines the essence of the absolute as speculative reality. The structure of the absolute, or "life," is revealed as tragic.

Reconciliation, then, is a distinct (and indeed the highest) possibility, so long as we elevate the standpoint of the understanding (*Verstand*) to that of reason (*Vernunft*) and immanently follow the movement of the concept in all its contradictions, tremors, and convulsions—in short, its crises—and understand them as the necessary moments of its unfolding. One could then see how a critique of the very notion of crisis would stem from the partial, one-sided standpoint that characterizes *Verstand*, and thus from the critical standpoint's inability properly to grasp crisis as a necessary moment of the unfolding of *Vernunft*. It is not a coincidence that the dialectical-materialist concept of crisis, inherited from Hegel and applied to our social and economic reality, is equivalent to that of contradiction, and came to be understood by many as the engine of history.[126] That equation is itself different from the one (already mentioned) between crisis and exception, especially as conceptualized by Carl Schmitt, including in his own interpretation of tragedy. But what Schmitt and the thinkers of the Tübingen *Schift* have in common in their appreciation of tragedy is the centrality of the question of time and history, of the nature of the event. Like medicine for Machiavelli and other political thinkers of the Renaissance, tragedy operates as a schema of crisis through which historical time can be thought.

At this point, it is useful to introduce in more detail Hegel's views on contradiction, insofar as they constitute the background to the Marxist and post-Marxist philosophies of crisis, which I analyze in Chapter 3. Common sense as well as most philosophers, whether logicians or metaphysicians, see contradiction not as essential or real, but as merely contingent and illusory. In this understanding, contradiction indicates a failure of thought, and is therefore "unthinkable" as a positive moment of thought itself.[127] It is a kind of "abnormality" or "sickness"—note the medical similes—that affects our ability to think or understand the way things are, but one that can be rectified or cured by applying the right method:

> In the first place, contradiction [*Widerspruch*] is usually kept aloof from things, from beings [*dem Seienden*], and from *truth* generally; it is asserted

that there is nothing that is contradictory. Secondly, it is shifted into subjective reflection by which it is first posited in the process of relating and comparing. But even in this reflection, it does not exist, for it is said that the contradictory cannot be represented [*vorgestellt*] or thought. *Whether it occurs in actual things or in reflective thinking, it ranks in general as contingency, a kind of abnormality and a passing paroxysm of sickness.*[128]

Contradiction, then, is normally thought to be on the side not of truth and reality, but of error and illusion. In fact, "representational" thought can only recoil in "horror" when faced with contradiction: it cannot look it in the eye. Looking away, it prefers to ignore it and pretend it is "nothing."[129] But Hegel disagrees. From the standpoint of real or "speculative" philosophy, contradiction is a category of thought in its own right and an *essential* moment of the productive logic of the concept. Classical logic sees identity as the most basic principle of thought, and defines it as the principle of non-contradiction. As such, thought excludes contradiction. But for Hegel contradiction is constitutive of identity and therefore more *essential* to thought and reality than identity:

> [I]t is one of the fundamental prejudices of logic as hitherto understood and of ordinary thinking that contradiction is not so characteristically essential and immanent a determination as identity; but in fact, if it were a question of grading the two determinations and they had to be kept separate, then contradiction would have to be taken as the profounder determination and more characteristic of essence. For as against contradiction, identity is merely the determination of the simple immediate, of dead being; but contradiction is the root of all movement and vitality [*Lebendigkeit*]; it is only insofar as something has a contradiction within it that it moves, has an urge [*Trieb*] and activity [*Tätigkeit*].[130]

Far from being opposed to reality, to life and truth, contradiction is its very engine or drive. Without contradiction, thought and being are merely static and purely immediate: dead. Contradiction is therefore truth *at work* for Hegel: it is the (painful) labor of the concept in thought, and of reason in history. It is the sign of the productivity of the negative, of sense seeking its own way. Contradictions point to their unsustainability, to the necessity of their transformation and overcoming, their negation and affirmation: their *Aufhebung*. They reveal the tensions that characterize any dialectical moment, and that will force it into a new configuration.

The brief period of German intellectual history, which extends from the mid-1790s to the very early 1800s, thus marks a turning point in the philosophy of history. Crisis remains at the heart of it. But, through its elaborate reconstruction of the tragic paradigm, early German idealism transformed the very meaning of crisis, associating it with the concepts of contradiction and reconciliation, inscribing it within a speculative-dialectical schema. That schema did not precede the tragic paradigm, but emerged alongside it. Crisis is now seen as embedded in the fabric of history and as a necessary moment of *speculatio*, understood as the *visio dei* or the intuition of the absolute. As such, the tragic, crisis-oriented paradigm also facilitated the transition from Kantian critique to dialectical critique, and prepared the ground for Engels's youthful *Outlines of a Critique of Political Economy* (1843), which was soon followed by Marx's critique of political economy. As we shall see in Chapter 3, the concept of crisis takes center stage with Marx, whose theory reveals the contradictions inherent to history and to the capitalist mode of production in particular. So long, he claims, as social relations are governed by a process of accumulation—that is, are driven by labor productivity understood as the rate of exploitation and the production of surplus value—and so long as wages increase more slowly than productivity, crises will prevail. Similarly, in the long run, the logic of capital, which is based on accumulation and relies on the endless appropriation and commodification of space and of natural resources, contradicts the logic of the earth and the biosphere: the expansion of capital cannot proceed indefinitely, since it relies on resources that are physically limited. Unlike Hegel, however, Engels and Marx see those contradictions as pointing to a horizon of resolution—socialism—in which capitalism will be left behind. The contradictions and repeated social crises of capitalism are themselves a call to action which, Marx believes, will necessarily take the form of revolution, understood as the turning or critical point that will eventually lead to reconciliation.

The Concept of Crisis in Twentieth-Century Philosophy

One can't help noticing the quasi-ubiquitous nature of the notion of crisis in twentieth-century philosophy, despite the radically different philosophical positions held by those who use it. In the last few years alone, the vocabulary of crisis has intensified. Prominent philosophers have spoken of "the crisis of the European Union,"[131] the "biopolitical crisis,"[132] "the crises of cynicism, racism, and liberalism" currently facing our democracies,[133] and the "unprecedented set of crises" facing us today.[134]

In the European context, the notion of crisis is often used to designate either a precise moment in European history broadly defined, or (and perhaps more importantly) something that threatens the very identity, "spirit," and even *existence* of "Europe." Let me mention a few familiar examples.

In two letters originally published in 1919 in an English journal, Paul Valéry spoke of "the spiritual crisis" and the "intellectual crisis" characterizing Europe following the "great" war.[135] A few years later, Edmund Husserl, reflecting on the fate of Western rationalism in Nazi Germany and the growth of anti-rationalism and anti-intellectualism in Europe, spoke of "the crisis of European humanity" and "the crisis of science" in terms of its loss of meaning for "life," understood not biologically but as the "life-world" that is the very object of philosophical (or phenomenological) investigation.[136] But this crisis, he insists, is the result of scientific reason itself. It is the very progress of scientific reason that produces the crisis, which Husserl calls naïve objectivism, and which consists in divorcing the world of facts from the world of values. As Derrida puts it: "It is reason that throws reason into crisis, in an autonomous and quasi-auto-immunitarian fashion."[137] Having said that, and whilst attributing the European crisis to "a misguided rationalism," Husserl refuses to conclude that "rationality as such is evil."[138] This, in turn, means that the failure of rationalism in its current form is only an "*apparent*" failure: it lies not in "the essence of rationalism itself," but "in its entanglement in naturalism and objectivism."[139] As a result, Europe is faced with an existential choice: either it allows itself to be further estranged "from its own rational sense of life," and to fall into "barbarity"; or, by reigniting the spirit of philosophy, it manages to rise again and, through "a heroism of reason [*Heroismus der Vernunft*]," "overcomes naturalism once and for all."¹⁴⁰

This crisis-oriented view of history, which forces history into an *either . . . or* and seals its fate, can also be found in Heidegger. Unlike Husserl, Heidegger sees this alternative not as a turning point *within* rationality, understood as the destiny of Europe, but as a twisting free (*Verwindung*) of rationality itself. In each instance "crisis" does not refer to a moment of disruption, or a caesura, through which the European process of civilization reaches a higher stage of development, and is thus a necessary stage in a process of *Vollendung* (as in Hegel, or in the optimistic and linear *Gechichtsphilosophie* of Friedrich Meinecke's 1936 *Historism*).¹⁴¹ Rather, it refers to a *decisive* moment and a "plight" (*die Not*), which defines the difference between life and death for Europe, and in turn requires a decision (*Entscheidung*). Crisis is not a key Heideggerian concept. Yet one could argue that the very structure of existence, and subsequently of history, that Heidegger puts forth is both critical *and* decisive, the site of the greatest "danger" *and* of "salvation." This critical schema is in place from the very early texts. It is particularly present in *The Phenomenology of Religious Life*, where Heidegger seeks to reveal the existential-ontological foundations of the religious experience.¹⁴² Drawing on Book X of Augustine's *Confessions*, Heidegger shows how ordinary life is the life of *tentatio* and *concupiscentia*, which distracts and disperses us, pulls us away from our spiritual calling.¹⁴³ For the most part, human life is *fallen* life, *Ruinanz* and *Zerstreuung*. Only through something like a *crisis* of existence, a religious (or existential) calling and the awakening of conscience (*conscientia, synteresis*), which involves a profound unease or *molestia*,¹⁴⁴ the deepest dread and anxiety,¹⁴⁵ can we stop forgetting who we *can* be; only by coming face to face with our own finitude can we tear ourselves away from fallen, inauthentic life and follow the path of authenticity. Only then are we truly free and fully human. The call of conscience—which, in *Being and Time*, comes not from God but from Dasein or existence *itself*, that is, from existence's ownmost and uttermost possibilities—requires a *decision* on our part, a decision *for* the new life and one's own freedom. It is, quite literally, the pivotal moment of existence, or the point at which existence becomes qualitatively different: defined no longer by the norms, conventions, and opinions of others, or by the passive acceptance of its own facticity, but by the affirmation of its own freedom and power as revealed by its own finitude.[146] Crisis is literally the moment of separation or scission (*Scheidung*) coextensive with the utmost decision (*Entscheidung*). I cannot think of a better formulation of what we might refer to as an existential crisis, insofar as it implied the profound transformation of one's entire existence.

This critical structure or schema is subsequently applied to History understood as the place of the most urgent decision in the face of a defining event, namely, the event of "metaphysics" as the forgetting and abandonment of the truth of being. This event, Heidegger tells us, began to unfold many centuries ago. Today, however, it rages in the form of certainty and objectification, in the all-encompassing, totalizing power of science and technics (*Technik*), in planetary domination, ecological devastation, and "the *transition to the technologized animal*."[147] As a result, the fate or destiny of Europe, its decline or salvation, revolves around an "*either . . . or*"—the *Kehre* or "turning"—that defines who we are *today*, and around which History pivots. Heidegger formulated this critical and decisive alternative in a series of texts from the late 1930s and early 1940s: we have entered the age of the *end* of metaphysics, which "means an age in which at some point and in some way the historical decision arises as to whether this final age is the conclusion of Western history or the counterpart to another beginning."[148] *Either* the co-belonging and mutual appropriation of the Human and the truth of Being is recognized and sheltered, *or* History descends ever more into the forgetting and abandonment of Being—in the use, abuse, and exploitation of the earth; in a calculative form of thinking that leads to ever-expanding cycles of planification, production, and consumption.[149] *Either* a "new beginning" rises, one in which human beings are finally able to *let go* of beings, "leap" into the truth (and abyss) of being, and "care" for it, *or* Europe (and the world) becomes a unified bureaucracy for which the planet is essentially a set of goods and values to be exchanged, and in which human beings are reduced to being "human resources."[150] *Either* the West continues on the path of the struggle for unconditional power (*Macht, Übermacht*)—which, for Heidegger, is not a human feature but an onto-historical horizon—and succumbs to the economic, social, political, and military violence (*Gewalt*) that comes with such a struggle;[151] *or*, turning away from beings in their effectiveness and efficiency, their producibility, productivity, and reproducibility—in short, their "rationalization"—human beings embrace the way of powerlessness, or of the otherwise than power (, *Machtlosigkeit*), the way of poverty (*Armut*) and thoughtfulness (*Besinnung*).[152]

In the 1950s, Hannah Arendt, concerned with the social and cultural problems of her time and with the distinction between life in a biological and a political sense, wrote essays on "The Crisis in Education" and "The Crisis in Culture"[153] befalling the United States and Europe. In the early 1970s, she also put together a series of essays to which she gave the title *Crises of the Republic*.[154] Whilst seemingly less dramatic and more local and specific than the crises of Spirit, Reason, or History already mentioned, and (in her own admission) less traumatic than the two world wars or the horrors of the concentration and extermination camps, the crises in question unfold against the backdrop of "the *general* crisis that has overtaken the modern world everywhere and in almost every sphere of life."[155] This general crisis is political through and through: it affects not a specific area of public policy or a particular question, but political life as such, or what Arendt calls "the world." At the same time, the crisis is always specific—that is, revealed in the context of particular problems, such as education, culture, or truth and lies in public life. The specific crises in question, which represent a profound "instability in modern society,"[156] concern the tension between the private and public spheres; between the family, which represents the security of a private life that shields the child against the *public* aspect of the world, and the world we need to share; between genuinely free time and time that is merely "left over after labor and sleep have received their due";[157] between past and future, or between authority and tradition on the one hand and rebellion on the other; between entertainment and culture.[158] Regarding the latter tension, Arendt's claim is that entertainment is a phenomenon of *mere life*, oriented toward needs and functionality, and a distinctive feature of *mass* society. It is what we fill our lives with once the basic functions and tasks of life have been fulfilled. Culture, on the other hand, is a phenomenon of the *world*, which transcends needs and functions and is defined by the fact that it *endures*. The enormous increase in "leisure" or "vacant time" does not change the nature of time, which is part of the biological life process of consumption, and is opposed to the genuinely free time of political and cultural life, of shared words, deeds, and works of art. We could, of course, complicate the picture by pointing to the rebellious and hedonistic counterculture of the 1960s and 70s, to the rejection of the traditional pillars of authority (including the military) and of the social, political, and cultural consensus that emerged from the Second World War in the United States. In each instance, Arendt believes, crisis signals an erosion or destruction of the *sensus communis* without which there is no political life: "In every crisis a piece of the world, something common to us all, is destroyed."[159] But, Arendt insists, a crisis is also an opportunity to delve into the "essence" of the matter: "a crisis forces us back to the questions themselves and requires from us either new or old answers."[160] Crisis, she seems to suggest, is an invitation to problematize anew, to think and act.

The Husserlian, Heideggerian, or Arendtian account of history relies on crisis, yet crisis is never defined as such. Crisis orients and organizes their assessment of the present, yet never becomes a central concept. Although those philosophers do not feel the need to clarify the sense in which they use the notion of crisis, or mobilize it only implicitly, they use it in ways that reveal distinctive features. Two fundamental, almost opposed tendencies seem to emerge. On the one hand, crisis signals a profound tension within a historical situation, if not something like its exhaustion or unsustainability. But it also signals something like a turning point: it points toward the future and demands that we transform the present. It involves a critical diagnostic as well as a moment of decision. It carries a sense of urgency and emergency, as well as a call to think differently.

Crises and Revolutions in the Natural Sciences

The final discourse of crisis I want to analyze is that of the history and philosophy of science. The articulation of contradiction, crisis, and revolution, which I will explore in detail in Chapter 3, is not exclusive to social and political movements, or indeed to the Marxist framework. It also provides a useful framework to think the history of science. Contrary to a well-established *doxa*, and even to the claims made by some philosophers of science (such as Lakatos, whom I discuss below), the history of science is not simply progressive, cumulative, or straightforwardly linear. Beyond the enlightenment narrative of a progressive history (be it of freedom or reason), a critical history of science, and of history in general, sees crises as turning points indicating the need for different norms and a new trajectory. Kuhn's seminal *Structure of Scientific Revolutions* is a work of that kind.[161] It questions the dogmatic image of scientific development as the progressive replacement of ignorance by knowledge, under the pressure of phenomena disclosing order in an aspect of nature where none had been seen before: "Cumulative acquisition of unanticipated novelties proves to be an almost non-existent exception to the rule of scientific development. The man who takes historic fact seriously must suspect that science does not tend toward the ideal that our image of its cumulativeness has suggested. Perhaps it is another sort of enterprise."[162]

Kuhn famously opposes "normal" and "revolutionary" science. For the most part, science is involved in "normal science," by which Kuhn means a puzzle- or problem-solving activity, as well as the crucial (and often fascinating) "mop-up work" that scientists carry out, sometimes for a long time, following the emergence of a new paradigm.[163] The work of normal science, Kuhn claims, consists in the "actualization" of the promise contained in the paradigm in question, or in providing answers to questions defined in advance.[164] As such, the aim of normal science is not to generate novelties, but to confirm predictions and work out the consequences of the paradigm. Normal research is a "highly cumulative" and "successful" enterprise that "owes its success to the ability of scientists regularly to select problems that can be solved within conceptual and instrumental techniques close to those already in existence."[165] Virtually every year, Nobel Prizes are awarded to scientists carrying out that kind of work. When faced with "anomalies" within an accepted scientific paradigm, normal science recognizes that "nature has somewhat violated the paradigm-induced expectations."[166] Yet it seeks to adjust or tweak the paradigm theory until "the anomalous has become the expected."[167] It does all it can to accommodate this anomaly within the paradigm. Normal science is intrinsically *conservative*.

The Hungarian-born philosopher of mathematics and science Imre Lakatos is one of the defenders of the *progressive* view of science, which he sees as an alternative to Kuhn's distribution of science around conservative and revolutionary poles. His forced exile from Hungary following the uprising and brutal repression by Soviet troops in 1956 may well have played a role in his eventual distrust of crises and revolutions. As Alan Musgrave and Charles Pigden emphasize, Lakatos was a dedicated opponent of Marxism in the later (and British) phase of his career, but had been a communist revolutionary in the earlier (Hungarian) phase of his life, an eager co-conspirator in the creation of a Stalinist state in Hungary in the late 1940s, and a committed denunciator of "deviationist" and "reactionary" professor and students.[168] In a nutshell, Lakatos claims that when faced with anomalies, proponents of what he calls a "research programme," which consists of a collection of experimental practices anchored in a "hard core" of theoretical assumptions that are deemed irrefutable (or at least resistant to refutation), build "auxiliary hypotheses" to protect the hard core. In Musgrave and Pigden's words, "a programme progresses theoretically if the new theory solves the anomaly faced by the old and is independently testable, making new predictions. A programme progresses empirically if at least one of these predictions is confirmed."[169] Lakatos suggests that change in the history of science occurs not through Kuhnian leaps and revolutions, but when "progressive research programmes replace degenerating ones."[170] In fact, the distinction between progressive and degenerating research programs corresponds to the distinction between "good" and "bad" science, or between science and non-science.[171] A research program is degenerating if the successive theories do not deliver novel predictions or if the novel predictions they deliver are systematically falsified. When a research program, such as the Linnaean tradition of natural history, clearly becomes degenerative, scientists do not immediately jump to a new, unverified paradigm but rather search within the fragments of the former theory for a novel way forward. In other words, novelty cannot be attributed solely to moments of crisis and the emergence of new scientific paradigms; a research program can be progressive—theoretically, empirically, or both— when changes to its auxiliary hypotheses are introduced and achieve greater explanatory or predictive power. I would argue that Lakatos's objections to Kuhn are a good reminder of how much work "normal" science can do, and the extent to which it operates within a progressive paradigm. But I would also claim that the nuance they invite us to use in our view of scientific practice does not invalidate Kuhn's distinction between normal and revolutionary science. For Lakatos, "a scientific revolution occurs when a degenerating programme is superseded by a progressive one," which then acquires "hegemonic status," without necessarily eliminating all other competing research programs.[172] In the end, even Lakatos's "progressive" interpretation of science as a practice does not conform to the purely cumulative and linear view of progress assumed by the doxa.

Sometimes, however, the anomalies are such that they can no longer be accommodated by the paradigm. They are then best understood as crises, and specifically as contradictions. For what is a crisis in science, if not the point at which phenomena stubbornly refuse to be assimilated to existing paradigms, the point at which a given paradigm or research program is no longer able to account for, or make sense of, certain facts or phenomena that it would itself expect to explain?[173] There must be a "conflict" between the paradigm that, despite the efforts, instruments, and specific aims of the researcher, "discloses anomaly, and the one that later renders the anomaly law-like."[174] The time is then ripe for a scientific revolution, such as Copernicus' theory of astronomy, which replaced the Ptolemaic system, or Lavoisier's chemical theory of oxygen, which replaced the phlogiston theory that had proven successful for a long time, or Einstein's special theory of relativity, which replaced Newton's theory of absolute space and the attempt, on the part of physicists such as George Stokes (1845), Heinrich Rudolf Hertz (1890), and Hendrik Antoon Lorentz (1892), to incorporate a complete aether drag model into Maxwell's theory of electromagnetism.[175] Faced with the persistence and increase of such anomalies, science is thrown into a state of growing crisis, which eventually (but not necessarily) leads to the emergence of new theoretical norms. As Kuhn puts it, "failure of existing rules is the prelude to a search for new ones."[176] A crisis is precisely the point at which a paradigm appears out of joint and the rules of normal puzzle-solving are loosened. Puzzles are no longer seen as problems to be solved within the norms of an already established paradigm, and through techniques of confirmation and falsification; instead they are seen as crises, as "counterinstances" or instances of *a different kind of problem*. A crisis, in that respect, is the sign or signal that the problem needs to be posed differently. A crisis in the strong sense indicates not a lack of solutions, but a badly posed or insufficiently well-posed problem. It is an invitation to *problematize anew* and see nature from a different perspective: "when paradigms change, there are usually significant shifts in the criteria determining the legitimacy both of problems and of proposed solutions."[177] It is the very grammar of the science that changes.

But why should a change of paradigm be called a revolution? What justifies the use of that political metaphor to describe the emergence of new scientific paradigms? And how far does this parallel go? Social, economic, and political crises reveal the limits of a given institutional framework. Confronted with the contradictions inherent to the system,

> individuals become increasingly estranged from political life and behave more and more eccentrically within it. Then, as the crisis deepens, many of these individuals commit themselves to some concrete proposal for the reconstruction of society in a new institutional framework. At that point the society is divided into competing camps or parties, one seeking to defend the old institutional constellation, the others seeking to institute some new one. And, once that polarization has occurred, *political recourse fails*.[178]

Crises of legitimation and authority follow. They in turn can lead to the demand for a radical reconstruction of society and the creation of a new political order. Revolution, in this sense, commits one to the idea that the norms and values governing the current system have reached a point of exhaustion, that it is not able to accommodate all the anomalies and problems it generates, that the problems of production and consumption, of one's relation to the world and others (and this includes relations of class, race, and gender, as well as eco-relations), of nationality and citizenship, of borders and the movement of populations, of education and the prison system, require a paradigm shift and the invention of new norms, which might mean the *abolition* of some institutions and the creation of new ones. The emergence of a new paradigm—of a counterproposition and counter-conducts—against the backdrop of crisis directly challenges the norms of the existing paradigm.

To speak of paradigms is to suggest that, contrary to popular belief, science is not merely or even primarily empirical. It is a theoretical, constructivist enterprise, which often goes against common sense; and the paradigms are tested not through empirical observation, but through the construction of experiments that can be reproduced and predictions that can be verified. To envisage the history of science as the history of competing paradigms is also to dispel the idea of scientific rationality as simply lifting the veil covering nature and revealing its hitherto undiscovered truth. First, a paradigm provides us with a new way of seeing the natural world. Kuhn is adamant about this point. He is also aware that it goes against a very usual way of describing scientific discoveries, rooted in a philosophical paradigm initiated by Descartes and developed at the same time as Newtonian mechanics. He even recognizes that the paradigm in question, which sees scientific discoveries as a matter of *interpreting* differently observations that themselves are fixed once and for all, "has served both science and philosophy well."[179] Nonetheless, he insists that "what occurs during a scientific revolution is not reducible to a reinterpretation of individual and stable data."[180] Rather than being an interpreter, "the scientist who embraces a new paradigm is like the man wearing inverted lenses."[181] To be sure, he confronts the same constellation of objects as before, and knows that he does so. Yet those objects are "transformed through and through in many of their details" as a result of the lens through which they are seen. The interpretation of data is central to research programs, and is a defining feature of normal science. Yet it presupposes a paradigm and makes sense only within it. A paradigm shift is thus a shift not in observation or interpretation, but in one's view or perception of the world: "during revolutions scientists see new and different things," and it is "as if the professional community had been suddenly transported to another planet where familiar objects are seen in a different light and are joined by unfamiliar ones as well."[182] The world itself has changed, like a visual gestalt: "What were ducks in the scientist's world before the revolution are rabbits afterwards."[183] At the very least, as a result of discovering oxygen, Lavoisier saw nature differently. Furthermore, the world has changed *irreversibly*: once the scientist's perception of his environment has been reeducated, the world of his research seems "incommensurable with the one he had inhabited before."[184] After Lavoisier, "where Priestley had seen dephlogisticated air and where others had seen nothing at all," chemists learned to see oxygen. And after Galileo, where, in the presence of a heavy body swinging back and forth on a chain until it finally came to rest, the Aristotelian (for whom a heavy body is moved by its own nature from a higher position to a state of natural rest at a lower one) saw a swinging body falling and achieving rest with difficulty, the new physicist sees "a pendulum, a body that almost succeeded in repeating the same motion over and over again ad infinitum."[185] At times of revolution, then, the scientist's vision of his environment must be retrained. However crucial and central to normal science, the work of interpretation can only articulate a paradigm, not question or correct it.

At the same time, and perhaps more controversially, or at least counterintuitively, Kuhn's idea of a scientific revolution involving a paradigm shift, and therefore a different way of seeing the world, also carries or generates its own blind spot: by making something visible, or making it visible *in that way*, I push other phenomena—or other, possibly equally legitimate ways of seeing them—into invisibility. Competing paradigms disagree about what is a problem and what a solution, or what is an urgent problem and what is not. Inevitably, they "talk through each other when debating the relative merits of their respective paradigms."[186] The proponents of competing paradigms live, trade, and practice in different worlds, and as a result see different things when they look from the same point and in the same direction. For example, the proponents of competing paradigms will disagree about what a theory of motion should cover: must it "explain the cause of the attractive forces between particles of matter or may it simply note the existence of such forces? Newton's dynamics was widely rejected because, unlike both Aristotle's and Descartes' theories, it implied the latter answer to the question. When Newton's theory had been accepted, a question was therefore banished from science. That question, however, was one that general relativity may proudly claim to have solved."[187] Something similar happened in the nineteenth century with the dissemination of Lavoisier's chemical theory: it dissuaded chemists from asking why the metals were so much alike, a question phlogistic chemistry had both asked and answered. In other words, the adoption of Lavoisier's paradigm had meant a loss not only of a legitimate question but of an achieved solution. Yet "in the twentieth century questions about the qualities of chemical substances have entered science again, together with some answers to them."[188] To take another example, "the laymen who scoffed at Einstein's general theory of relativity because space could not be 'curved'—it was not that sort of thing—

were not simply wrong or mistaken."[189] With Einstein, and the Riemannian geometry on which he relied, the meaning of space itself changes: "What had previously been meant by space was necessarily flat, homogeneous, isotropic, and unaffected by the presence of matter."[190] Newtonian physics depended on it. Einstein's paradigm shift requires that space, time, matter, force, and so on be understood differently and laid down on nature again. We could provide many more examples. The fundamental point is that "paradigm debates are not really about relative problem-solving ability," facts, or truth.[191] Rather, they are about the construction of problems, and this in such a way that they cannot be resolved by proofs or even arguments. They require an act of faith, a leap of some kind, similar to that required in political revolutions:

> Like the choice between two competing political institutions, that between competing paradigms proves to be a choice between *incompatible modes of community life*. Because it has that character, the choice is not and cannot be determined merely by the evaluative procedures characteristic of normal science, for these depend in part on a particular paradigm, and that paradigm is at issue.[192]

Contrary to what we would tend and like to believe regarding the procedures of science at that crucial juncture, a *decision* in favor of the paradigm is required for the paradigm to become persuasive:

> The man who embraces a new paradigm at an early stage must often do so in defiance of the evidence provided by problem-solving. He must, that is, have *faith* that the new paradigm will succeed with the many large problems that confront it, knowing only that the older paradigm has failed with a few. A *decision* of that kind can only be made on *faith*.[193]

The transition to the other side is made not one step at a time, "forced by logic and neutral experience," but "all at once (though not necessarily in an instant)."[194] In other words, when paradigms enter into a debate about paradigm choice, their argument is necessarily circular: each group uses its own paradigm to argue in that paradigm's defense. Once again, it is not as if the resulting circularity made the arguments in question wrong or even ineffectual. The scientist's defense of the paradigm provides a clear image of "what scientific practice will be like for those who adopt the new view of nature."[195] That image might even be persuasive. Yet so long as one refuses to step into that circle and adopt the perspective of the new paradigm, the circular argument "cannot be made logically or even probabilistically compelling."[196] This literally and in every sense paradoxical view brings the parallel between science and politics to yet a different level. For Kuhn is not afraid to draw for science a conclusion borrowed from competing models of political life: "As in political revolutions, so in paradigm choice—there is no standard higher than the assent of the relevant community." There is no ultimate authority, no definitive argument to end the dispute over competing paradigms. As in politics, the dissensus ends with the formation of a consensus, which is ultimately a matter of persuasion and decision rather than proof: "this issue of paradigm choice can never be univocally settled by logic and experiment alone."[197] To be sure, one cannot discover how scientific revolutions happen without considering the impact of nature and of logic. But one also needs to take into consideration "the techniques of persuasive argumentation effective within the quite special groups that constitute the community of scientists."[198] In other words, in science as in politics there are techniques of the heart as well as of the mind. Most often, though, the conversion is a deeply personal and even aesthetic decision: "sometimes it is only personal and inarticulate aesthetic considerations" that convince the scientist to shift paradigms.[199] Slowly, as the paradigm is improved, as its research possibilities and program become clearer, and as a sense of what it would be like to belong to the community guided by it emerges, more scientists join it, and the strength of the persuasive arguments in its favor increases. That dynamic, in turn, puts it on the path to becoming a normal science.

With more time, one could show that the same dynamic animates the history of art, literature, and music. They too produce paradigms, within which something like normal art is practiced and traded. Yet, at certain critical times, and often (but not necessarily) in conjunction with social, political, economic, or ecological crises, they go through revolutions, at the end of which the rules of their artform are redefined. What I said about Mallarmé in my introduction could be said of the birth of modern painting (Cézanne) in response to the crisis of perspective, or Schönberg's dodecaphonic music as a response to

Wagner (to whom Mallarmé also responds). The history of art undergoes paradigm shifts as a result not of subjective taste or arbitrary decisions, but of crises internal to individual artforms.

However, while on the whole convincing, the parallel Kuhn draws between scientific and political hegemony does not go all the way. That is because political consensus and hegemony will never be able to rely on the rigorous and ultimately indisputable procedures of science: the role of affects and imagination, of myth and superstition, is irreducible in political community-building. Ideas alone, no matter how powerful, will never be sufficient to federate the multitude. Kuhn seems to grant the point when he writes: "Because they differ about the institutional matrix within which political change is to be achieved and evaluated, because they acknowledge no supra-institutional framework for the adjudication of revolutionary difference, the parties to a revolutionary conflict must finally resort to the techniques of mass persuasion, often including force."[200] Does science not operate differently in the end? To be sure, Kuhn emphasizes the nonrational element in the scientist's decision to embrace a new paradigm. He speaks of that decision as involving aesthetic preferences and even a leap of faith. His point, though, is that the success of the paradigm in question depends not on aesthetic preference or a Damascus moment, but on the hard work and slow improvement of the paradigm—its ability to withstand challenges, objections, and criticisms, and to persuade an ever growing number of scientists. In other words, while not entirely devoid of passions and/or aesthetic considerations, the consensus and community-building force of the paradigm rests on scientific rationality. It minimizes the role and impact of the imagination and the world of affects. As such, it differs from the ways in which the political multitude tends to come together. It also provides, perhaps, a model for the multitude.

But there is another, perhaps more fundamental reason why the parallel between scientific and social revolution can only go so far. It is clearly expressed by Georg Lukács, whose lectures and seminars Lakatos attended in 1945–7.[201] Following Marx, Lukács claims that, in the case of social reality, contradictions are not the sign of an imperfect understanding of the whole, but "belong to the nature of reality itself and to the nature of capitalism."[202] This means that when the totality is known—dialectically, and from the point of view of the working class—these contradictions will not vanish and cease to be contradictions. On the contrary, they will appear as necessary contradictions, arising out of the antagonisms of this system of production."[203] But in the case of the natural world, contradictions between theories do not have the same status: they are a sign of their incompleteness:

> The methodology of the natural sciences and every kind of Revisionism rejects the idea of contradiction and antagonism in its subject matter. If, despite this, contradictions do spring up between particular theories, this only proves that our knowledge is as yet imperfect. Contradictions between theories show that these theories have reached their natural limits; they must be transformed and subsumed under even wider theories in which the contradictions finally disappear.[204]

Lukács' conclusion is therefore clear: "When the ideal of scientific knowledge is applied to nature it simply furthers the progress of science. But when it is applied to society it turns out to be an ideological weapon of the bourgeoisie."[205] The contradictions of capitalism, it claims, are "purely surface phenomena, unrelated to this mode of production."[206] I will return to these contradictions in Chapter 3.

Conclusion

In addition to providing an overview of the history of the notion of crisis, from its legal, religious, medical, and tragic origins to its mutations in the modern and contemporary discourses of political economy, philosophy, and science, this chapter laid the foundations for the typology that will concern me for the remainder of the book. "Crisis" occurred alongside other key concepts—deviation, exception, contradiction, extinction—which indicate that a critical history of crisis cannot be only a matter of semantics or hermeneutics, but must also incorporate an archaeology, the aim of which is to reveal crisis as a historically differentiated process involving different *regimes*. It is to an analysis of those regimes that I now turn. To be more precise: I will focus on the regimes of exception, contradiction, and eventually extinction (or collapse), and leave aside the regime of deviation and the liberal technique of management that corresponds to it, returning to it occasionally and by way of contrast. The reason for that is simple: whilst often designated as such, and by virtue of their expected return to a "normal" situation, crises of deviation are not crises in any fundamental sense. Naturally, there is bound to be some disagreement over the nature of the crisis itself (and part of the democratic politics of crisis, I have argued, consists in keeping open the space of such a disagreement). It is the work of critique to take managerial power to task on that front, that is, to dispute the response to crisis as being *de facto* one of "management," to question the broader liberal and neoliberal framework—its discourse of truth, its hermeneutic power, its authority, its national and international institutions, its instruments, and its technologies of the self—within which crisis is inscribed. But where and when there is agreement—say, on the need to raise or lower interest rates—the measures to facilitate a return to "normality" are of a purely technical nature.

Another aim of this introductory and historically oriented chapter was to show that, whilst present in a number of discourses, and with roots in Greek law, tragedy, and medicine, the vocabulary of crisis arrived on the philosophical scene relatively late. In addition, crisis remained largely unthematized. To be sure, it became increasingly important as an organizing or background notion. But it was rarely defined. As such, it operated more like a philosopheme, which carried with it a more or less explicit understanding of the event and, more broadly, history. The paradox, then, is that while the schema of crisis became the fundamental mode of interpreting historical time, it was most often as an unthought that rarely translated into an actual *concept* of crisis. The two exceptions I will now turn to, but already alluded to, concern the status of crisis as exception in legal theory and philosophy, and, following Hegel and especially Marx, as contradiction in the philosophy of history and social relations. What is at stake in the former, from a philosophical point of view, is the singularity of sovereign power. What is at stake in the latter is the long-term sustainability of the economic regimes of accumulation that have dominated the world over the last five hundred years.

2

Crises of Exception

I now turn to an area in which the notion and, more importantly, the schema of crisis has played, and continues to play, an important role: namely, legal and political theory, especially in relation to what is known as the state of exception. Although the term translates the German *Ausnahmezustand*, or *Notstand*, equivalents exist in other languages and constitutions. In French law, it is known as the state of emergency or siege (*état d'urgence, de siège*), in Italian law as emergency decrees, and in Spain as the *estado de excepción*. A version of it also exists in Anglo-Saxon law, which allows for the declaration of martial law, or emergency powers, under specific circumstances. The type of crisis in question signals an exceptional situation that requires exceptional measures and powers. As such, its difference from crises of deviation is a difference of kind rather than degree. To be sure, both presuppose a norm and a normal state. But the crisis of exception—or, better said perhaps, the social or political crisis that leads to the decision regarding the state of exception, or the legal suspension of the rule of law—is not analogous to the management of a crisis of deviation. In this chapter I analyze the sources and history of that legal mechanism, and its formulation by Carl Schmitt, who sees it as the prerogative of sovereign power. But I also question its increasing use in democratic regimes and argue that the "normalization" of the state of exception is often (but not always) the sign of a failure properly to identify the nature of the crisis with which they are faced.

According to Agamben, the archetype for the modern *Ausnahmezustand* can be found in Roman law, and in the institution of the *iustitium* under the

Republic in particular.¹ From *ius sistere*, "suspending legal business," *iustitium* designated the temporary cessation of jurisdiction and judicial operations by magistrates and judges in civil and criminal matters.² In other words, the law made provisions for a cessation of the rule of law and the introduction of exceptional measures. *Iustitium* was a response to a time of deep crisis, usually defined by an external war, a civil war, or an insurrection (such as a slave uprising). Those crises manifested themselves as a profound disorder or agitation (*magna trepidatio*), which justified the proclamation of a state of *tumultus*. The *iustitium* could only be canceled by the authority that ordered it—a consul or dictator.³

But the identification of the state of exception with sovereignty is more recent and a distinctive trait of political modernity. Let me return briefly to Gabriel Naudé's *Considérations politiques sur les coups d'État*. As Louis Marin puts it, "the 'baroque' essence of the political act is the *coup d'État* of the prince."⁴ In the seventeenth century, the *coup d'État* meant something different from what it came to designate with the revolutions of the eighteenth and nineteenth century, namely, the violent overthrow of a regime by an individual or group. The "baroque" *coup* designates "the action that decides something important for the good of the State or the prince, the extraordinary act which a government carries out to preserve the security [*salut*] of the state."⁵ This action is decisive, extraordinary, and violent. It is also liminal in that it happens at the limit—and reveals the limit—of sovereign power. Hence, Marin notes, its violence, "which introduces the fundamental question of its justification and legitimacy."⁶ Foucault argues something very similar in *Security, Territory, Population*, a lecture course in which, pivoting away from his focus on disciplinary and biopower, he sketches a genealogy of a broader problem, that of "governmentality," and identifies a key shift in the art of governing, from pastoral power in the Middle Ages to the "reason of state" in the late fifteenth and early sixteenth centuries. In the modern period, the *coup d'état* becomes the very reason or essence of the state, beyond substantive law, which it also and otherwise recognizes (*excessus iuris communis*, says Naudé⁷). "Necessity," the theorist of absolute sovereign power Cardin Le Bret (1558–1655) argues, "silences the laws."⁸ The engine of governmentality—of what Carl Schmitt eventually called "the political"—is not legality, but the "necessity" and "safety" (*salut*) of the state. Far from breaking with the *raison d'état*, then, the *coup d'état* is its "assertion" and "self-manifestation."[9]

The Legacy of Carl Schmitt

Yet the most important and influential theorist of the state of exception in modern times is arguably Carl Schmitt (1888–1985), whose extensive and diverse body of work—I counted forty-four books and close to two hundred articles—continues to influence debates in constitutional law (as well as political theory), and even underwent something of a revival following the 9/11 attacks on the World Trade Center and the Pentagon, related attacks in the United Kingdom and Spain, and the "Global War on Terror" waged by the George W. Bush administration.[10] As Michael Hoelzl and Graham Ward note in the introduction to their translation of *Dictatorship*, even during the First World War, which he spent mostly in Munich, Schmitt, then a constitutional lawyer in his twenties, had found the time to reflect upon what was happening around him and upon the work in which his own office was involved— namely, implementing the Bavarian state of law of 1912 and administering martial law.[11] This gave rise, in his mind, to an important distinction between "law" (*Gesetz*) and the necessary "measures" (*Maßnahmen*) that were called for in times of crisis. In 1916 he published a long essay titled "Diktatur und Belagerungszustand: Eine staatsrechtliche Studie" ("Dictatorship and State of Siege: A Study in Public Law"), and in 1917 he followed it with another essay, "Die Einwirkungen des Kriegszustandes auf das ordentliche strafprozesualle Verfahren" ("The Impact of the State of War on Ordinary Criminal Law Procedure"). Both essays, Hoelzl and Ward remark, "dealt with the legality of the state of siege in Germany," and both "discussed the suspension of constitutional law in a time of danger to the security, stability, and union of the nation."[12] In the words of another scholar, the articles "outlined ways relatively traditional legal instruments—most important, the state of siege—could be theoretically retailored to fit novel conditions."[13] This means that, while not necessarily a political reality, the state of exception and the need for a strong leader—a "commissary dictatorship" or a power delegated by a constituted sovereignty—remained a political possibility in Schmitt's conception of constitutional law.[14] This is how Schmitt himself puts it in a 1926 article entitled "Diktatur":

> Dictatorship is the exercise of state power freed from any legal restrictions, for the purpose of resolving an *abnormal* situation—in particular, a situation of war and rebellion. Hence two decisive elements for the concept of dictatorship are on one hand the idea of a *normal* situation that a dictatorship restores or establishes, and on the other the idea that, in the event of an abnormal situation, certain legal barriers are *suspended* in favour of resolving this situation through dictatorship.[15]

In other words, dictatorship is justified by the fact that, although it ignores the law, it does so with a view to saving it. This is what Schmitt calls the "saving" or "rescuing" action of state authority (*die rettende Tat der Staatsgewalt*)— namely, the exercise of state violence through the otherwise unacceptable suspension of the law. This moment is the purest expression of sovereignty and the manifestation of the political without law. The question of sovereignty, he writes in *Dictatorship* as well as in *Political Theology*, is "the question of the decision on the exception"; and what characterizes exception as exception is precisely "the suspension [*Suspendierung*] of the entire existing order."[16] To be more precise, and as Agamben notes, the state of exception suspends not the legal norm as such, but its *application*: the *force* of law remains in place. The distinction between norms of law and norms of realization of law (or between the potentiality and the actuality of law) matters, because it makes the legality of the suspension of law possible. In any event, crisis signals a *liminal* state in which the normal juridical order is "suspended," even "destroyed," and the political itself or *as such* is revealed.[17] What Schmitt calls "the political," and distinguishes from politics as the negotiation between interests or groups, is the exception that confirms the rule, the state of crisis that exceeds positive law. The exception can never be "subsumed under," nor "derived from," the norm:[18] "The exception is more interesting than the rule. The rule proves nothing; the exception proves everything. It confirms not only the rule but also its existence, which derives only from the exception. In the exception the power of *real life* breaks through the crust of a mechanism that has become torpid by repetition."[19] This, I believe, is another crucial difference between the crisis of exception and the crisis of deviation, which is entirely derived from the norm. Real or sovereign political life, as embodied in the state of exception, suspends, interrupts, and exceeds the liberal administrative state governed by legal, iterable norms. Conversely, "a jurisprudence concerned with the ordinary day-to-day questions has practically no interest in the concept of sovereignty. For it, only the normal can be recognized [*Auch für sie ist nur das Normale das Erkennbare*]; everything else is a 'disturbance' [*eine ,Störung'*]."[20] By contrast, the decision "frees itself from all normative ties [*macht sich frei von jeder normativen Gebundenheit*] and becomes in the true sense absolute [*absolut*]."[21] In that respect, it is "analogous to the miracle in theology."[22] And that is why it is a "borderline concept" (*Grenzbegriff*).[23]

Schmitt on *Hamlet* as a Site of Exception

Schmitt's views on the state of exception can be further illustrated by turning to his interpretation of *Hamlet*.[24] In Chapter 1, I introduced Shakespeare's play as an example of a crisis of pollution, consistent with the Greek tragic paradigm. But Schmitt reads *Hamlet* (and tragedy more broadly) differently. For Schmitt, tragedy is the literary schema—I use the word in its Kantian sense—of anomie. It is the expression not of a punishable offense, but of political modernity, that is, of sovereignty defined as the decision regarding the state of exception. The following remarks will shed further light on Schmitt's conception of sovereignty. But they will also clarify Schmitt's decades-long confrontation with Walter Benjamin on the difference between tragedy and the German baroque tragic drama, or *Trauerspiel*, which grew out of the religious civil wars in Germany.[25] In that respect, my remarks anticipate my reading of Benjamin on political violence and the general proletarian strike in Chapter 3, devoted to the crisis regime of contradiction. But they also anticipate Chapter 4, in which I read Derrida's emphasis on the motif of spectrality in *Hamlet* as an implicit critique of Schmitt on tragedy and, more broadly, of crisis as a critical-historical concept.[26] Insofar as Derrida's reading of *Hamlet* allows him to frame his own idiosyncratic (and in my view problematic) reading of

Marx, against whom Schmitt develops (at least in part) his own concept of the political, it becomes increasingly clear that Shakespeare's play can be seen as a battleground on which different types and conceptions of crisis (as pollution, exception, or contradiction), as well as a certain reticence or skepticism regarding the vocabulary of crisis, engage each other.

Two preliminary remarks are in order.

First, and as Victoria Kahn notes,

> Schmitt takes issue with a narrow, literary critical approach to the play, one that focuses on the genius of the author, the psychology of the title character, and the aesthetic autonomy of the work of art. This aesthetic approach might be appropriate to the lyric poet, whose 'creative freedom' is unconstrained by external forces, but the dramatist's invention is limited by historical circumstances, a very real audience, and the 'public sphere.'[27]

In the section of the book titled "Sources of the Tragic," Schmitt contrasts the historical or mythic "reality" of tragedy with the mere aesthetic "play" of the *Trauerspiel*. The "surplus value" of tragedy, Schmitt argues, consists in its ability to include historical reality: it "lies in the objective reality of the tragic action itself, in the enigmatic concatenation and entanglement of indisputably real people in the unpredictable course of indisputably real events," and "forms the mute rock upon which the play founders, sending the foam of genuine tragedy rushing to the surface."[28] And this, Schmitt claims, is the reason why Shakespeare does not want us to weep for Hamlet as the actor of the play within the play, to which I'll turn in a moment, weeps for Hecuba: to weep for Hamlet would be to turn the historical into the sentimental, to succumb to the aesthetic, and to reduce tragedy to *Trauerspiel*.[29] On this point, Schmitt agrees partly with Benjamin, whose *The Origin of German Tragic Drama* had established a key distinction between Greek tragedy, which "depicts mythied stories from the recent past," and *Trauerspiel*, which "despite often being set in far-flung places and times, concerns the political circumstances of historical life."[30] Or, in Benjamin's own words: "the object of tragedy is not history, but myth, and the tragic stature of the *dramatis personae* does not derive from rank—the absolute monarchy—but from the pre-historic epoch of their existence—the past age of heroes."[31] Unlike Benjamin, though, Schmitt sees myth as the "intrusion" (*Einbruch*) of time onto the scene of play, or the "incontrovertible core of a single historical reality that transcends every subjective invention."[32] Myth, according to Schmitt, is clearly on the side of the exceptional and the historical: "*myth is literature's exception*, embodying the piece of historical reality that is in literature but more than literature. . . ."[33] In this respect, his appreciation of Shakespeare echoes Herder's 1773 seminal essay on the English playwright, and its insistence that, by virtue of its historical context and situatedness, the meaning of the Shakespearean (and Elizabethan) drama is radically different from that of Greek tragedy, and its aesthetic rules and standards radically different from those established by Aristotle in the *Poetics*.[34] For Schmitt, the modern, Shakespearean drama creates myth from history, rather than taking myth as its point of departure and turning it into history: "While ancient tragedy is simply faced with myth and creates the tragic action from it, in the case of *Hamlet* we encounter the rare (but typically modern) case of a playwright who establishes a myth from the historical reality that he immediately faces."[35]

In *The Concept of the Political*, written some thirty years before *Hamlet or Hecuba*, Schmitt already made clear the view that a world without the political is merely one "of culture, civilization," and above all "entertainment."[36] This world might be very "interesting," but it cannot claim to be "serious." This key distinction is most likely a reference to Kierkegaard, for whom the search for the "interesting" (the exciting, the unusual, the surprising, the original) is "a border category, a *confinium* between aesthetics and ethics"[37] and a strategy to avoid "boredom," the basic and "infinitely repulsive state" from which one tries to escape through the aestheticization of existence.[38] Ultimately, though, the strategy of enjoyment, however imaginative and sophisticated, fails: the life of the aesthete and the hedonist, which replaces one set of pleasures with another, more refined set, ends up reproducing the *ennui* it seeks to avoid.[39] Those pursuits—*divertissements*—are ways of refusing to engage with existence seriously (i.e., to decide in favor of, and commit to, a specific form of life). Naturally, for Kierkegaard, it is not the ethical-political but the religious form of life that is the highest, and therefore the ultimate mark of a "serious" existence.[40] The tragic, for him, is an ethical category that signals a stage of existence higher than the aesthetic, but still not as significant or "serious" as the religious. Still, Schmitt's views on tragedy resonate strongly with one aspect of Kierkegaard's account. In *Either/Or*, Kierkegaard depicts modern life as a loose association of discrete individuals who never manage to overcome their isolation. Kahn puts it like this: "In contrast to the ancient Greek individual, who 'still rested in the substantial categories of state, family, and destiny,' the modern individual is characterized by anxiety, melancholy, and despair."[41] By emphasizing "responsibility and individual self-fashioning," Kahn explains, the modern age "is in danger of losing a sense of the tragic altogether—a sense, that is, of something that transcends the individual."[42] Modern tragedy is confined to the sphere of "subjective reflection and decision."[43] As such, Kahn concludes, modern tragedy falls short of the tragic in the strong sense, which, according to Kierkegaard, represents the conflict between free will and necessity (or external circumstances).

Schmitt's own distinction between *Trauerspiel* and tragedy mirrors his distinctions between aesthetics and politics, playfulness and seriousness, pure representation and action, the norm and the exception. To be sure, "in the already baroque atmosphere around 1600," the world had become a stage.[44] "Men of action in this epoch," he writes, "saw themselves on center stage before spectators and understood themselves and their activities in terms of the theatricality of their roles. . . . Action in the public sphere was action on a stage and thus role playing."[45] And Schmitt reminds us that James I, as well, "admonished his son to always remember that as king he would be on stage and all eyes would be focused on him."[46] But, Schmitt insists, the baroque theatricalization of life was still rudimentary in Elizabethan England—"not yet incorporated into the strict framework of the sovereign state and its establishment of public peace, security, and order, as was the theater of Corneille and Racine in the France of Louis XIV."[47] In seventeenth-century France, the irruption of the *coup d'état* as the liminal expression of the *raison d'état* required its own representation and dramatization. As Marin notes in his reading of Naudé, the transformation of force—of "the radiance [*éclat*], violence, absolute choc of force"[48]—into power, and of power into absolute power, made this moment of representation necessary. It is therefore perhaps not a coincidence if much of seventeenth-century drama revolves around this question, works like a mirror in which sovereign, absolute power contemplates itself.⁴⁹ Benjamin, as well, insists on this dimension of representation in his analysis of the German baroque tragic drama: the object of *Trauerspiel* is not merely "historical life," but "historical life as represented by its age."⁵⁰ And the figure who represents or schematizes the baroque age is the sovereign: "The sovereign represents history. He holds the course of history in his hand like a sceptre."⁵¹ As we have seen, Schmitt also locates the value and even essence of tragedy in historical reality. But the historical reality of Shakespeare's play, he argues, is one that staged the whole of society, "without artificiality," and "the immediately present play of real life."⁵² Somehow, "the play on stage could magnify itself without detaching itself from the immediate reality of life."⁵³

Second, Schmitt disagrees with Walter Benjamin's interpretation of the relation between sovereignty and decision in the seventeenth-century *Trauerspiel*.⁵⁴ Drawing on Schmitt's own notion of sovereignty, and the idea that "the ruler is designated from the outset as the holder of a dictatorial power if war, revolt, or other catastrophes should lead to a state of emergency,"⁵⁵ Benjamin argues that "tragedy turns on the decision of an individual character, whereas the baroque play of mourning involves a dislocation of sovereignty and thus of a world in which decisions can take place. This is a world in which character is not unified or consistent, and in which history is no longer the medium of significant action":⁵⁶ baroque drama progresses "no further than the painstaking analysis of political intrigue"; it knows "no other historical activity than the corrupt energy of schemers."⁵⁷ There is widespread "discontent" but not a "trace of revolutionary conviction."⁵⁸ Action has been replaced by acting; the sovereign has become a despot or Machiavel, who governs by manipulating the instincts and emotions of his subjects;⁵⁹ and the temporal disjunction of decision-making has been replaced by a spatial dislocation in which everything is exceptional, so nothing is. In the baroque "the state of exception is impossible, not because it is superfluous, but because it exists permanently as a perpetual state of lawlessness,"⁶⁰ because there was no authority that could instate or end it. "The most important function of the prince," Benjamin argues, is to "avert" the state of exception, not to implement it, as Schmitt will argue.⁶¹ As Bredekamp puts it, "the symbol of the epoch is neither the clarity and permanence of the laws nor the moment of the sovereign's decision," but the inability to decide and the torment of hesitation.⁶²

Despite his praise of Benjamin's treatment of the allegorical dimension of Shakespeare's play, Schmitt feels that Benjamin's conception of *Trauerspiel*, which locates crisis in the absence of crisis (as exception), fails to capture the truly tragic dimension of *Hamlet*.

How, exactly, does time (as history) erupt in *Hamlet* and become myth? In two ways, or on two intertwined levels.

First, and in relation to an immediate past, in the obvious parallel between the fictional characters of Gertrude, Claudius, and Hamlet, on the one hand, and the historical figures of Mary Queen of Scots, her son James, and the Earl of Bothwell, on the other. On February 8, 1587, Bothwell murdered Mary's husband, Henry Lord Darnley. Less than three months later, he married Mary. The first performance of *Hamlet* probably dates from 1600 or 1601, which means two or three years before James VI of Scotland became James I of England and Ireland.[63] There is also the broader historical background of the bloody war of religions, which tore Europe, and specifically the British Isles, apart. The myth of *Hamlet* is that of a schism or conflict between the Catholic Don Quixote and the Protestant Faust.[64] It is the myth of the Reformation and the wars of religion prior to the treaties of Westphalia and the emergence of the modern, sovereign state.[65] As such, it is perhaps best embodied by the personality of James: baptized as a Catholic by his mother Mary Stuart, yet removed from her and raised as a Protestant by her enemies, James is "a king who in his fate and character was the product of the strife of his age," a man "literally from the womb immersed in the schisms of his era."[66] Like James, and contrary to what Benjamin claims, "Hamlet is not Christian in any specific sense."[67] Hamlet is no longer Christian or religious "in the medieval sense."[68] But this does not mean that he (or James) is religiously neutral in the sense of the modern state, "which emerged from the overcoming of confessional civil war."[69] *Hamlet*'s time—the time of the play and of its main protagonist—is a time out of joint and in-between: "between Catholicism and Protestantism,"[70] between the Middle Ages and modernity, between religious fanaticism ("the barbaric") and "the political," between the transcendence of a "commonwealth forged by God"[71] and the immanence of sovereign power, between the (French) power of terrestrial statehood and the maritime existence to which England was eventually destined. Hence Hamlet's melancholy, a mood that is not a subjective, merely psychological trait, but the reflection and embodiment of a historical reality.[72] As one commentator puts it, "the melancholy paralysis of modernity stands in contrast to the active vengeance of the ancient."[73]

Let me expand on how Schmitt views this historical-political context. In his 1938 study of Hobbes' *Leviathan*, Schmitt notes the presence of the figure of the leviathan in Shakespeare, but insists that it does not prefigure the Hobbesian one: "The leviathan is cited a few times in Shakespeare's dramas, but always objectively, as a powerful, enormously strong, or quick sea monster, without any symbolism pointing toward the politico-mythical."[74] As Navarette aptly notes, Shakespeare's leviathan is pre-political in the Schmittian sense, that is to say, "barbaric," whereas Hobbes' leviathan is "political."[75] It is the mythical representation of modern sovereignty, that is, of the ordering of Church and State which Shakespeare, who died a quarter of a century before civil war broke out in England, never experienced. By contrast, Navarette claims, Hobbes conceived his *magnus homo* against the backdrop of this concrete historical situation and as a response to it. Neither Hamlet, on the theatrical stage, nor James, on the historical stage, were able to assert "*L'État, c'est moi*," as Louis XIV is supposed to have said. They were not sovereigns. To be sure, they lived and suffered in their flesh the tensions which had not yet broken out as war. But they were not able to resolve them, that is, precisely to decide on security, peace, and public order, as the French absolute monarch did. They were not able to exercise the dictatorship which, three decades after the death of James I, Cromwell eventually brought about. For only under Cromwell's protectorate did Hobbes' leviathan become historically concrete in England. But it did so only briefly. As Schmitt puts it, "the image of the sea monster leviathan as a symbol of the English state held for a brief historical moment" and "the continental—that is, the Spanish-French—doctrine of the state" came close to being realized in England.[76] The English nation mastered the seas "and grew into the position of a world power without using the forms and means of state absolutism. The English leviathan did not become a state."[77] In the end, "the evolution of England proceeded in a direction contrary to the concept of the State advanced by Hobbes."[78] As a maritime and deterritorializing power "the English Isle and its world-conquering seafaring needed no absolute monarchy, no standing land army, no state bureaucracy, no legal system of a law state such as became characteristic of continental states."[79]

Without such a historically potent core, which signifies the intrusion of real sovereign presence, albeit negatively, under the sign of taboo and scandal, "the doubling would simply make the play more playful, more unlikely and artificial—more untrue as a play, until finally it would become a 'parody of itself.'"[80] For Benjamin, baroque theater always runs the risk of lapsing into parody because the world it describes is one of decadence and closed off from the possibility of transcendence. While recognizing the radical immanence of this fallen world, perhaps best represented by the corrupt court of Claudius, Schmitt insists that the truly tragic or "political" moment in the play resides in "the *objective reality* of tragic action itself, . . . the enigmatic involvement and entanglement of indisputably *real* people in the unpredictable course of indisputably *real* events."[81] "In tragedy," in other words, "the common public sphere (which in every performance encompasses the author, the actors, and the audience) is not based on the accepted rules of language and play, but upon the living experience of a shared historical reality."[82] A merely "invented fate," he concludes, "is not fate at all."[83]

At the second and specifically dramatic level, the mythic dimension of the play is made more palpable by, and is as it were concentrated in, one of the two plays within the play. The first (Act II, sc. 2) has no title, but the second (Act III, sc. 2) has two, *The Murder of Gonzago* and *The Mousetrap*. Although the title of Schmitt's essay is borrowed from the first—a bloody farce, Bloom tells us, of "a poetic badness not to be believed," and which could be called *The Slaughter of Priam, with the Lamentation of Hecuba*[84]—its argument resonates more with the second play, which Hamlet puts on to test the reaction of the Queen and King, and establish their guilt (or innocence) in the assassination of his father. At first glance, *The Mousetrap* is a *mise en abyme* of play, a (typically baroque) doubling of the play that runs the risk of lapsing into parody. No doubt, "mere play may endlessly reproduce and refract itself."[85] But this, for Schmitt, is unacceptable and the sign of an inability to grasp the truly tragic within the play. Far from offering a mere parody of the play, far from being mere ὑπόκρισις (*hypokrisis*) or *simulatio*, *The Mousetrap* intensifies the "realistic core of the most intense significance and timeliness."[86] The true taboo behind the question of the innocence or guilt of Hamlet's mother, and which is never quite settled, is the unsayable yet recognizable presence of Mary, Queen of Scots, and the question of her involvement in the plotting of the brutal and scandalous assassination of her husband. This is a question that is left hanging and haunts the contemporary audience. The presence/absence of Mary Stuart in the figure of Gertrude resonates in us, even today, in a way that Greek tragedy cannot:

> Mary Stuart is still for us something other and more than Hecuba. Even the fate of the Atreidae does not affect us as deeply as that of the unhappy Stuarts, since it coincides with the fate of the European religious schism.[87]

Kahn puts it like this:

> Hecuba—a figure from the world of Greek myth—now appears as a mere literary invention, while Hamlet—Shakespeare's most famous literary invention—rises to the stature of tragic myth. As a result, Schmitt argues, Shakespeare's audience comes to understand the difference between mere aesthetic appreciation of *Hamlet* the play and the necessity of a genuinely tragic decision in the face of a state of emergency.[88]

It is clear that Shakespeare's play—unlike, say, the *Oresteia*—neither resolves nor indicates ways of resolving the crisis. Hamlet's own indecision, Gertrude's ambiguous role in the death of her husband, and even the cascade of deaths that bring the play to an end do not amount to anything like a resolution. But what the play does, as Kahn emphasizes, is to make the historical crisis "powerfully real to the audience."[89] This is what led Löwith to conclude that the tragic in *Hamlet* consists in its ability to represent "a decision in favour of decisiveness."[90]

Beyond the specific historical context of the play and of the moment of decision it signals, Schmitt's interest in *Hamlet* speaks to his own historical situation, his own crisis, one that is perhaps also *ours*. We saw how Schmitt's affirmation of the force of the sovereign decision arises, in part, as a reaction against what he considers to be the "contradictions and compromises," "negotiations" and "half-measures" of the modern, liberal state, its endless suspension of the moment of decision and "everlasting discussion."[91] For

Schmitt, the parliamentary democracy of the Weimar period, and liberal democracy more broadly, lead to a state of chronic indecision and represent an "onslaught against the political."[92] Moreover, the technocratic state and managerial-administrative techniques of government simply ignore the political. For the liberal state, "there must no longer be political problems, only organizational-technical and economic-sociological tasks."[93] This primacy of the economic over the political is what defines the era, beyond its liberal incarnation: "American financiers, industrial technicians, Marxist socialists, and anarchic-syndicalist revolutionaries unite in demanding that the biased rule of politics over unbiased economic management be done away with."[94] This "vanishing" of the political "into the economic or technical-organizational," Schmitt seems to suggest, always comes at a price, one that the world paid in the 1930s and continues to pay today, at a time when various forms of fascism, dictatorships, and populist-decisionist regimes are on the rise. Were he alive today, he would no doubt see in such phenomena the return and revenge of the political, or at least of our irreducible, ineliminable thirst for it. He would see the most profound crises of the time as crises of the liberal, technical-managerial paradigm, rather than as crises the liberal order can "manage."

While agreeing with Schmitt's diagnosis of the limits and unsatisfactory nature of liberal governmentality, one that I have explored elsewhere,[95] and while recognizing the aspiration to a different way of governing ourselves and others, should we understand and embrace it as politics in the Schmittian sense? What other reading of *Hamlet*, of the aesthetic, and of its relation to politics might be possible? Would it uncover yet a different sense or regime of crisis, or take us beyond crisis, beyond its schema, its economy, and its temporality, and toward a renewed sense of democracy? What articulation of the aesthetic and the political—other than that of myth (or tragedy) and sovereignty—might be conceivable? I will return to at least some of those questions in Chapter 4, where I discuss Derrida's own idiosyncratic reading of *Hamlet*, rooted in the ghostly, spectral figure of the King, and centered on the question of the relation between decision and the undecidable.

Contemporary Regimes of Exception

Schmitt is not the only one who holds an exceptionalist view of the law. In *Constitutional Dictatorship: Crisis Government in the Modern Democracies* (1948), the American historian and political theorist of the state of exception, Clinton L. Rossiter, defended the principle according to which "in time of crisis a democratic, constitutional government must temporarily be altered to whatever degree is necessary to overcome the peril and restore normal conditions."[96] This is entirely consistent with (at least a certain interpretation of) the US Constitution, especially as interpreted by Abraham Lincoln. Of all the US presidents (other than George W. Bush), Lincoln is the one who pushed executive power the farthest and whose presidency Rossiter labeled a "constitutional dictatorship." Faced with the secession of the Deep South and its refusal to accept the end of slavery, Lincoln adopted a radical interpretation of the Constitution and crushed the rebellion. Invoking Article II.3 of the Constitution (on "extraordinary occasions"), he took a series of measures, some of which were normally the prerogative of Congress, which he did not consult. He issued a call for volunteers, increased the size of the regular army, ordered the navy to enlist more sailors and purchase warships, and diverted millions from the Treasury to recruit and pay troops. More radically, and to respond to attacks against military units from Massachusetts in Baltimore, Maryland, which was a slaveholding and pro-Confederacy state, he suspended the writ of habeas corpus, replacing civilian law enforcement with military detention without trial.[97] In his book, Rossiter also predicted that, in an increasingly dangerous world—the Atomic Age at the time, or the Age of Terrorism, biothreats, and mass migration today—the state of exception might very well become the norm and open the way to a *permanent* state of exception: "The instruments of government depicted here as temporary 'crisis' arrangements have in some countries, and may eventually in all countries, become lasting peacetime institutions."[98] This has indeed turned out to be the case as crises of all kinds—economic, demographic, or health-related—are increasingly "securitized" and even militarized, that is, declared a threat to the population as a whole, and conflated with politico-military crises. The consequence of this is the blurring of the line separating war and peace, exceptional and normal situations, the legal nomos and anomie.

Closer to us, John Yoo, a lawyer in the Office of Legal Counsel of the Department of Justice between 2001 and 2003 and now the Emanuel S. Heller Professor of Law at the University of California, Berkeley, defends the growth of the executive powers of the US presidency. In a long book review from 2010, he claims that, following Locke, the framers of the Constitution "created the Presidency so that a branch of the government would always be 'in being' and could exercise substantive powers *in times of crisis and emergency*."[99] In addition to Lincoln, he mentions Jefferson, who profoundly influenced the presidency by introducing the concept of the prerogative: following §160 of Locke's *Two Treatises of Government* on prerogative power, he advanced the theory that the president "could act outside the Constitution to protect the national interest in moments of great crisis. . . ."[100] Yoo concludes his review by saying that, under the Constitution, "it becomes clearly apparent that the executive power encompasses much more than *managing* those who enforce the law. Article II vests powers of substance that come to the fore during *crises*."[101] In that way, Yoo confirms the distinction I have been using between crises of deviation and crises of exception—between a certain violence to norms, which can be managed, and another kind of violence, which calls for the suspension of the norms.

Let me now refer to a few recent examples of crises giving rise to the declaration and implementation of the state of exception.

Consider President George W. Bush's response to the attacks of 9/11 and the "war on terror." The military order signed by the president on November 15, 2001, introduced the notion of "indefinite detention," which in effect stripped "enemy combatants" of all rights. They were neither prisoners of war protected by the Geneva Convention nor charged with a specific crime and therefore protected by the rule of law. They were "detainees" placed outside judicial control, reduced to the state of bare life, and confined to a political no man's land. Unsurprisingly, this extrajudicial status made possible the torture memos produced by the Justice Department condoning practices such as waterboarding, stress positions, and inhumane deprivations. This, Agamben notes, is something not seen since Nazi Germany's downgrading of the Jews' legal status, which made their arrest and extermination possible. In this context, John Yoo's work is again relevant. Yoo was the author of the "torture memoranda" of 2002 and 2003, also known as the Bybee memos, named after Assistant Attorney General Jay S. Bybee. They were rescinded by President Obama in 2009 (Executive Order 13491).[102] The memos stipulated that Congress has no constitutional right to interfere with the president in his role as commander-in-chief, including making laws that limit the ways in which prisoners may be interrogated. They also authorized CIA agents to employ "enhanced interrogation techniques." According to Horton, Yoo's public arguments and statements suggest the strong influence of one thinker: Carl Schmitt. There is no direct evidence to support Horton's claim. Similar claims were made about David Addington, legal counsel to Vice President Dick Cheney between 2001 and 2005.[103] What really matters is the persistence of a line of thinking amongst constitutionalists that advocates the declaration of the state of exception and the prerogative of exceptional powers in times of crisis. I therefore agree with Linker, who writes: "Whether Yoo and Addington formulated their views on their own, by radicalizing the doctrine of the 'unitary executive,' or reading Schmitt by flashlight in a White House broom closet is irrelevant. The ideas are nearly identical, whatever their origins."

My second example concerns migrant camps, about which much has been written. I speak of migrant camps but have in mind camps in the broad sense, which include, in the words of Mbembe, "refugee camps, camps for the displaced, migrant camps, camps for foreigners, waiting areas for people pending status, transit zones, administrative detention centers, identification or expulsion centers, border crossings, temporary welcome centers..."[104] They too are spaces of exception, in which "bare life and the juridical rule enter into a threshold of indistinction."[105] Such spaces without place—thresholds that lead nowhere, "zones of indifference,"[106] or "out-places"[107]—reinforce an already existing precarity and add the insult of exclusion to the injuries of economic hardship, persecution, and war. The Australian case is particularly striking. Operation Sovereign Borders (OSB), led by the Australian Defence Force, is a border protection effort that was set up under the Abbott coalition government in 2013. Its aim is to implement a "zero tolerance" policy toward "Illegal Maritime Arrivals"—a radicalization in terminology from the previous government's "Irregular Maritime Arrivals." This has led to the principle of *mandatory* detention in offshore Immigration Detention Centres, some of which, like Christmas Island, are operated by private companies (the combination of offshoring and outsourcing security is a hallmark of neoliberal states). Migrants can be held up in such camps for months, even years. In fact, under the 1994 amendment to the Migration Act of 1958, there is no time limit on this detention, and only very limited review by the courts is available.[108] Unsurprisingly, severe violations of international law and human rights have taken place in these camps, and are being challenged in courts. High rates of suicide and self-harm are also commonplace.

A very similar situation can be found in the United States, which has the largest immigration detention system in the world. Although this situation cannot be attributed to the Trump administration, the latter certainly created the most hostile environment possible for migrants, similar to the official policies established in Australia, the UK, and Hungary. It perpetuates the white supremacist agenda (often disguised behind the theory) and perceived threat of the "demographic shift" driven by Latino immigration (a similar idea, known in France as the "*grand remplacement*," announces the takeover of Europe by north and sub-Saharan Africans). The Customs and Border Protections (CBP) holding cells, commonly referred to by CBP agents as *hieleras*, or iceboxes, and the ICE (Immigration and Customs Enforcement) "Service Processing Centers" are regularly in breach of their legal obligations. The living conditions in the holding cells (for that is what they are) have been described as "deplorable" and "inhumane," and found to be in violation of a two-decades-old settlement in *Flores v. Reno*.[109] Operated by a couple of private companies (CoreCivic, Geo), ICE detention centers are a very large, growing, and highly lucrative industry that criminalizes *and* commodifies human displacement.[110] They are part of a trend that outsources security and extracts value from populations fleeing poverty or war zones, or simply seeking to be reunited with their families. The scale of the centers is impressive and reminds one of Amazon mega-warehouses. But they also have been overcrowded, and the conditions imposed on detainees, especially children, have been likened to torture by doctors and independent observers.[111]

The situation in Europe is not altogether different. Once a continent of hospitality and asylum, it has largely become a hostile environment that dreams of itself as a "fortress."[112] Hostility toward migrants—as attested by the Home Office Hostile Environment Policy in the UK since 2012, and recently reinforced by Priti Patel's deal with Rwanda and Suela Braverman's efforts to offshore and outsource all unlawful arrivals in the UK—has become official policy in many European countries and parties, including on the left. In 2015 alone, close to 725,000 migrants in search of a better life—some would say a life *tout court*—and a minimum degree of security traveled by sea to reach Europe. More than 3,300 died.[113] Europe responded by privileging its own security and multiplying zones of exception where *human* life, associated with the principles of dignity and autonomy, and the discourse of rights, is denied and rendered more precarious.[114] Borders are subjected to a strict dispositive of securitization and an exclusive logic of sovereignty: outsourced, offshored, and militarized, the borders of Europe are constantly moving and have turned into increasingly dangerous environments. Extending as far as Turkey and Libya, they are protected by detention centers that have been condemned by various human rights organizations, including Human Rights Watch. But they are also multiplied within Europe itself, through checkpoints, massive technological surveillance, and close monitoring. Hospitals, universities, and even charities are now asked to monitor and provide data regarding those they help or harbor, as if they were enemies. Borders are extended beyond the recognized "physical" borders of Europe, and at the same time endlessly reinscribed within its space. Meanwhile, the *reality* of those they affect—their emotional journey and ordeal—is rendered invisible, or as invisible as possible. These lives are marked by loss, violence (often state-sanctioned), intimidation, fear, trauma, and death. Paradoxically, the hostile environment is itself construed as a matter of life and death, of preserving the life and livelihood of those *inside*, of defending them against other forms of life—of *immunity*. Writing in *The Sun* at the height of the migration crisis in 2015, Katie Hopkins suggested that migrant vessels coming to Europe be forcibly returned to their country of origin and sunk as a deterrent to the "cockroaches" trying to reach its shores.[115] Under Matteo Salvini, Italy criminalized rescue operations in the Mediterranean and abrogated "humanitarian protection."[116] Unsurprisingly perhaps, philosophers despair and speak of "the end of hospitality."[117] The humanitarian policy of rescuing migrants, the goal of which is simply to not let them die, is a far cry from a politics of hospitality. Yet it seems infinitely more humane and faithful to the EU Charter of Human Rights than the current sovereignist position, which is increasingly becoming a necropolitics.[118]

This securitizing tendency also surfaced in the context of Covid-19, which combines the worst health crisis the (Western) world has known since the Spanish flu and the worst economic downturn since the Great Depression.[119] In his first speech to the nation, in which he announced the lockdown of the country and declared the state of emergency, President Macron said that France was "at war" against Covid-19, thereby justifying the extreme measures he was imposing.[120] Between November 2015 and the end of 2021, France lived under the state of emergency for almost two-thirds of the time.[121] The martial language was subsequently abandoned. But the principle remained. To exercise its mandate and function as biopower—a form of government whose aim is not merely *laisser vivre*, but *faire vivre* (i.e., to care for the health of its population)—governments felt the need to activate their sovereign right to limit the liberties they normally guarantee. In a time of pandemic, the right of the people gives way to the right of the population. But the necropolitics of *laisser mourir* have not disappeared. The Covid-19 pandemic has been particularly cruel to migrants, who found themselves excluded from vaccine programs, that is, from the positive aspects of biopower, and further reduced to bare life.[122] Spaces of exception—refugee camps, indeterminate spaces between political places, and border controls outsourced and offshored by rich states—are rendered yet more precarious and exclusionary by a global health crisis, thus revealing a toxic nexus of sovereign power, biopower, necropolitics, and climate change. Some lives really are cursed, almost entirely reducible to the many crises that traverse them. Let me return to the example of the ICE detention centers. The precariousness of those detained lives has increased considerably during the Covid-19 crisis, and as a direct result of the criminalization, securitization, and deplorable conditions of detention to which they are subjected: between June 2020 and March 2021, the rates of infection inside the centers were twenty times that of the general US population, and five times that of the US prison population, which is also the largest in the world.¹²³ Detainees exhibiting Covid-19 symptoms were systematically denied tests and needed to become gravely ill before receiving treatment. As a direct result of an immune response to the threat of immigration, entire communities of ICE detainees, staff, and those with whom they came into contact outside the confines of the detention centers saw their health and even their lives endangered, considerably more than in other parts of the country. Thus, the systematic suspension and violation of a normal legal framework in the name of crisis (the migration crisis) led to an even greater toll in a time of pandemic: the precariousness of those lives was increased during the Covid-19 crisis, their bareness made even more palpable.

Viktor Orbán's Hungary is another example of the abuse of emergency measures and the introduction, from 2023, of a "permanent state of exception."¹²⁴ According to a Friedrich Naumann Foundation for Freedom report from 2020, when the Covid-19 crisis ended, Prime Minister Viktor Orbán's government announced that it would end the "state of danger" and return its special powers to parliament.¹²⁵ However, and according to the same report, "critics described the move as a political ploy," since parliament also voted in favor of an amendment of the "state of medical emergency" provisions in the Health Act. According to this bill, "the government would be able to govern by decree again in such a case, with even less control than before." Both bills were adopted by parliament on June 16, 2020. The law on "terminating the state of danger" is merely a call to the government to end the state of emergency and thus the extraordinary legal order. However, the draft law does not set a deadline and the government can decide on the timing itself. The second legislative proposal stipulates that

> the government may declare a "medical emergency" on the recommendation of the chief medical officer and following a ministerial proposal. The beginning and end of the medical emergency, which is not laid down in the constitution, depends on the government's decision. According to the law, during the medical emergency the government may, by decree, restrict the exercise of fundamental rights such as freedom of movement or assembly. The restrictions can initially last for six months but can then be extended practically indefinitely. Parliamentary approval is no longer required.

According to Mészáros, "the ninth amendment to the Fundamental Law of Hungary has raised concerns about the government's use of emergency powers, granting the executive branch even more authority during exceptional times by allowing the government to prolong the 'state of exception' indefinitely and maintain pandemic-related emergency measures to respond to potential consequences of the war in Ukraine."[126] Unsurprisingly perhaps, the abuse of emergency powers had started with an aggressive campaign against migrants in 2015, which led to a series of amendments to the Migration Act, namely, the "State of Migration Emergency," the "Temporary Appropriation Applicable during a State of Mass Migration Crisis," and "Other Regulatory Actions Applicable during a State of Mass Migration Crisis."[127] But the extension of the state of exception and the rule by emergency decree does not stop at the medical and migration "crisis." Following another amendment on "humanitarian catastrophe," which entered into force on May 24, 2022, the Hungarian government is now authorized to declare a state of emergency in response to a humanitarian crisis that is happening not in its own country, but in a neighboring one (Ukraine). This, Mészáros argues, "is unique in modern constitutional democracies."[128] Orbán immediately used the new state of danger to tackle what he saw as a growing economic and fiscal crisis.[129] Orbán's Hungary is therefore a prime example of a formally democratic regime for which crisis has become a legal, political, and even economic discursive event, and the state of exception a generalized technique of government.

But the most striking and longest-standing state of exception is arguably that of Israel. Since its inception in 1948, and the war that followed against Arab neighboring states, the state of Israel has existed in a continuous state of emergency. Established by Section 9 of The Law and Administration Ordinance of 1948, and by Sections 38 and 39 of the Basic Law: The Government (as amended in 1992), the state of emergency has been renewed annually almost automatically since 1992 (before that, it remained in force so long as the Knesset did not formally revoke it). As a result, and to use just one example, Israel does not consider itself bound to comply strictly (especially in the territories it has occupied since 1967) with article 9 of the International Covenant on Civil and Political Rights (1966), which it ratified in 1991. The article in question gives any person a right to be informed upon arrest of the reasons for the arrest and to be notified promptly of the charges they face. It also guarantees the arrested person a right to be brought promptly before a judge and to be tried within a reasonable time.[130] According to one legal scholar, Israel's "convoluted emergency jurisprudence" is less "the accidental outcome of trying times" than a flexible "governing tool" and "an enduring condition."[131] The political aim of this extension of sovereign power, which "maintains a degree of legitimacy by operating behind a veil of legality," is the "systematic discrimination against Palestinians" and the endless deferral of Palestinian sovereignty.[132] The situation is therefore similar to the colonial context, where exceptional emergency powers became the governing norm and where, in the same territory, the colonizing subjects were protected by state law (as an extension of personal law), whereas the colonized subjects lived under military rule.[133] According to B'Tselem, in 1948, Israel incorporated into its law the Defense (Emergency) Regulations which the British Mandate government had introduced in 1945. They included "provisions against illegal immigration, establishing military tribunals to try civilians without granting the right of appeal, allowing sweeping searches and seizures, prohibiting publications of books and newspapers, demolishing houses, detaining individuals administratively for an indefinite period, sealing off particular territories, and imposing curfew."[134] As Edward Said points out, "these laws were openly racist in that they were *never* used in Israel against Jews."[135] After 1948, when Israel retained them, they were used to "forbade Arabs the right of movement, the right of purchase of land, the right of settlement, and so forth."[136] The irony, Said concludes, is that "under the mandate the regulations were regularly denounced by the Jews as colonial and racist. Yet as soon as Israel became a state, those same laws were used against the Arabs."[137] Since the beginning of the war in Gaza following the massacre of October 10, 2023, the crisis of exception, which had kept Palestinians in a state between life and death for decades, has morphed into a crisis of extinction, collapse, and extermination, the logic of which I will analyze in detail in Chapter 5.

My conclusion regarding the particular legal response to crisis is that its deep tendency is to move beyond the realm of extraordinary measures and become a technique or technology of government: the suspension of the rule of law in the name of safety and security, whether understood in a classical political way as an internal or external threat to the integrity of the body politic, or biopolitically as a threat to the *living* population, is gaining ground. Those two aspects of security are sometimes combined. This is the case with the so-called immigration crisis, seen as a threat to both territorial sovereignty and the health of the population. In both cases, the exceptionalist response to crisis *produces* a kind of life, somewhere between the ethical-political life of rights and bare, biological life. But this convergence is not a coincidence. Although sovereign power and biopower have two different origins, they quickly became intertwined and produced a highly toxic mix, one that involved state racism, racial laws, the dehumanization of certain populations, and forms of necropolitics that include (but are not reducible to) genocides.

Let me take a step back. I can summarize our itinerary thus far by saying that crisis signals a decisive moment, a critical point, or a point of bifurcation: it signals an *event* in the strong sense of the term. In terms of its regimes, a moment of crisis can reveal an unusually significant *deviation* from the norm, which requires unusual measures aimed at restoring the norm. This is the liberal, *managerial* response, which sees crises as *anomalies*. But, as we saw in this chapter, a crisis can also be perceived as an *anomie*, and met with the (more or less temporary) suspension of the legal nomos. This response is not liberal but *sovereignist*, not managerial but *political* in a Schmittian sense. In Chapter 3, I will look at a different kind of crisis, already alluded to in Chapter 1: the crisis of *contradiction*, which calls for neither the management nor the suspension of the nomos, but its *overturning* or replacement. It is driven by a revolutionary logic, born of the conviction that the contradictions inherent to the system in question are such that only a change of norms, and therefore of system, will be able to solve them. Another, slightly different way of summarizing our itinerary thus far is by emphasizing the articulation of types of crisis and regimes of power. The response of sovereign or state power to crisis is *exception*. Its particular form of violence is anomie (which is not outside the law). Its target is citizens, even if negatively, through the suspension of rights. The response of biopower to crisis is *management*. Its particular form of violence is normalization. Its target is the population. The response of popular power, or of the power of the people, to crisis is *uprising*. By uprising, I mean not the capturing of state power, but the overthrow of a normative framework and the invention of new forms and norms of life. Its violence is that of antinomy and law-giving. It is the exercise of violence outside the law. But it is also the exercise of the natural right of the multitude. Whereas the first two responses to crisis are conservative in nature (they seek to restore the norm), the third is revolutionary or anarchic (it seeks to replace the norms). Those responses are not mutually exclusive, as we saw in the Covid-19 pandemic, or in the case of the Nazi revolution, which suspended indefinitely the constitution of the Weimar Republic.

3

Crises of Contradiction

Crisis-Tendencies in Capitalism: The Marxist Legacy

The schema of crisis is nowhere more present than in the tradition of critical social theory and social philosophy, inherited from Marx. From Horkheimer to Habermas and Jaeggi, from Arrighi to Foster and Fraser, from Gramsci to Laclau and Mouffe, the notion of crisis is ubiquitous and operates as a genuine philosophical concept. Critical social theorists speak of crises of accumulation, legitimation, motivation, representation, democracy, and hegemony. In fact, as Balibar notes, it would not be an exaggeration to say that the concept of crisis, and the paired terms crisis-critique, determined the program of the various social philosophies (Marxism included) that have sought to define the objectives and practical functions of the social sciences since the beginning of the nineteenth century.[1] This, Balibar argues, is because critique is concerned with two different types of phenomena. On the one hand, it is concerned with phenomena of conflict, alienation, or pathology, which are all symptoms of deep-seated contradictions. In that respect, critical theory broadly defined is largely (but not exclusively) indebted to the speculative and especially Hegelian understanding of crisis I sketched in Chapter 1. Contradiction is the invisible lining of social relations, or the hidden truth that *regulates* them. But critique is also concerned with the phenomena that *interrupt* the reproduction of those social relations, whether provisionally or definitively. Hence the privilege enjoyed by the idea of revolution.[2] What we have, therefore, is a conception, and indeed a *concept* of crisis, which signals the manifestation of inherent contradictions and forms of social alienation, the resolution of which necessarily takes the form of revolution—or takes the form of a necessary revolution, by which we should understand the rejection of the norms constitutive of the system of accumulation in question and the attempt to replace it with another. As Clarke puts it: "The distinctiveness of the Marxist perspective is that it looks for the causes of crisis not in natural or quasi-natural economic, psychological or ecological limits, but in the social relations of the capitalist mode of production, and it looks for the resolution of crisis through the transformation of those social relations not from above but from within."[3]

By contrast, and as I have already indicated, neoclassical economics generates ever more abstract and mathematized models which, in their attempt to produce an ideal picture of the market, systematically exclude its contradictions and crises. This mathematical idealism bears little resemblance to the economic reality, yet the latter is always measured against, and is meant to mirror, the former. Because liberal governmentality conceives of crises as simple deviations from the norm, its response to crisis is *managerial*. It seeks to tweak or reform the system, without calling its norms into question. This also means that politics itself has become managerial, and government has been replaced by governance and technocracy, thus leaving a gap at the heart of the political, or depoliticizing crisis. Following the major economic and social crises of the last fifteen years, however, this technocratic form of governance has been increasingly rejected in favor of a return of politics, albeit of a populist, sovereignist, and at times neo-fascistic kind. Far from leading to the outcome hoped for by critical theorists, the recent crises have (once again) given birth to a range of reactionary movements. The social and political movements, often violent, of the last decade can be attributed on the one hand to the economic crisis of 2008–2009, which brought the world to its knees, and on the other to its managerial, rather than truly political, response. Where we have seen a return of politics, it is mostly in the form of ultra-nationalism, often combined with religious extremism, or of spontaneous riots, many of which are also weaponized by the Far Right.

In the absence of a clear theory of crisis as such in Marx's writings, the question regarding the root causes and mechanics of crisis was (and continues to be) a matter of intense debate in Marxist theory. It includes Engels's theory of the tendency to overproduction, according to which the expansion of production necessarily runs ahead of the growth of the market; Rosa Luxemburg's theory of underconsumption on the part of the working class, which leads to the imperialist, disruptive, and destructive expansion of the capitalist forces of production to other, non-capitalist parts of the world, where capital finds both the labor power to produce more, cheaper goods, and a new market to consume them; the theories of disproportionality of Tugan-Baranofsky and Rudolf Hilferding; Gramsci's distinction between economic life, for which internationalism, or cosmopolitanism, is a necessary condition, and the life of the state, which moves ever more toward nationalism; and last but not least, Marx's so-called law of the tendency of the rate of profit to fall.[4] The crux of the argument, for Marxist and post-Marxist thought, is that crisis is capitalism's basic state, its ontological feature: capitalism is *structurally* in crisis, it is crisis itself—for the simple reason that its basic form, that of commodity, by which Marx means the transformation of the product and its use value into exchange value, and even *pure* exchange value, or *money*, and its basic logic, that of profit, accumulation, and cut-throat competition, contain within themselves their own contradiction, and, *in nuce*, all other contradictions.[5] Capitalism is therefore defined by cycles of accumulation, which are themselves responses to the specific contradictions and crises generated by any given cycle.

The consequences of this view are expressed perhaps nowhere more lucidly than in "The Chapter on Capital" in *Grundrisse* (probably from July 1857), in which Marx follows the logic of the necessary expansion of the sphere of circulation to its logical and ultimately destructive conclusions. To be sure, Marx dreams of an economic order that would stay as aligned with use-value as possible and would be based on a precise and reasonable assessment of human needs and natural resources. And there is no doubt that he saw in capitalism an infernal machine forced to create artificial needs (in fact, desires) in order to continue to expand, and unable to rest until it has conquered every corner of the world and of the human soul. This is how he puts it in a remarkably prescient passage, in which he foresees the phenomenon known today as globalization, and the principle of "desirability" that governs consumption in a globalized, marketing-based, and highly competitive environment:

> The tendency to create the *world market* is directly given in the concept of capital itself. Every limit appears as a barrier to be overcome [*Jede Grenze erscheint als zu überwindende Schranke*]. Initially, it is a matter of subjugating every moment of production itself to exchange and to suspend the production of direct use values not entering into exchange. . . .
>
> On the other side, the production of *relative surplus value*, i.e. production of surplus value based on the increase and development of the productive forces, requires the production of new consumption; requires that the consuming circle expands with the expansion of the circle of production. Firstly, quantitative expansion of existing consumption; secondly: creation of new needs by propagating existing ones in a wide circle; thirdly: production of *new* needs and discovery and creation of new use values.[6]

Marx also defines this process as "the annihilation of space by time,"[7] or the creation of a world in which the speed of flows of accumulation constantly accelerates. In other words, capitalism can survive only if it continues to overcome its own internal limits and to expand. Yet this expansion is not limitless: the process of self-overcoming, or *Überwindung*, eventually leads to its own destruction, or *Aufhebung*.

Occasionally, Marx foresees capitalism's threat to the environment and the planet's resources. A couple of paragraphs down from the passage I just quoted, he touches on this key issue, and thus on the possibility of bringing into focus yet another kind of value, irreducible to either use or exchange.[8] In the end, however, he focuses on what he sees as the inevitable destruction of capitalism itself under the weight of its own contradictions, rather than on the destruction of natural resources and the planet. The argument is the following: the necessary expansion of the market and "universal industry" through value-creating labor goes hand in hand with "a global system of exploitation of all natural and human resources [*ein System der allgemeinen Exploitation der natürlichen und menschlichen Eigenschaften*]" or with "the universal appropriation of nature [*die universelle Aneignung der Natur*]" through science and technology.[9] Indeed, everything happens as if "the theoretical discovery of the autonomous laws of nature" were merely "a ruse so as to subjugate it under human needs, whether as an object of consumption or as a means of production."[10] In other words, the advent of modern science coincides with the Promethean and specifically capitalist project of the subjection of nature by humankind.[11] With the advent of capital, "nature becomes purely an object [*Gegenstand*] for humankind, purely a matter of utility," and ceases therefore to be recognized as an independent power.[12] With a degree of irony, as the words appear in English, Marx sees in this tendency "the great civilising influence of capital" and "a stage of society in comparison to which all earlier ones appear as mere *local developments* of humanity and as *nature-idolatry* [*Naturidolatrie*]."[13] The particular assemblage of capital, science, and technology, therefore, appears as the overcoming of nature-fetishism, understood this time as the urge to endow nature with divine agency and powers. Marx's assessment becomes even more ambiguous, if not ambivalent, when he recognizes capital as a force that "drives beyond national barriers and prejudices as much as beyond nature deification and worship [*Naturvergötterung*], as well as all traditional, confined, complacent, encrusted satisfactions of present needs, and reproductions of old ways of life."[14] Ultimately, however, the original fetishization of nature, which capitalism overcomes, is replaced by the fetishization (and idolatry) of the commodity form and of an almighty subject, bent on taming and exploiting nature *qua* resource: capital, he claims, dismisses this deification of nature; it is "destructive [*destruktiv*] towards all of this, and constantly revolutionizes it, tearing down all the barriers which hem [*hemmen*] in the development of the forces of production, the expansion of needs, the diversification [*die Mannigfaltigkeit*] of production, and the exploitation and exchange of natural and mental forces."[15] There is something intrinsically disruptive, destructive, and revolutionary about capital. There is no sphere of life, social and more generally cultural, which it leaves untouched. It alters our view of other human beings, our place in the world, and our relation to nature. In the end, Marx emphasizes the contradictions inherent to such a position, and recognizes the seeds of self-destruction and permanent crisis planted by capital itself:

> But from the fact that capital posits every such limit [*Grenze*] as an obstacle [*Schranke*] which, *ideally*, it would overcome, it does not by any

means follow that it has *really* overcome [*überwunden*] it; and, since every such barrier [*Schranke*] contradicts its character, its production moves in contradictions which are constantly overcome [*überwunden*] but just as constantly posited. Furthermore, the universality towards which it irresistibly strives encounters barriers in its own nature, which will, at a certain stage of its development, allow it to be recognized as being itself the greatest barrier to this tendency, and hence will drive it towards its own suspension or destruction [*Aufhebung*].[16]

In the long run, Marx claims, capitalism is unsustainable, and destined for destruction (of the earth's forests, soils, oceans, and atmosphere, and possibly of itself), because the process of overcoming and conquest that characterizes it will eventually reach and meet its end: it will collapse under the weight of its own contradictions. It could be argued that the current ecological and climate crisis signals such an end and announces the imminent collapse of capitalism: an *epochal* rather than an ordinary developmental crisis.[17] Long-distance trade in food and fiber for clothing, and the use of chemicals for agricultural purposes, amounts to "a progress in the art, not only of robbing the worker, but of robbing the soil."[18] The frontier economy, central to the expansion and reproduction of capital, is intrinsically predatory and destructive. What is highlighted here is the looming demise of an entire system, and the need to think of the earth as such and for itself—that is, as the fragile ground of human existence and the estate with which we are entrusted. With hindsight, we can wonder whether the ultimate idolatry and fetishism wasn't—isn't still?—that of a certain conception of the human being as "sovereign" of the earth; and that of a mode of production, accumulation, conditioned upon access to, and exploitation of, cheap labor, cheap energy, cheap raw materials, and cheap food.[19] In this context, the question of agriculture is particularly revealing. I will return to it, and to the environmental collapse to which it contributes, but which also affects it negatively, in the final chapter. But for the time being, let me simply say that, for the most part, and throughout the world, the peasant class is, like the soil it cultivates, increasingly impoverished.

According to Marx, however, the strongest indication of the contradiction inherent to capitalism, and thus the strongest force of self-destruction inhabiting it, is the "law" of the tendency of the rate of profit to fall (TRPF)—one that is much debated and highly controversial, even within Marxist circles.[20] According to one commentator, the TRPF "has been regarded, by most Marxists, as the backbone of revolutionary Marxism," so much so that its refutation or removal would lead not to revolution but to "reformism in theory and practice."[21] In the eyes of another scholar and Marxist economist, the TRPF "remains one of the most important and highly debated issues of all of economics" because it raises "the question of whether, as capitalism grows, this very process of growth will undermine its conditions of existence and thereby engender periodic or secular crises."[22] Marx himself calls the TRPF "in every respect the most important law of modern political economy."[23] In a nutshell, the law stipulates that the rate of profit—the ratio of the profit in relation to the amount of invested capital—decreases over time. Technological innovation, which capitalists pursue relentlessly to reduce costs of production and give them a competitive advantage, will reduce their rate of profit in the long run, since profit (or "surplus value") can only come from human labor (or "variable capital"). As the ratio of fixed or "constant capital"—the portion of total capital invested in physical assets such as land, factories, machinery, vehicles, livestock, or technocratic—increases, and the ratio of "variable capital" decreases, surplus value also decreases. Concretely, this means that "beyond a certain point, the development of the powers of production becomes a barrier for capital; hence the capital relation a barrier for the development of the productive powers of labour."[24] Otherwise stated, in the short run productivity increases as a result of competition, technological innovation, and the introduction of more efficient means of production. In the long run, however, and so long as demand does not increase and the more efficient methods are adopted widely, the amount of labor required will inevitably decrease. But since value comes from the amount of labor that is socially necessary to produce a given commodity, the average rate of industrial profit will tend to decline as new machinery is introduced, productivity is increased, or costs are reduced. When it reaches that point, Marx argues, the entire edifice crumbles, and the final form of servitude (namely wage labor in relation to capital) disappears:

> Capital, i.e. wage labour, enters into the same relation towards the development of social wealth and of the forces of production as the guild system, serfdom, slavery, and is *necessarily* stripped off as a fetter. The last form of servitude assumed by human activity, that of wage labour on one side, capital on the other, is thereby cast off like a skin, and this casting-off itself is the result of the mode of production corresponding to capital.[25]

In other words, the material as well as mental conditions of the "negation" (and collapse) of wage labor and of capital, which were themselves the "negation" of earlier forms of unfree social production, are results of the mode of production of capital itself. On the side of the end of the form of alienation specific to wage labor, Marx's image of the stripping-off of its "fetters" situates it in a line of other forms of alienation and their necessary demise. But the biological image of the old skin being "cast off" as a direct result of the process that generated it in the first place illustrates yet more powerfully what Marx, after Hegel, calls *Aufhebung*: it is as if, unbeknownst to the system of production in question, its development had in fact been a slow movement toward its own demise, one that does not take the form of a smooth transition—the new skin, whatever its form, does not replace the old in a purely organic manner—but involves "bitter contradictions, crises, spasms."[26] The *violence* inherent to the "destruction of capital" is caused not by forces external to it, but by its own drive for self-preservation. This means that the "higher state of social production" to which it will eventually lead is due not to its benevolence, or to the realization of its own shortcomings and self-reformation, but to its internal logic, which is logic *as such*—that is, the Hegelian "logic of the content," or the dynamic of thought and material processes driven by the power of contradiction and negation. One can subscribe to Marx's critique without subscribing to its predictive claims, its teleology, and the idea of an inevitable "higher" state of social production. If anything, the last hundred years seem to point to capitalism's limitless ability to generate economic, social, and political crises of the gravest kind and survive them. Unlike previous historical configurations, it rises from its own ashes.

To put the terms of Marx's "law" slightly differently: with the growth of scientific power, technological innovation, competition, and the development of the population, capital faces a difficulty: namely, its ability to increase its profit margins. This, in turn, forces it to increase the productivity of its labor force, which translates into greater pressures on it: "Hence the highest development of productive power together with the greatest expansion of existing wealth will coincide with the depreciation of capital, degradation of the labourer, and a most straightened exhaustion of his vital powers."[27] To be sure, the fall of the rate of profit can be slowed down and the moment of truth in the form of crisis can be delayed, for example through "the constant devaluation of a part of the existing capital," such as "the transformation of a great part of capital into fixed capital which does not serve as agency of direct production"; the lowering of taxes or reduction of ground rent; the "creation of new branches of production in which more direct labour in relation to capital is needed," or where the productivity of labor is not yet developed.[28] In other words, one needs to take into account "counteracting factors" that raise the rate of profit without calling into question the TRPF. In his draft manuscript of Volume 3 of *Capital*, Marx cites the following five factors: the more intense exploitation of labor; the reduction of wages below their value; the cheapening of the elements of constant capital by various means; the creation of a "relative surplus population" or "industrial reserve army," which consists of the unemployed and underemployed; and the reduction of the cost of industrial inputs and commodities through the expansion of foreign—especially colonial—trade.[29] To this list, and looking at how the capitalist economy has continued to grow in the last decades, we could add systematic debt, public or private, as a key instrument of the creation of surplus value.

But the contradictions of capitalism do not end there. Its more recent—financialized and globalized—form has introduced some further contradictions and exacerbated some that already existed. Let me mention a few. Markets, we are told, are intrinsically rational and efficient. That is because they are governed by quasi-natural laws, which seek equilibrium. Yet whenever the laws in question are transgressed, or the market doesn't behave according to its abstract, ideal form and wreaks havoc, the state, which under "normal" conditions is kept outside the free play of the market, is called upon to save it. The state is thus not only the condition of possibility of capitalist accumulation—through a legal system that guarantees and enforces property rights, market exchange, and free international trade; a police apparatus that guarantees social order; and an economic policy that guarantees "the full faith and credit" of the money supply—but also the force that saves it, whatever the cost. Another way of describing the contradiction inherent to the separation between economic and political power under capitalism would be this: the power to organize production and cover our basic needs is privatized, while "the task of governing the remaining, 'non-economic' order, including the external conditions for accumulation, falls to the public power."[30] As we know, this distinction is constantly violated, but only when it is a matter of protecting capital: privatize the profit, socialize the risk. The market is therefore an odd kind of system, in that it requires a constant input of energy, at the level of both its conditions of emergence and its negative effects or accidents, by another, officially endogenous source—namely, the state. Today's corporations are allowed to externalize as many costs as possible, to extract as much value from workers, nature, society, and even future generations as they can, and pay as little as possible. In the case of nature and future generations, the cost is exactly zero. Liberal economists speak of the "laws" of the market, where one should really speak of the norms of an entirely constructed assemblage, the state/market assemblage.

Another contradiction and source of considerable political tension stems from the fact that, with the globalization and de-territorialization of capital, the economic and transnational "world-system" is increasingly at odds with the territorial logic that defines states and the international relations between states. Often, states find themselves forced to lower their taxes to "attract" companies and be more competitive. At the same time, states expose their sovereignty to the will and power of financial markets, which thus limit the power of the states to act as a condition of possibility of accumulation. This contradiction can take various forms, but invariably generates frustration and anger on the part of citizens (and economic agents) who see their autonomy, sovereignty, and agency slip away from them and into the hands of a force (they believe) they cannot control. They then turn against the political class, the "establishment," the "elite," the "bureaucrats"—in short, against those they can still act on. But the tension can also take the form of a conflict between states, or between states and international organizations such as the World Bank, the IMF, or the WTO.

Inevitably, and despite the multiplication of the countermeasures I just mentioned, Marx believed, and Marxists believe, that the contradictions inherent to the system lead to a succession of "catastrophes," of "explosions, cataclysms, crises," and "to their repetition on a higher scale," which finally leads to the "violent overthrow" of the capitalist order.[31] The century of crises and revolutions, which Rousseau announced in *Émile*, finds in Marx a new impetus and orientation: they will, he claims, be a direct and almost inevitable effect of the contradictions inherent to the capitalist mode of production.

Social Struggles and Subaltern Strategies

Walter Benjamin on the General (Revolutionary) Strike

As Nancy Fraser notes, and despite its structural invariants, capitalism does not exist as such, but only in historically specific forms or "regimes of accumulation."[32] This means that the contradictions inherent to capitalism as a totalizing social order evolve and give birth to different phases of development. Fraser identifies three such regimes (in addition to the early, merchant form of capitalism):

> a nineteenth-century regime of liberal or competitive capitalism in which the public powers of territorial states were used to constitute the capitalist economy; a twentieth-century regime of state-managed monopoly capitalism in which state-level public power was additionally deployed in efforts to forestall or mitigate economic crisis by disciplining capital for its own good; and the current regime of globalizing financialized capitalism in which state power is increasingly used to construct transnational governance structures that empower capital.[33]

In each case, the changes were forced by major crises, such as the financial crash of 1929, or the oil crisis of 1973 and 1974. The financial crash and near collapse of the world economy in late 2008, combined with the economic policies developed in response to the COVID crisis and the war in Ukraine, discredited almost entirely the neoliberal ideology of market efficiency and rationality, and repeatedly violated its basic principles. As a result, the question regarding the future of the current regime of accumulation remains entirely open. Will it lead to a new, post-financial phase of capitalism; a postcapitalist society, which would not necessarily be better than the one it replaces; or a long period of social disintegration punctuated by the appearance of morbid symptoms, including old or new types of revolutions, whether of a secular or a religious kind? It is impossible to say. At this stage, it is the third scenario that seems the most likely, given the number of morbid symptoms currently on display in capitalist societies (more on these later).

As the political contradiction of capitalist society finds expression in a different set of crises, so too do the forms of social struggle. In periods of relative stability, ordinary political struggles, which take place within the terms of a given regime, tend to prevail. But in times of crisis, extraordinary struggles seek radically to transform the regime in question. "In the first case," Fraser writes, "subaltern strata seek to use the public power to improve their conditions within it, while the most far-sighted fractions of the ruling class would use that power to institute piecemeal, system-conforming reforms to patch up the rough spots."[34] And insofar as the respective aims of those two groups converge, ad hoc reforms can serve, for a while at least, to counteract the system's inherent tendency to crisis. In periods of profound crisis, by contrast, "the dysfunctionalities metastasize, exceeding the reparative capacities of piecemeal reform and inciting demands for deep structural change."[35] What we have, then, is a revolutionary dynamic, which can lead to two different outcomes: "In these periods, competing groups of social actors struggle to develop and realize their respective projects for resolving the crisis—whether by devising a new regime of accumulation or by creating a postcapitalist society."[36] As the regimes of accumulation differ, so too do the struggles.

In this chapter, I look at the phenomenon of the general or revolutionary strike, which I interpret as the paradigmatic form of the social struggle of nineteenth-century capitalism. Following Sorel and Benjamin, I distinguish it from the "local" or system-conforming strike, which seeks to extract concessions from capital. In a subsequent section, I will discuss the riot and other forms of struggle, including the "antiwork" movement, as typical of the third, globalized and financialized form of capitalism. This is not to say that one form of struggle simply replaces another. For one regime of accumulation does not simply replace another either: it is more a matter of a transformation, or a mutation, which retains some aspects of the previous regime while eliminating, adding, or replacing others. I choose to approach this question from the perspective of Walter Benjamin for several reasons. First, Benjamin's analysis of the general strike takes place in the context of a broader reflection on the legitimate use of violence and on the state of exception, which he understands differently from, and in opposition to, Carl Schmitt. Second, Benjamin's analysis is singular in that it opens onto a philosophy of history that is messianic rather than eschatological, and underpinned by an idea of justice irreducible to the system of right—which, as I'll show in Chapter 4, Derrida also draws on. Finally, Benjamin's view of critique and revolution is carried out in the name not of a universal class, but of all the subaltern classes. As such, it paves the way for my discussion of further subaltern strategies, based on the works of Gramsci and W. E. B. Du Bois.

In 1930, Walter Benjamin and Bertolt Brecht drafted a proposal for a new journal titled *Krise und Kritik*, the program of which was expressed in the following terms: "The journal's field of activity is the present crisis in all areas of ideology, and it is the task of the journal to register this crisis or bring it about, and this by means of criticism."[37] Critique, in this instance, is both diagnostic (i.e., directed at the ideological expression of crisis in science and art) and praxical (i.e., oriented toward the *provocation* of crisis in a revolutionary sense). A decade earlier, Benjamin had published his now famous "Critique of Violence" (1921).[38] His point of departure—namely, the question of violence in politics, especially in connection with the general, revolutionary strike—is crucial if we are fully to grasp the nature of his disagreement with Schmitt.

Apart from the state, which has the monopoly on violence (*Gewalt*), organized labor is probably the only legal subject entitled to exercise it. To be sure, one might immediately object that a strike cannot be described as violent, insofar as it is a withdrawal, an omission of action, or a nonaction, and that state power recognizes it as a right on this basis alone. The moment of violence, however, "is necessarily introduced, in the form of extortion, into such an omission, if it takes place in the context of a conscious readiness to resume the suspended action under certain circumstances that either have nothing whatever to do with this action or only superficially modify it" (p. 239). Following Sorel's *Réflexions sur la violence* (1908), Benjamin qualifies this kind of strike as *political*, or as a political *partial* strike. It is *partially* political, since "it causes *only* an external modification of labour conditions."[39] It is part of a calculation "to resume work following external concessions and this or that modification to working conditions."[40] As such, it is essentially *extortionate* and *law-making*. And law-making, Benjamin adds, "is power-making, assumption of power, and to that extent an immediate manifestation of violence."[41] There is no power struggle that does not involve *some* force or violence. Understood in this way, "the right to strike constitutes in the view of labour, which is opposed to that of the state, the right to use force in attaining certain ends" (p. 239). Under normal circumstances, these antithetical rights lead to a resolution of one kind or another, in which the state loses none of its power.

But the revolutionary proletarian general strike—which, oddly enough, and still with reference to Sorel, Benjamin describes as *nonpolitical* and *nonviolent*—signals the point when "the antithesis between the two conceptions emerges in all its bitterness" (p. 239). What we have, then, is the expression of an objective contradiction within the form of the state, one that Benjamin has no choice but to call a *crisis*: "In this difference of interpretation is expressed the objective contradiction in the legal situation, whereby the state acknowledges a violence whose ends, as natural ends, it sometimes regards with indifference but in a crisis (the general revolutionary strike) confronts inimically."[42] Since the state views the interpretation and exercise of a right that it granted in the first place as a violence toward itself and its legal system, which it believes the general strike aims to overthrow, it reserves the right to meet the strikers with equal or greater violence. What it does, in effect, is silence the only possible critique of its own violence—that is, the critique that stems from the strikers' ability "to found and modify legal conditions."[43]

What makes the general strike radical, revolutionary, and unacceptable in the eyes of the state is precisely its *general* and *nonpolitical* character, by which I think we should understand the fact that it is nonnegotiable. For labor, it is a right, and one it intends to exercise to the full. For the state, it is an abuse, and therefore illegal, since the right to strike was never "intended" in that way: the specific reason for strikes admitted by legislation cannot be prevalent in every workshop or company. As a result, the state will take "emergency measures" and push its *own* sovereign or *law-preserving* right to its limit. For what we have is a strike, the object of which is not material gain of any kind, or specific demands regarding the workplace, but the abolition and destruction of state power. Its aim is "to resume only a wholly transformed work, no longer enforced by the state."[44] As such, it is "anarchistic."[45] By contrast, Schmitt insisted that the state of exception, while an exception to the norm, "is different from anarchy and chaos."[46] For Benjamin, the revolutionary moment, as embodied in the general strike, is not so much a temporary suspension of the law as an overturning or deposing (*Entsetzung*) of the legal order, understood as the dialectic between law-making and law-preserving violence (*rechtsetzende und rechtserhaltende Gewalt*), or executive (*schaltende*) and administrative (*verwaltete*) violence. At the same time, this "pure immediate" or "revolutionary" violence is the founding of "a new historical epoch [*ein neues geschichtliches Zeitalter*]."[47] In that respect, it can be said to be supremely or radically historical. It is, Benjamin says, divine (*göttliche*) or sovereign (*waltende*) violence. As such, it is to be distinguished from both "mythic" violence, which is law-making and "assumption of power," and law-preserving, "administrative" violence.[48]

This theological-political equation would seem to indicate a proximity between Benjamin and Schmitt. Both equate sovereignty with the exceptional and the singular, with the divine. But did we not establish that Schmitt equates the state of exception with the *suspension* of the legal norm, whereas Benjamin equates it with the *creation* of an entirely new social, political, and legal order? In addition, Schmitt's conception of the exception is "miraculous," whereas Benjamin's is messianic. Finally, Schmitt's position seems to be conservative through and through, whereas Benjamin's is clearly revolutionary. On this last point, and on closer inspection, however, things are more complicated than they appear to be. For Schmitt makes a crucial distinction between two types of dictatorship, which I have thus far ignored: *commissary* dictatorship, to which I have already referred, and which is limited and constitutional; and *sovereign* dictatorship, which is unlimited and transformative. This is how Schmitt puts it in "Diktatur" (1926):

From the historical development of the regulation concerning the state of emergency it is obvious that essentially two types of dictatorship exist: namely a dictatorship that, despite all its extra-legal authorisation, remains within the prescriptions of a constitutional order and in which the dictator is constitutionally mandated (commissary dictatorship); and on the other hand a dictatorship in which the whole legal existing order is rendered obsolete and a completely new order is intended (sovereign dictatorship). This sovereign dictatorship is exercised by a national assembly that has at its disposal state power without legal limitations when the existing constitutional order has been abolished—say, after a revolution—and the new constitution has not yet been implemented.[49]

Scheuerman clarifies the difference in the following terms:

Commissarial dictatorship allows emergency authorities to do whatever they consider necessary to overcome concrete threats at hand. Yet their acts are not supposed to possess the character of ordinary law: individual emergency measures are strictly delimited from standing general laws. In contrast, sovereign dictatorship entails full-scale *revolutionary* dictatorship, along the lines of the Jacobins and more recent political conjunctures, including the 1918 German Revolution. Its legal acts are *transformative* and thus also effectively permanent.[50]

According to Schmitt, the Weimar Constitutional Assembly exercised the powers of sovereign dictatorship when it created Germany's first republican system. Acting in the name of the people as a whole, conceived as a constitutionally unbound *pouvoir constituant*, postwar Germany's revolutionary dictatorship destroyed the preexisting political order to create a new one. This clearly shows that the Schmittian state of exception, and therefore his conception of political sovereignty, is not exclusively conservative, but can also be revolutionary. At a formal level, this position would make it compatible, if not identical, with that of Benjamin. And yet, Benjamin and Schmitt are on separate ends of the political divide, the first embracing a leftist view of social relations, the second embracing the National-Socialist revolution and its anti-Semitic worldview.

Wherein, then, lies the difference between the two, aside from their actual politics? In what sense does their view of *Ausnahme* differ?

The debate, both exoteric and esoteric, which took place between the two thinkers in the 1920s is now well documented and summarized in Agamben's *State of Exception*.[51] Agamben's most compelling (and convincing) claim is that Schmitt's theory of sovereignty and the state of exception in *Political Theology* is an answer to Benjamin's essay on violence, and an attempt to neutralize the possibility, and indeed legitimacy, of a *pure* form of violence. According to Agamben, the distinction between law-making and law-preserving violence, which was Benjamin's target, "corresponds to the letter" to the opposition between constitutive and constituted power.[52] The distinction between the two types of power has governed the great political transformations of our time since the French Revolution. It was also the foundation of Schmitt's theory of sovereign dictatorship in *Die Diktatur*, published only one year before *Politische Theologie*.[53] "The sovereign violence in *Political Theology*," Agamben writes, "responds to the pure violence of Benjamin's essay with the figure of a power that neither makes nor preserves law, but suspends it."[54] In other words, and as we saw in Chapter 2, suspension is the Schmittian, sovereignist response to anarchist or revolutionary violence. Schmitt seeks to neutralize one extreme or liminal form of violence (the general strike) with another (the state of exception), which, far from being outside the law, fuses together the law and the sovereign. For Benjamin, by contrast, "the most important function of the sovereign is to exclude" the juridical order [*den auszuschließen*].[55]

"On the Concept of History," which Benjamin wrote shortly before dying by suicide on September 26, 1940, articulates the essential difference between the two thinkers on the question of the use and specific meaning of political violence, and its connection with the state of exception.[56] In section VIII of the essay, Benjamin states: "The tradition of the oppressed teaches us that the 'state of emergency' [*Ausnahmezustand*] in which we live is not the exception [*Ausnahme*] but the rule." He then adds that the task is to "attain a conception of history that is in keeping with this insight." In other words, historical materialist consciousness *requires* that one adopt the standpoint of the oppressed (the proletariat, the Jews, the communists, the Roma, the disabled, etc.). And that, in turn, requires that we "bring about a real state of emergency [*wirklichen Ausnahmezustands*]." What, then, we should ask, distinguishes the "real" state of emergency from the "fictitious" or fascist one, which was introduced in Germany in 1933 and lifted only after the defeat and collapse of the Third Reich? The fascist state of emergency corresponds to the *indefinite* suspension of the rule of law, which the Nazis, having set fire to the Reichstag, introduced by invoking Article 48 of the constitution of the Weimar Republic and forcing President Hindenburg to sign the Presidential Decree for the Protection of People and State (*Verordnung des Reichspräsidenten zum Schutz vom Volk und Staat*). As Agamben puts it: the confusion between the exception and the rule, which Schmitt was very careful to distinguish, "was precisely what the Third Reich concretely brought about."[57] Yet contrary to what Agamben claims, I don't think that the "real" state of emergency refers to the situation that prevailed in Germany at the time, and the "fictitious" one to the state of exception regulated by law. Agamben is arguably too formalistic in his reading, and tends to ontologize violence: "Here, pure violence as the extreme political object, as the 'thing' of politics, is the counterpart to pure being, to pure existence as the ultimate metaphysical stakes; the strategy of the exception, which must ensure the relation between anomic violence and law, is the counterpart to the onto-theo-logical strategy aimed at capturing pure being in the meshes of logos."[58] This, I believe, holds for Schmitt, whose vision of praxis as a *jurist* is motivated by the decision concerning the state of exception, primarily from the point of view of constitutional law. "If law is decision," Agamben writes, "the jurist is not only an impartial interpreter of the existing norms, he is also a vehicle contributing to the formal elaboration of a new substantive law created through social praxis. . . . Schmitt argues without reservation for this involvement of the jurist in the material constitution of his times."[59] This is true. But Benjamin's vision of praxis is motivated by a sense of justice for the oppressed and falls clearly in the realm of what, in *Dictatorship*, Schmitt identifies as a position for which the norm is defined by a "political ideal" rather than by "an existing constitution."[60] Remarkably, in his reading of "Critique of Violence," Agamben fails to mention the issue of class struggle and the exceptional case of the general strike as not simply an example of "pure" violence, but its paradigm. The *form* of the general strike is the foundation for the critique of state violence. "In a strike," Benjamin writes, "the state fears above all else that function of violence which is the object of this study to identify as the only foundation of its critique." As a result, Agamben can't see that the "real" state of emergency is the *revolutionary* one, through which a classless society is achieved and oppression, including of a biopolitical kind, is overcome.

This is precisely the situation Schmitt discusses in *Dictatorship*, while distinguishing it from the one he seeks not only to analyze but also justify: the state of exception as revolution differs in kind from the state of exception as the suspension of the "constitutional" or "lawful" state [*Rechtstaat*].[61] The dictatorship of the proletariat and that of the sovereign cannot be said in the same sense. Or, as he puts it, the concept of class has profoundly changed the concept of sovereignty. Hence his preference for what he called a "countertheory of sovereign dictatorship," or a right-wing authoritarian response to modern left-wing revolutionary dictatorship. This also explains why, in the 1930s, Schmitt increasingly blurred the distinction between the two types of dictatorship introduced in the 1920s and came out in favor of Nazism as a rescuing form of sovereign dictatorship: facing a full-scale existential crisis and the imminent loss of the most basic political unity, Germany had no choice but to turn its back on modern constitutionalism and decide in favor of the Nazi state of exception.

But the picture on Benjamin's side is yet more complicated. His conception of the revolutionary moment is idiosyncratic and rooted in his no less idiosyncratic and specifically messianic conception of history, developed in his "Theses on the Philosophy of History." The state of emergency, which stems from a "situation" and "moment" of *danger*—structurally similar to the one Heidegger speaks of in his private manuscripts from the late 1930s and early 1940s—*rescues* the past, tradition, and memory from "the ruling classes" and their "conformism" (section VI), in what amounts to a blasting open of the continuum of history: "The awareness that they are about to make the continuum of history explode is characteristic of the revolutionary classes at the moment of their action" (section XV). "Universal history," which tells "the sequence of events like the beads of a rosary" and establishes "causal connections" between events, gives way to a history of the "moment," understood as a "shock" in which history is "crystalized," that is, "shot through with chips of Messianic time" (sections

XVII and XVIII A). For the Jews, "every second of time was the strait gate through which the Messiah might enter" (section XVIII B). The materialist history that is proposed here is unorthodox, in that it is not of the "universal class," but of the subaltern, the forgotten minority, the victims of the past. In addition, the time at issue escapes the arche-teleological structure of universal history as well as the causal structure of mechanical history: messianic time is fragmentary, untotalizable, surprising. It is one for which every moment is potentially pivotal (and therefore critical), indeed inhabited by a virtual presence that tears open the continuum of history and announces "justice." This means that any attempt at constructing a purely causal, mechanistic view of history, and thus of historical materialism, is doomed: "universal" history cannot account for the "shock" of the singular; the totalizing image of time fails to recognize and therefore do justice to its crystal-image.

The state of emergency in the "real" sense is indeed a state of exception, but the exception signals the singular to which the universal cannot do justice, the voice it cannot hear; and what is "rescued" is not the state, or the law, as Schmitt believed, but justice. As such, it is defined not by a moment of suspension of the law, destined to a return to its "normality," nor indeed by a mere exclusion, but by a moment of creation, in which the law is given anew, albeit not as a universal. The opening sentence of section VIII now takes on a different and clearer sense: if "the *tradition* of the oppressed teaches us that the 'state of emergency' in which we live is not the exception but the rule," it is because beneath and before the state of emergency as a legal and supposedly temporary measure lies the state of exception of the oppressed and the subaltern, who cannot speak. This exception *is* the rule or is necessarily embedded (and concealed) in it. History is necessarily written by the victors; yet the presence of the victims can never be entirely erased, thus opening up the space for another writing of history, in which the exception is the rule:

> Whoever has emerged victorious participates to this day in the triumphal procession in which the present rulers step over those who are lying prostrate. According to traditional practice, the spoils are carried along in the procession. They are called cultural treasures, and a historical materialist views them with cautious detachment. For without exception the cultural

treasures he surveys have an origin which he cannot contemplate without horror. They owe their existence not only to the efforts of the great minds and talents who have created them, but also to the anonymous toil of their contemporaries. There is no document of civilization which is not at the same time a document of barbarism. And just as a document is not free of barbarism, barbarism taints also the manner in which it was transmitted from one owner to another. A historical Materialist therefore dissociates himself from it as far as possible. He regards it as his task to brush history against the grain. (section VII)

Let me return to the example of the general strike as a state of exception, radically different in nature from the exception in the sense of the suspension of the normal legal order. At times, a political partial strike (to use Benjamin's terminology) can evolve into a political radical or revolutionary strike. In addition, it need not pit the working class against the bourgeoisie. This is what happened in Poland in 1980 and 1981 with the rise (and eventually brutal repression) of the Solidarity movement.[62] The context in which the strikes occurred matters: Poland was going through its deepest economic crisis since the end of World War II, and a severe debt crisis, which eventually turned into a sovereign debt crisis. At the same time, wages were too high in relation to prices, which had been kept frozen since the early 1960s. In 1980, the government reached the conclusion that prices and wages needed to be adjusted. This led to massive social unrest, which in turn created more market instability.

The Polish case is interesting and unusual in at least two ways. First, it happened in a socialist state, in the eyes of which the sovereign was the working class, as embodied in the Leninist Polish United Workers' Party. In this context, independent unions had no reason to exist: the interests of the workers were represented at all times and at the highest level. The strikes began as a set of twenty-one demands, which included the right to create unions, to strike, and to speak freely. But they became politically more radical as Solidarność gained an ever broader membership base, which ultimately reached ten million members, compared to three million Party members, in a population of thirty-five million. They eventually paralyzed the entire country.

The movement was therefore doubly unacceptable: first because it threatened the integrity of the Polish state, and second because it called into question the state's Leninist *ideological* foundations, according to which the Party dominated the state (the Polish People's Republic) and the state dominated the economy. According to one commentator, the demands of Solidarity amounted to a mixture of anarcho-syndicalism, which included the introduction of worker self-management, socialized planning of the economy, and ownership of the media; political liberalism, in the guise of political pluralism, judicial and prosecutorial independence, and academic and religious freedom; and direct democracy, in the form of referenda to settle disputes between Solidarity and the Party.[63] In the eyes of the Leninist hegemonic Party and its allies in the Warsaw Pact, those positions were alarming and unacceptable: they amounted to the creation of a new *pouvoir constituant*, the aim of which was the abolition of Leninist power in Poland. The "state of emergency" or "state of war" (*stan wojenny*), generally referred to as "martial law," was declared on the night of December 12–13, 1981. Its aim, in the words of the Presidium of the National Coordination Commission of Solidarity, was to crush the movement "through terror" and "force." And that is exactly what it did.

The conclusion I wish to draw regarding the Polish example is that the Solidarity movement was directed at the proletariat as an *abstract* universal class and the hegemonic rule of the Polish United Workers' Party. But it was a working-class movement, which didn't call for bourgeois hegemony, the introduction of capitalism, or even market mechanisms. As another commentator puts it, Solidarity "not only was not an anti-communist movement . . . but was also, in itself, a communist event *par excellence*."[64] It was an act of sovereignty on the part of an entire people, which disputed the power of the official sovereign (the Party) and sought to replace an abstract or "fictitious" state of emergency with a "concrete" one. Naturally, one can also analyze the situation from the point of view of the legality then in place, and the significance of the martial law introduced by General Jaruzelski. The question, which Manko raises by adopting a Schmittian lens, becomes one of knowing whether Jaruzelski's dictatorship was a sovereign or a commissary dictatorship. His answer is that "on the level of the *lex scripta* it was merely commissary, but if we take the constitution as a whole, in its substantive and not only formal sense it had clear elements of a sovereign dictatorship."[65] Already in 1982 the general began to introduce elements of the liberal rule of law and to implement far-reaching economic reforms, such as the adjustment of prices (by as much as 400 percent), a reduction of real wages, and the introduction of elements of a market economy. Still, it is likely that none of this would have happened without the massive mobilization and strikes orchestrated by the Solidarity movement.

Tactical Alliances and Hegemony-Formations: On Gramsci's *Prison Notebooks*

Gramsci's concept of hegemony first appeared in *Notes on the Southern Question* (1926).[66] There, in keeping with the Leninist approach, Gramsci defines hegemony in purely political and specifically tactical terms: "The proletariat can become the leading and the dominant class to the extent that it succeeds in creating *a system of alliances* which allows it to mobilize *the majority of the working population* against capitalism and the bourgeois State."[67] In the Italian context, this tactical alliance was to take place between the proletariat and the peasant masses. As in Lenin, the alliance was not "moral and intellectual," but strictly political—that is, motivated by intersecting class interests.[68] It is precisely the move from a purely tactical-political sense of hegemony, based on class alliance, to hegemony in a moral and intellectual sense, that the *Prison Notebooks* enact.[69] This move signals, in turn, a profound transformation of the meaning and role of ideology, if not its rehabilitation. As Laclau and Mouffe put it: "Ideology is no longer identified with a 'system of ideas' or with the 'false consciousness' of social agents; it is instead an organic and relational whole, embodied in institutions and apparatuses, which welds together a historical bloc."[70] This means that ideology is itself material, and not a mere surface effect of class interests or determinations.

According to Gramsci, a hegemonic class or group exercises political leadership over "subordinate" or "subaltern" classes. It does so first through the coercive, legal apparatus of the state (*dominio, coercizione*), which secures the "discipline" of the subaltern groups: Gramsci is clear about the fact that, in a *democratic* regime, in which political authority is not arbitrary or imposed from without but the result of a free decision, "discipline is a necessary element of the democratic order, of liberty."[71] More importantly, however, hegemony is established through consent—that is, by winning those groups over, by constructing a "collective will" from a number of dissimilar perspectives, dispersed wills, and heterogenous aims, which are never reducible to class (and therefore fixed) determinations.[72] Now the consent in question is precisely the product of an "organic ideology" or common worldview—a "common sense" or "conformism" (Notebook 11, §12)—which involves the participation of those whom Gramsci calls the "organic intellectuals," by which he means intellectuals, journalists, scholars, and artists, as well as functionaries, administrators, managers, and politicians. This is how, in addition to economic and political unity, intellectual and moral cohesion are achieved on a universal level. Hegemony, in that sense, corresponds to the third and most "political" phase of the relation of forces between groups—the first being the primitive solidarity and homogeneity between professional groups (the merchant feels in solidarity with other merchants, but not with the manufacturer), and the second the social solidarity between the members of the same social group, bound by a community of interest. It corresponds to the level of *superstructure*, which slowly emerges from the *structural* level, or from the relation between social groups—from their function and position—as defined by the material forces of production. The latter is easily defined scientifically, mathematically even, since it designates an *objective* relation, a *naturalistic* phenomenon. But the critique of the constitution of the sphere of ideology requires a different kind of analysis and the creation of specifically designed conceptual tools. Gramsci is careful to distinguish philosophy as he understands it from "the conception of the world that is most widespread among the popular masses in a historical period,"[73] by which he means "the ensemble of all the philosophies of individuals and groups, as well as scientific opinions, religion, and common sense,"[74] which taken together make up popular culture.[75]

Ideology *critique*, as Gramsci understands it (and understands Marx on the topic), makes sense only from the point of view of what he opposes to ideology, which he terms "the philosophy of praxis."[76] But this opposition is an internal one, insofar as philosophy itself, on Gramsci's reading, is an ideology or a superstructure. The distinction that needs to be made, therefore, is not between ideology and another realm, but between types of ideology. From the standpoint of the philosophy of praxis, "ideologies are anything but arbitrary," or simple illusions: while not the mainspring of history, they are "an objective or operative reality," "real historical facts that one must fight against and unmask as instruments of domination—not as a matter of morality, etc., but as a matter, precisely, of political struggle in order to make the ruled intellectually independent of the rulers, to destroy a hegemony and create another as a necessary moment of revolutionizing praxis."[77] The philosophy of praxis is and needs to be a superstructure, because ideology is the terrain on which subaltern groups become conscious of their social position, their own strength, and their own tasks. There is, however, a fundamental difference between the philosophy of praxis and other philosophies or worldviews; and this difference has everything to do with crisis, contradiction, and the possibility of eliminating the former by overcoming the latter:

> Other ideologies are nonorganic creations because they are contradictory, their aim is to reconcile opposed and contradictory interests. Their "historicity" will be short lived because contradiction will surface after every event of which the ideologies have been an instrument. The philosophy of praxis, on the other hand, does not seek the peaceful resolution of existing contradictions in history; it is, rather, the very theory of such contradictions. The philosophy of praxis is not the instrument of government [and, more generally, of power—MB] by means of which the dominant groups obtain the consent of the subaltern classes and exercise hegemony over them; it is rather the expression of these subaltern classes who want to educate themselves in the art of government [the groups who want to be governed less, differently—MB] and who have an interest in knowing all truths, including unpleasant ones, and avoiding the "impossible" deceits of the upper class and, even more, their own.[78]

To illustrate Gramsci's point with examples from our more recent history, let me turn briefly to the efforts on the part of Western capitalist democracies to federate their population around new forms of consensus and hegemony, as described by Habermas in *Legitimation Crisis* (1973).[79] Habermas's preliminary aim is "to introduce systematically a *social*-scientifically useful concept of crisis," as opposed to the merely *systems*-theoretic concept of crisis found in Luhmann and other sociologists of self-regulated systems, for whom crises are seen as "persistent disturbances of *system integration*" and thus failures on the part of a given system properly to integrate or solve the problems with which it is faced.[80] By contrast, Habermas defines crisis as a failure of *social* integration—that is, as the point at which consensual foundations of normative structures or social institutions are so impaired that they disintegrate. His basic argument is that capitalism, understood as a regime of accumulation, underwent a decisive shift in the postwar period— one, I hasten to add, that was challenged from the start by the Vienna school of economics and by German ordoliberalism, the ideas and policies of which eventually triumphed in the late 1970s and early 1980s under the governments of Margaret Thatcher, Ronald Reagan, and Augusto Pinochet. Whereas the role of the state in the early, liberal or competitive stage of capitalism was limited to constituting the capitalist economy and repressing the forces that threatened it, state power was deployed anew in the roughly thirty-year period between the end of the war and the oil crises of the 1970s. In Fraser's terms, the state took it upon itself "to steer national economic development, to compensate market failures, and to manage economic (and political) crises."[81] State-capitalism sought to soften boom-and-bust cycles by creating the welfare state (through significant taxation), by planning the economy and creating a public sector that partially replaced the market, by improving labor/capital relations through negotiations, and by controlling monetary policy. Keynesian economics and crisis management were the doxa of the day. However, like its predecessor, this regime too proved unsustainable over the long run, and generated a series of economic and especially political crises. Why? Because state-capitalism did not resolve capitalism's contradictions, but only displaced them by "shifting the locus of crisis from the market to the state, or from the economic to the political field."[82]

How does Habermas describe this specifically political contradiction? To answer this question, we need to mention the three (or four, depending on how we count) crisis-tendencies he introduces: the economic crisis-tendency, the political crisis-tendency (which can take the form of either a "rationality" or a "legitimation" crisis), and the sociocultural crisis-tendency (or the crisis of motivation). The general point here is that in a system in which the state takes it upon itself to replace and supplement tasks that were once, under a purely liberal system, a matter for the market only, class relationships are repoliticized (become a matter of public concern and negotiation), and crisis-tendencies shift from the economic into the administrative. In other words, they become crises of rationality and/or legitimation: "The political system requires an input of mass *loyalty* that is as diffuse as possible. The output consists in sovereignly executed administrative decisions. Output crises have the form of a *rationality crisis* in which the administrative system does not succeed in reconciling and fulfilling the imperatives received from the economic system."[83] *Input* crises, by contrast, have the form of a *legitimation* crisis. They happen "when the legitimizing system does not succeed in maintaining the requisite level of mass loyalty while the steering imperatives taken over from the economic system are carried through."[84] A "rationality deficit" in public administration occurs when "the state apparatus cannot, under given boundary conditions, adequately steer the economic system." A "legitimation deficit" occurs when "it is not possible to maintain or establish effective normative structures to the extent required by administrative means."[85] Finally, a motivation crisis occurs when "the socio-cultural system changes in such a way that its output becomes dysfunctional for the state and for the system of social labor."[86] The economic and political crisis-tendencies can themselves break out only through the sociocultural system, understood as the set of "purchasable and collectively demandable goods and services, legal and administrative acts, public and social-security, etc."[87]

Now in the case of state-capitalism government activity "pursues the declared goal of steering the system so as to avoid [economic] crises," with the consequence that "the class relationship" does not disappear, but loses its "unpolitical form."[88] At the same time, and in the long run, to the extent that the "interventionist" state "does not suspend the spontaneous working of the law of value but is rather subject to it," its administrative activity can only intensify the crisis-tendency inherent to capitalism.[89] As a result, even the class struggle, "which can lead to regulation in the interests of wage labour, remains 'a moment of the movement of capital.'"[90] Now faced with the huge economic cost of its own interventionism and social appeasement, and to avoid the crisis-ridden disturbances of growth, the state apparatus relies heavily on taxes. This, in turn, introduces the risk of a crisis of a different kind—namely, a crisis of legitimation: "the selective raising of taxes, the discernible pattern of priorities in their use, and the administrative performances themselves must be so constituted that the need for legitimation can be satisfied as it arises."[91] This absence of consensus results in a deficit in legitimation. Now the question and challenge state-capitalism had to face was: "Could the state get sufficient backing for expanded administrative functions aimed at preserving class domination, without provoking a legitimation crisis—without, that is, activating the citizenry and causing it to question the use of public power in the service of private interests?"[92] While an inherent tendency of state-capitalism, Fraser goes on to argue, "a legitimation crisis was by no means inevitable. Such a crisis would arise, rather, only if an administrative crisis were accompanied by a *motivation* crisis."[93] We can speak of a motivation crisis, Habermas argues, "when the socio-cultural system changes in such a way that its output becomes dysfunctional for the state and for the system of social labor."[94] Only on the condition that a critical mass of citizens "reject the privatized, consumerist, and careerist orientations that undergirded their loyalty to the regime," and "question the legitimacy of class domination," was a legitimation crisis possible.[95] So long as a critical mass retained the social and moral disposition "to insist that domination be justified or abolished, a motivation-cum-legitimation crisis was possible. If, however, this orientation were to be sapped or disabled, even a full-blown administrative crisis would not translate into legitimation crisis."[96]

Naturally, one could imagine such a cascade of crises leading to a radical rejection of not only state-capitalism, but capitalism as such. And it is true that, "for a time in the late 1960s and early 1970s, the conditions for a full-scale legitimation crisis seemed to be in place," especially in the West and in the young generation, through the rejection of consumerism and post-colonial wars.[97] Instead, what happened was a rebooting or reinvention of capitalism through the neoliberal paradigm, which has now also run its course and exhibits a range of morbid symptoms. In other words, the cycle of crises extends. It is made worse—*much* worse—by the ecological crisis, in which it finds its most acute expressions, and to which I will eventually turn.

Let me circle back to Gramsci's opposition between "nonorganic ideologies" and "organic" ideology, or the "philosophy of praxis." Unlike the former, the fully "organic" ideology confronts contradictions head on—that is, by recognizing them as the forces of "historical becoming." The philosophy of praxis does not seek to resolve the contradictions inherent to the ideology, and the structure it reflects, by tweaking or bending the hegemonic paradigm in place, as if they weren't contradictions in the strong sense. Rather, it *exposes* those contradictions—especially the contradiction between ideologies and actual reality—and seeks to overcome them by replacing the paradigm that produced them in the first place. Similarly, it exposes the many ways in which superstructures "aim to hide reality—that is, struggle and contradiction—even when they are 'formally' dialectical," as in Croce.[98] The philosophy of praxis seeks to sever the link between knowledge and domination (*dominio*) in order to establish a different kind of connection, between critical thinking—including its own illusions, deceits, and prejudices—and government, in what amounts to an "organic" and fluid assemblage. Critique, then—of one's common sense, historical situation, and sphere of activity—is what distinguishes philosophy from religion and other forms of philosophy, "the philosophy of the intellectuals, out of which the history of philosophy arises."[99]

Gramsci insists that the "universal" or "consensus" achieved in hegemony is an "unstable equilibrium," open to challenge. In "normal times"—that is, when the conduct of a subaltern group is not independent and autonomous, but precisely submissive and subordinate, the group does not think or act "as an organic whole." Instead, it models itself after the interests and ideology of another, hegemonic group.[100] An "organic crisis" occurs when a subaltern group strives to attain hegemony by challenging the dominant class, while taking into consideration the interests and aspirations of other subaltern classes. This, according to Gramsci, was the case of the French Revolution: contrary to popular belief and "vulgar traditional history," the revolution was not the result of a crisis of impoverishment. In fact, the economic situation in France in 1789 was rather healthy, and the bourgeoisie was thriving.[101] The collapse of the existing equilibrium was the result of a larger conflict over group "prestige." But as we know from Hegel's *Phenomenology of Spirit*, the struggles for prestige are amongst the most violent. Hegemonies are therefore subject to crises of "authority" or "legitimacy." What characterizes such crises—we can also refer to them as crises of representation—is a detachment, on the part of social groups, from the traditional forms that are meant to represent them. Speaking of political parties, Gramsci writes:

> At a certain point in the course of history, classes become detached from their traditional parties. In other words, the traditional parties in their particular organizational form, with the particular men who constitute and lead them, no longer represent their class or their class fraction. *This is an extremely delicate and dangerous crisis* because it opens the field to men who are charismatic or claim to be sent by providence.[102]

The crisis, which consists in a contradiction or conflict "between the represented and the representatives," becomes particularly dangerous when it spreads to all the political parties and among all the different classes, "when the rank and file of one or more parties does not quickly go over to another party that better epitomizes the general interest."[103] In the absence of this quick shift from one party to another, or even from all parties to a single one, in what amounts to "the fusion of a class under a single leadership in order to resolve an overwhelming problem affecting its existence"—in the absence, therefore, of an "organic" and "normal," albeit sudden and extremely rapid transition from one party to another—"no class, neither the conservative nor the progressive class, has the strength to win."[104] In other words, the crisis of representation leaves a political vacuum, which, in the absence of a quick realignment of political parties, runs the risk of being filled by "the man sent by providence," or the "master," rather than by a communist-led revolution. This is how political parties "lose their historical social base and find the ground taken from under their feet. This is what happened in Germany, especially with the rise of Hitlerism."[105] It is also what happened in Italy, with the rise of Mussolini. And it is what is happening today: with the collapse of the neoliberal consensus, which had governed much of the world between the late 1970s and the financial and economic crisis of the late 2000s, providential and authoritarian figures—at times secular, at times religious—have sprung up in every corner of the earth. The current crisis of legitimacy and representation, which takes the form of "anti-establishment" rhetoric and rejection of the "corrupt" political class, has led to the return of the figure of the savior, the "strong man," and the permanent state of exception. On the Marxist and specifically Gramscian reading, which I believe is correct, the current tendency toward a prolonged state of emergency is not the manifestation of the essence of the political but the symptom of an economic and political crisis of contradiction. In addition, we see an increasing distrust in party politics, a volatility in party loyalty, and, as a response to these phenomena, the constant creation of parties devoid of substance and with meaningless names, whose sole purpose is to capitalize on the Zeitgeist. This phenomenon is another symptom of the same crisis.

These "dangerous crises" open the field to "violent solutions" and to "the activities of dark forces," from which democracy recovers only with great difficulty.[106] In Notebook 13, written between 1932 and 1934, Gramsci extends his explanation regarding the "crisis of the hegemony of the ruling class," or the "crisis of the state as a whole," by claiming that they occur

> either because the ruling class has failed in one of its major political initiatives (such as war) for which it has requested or obtained through coercion the consent of the great masses, or because the huge masses . . . have shifted suddenly from political passivity to some kind of activism, putting forward demands that taken as a whole, even though disjointed, constitute a *revolution*.[107]

The picture that emerges, then, is that of crises of hegemony that can yield different outcomes. To be sure, they can lead—organically as it were, and through the formulation of demands—to the emergence of a new ruling class. The class in question can be the working class united with the intellectual class, as classical Marxism had anticipated. In a post-Marxist sense, however, and at a time when social and political struggles of many different kinds have exploded, no class can be singled out as the universal subject of History, and therefore of Revolution. Subaltern, marginal groups are manifold, and each—whether in relation to gender, race, post-coloniality, or class—needs to develop its own revolutionary, hegemonic strategy. But in the absence of such an "organic" or "normal" response, crises of hegemony can lead to deeply antidemocratic "solutions," and to the emergence of "providential figures" or "masters" who replace the socially and politically mediated space with a fusional one. All too often, though, the traditional ruling class, "with its large body of trained personnel," responds to crises of hegemony by clinging to power in whatever way it can—that is, by "changing men and programs," making "demagogic promises" that "expose it to an uncertain future," and by dispersing the leadership ranks of its adversaries. Those political tactics, tried and tested, are nonetheless doomed, and produce further crises.[108]

Organic crises, then, can lead to the emergence of new hegemonies or new forms of leadership, based on consent (*consenso*). But they can also generate "morbid" symptoms, which accentuate and radicalize the contradictions constitutive of the crisis, rather than solving them: "The crisis consists precisely in the fact that the old is dying and the new cannot be born; in this interregnum, morbid phenomena of the most varied kind come to pass [*si verificano i fenomeni morbosi piú svariati*]."[109] As one commentator puts it, those symptoms are morbid because

> they show that the existing order suffers from existential problems that are unlikely to be solved within the existing framework. At the same time a new, hegemonically stable order does not seem to be on the rise, ready to supplant the old one. This crisis period is thus shaped by morbidities that cannot be managed but at the same time do not represent a viable alternative.[110]

One such morbid symptom is what Gramsci calls "bureaucratic centralism," which he opposes to "organic centralism." Gramsci equates the latter with "democratic centralism," insofar as it is "in motion," or continuously adapting to historical movements, while taking into account something that is relatively stable and permanent—namely, the organic development of the leading class within the state. Democratic centralism thus defined always runs the risk of being overturned or perverted by "bureaucratic centralism," which "is indicative of the formation of a small privileged group that seeks to perpetuate its privileges by controlling and even stifling the emergence of oppositional forces at the base, even if those forces have the same interests as the dominant group."[111] No institution is immune from such a tendency, which progressively transforms relations of consent into relations of domination, or hegemonies into bureaucracies. The risk comes from the weight of "habitude"—that is, from a "tendency to become mummified and anachronistic," to "execute" rather than "deliberate" and "know how to adapt to new tasks and new epochs."[112] The great danger of bureaucratic centralism, whether it affects institutions of the state such as the electoral-parliamentary field, political parties, trade unions, or the media, is one that threatens every hegemony and every democratic movement. In many liberal democracies (and the European Union), it takes the form of a technocracy increasingly disconnected from the reality of those it governs, and increasingly rejected by citizens. But this bureaucratic sclerosis was particularly pronounced in the Communist Party of the Soviet Union in the Third Period of the Communist International (Comintern), which terminated the New Economic Policy (NEP), began the rural collectivization in the Soviet Union in November 1929, and consolidated the Stalinist control of the country and the Comintern. Gramsci is often thought to have had the rise of fascism in mind in 1930 when he wrote his now famous sentence regarding the "morbid symptoms" of the interregnum. And there is no doubt that he saw the rise of fascism in Italy as the result of a crisis of authority and legitimacy afflicting capitalist societies after the Wall Street crash of October 1929 and the Great Depression that followed. But he also (and perhaps mostly) had in mind the ultraleft, "bureaucratic" turn that began in 1928 and forced the Italian Communist Party to undergo a similar turn in 1930.[113] What he clearly saw, then, was the danger of sclerosis of a "scientific" Marxism that identified the subject of history and truth with a single class, the proletariat, which could gain class- or self-consciousness only through the Party. Gramsci's opposition to such a turn, and to the rejection of the democratic perspective in the fight against Mussolini's rule, is well documented.[114] The situation that Gramsci feared and predicted is precisely the one that came to dominate the socialist states of the twentieth century. As we saw earlier in the case of Poland and Solidarity, it is also one that was met with a subaltern, working-class strategy that led to the generation of a new hegemony.

Today, the morbid symptoms emanating from the interregnum period, in which the old order is "already" dying and the new one can "not yet" be born, take again the form of nationalism, xenophobia, and, more broadly, the politics of stigmatization and exclusion. The financial crash of 2008 and the severe economic crisis that ensued translated into a huge loss of legitimacy (hegemony, consent) of the liberal order, and a loss of prestige of its intellectual and bureaucratic class. That disenchantment led not to a new hegemony of the anti-capitalist Left, but to a range of right-wing populisms and nationalisms, some of which emerged from the fringes of the political establishment, others from its own ranks, in what amounts to a desperate and deeply opportunistic move, making once again "demagogic promises" and exposing us to "an uncertain future." What Marx said of Bonapartism, and Gramsci saw as a clue in his own analysis of fascism, seems to repeat itself today, across the world:

> The Empire, with the *coup d'état* for its certificate of birth, universal suffrage for its sanction, and the sword for its sceptre, professed to rest upon the peasantry, the large mass of producers not directly involved in the struggle of capital and labour. It professed to save the working class by breaking down Parliamentarism, and, with it, the undisguised subserviency of Government to the propertied classes. It professed to save the propertied classes by upholding their economic supremacy over the working class; and, finally, it professed to unite all classes by reviving for all the chimera of national glory. In reality, it was the only form of government possible at *a time when bourgeoisie had already lost, and the working class had not yet acquired, the faculty of ruling the nation.*[115]

Contradictions can fester and rot. They can lead to cycles of violence and hatred, which reinforce one another. They can metamorphosize and metastasize. Oftentimes, the work of the negative is simply ... negative, and contradictions, far from signaling their own *Aufhebung*, descend further into nihilism.

Not all crises are "organic" crises of legitimacy, or representation. All, however, are crises of contradiction. Gramsci considers the example of the "crisis" and "catastrophic" events of 1929.[116] From the point of view of critique, it is crucial, he argues, to resist the urge to give a unique definition of the events that led to such a catastrophe, or attribute them to a single cause or origin. Similarly, it would be wrong to ask about when the crisis started, given the fact that we're dealing with a process, rather than a single event: crises develop a life of their own. The financial crash did indeed happen in the autumn of 1929. But the crisis that triggered it encompasses the whole of the postwar era. Some, with good reason, even saw the war itself as a crisis, and indeed as its most acute manifestation. But the crisis cannot be understood as such without a clear sense of the modes of production, rather than the political or judicial facts, underpinning Western societies. And this is where, once again, the vocabulary of contradiction reappears: if capitalism has unfolded as a series of crises, it is because of its internal contradictions, such as the contradiction between *la vita economica*, for which internationalism, or cosmopolitanism, is a necessary condition, and *la vita statale*, which moves ever more toward nationalism. This is a contradiction of which we are constantly reminded; it defines national politics and international relations today. So long as countries remain under certain "structural conditions," by which Gramsci means conditions of production *and* national identification, they will go through such crises.

A question of political strategy (or strategies) follows. Since crises of hegemony involve the struggle between subaltern and dominant groups, the question (for the subaltern) becomes that of knowing how they can constitute a new popular hegemonic bloc, build their own common sense, and establish their own ideology or mythology. By contrast, for the dominant class, the question is that of perpetuating the consent it managed to obtain in the first place, to do what it takes to remain in power, whether in "normal" times or in times of crisis; and as we saw, it responds to organic crises by clinging to power in whatever way possible, for example by replacing ministers or heads of major institutions, making empty promises, distracting the masses, or sowing division in the ranks of its adversaries. This is how the dominant/subaltern dichotomy is translated into two different political strategies. However, there is, and I believe always has been, a debate around the nature of the aspiration of the subaltern, the terms and norms of their claim to power, and the manner of their struggle against the dominant class.

On the one hand, and assuming that crises are intrinsically organic crises of hegemony, all political strategies are strategies of hegemony, and there is an isomorphism between the strategies of the dominant and subaltern classes. The meaning of the concept of strategy is the same in the hegemonic or majority strategy and the subaltern or minority strategy. They are the specific differences of an identical generic category. To be sure, their respective tactics will differ. But their strategy is identical, insofar as they are both informed by the schema of hegemony. This Gramscian line of thought is clearly visible in Laclau and Mouffe's early work: the (then nascent) neoliberal hegemony was to be challenged and hopefully replaced by a truly socialist hegemony and a radical democratic politics.[117] Any form of consensus is the result of a hegemonic articulation, and hegemony is what groups struggle to achieve. "Our motto," they say, is "'back to the hegemonic struggle.'"[118] But hegemonic formations, they argue, are intrinsically fragile, for they are rooted in historical contingencies irreducible to fixed class determinations. They unfold in a space of "undecidability" in the Derridean sense, in which no single *class* can ever be identified as "universal." By the same token, and contrary to what orthodox Marxism asserted, the hegemony of one class—the proletariat—can never translate into a total disappearance of antagonisms or dissensus, and politics cannot be reduced to the struggle between class interests or their representation (in the Party and ultimately the State). According to Laclau and Mouffe, the *possibility* of this "authoritarian turn" was present "from the very beginning of Marxist orthodoxy; that is to say, from the moment in which a limited actor—the working class—was raised to the status of a 'universal class.'"[119] And this elevation, they argue, was as much epistemological as it was ontological: "The centrality attributed to the working class is not a practical but an *ontological* centrality, which is, at the same time, the seat of an *epistemological* privilege: as the 'universal class' the proletariat—or rather its party—is the depository of science."[120] This classism translates into a permanent and deeply antidemocratic schism between class identity and the identity of the masses, between political (or party) leadership, which represents the scientific truth of the "universal class," and the democratic demands emanating from the multitude, which do not have a necessary class or "bourgeois" character. All of this is to say that the key distinction for the advocates of politics as struggles of hegemony is that between a democratic and an authoritarian practice of hegemony. Through the practice of democratic hegemony, Laclau and Mouffe argue in their reading of Gramsci, "a class does not *take State power*, it *becomes* State."[121]

On the other hand, some argue for a strategy of minority politics that is *sui generis* irreducible to the strategy of hegemony, for the simple reason that "minority" designates the irreducible excess of heterogenous forces that cannot be identified with, or assimilated within, a common sense, consensus, or majority. In this instance, the distinction between a majority and a minority strategy is broached by the minority viewpoint itself, which reveals and analyzes the problems affecting majority strategies, whereas from the point of view of the majority there can be no minority *politics*, for the simple reason that there can be no minority *strategy*. At best, there can be minority *tactics*, such as acts of resistance or counter-conducts.

Naturally, it is not a matter here of affirming one strategy over the other, of declaring one more legitimate, adequate, or effective than the other. They are context dependent. But it is a matter of distinguishing between a "hegemonic strategy," such as the one proposed by Gramsci, Laclau, and Mouffe, and the idea of a "minority-becoming" as proposed by Deleuze and Guattari. But that clear-cut opposition is itself perhaps too reductive and simplistic. For I would argue that what I have just referred to as the heterogeneous forces resistant to common sense, and which Deleuze—from his early critique of common sense in *Difference and Repetition* to his political work with Guattari—defines as "singularities," is already at work in Gramsci's use of "philology" as a critical method and an alternative to the molar tools of both philosophical materialism and idealism.[122] In his vocabulary and critical practice, philology—a method traditionally constitutive of the Italian school of philosophy—designates the science of the singular. It is, he writes, "the methodological expression of the importance of particular facts understood as definite and specific 'individualities.'"[123] It requires minute attention to details; it records history in its infinite variety and multiplicity; it seeks to ascertain the specificity of the particular, without subsuming it under a pre-given universal. Yet the particular, I would argue, is not necessarily the particular of the universal, or, in the political context, of the hegemonic norms and common sense. As the singular, it escapes the play of the universal and the particular altogether—a play which, according to Laclau and Mouffe, designates the "hegemonic relation" itself, by which "a certain particularity assumes the representation of a universality entirely incommensurable with it," and with which it remains in a kind of "unresolvable tension," such that the hegemony is "always reversible."[124] There is no question, then, that the Gramscian idea of hegemony, especially as interpreted by Laclau and Mouffe, complicates the nature of the relation between particular and universal, insofar as it sees the latter as the fragile and specifically *political* articulation of the differential positions and roles assumed by social actors who, under specific and contingent conditions (of oppression for example), come together and establish relations of equivalence between themselves. Yet the revolutionary potential of the subaltern *qua* singularity is of a different kind. What Deleuze and Guattari call minority or revolutionary becoming is precisely the power of transformation contained in the folds and margins of the universal (or the hegemonic), which the latter cannot *recognize*, for the simple reason that one can recognize only what one already knows, or what one can apprehend from within a previously and well-established ideological and normative horizon. As singularities, the subaltern represent a revolutionary force that exceeds the basic mechanics (and therefore crises) of contradiction, which are limited to the relation between the particular and the universal. Crises of singularities, I would argue, designate crises of a different kind, or crises that are precisely not of any kind, or genus, not of the kind "kind," but throw kind—genus, the universal, the common, hegemony—into question, in the name of another assemblage, another constitution, another politics. A shift in strategy ensues, from an antagonistic and confrontational model, following a military or warlike model, associated with the form of the state, the state apparatus, and the conquest of state power, to a model defined by lines of flight and creation, assemblages, groups, and organizations that bypass state (or class) codification. It is not even, or no longer, a matter of "becoming State," as Laclau and Mouffe claimed in their reading of Gramsci. The claims of the subaltern *qua* "*devenir-minoritaire*" cannot be translated in the idiom of common sense, or in the key signifiers of the universal (the state, the proletariat, the market, the white male, or technocratic). This is why they cannot be recognized, or can be recognized only at the cost of reducing their heterogeneity. Their heterogeneity, by which I mean their power of differentiation, requires the constitution of a new idiom and a new political grammar, necessarily at odds with, yet traversing or cutting through, those of the state.

Hence the question "Can the subaltern speak?"[125] If so, how—that is, in what idiom, with what words, and from what position? These questions animate the work of many postcolonial thinkers, and especially of those who, like Spivak, have adopted the category of the subaltern to analyze and question the colonial and postcolonial condition. In her long and seminal essay, Spivak is quite critical of Deleuze (as well as Foucault). She sees herself—the postcolonial position from which she speaks, the problem for which she stands—as having more in common with Derrida, who recognizes the constitution of the Other, notably through the elaboration of a science of writing and the logocentrism underpinning it, as a genuinely *European* problem. I will leave aside the question of the pertinence of Spivak's critique of Deleuze and Foucault, which is almost entirely based on an interview they gave on March 4, 1972,[126] and focus instead on her positive (yet not unconditional) appreciation of Derrida's early work.[127] Despite acknowledging a debt of gratitude toward Derrida's *Of Grammatology*, and specifically toward his deconstruction of the Eurocentric schema, through which the Other is both included and excluded, or produced in the margins of its text, she criticizes him for failing to attribute this schema to specific historical circumstances, preferring instead to transcendentalize (or *quasi*-transcendentalize) it. She points to Derrida's inability to recognize in the ethnocentrism of the European science of writing in the late seventeenth and early eighteenth centuries a symptom of a "crisis" greater than "the general crisis of European consciousness," greater even than the "structural" or "originary" violence Derrida describes and deconstructs in detail. The "originary" violence in question traverses and structures the debates of the eighteenth century concerning the possibility of a science and history of writing, which presuppose a series of oppositions—between "living speech" (*la parole vivante*) and "writing" (*l'écriture*), and the threat the latter presents for the former; between the metaphysical, Western drive to presence that animates the former, and the obscure, disruptive, and *originary* force that frustrates it, forever suspending and deferring the moment of its closure; between the logo- and phonocentrism of an *episteme*, the *metaphysical* roots of which reveal a subjectivity animated by a desire to experience, conceive, and feel itself as substance, that is, as a self-present, self-identical and autonomous being, and this "dangerous" yet necessary "supplement" that is writing, which carries within it the "trace" of an Other. It is, Derrida argues, with this transcendental-historical, phono- and ethnocentric schema in place that "European" science approaches, analyzes, classifies, and assesses other, non-European forms of writing, and even other civilizations.[128] It is also through the construction and exclusion of this Other that it reaffirms its own identity—that is, identity itself, in the form of auto-affection. While recognizing the pertinence and value of the structural tension underpinning the epistemic crisis Derrida analyzes in *Of Grammatology*, Spivak points to his blindness regarding a crucial event, without which his critique of the place and role of the Other, whether in the form of writing or of the non-European civilization, remains incomplete: namely, "the slow turn from feudalism to capitalism via the first waves of capitalist imperialism."[129] The Marxist and post-colonial critique, then, concerns the manner in which the question and history of writing, as it broke out in Europe in the late seventeenth and early eighteenth centuries, is attributable not just, or not simply, to European phono- and logocentrism, and to the metaphysics of presence underpinning it, but to an "epistemic violence" toward Europe's "others" rooted in the (equally violent) capitalist and imperialist division of labor.

If, returning to Gramsci, and possibly in agreement with Laclau and Mouffe, one were to retain the idea of the subaltern, it would be precisely to wrest it from the hegemonic paradigm altogether, or to recognize in it an excess or residue that escapes the logic of hegemony. As such, the strategy corresponding to the subaltern position would not be one of counter-hegemony, of competing normativities and common sense, of negotiating the articulation of the universal and the particular. Rather, it would ascribe to the subaltern the position of the singular or the minor—a potentially disruptive, revolutionary position, a revolutionary becoming inscribed within the folds or margins of the hegemony, rather than simply outside it. To try and illustrate what a revolutionary yet minority strategy (rather than tactics) can look like, I now turn to the case and writings of W. E. B. Du Bois. The African American critical theorist is, I believe, a good case study precisely because one can trace a certain evolution in his strategic approach to "the race problem" in America, from a hegemonic to a minor strategy, from a liberal to a cooperative paradigm, the latter being, in the end, more effective than the former.

A Nation Within a Nation: W. E. B. Du Bois on Cooperation as a Subaltern Strategy

The Crisis is the official publication of the National Association for the Advancement of Colored People (NAACP), and one of the oldest African American publications. Founded in 1910 by W. E. B. Du Bois, who served as its editor until 1934, *The Crisis* stood, and in many ways still stands, for a diagnosis regarding the shortcomings—one could say the contradictions—inherent to the social, economic, and ideological American "system." Equally, it promotes the critique of the constitution and reproduction of subaltern groups, and the abolition of racial segregation and prejudice in all its forms. Du Bois qualifies this system as an "anomaly."[130] For reasons that should by now be obvious, I prefer to designate it as an antinomy, insofar as the crisis generated by the system can be solved only by radically transforming the norms of the system, by constructing a new set of norms. This is a point Du Bois himself makes when he claims that "human slavery in the South pointed and led in two singularly contradictory and paradoxical directions—toward the deliberate commercial breeding and sale of human labor for profit and toward the intermingling of white and black blood."[131] This contradiction led to a civil war, followed by a brief period of "reconstruction," soon betrayed by the return of a brutal system of racial segregation, prejudice, and economic exclusion ("Jim Crow"), the long-term effects of which are still felt today.[132] Now the key question, for Du Bois, was precisely that of the new norms at issue: the form they needed to take, and the nature of their relation to the white, capitalist order.

Immediately after Woodrow Wilson's inauguration in 1913, Du Bois sent the newly elected president of the United States an open letter. The letter singles out "the Negro problem" as "the greatest problem facing the nation," and one that, *The Crisis* believes, Wilson is in a unique position to begin to solve since, "while a Southerner in birth and tradition, you have escaped the provincial training of the South and you have not had burned into your soul desperate hatred and despising of your darker fellow men."[133] In a subsequent letter from the same year, Du Bois expresses his deep disappointment and frustration: in the six months following the president's inauguration, "not a single act and not a single word of yours since election has given anyone reason to infer that you have the slightest interest in the colored people or desire to alleviate their intolerable position."[134] On the contrary: as historians have shown, Wilson purged his administration of all Black officials, thus confirming *The Crisis*'s fear that he was indeed behind this new wave of segregation: "Public segregation of civil servants in government employ, necessarily involving personal insult and humiliation, has for the first time in history been made the policy of the United States government."[135] This policy, Du Bois concludes, constitutes "the gravest attack on the liberties of our people since emancipation."[136] The letter ends with a renewed appeal to Wilson's "sense of fairness and broad cosmopolitan outlook on the world."[137]

Those words were consistent with the rhetoric used to present the first issue of *The Crisis* and justify its title: "The object of this publication is to set forth those facts and arguments which show the danger of race prejudice, particularly as manifested to-day toward colored people. It takes its name from the fact that the editors believe that this is a critical time in the history of the advancement of men."[138] Crisis, in this context, is understood as a historical turning point in racial relations in America, the fate of "Negro-Americans," and, more broadly, "the rights of men, irrespective of color or race." Either "tolerance, reason, and forbearance can to-day make the world-old dream of human brotherhood approach realization"; or "bigotry and prejudice, emphasized race consciousness and force can repeat the awful history of the contact of nations and groups in the past." Twenty-five years later, Du Bois formulates this alternative, and the language of the Enlightenment in which it was couched, in yet more radical terms:

> This the American black man knows: his fight here is a fight to the finish. Either he dies or wins. . . . He will enter modern civilization here in America as a black man on terms of perfect and unlimited equality with any white man, or he will enter not at all. Either extermination root and branch, or absolute equality. There can be no compromise.[139]

In the face of the greatest crisis of his time, or "the last great battle of the West,"[140] Du Bois adopts the classical trope of resolve—that is, the determination to stand firm on his principles and to act accordingly, without compromise, and whatever the cost. In a text from January 1912 entitled "I Am Resolved," Du Bois lists seven resolutions, all of which begin with "I am resolved...." Let me cite just one:

> I am resolved *to be ready at all times and in all places to bear witness with pen, voice, money and deed against the horrible crime of lynching, the shame of 'Jim Crow' legislation, the injustice of all color discrimination, the wrong of disfranchisement, for race or sex, the iniquity of war under any circumstances and the deep damnation of present methods of distributing the world's work and wealth.*[141]

But Du Bois's resolve exceeds the limits of "bearing witness." Or, if we take seriously the etymology of the Greek martyr, "bearing witness" is an attitude and commitment that implicates the whole of one's life. Du Bois concludes his list of New Year's resolutions with the following words:

> *For all these things*, I am resolved *unflinchingly to stand, and if this resolve cost me pain, poverty, slander and even life itself, I will remember the Word of the Prophet, how he sang*:

> "Though Love repine and Reason chafe,
> There came a Voice, without reply,
> 'Tis man's Perdition to be safe
> When for the Truth he ought to die."[142]

The crisis at hand is indeed a matter of life and death, of truth and falsehood, of good and evil. It manifests itself clearly, in the form of a Kierkegaardian *either . . . or* that excludes all compromise. The resolve in question implies a perfect alignment of word and deed, of voice and gesture. It is ethical in the strongest sense of the term. But it is also political, insofar as it seeks to transform social relations and overturn deeply rooted forms of injustice. As such, it connects with the following verses from *The Present Crisis*, a poem written at the height of the American Civil War by the ardent abolitionist James Russell Lowell that inspired the title of *The Crisis*:

> Once to every man and nation comes the moment to decide,
> In the strife of Truth with Falsehood, for the good or evil side;

> Some great cause, God's new Messiah, offering each the bloom or blight,
> Parts the goats upon the left hand, and the sheep upon the right,
> And the choice goes by forever 'twixt that darkness and that light.
> Hast thou chosen, O my people, on whose party thou shalt stand,
> Ere the Doom from its worn sandals shakes the dust against our land?
> Though the cause of Evil prosper, yet 'tis Truth alone is strong,
> And, albeit she wander outcast now, I see around her throng
> Troops of beautiful, tall angels, to enshield her from all wrong.
> Backward look across the ages and the beacon-moments see,
> That, like peaks of some sunk continent, jut through Oblivion's sea;
> Not an ear in court or market for the low, foreboding cry
> Of those Crises, God's stern winnowers, from whose feet earth's chaff must fly;
> Never shows the choice momentous till the judgment hath passed by.

As Du Bois himself acknowledges, his life—the life he was willing to sacrifice—was of interest and significance only "because it was part of a Problem," namely the "race problem."[143] His life, like those of millions of African Americans, was indistinguishable from that problem. Such is the reason why *Dusk of Dawn* is more "an autobiography of a race concept" than of Du Bois "the man." And if the problem in question can be qualified as a crisis—not all problems are crises—it is because its solution requires the suspension of one social, economic, and ideological order, as well as the invention of another. It calls for the creation of new ethical norms, the profound transformation of race, class, and gender relations. To be identified as such, the problem requires a critical attitude, one that questions the status quo, rooted in racial discrimination, pseudo- or imperial science, and economic inequality. But given the system of oppression for which the problem stands, given the suffering, the humiliation, the killings, the punishments endured by Black Americans, the problem also calls for a radical form of praxis, embodied in the idea of peaceful revolution. To be sure, and as we'll see, Du Bois began by seeking and believing in a solution "to the race problem" within the liberal order and by following its norms. He began by seeking acceptance and recognition on the part of the white man through patient education. Progressively, however, he arrived at the conclusion that the race problem was the expression not of a marginal flaw, but of an entire system: a social, economic, and ideological order. As such, the issue of race required a radical overhaul of the order in question.

"Revolution" is the title of the ninth and final chapter of *Dusk of Dawn*. Looking back at the first twenty years of his life as an activist, Du Bois notes how, initially, his "basic theory had been that race prejudice was primarily a matter of ignorance on the part of the mass of men, giving the evil and antisocial a chance to work their way; that when the truth was properly presented, the monstrous wrong of race hate must melt and melt quickly before it."[144] Initially, then, Du Bois believed that racial prejudice was an epistemic problem and vice. And some facts seemed to prove him right: much of the thought and attitude that saw the "Negro" race as degenerate and essentially barbarian had passed away. Statistical proof had invalidated the practice of lynching as a response to the rape of white women. Full citizenship rights had been recognized by the Supreme Court. Yet "the barriers of race prejudice were certainly as strong in 1930 as in 1910 the world over, and in certain aspects, from certain points of view, even stronger."[145] This demoralizing realization meant that forces "stronger and more threatening" than "ignorance and deliberate ill-will" were responsible for race prejudice, forces that Gramsci would designate as ideological in the broad, organic sense. A more systemic racism, a more deeply rooted form of hate, was at stake. As a result, a different kind of struggle and a different attack on the causes of racism were called for. And in that respect the Russian Revolution, in its attempt to tackle "the problem of the poverty of the mass of men when an abundance of goods and technical efficiency of work seemed able to provide a sufficiency for all men, so that the mass of men could be fed and clothed and sheltered, live in health and have their intellectual faculties trained," proved to be an inspiration.[146] Du Bois was "painfully sensitive to all its failures, to all the difficulties which it faced."[147] Furthermore, he "could never regard violence as an effective, much less necessary, step to reform the American state."[148] Nonetheless, the Russian Revolution, together with the reading of Marx and Lenin, whom he discovered on his trip to Russia in 1928, revealed to Du Bois the theoretical and tactical limits of the liberal politics of emancipation favored by the NAACP between 1910 and 1930. So long as the struggle for political rights was seen "as an end in itself rather than as a method of reorganizing the state"; so long as the economic struggle consisted in "a continued agitation" aimed at providing "free entrance into the present economy of the world," rather than profound changes "in the organization of industry," democracy would remain an empty promise, and the "Negro race" would not be free.[149] In other words, the struggle against racism goes hand in hand with the struggle against economic inequality. At the same time, and for reasons we have yet to explore, Du Bois believed that a revolution of the Bolshevik kind would never be sufficient to eradicate racism: the conquest of state power by the proletariat as the universal class would in itself never guarantee the end of racial prejudice.

Let me briefly diverge from my reading of Du Bois and broaden the discussion to South Africa during apartheid. Nelson Mandela faced a situation very similar to that of Du Bois and expressed an identical resolve in the face of the institutional injustice that is state racism. The law of his conscience took precedence over the law of the land and led to a confrontation with the state. Only the total overhaul of the country's constitution and the creation of a social contract, he felt, could eradicate that order. What should replace it? On the one hand (and unlike Marxists), Mandela expressed his deep admiration for the liberal parliamentary system that produced the doctrine of the separation of powers, the Petition of Rights, and the Bill of Rights.[150] At the same time, he felt "attracted by the idea of a classless society."[151] That attraction stemmed in part from his reading of Marx and Marxist authors.[152] But it also stemmed from his "admiration" of and even "fascination" with "the structure and organization of early African societies in this country."[153] In those societies,

> the land, then the means of production, belonged to the whole tribe, and there was no individual ownership whatsoever. There were no classes, no rich or poor and no exploitation of man by man. All men were free and equal and this was the foundation of government. Recognition of this general principle found expression in the constitution of the council, variously called Imbizo, or Pitso, or Kgotla. . . .[154]

The question of economic equality as a way of truly overcoming the legacy of institutional racism remained a central topic and a source of intense debate in the post-apartheid era, in the same way that it did in America, and for Du Bois in particular. In his 1998 "Two Nations" speech, Thabo Mbeki emphasized the deep and structural divisions between Black and white, which, he argued, required greater economic redistribution. One nation, "white, relatively prosperous," lives alongside the other, "black and poor." The situation, he adds, is "underwritten by the perpetuation of the racial, gender, and spatial disparities born of a very long period of colonial and apartheid white domination."[155] In that same speech, and four years into the process of reconciliation, Thabo Mbeki presents the fundamental question, the one that will allow for a true reconciliation and the overcoming of the Blacks' *ressentiment*, in straightforward terms: "Are the relatively rich who, as a result of an apartheid definition, are white, prepared to underwrite the upliftment of the poor who, as a result of an apartheid definition, are black?" It is only at that cost—that is, at the cost of an economic sacrifice and a loss of economic power—that the suffering inflicted on Black South Africans can be alleviated.

By 1930, Du Bois had become convinced that "the basic policies and ideals of the Association must be modified and changed; that in a world where economic dislocation had become so great as in ours, a mere appeal based on the old liberalism, a mere appeal to justice and further effort at legal decision, was missing the essential need."[156] The essential need is economic: it is "to guard and better the chances of Negroes, educated and ignorant, to earn a living, safeguard their income, and raise the level of their employment."[157] In other words, education, litigation, and the appeal to the benevolence of the whites were insufficient, and in fact vain, so long as the economic dimension was not fully integrated in the struggle. So long as the wealth and power of the white majority continue to benefit, or indeed be derived, from racial inequality, racial prejudice will remain firmly in place. The "change of emphasis," which Du Bois began to advocate following the Great Depression, and which consisted in replacing a liberal with a more revolutionary paradigm, signals an evolution of the articulation of crisis and critique. No longer, Du Bois argues, can the struggle for emancipation take place within liberal normativity. A new set of norms, both theoretical and practical, needs to be introduced. They are economic first and foremost, and I will return to this point in a moment. But they are also libidinal.[158] Du Bois saw his own study of psychology under William James as preparing him for the deepest insights of Freudian metapsychology: "I now began to realize that in the fight against racial prejudice, we were not facing simply the rational, conscious determination of white folk to oppress us; we were facing age-long complexes sunk now largely to unconscious habit and irrational urge."[159] In that respect, Du Bois follows in the footsteps of Wilhelm Reich and anticipates the work of Herbert Marcuse by establishing a strong connection between ideology and the unconscious of the masses.[160]

Du Bois did not embrace the ideas of socialist collectivism, the dictatorship of the proletariat, or the end of pluralism: "I was not and am not a communist."[161] He rejected "extreme communism and violence" as much as "extreme reaction toward plutocracy."[162] On the one hand, he saw "disaster for American Negroes" in following the path of one nation, Russia, and adhering to one dogma, Marxism-Leninism, which tends to ignore "race hate" as a fundamental constitutive problem. But in his view it was equally "nonsensical" to assume that the program he had espoused in 1910 was going to work in 1950.[163] The original liberal attitude failed to yield the expected results. Yet economic determinism and violent insurrection were equally ill-suited for America. Where did that leave him? On the one hand, Du Bois subscribed to the Marxist view according to which "economic foundations" are "the determining factors in the development of civilization, in literature, religion, and the basic pattern of culture."[164] But he did not believe that class consciousness (or interest) alone, or even the transformation of economic conditions, would be sufficient to lead to the disappearance of racial prejudice. Certain forms of prejudice, born of economic structures established many centuries ago, can override all social interest and even outlive those structures. This is how he puts it in *Black Reconstruction in America*, published the same year as "A Negro Nation Within the Nation:"

> The theory of laboring class unity rests upon the assumption that laborers, despite internal jealousies, will unite because of their opposition to exploitation by the capitalists. According to this, even after a part of the poor laboring class became identified with the planters, and eventually displaced them, their interests would be diametrically opposed to those of the mass of white labor, and of course to those of the black laborers. This would throw white and black labor into one class, and precipitate a united fight for higher wage and better working conditions.

> Most persons do not realize how far this failed to work in the South, and it failed to work because the theory of race was supplemented by a carefully planned and slowly evolved method, which drove such a wedge between the white and black workers that there probably are not today in the world two groups of workers with practically identical interests who hate and fear each other so deeply and persistently and who are kept so far apart that neither sees anything of common interest. . . .
>
> Thus every problem of labor advance in the South was skillfully turned by demagogues into a matter of inter-racial jealousy.[165]

The tactics and history of racialization, and the racial divide thereby introduced, have been so successful that the recognition of common interests between white and Black workers is either impossible or insufficiently powerful to neutralize racial prejudice. Writing in 1935, Du Bois notes how, in the South, Black Americans are "restricted more and more to common labor and domestic service of the lowest paid and worst kind," excluded from "textile, chemical and other manufactures."[166] In the North, the situation isn't much better. Following the First World War, "two million black workers rushed North to work in iron and steel, make automobiles and pack meat, build houses and do the heavy toils in factories," but only to meet first "closed trade unions which excluded them from the best-paid jobs," and then the Great Depression, which hit them harder than the white population.[167] Racism within the white working class is, he claims, an almost insurmountable obstacle, and certainly "the greatest problem facing the African-American community."[168] In Du Bois's eyes, racial integration in the 1930s seemed a more distant prospect than ever. It is possible, as he says, that racism is ultimately a matter of an unconscious force or *Trieb*, rooted in ancestral complexes and now settled as habit. The "urge" in question might be the product of a specific history, that of slavery and economic exploitation. Or it might be the product of a more primordial, constitutive complex. In a sense, the explanation is irrelevant, as it cannot bring about a concrete solution.

How can the race problem be overcome in the absence of either a liberal or a Bolshevik (revolutionary) solution? What strategy can be adopted when the politics of pedagogy, recognition, and assimilation turned out to be as unsuccessful as the politics of violent overthrow? Du Bois proposes a third way, which gives equal weight to the problems of racial prejudice and economic inequality. It is most succinctly formulated in a speech he gave in New York on June 26, 1934. The historical circumstances matter. There is, of course, the matter of Du Bois's resignation from the NAACP and *The Crisis*, caused by a disagreement regarding the nature of the crisis and the strategy required to overcome it.[169] But the deeper underlying circumstances concern the way the Great Depression threatened the economic survival of African Americans. In other words, the issue at the time was a double crisis, and the way to address it: the systemic crisis of racial prejudice and discrimination was aggravated by an economic crisis of phenomenal proportions. Du Bois's conclusion (and proposed strategy) was that African Americans must recognize *and* organize themselves as "a nation within a nation," according to a cooperative model. The need, then, and to paraphrase Bernard Harcourt, was no longer to fight segregation, as many activists and thinkers still advocated, nor to wait for humanitarian benevolence from white people in the hope that African Americans would eventually be integrated into white industry; it was to create a separate Black cooperative nation within the nation.[170] Du Bois' long-term aim was to turn the United States into a unified country, which required that class and racial barriers be overcome. But that started with the construction of a model of integration internal to the Black American community. With the constitution of a Black cooperative nation, Du Bois believed, Black Americans would no longer be "refused fellowship and equality in the United States."[171] As Harcourt puts it, Black separatism was intended to demonstrate the economic and technical abilities of African Americans, "ensure their economic advancement, and put them on equal footing with whites within the current industrialized society."[172]

Du Bois proposed to use the cooperative form—an existing legal form, in the United States and abroad—to encourage economic exchanges among African Americans.[173] As Harcourt notes in his recent book on cooperation, debates around the cooperative form as an alternative model of production were very much in the air at the time.[174] Du Bois was drawn to such alternatives. For him, "cooperation" represented both a means and an end: a means to achieve economic advancement, to be sure, but also an end in itself, as well as a way of being (a question to which I'll return in my discussion of the ecological crisis). It responded to a double crisis, economic and ideological, by rethinking the nature of labor relations and the conditions of production, and by transforming Black consciousness. In this regard, Du Bois was closer to nineteenth-century utopian socialists—who imagined, and in some cases built, utopian workshops, factories, and company towns intended to provide for the welfare of workers—than he was to Marx and Engels. For Marx and Engels, worker cooperatives—even self-governing worker cooperatives—were at best a first step toward a communist horizon; they had to be overcome because they retained elements of self-interest and proprietorship. For Du Bois, they were both a means and an end: the final horizon of "abolition democracy" was tied to cooperative association. In that respect, his economic and social model resonated with the models promoted by a range of social visionaries, such as Robert Owen, Charles Fourier, Pierre-Joseph Proudhon, or Louis Blanc.[175]

The cooperative legal form has existed for centuries and surrounds us today.[176] It includes "worker cooperatives for producing and manufacturing; credit unions for banking; housing cooperatives for living; mutuals for insuring; producer, retailer, and consumer cooperatives for commercial exchange; and nonprofit organizations for good works and learning."[177] These forms of cooperation provide a new framework that allows the wealth generated from production and consumption to be shared equally, and profit to be reinvested. But they may also be the best way to address head-on the global climate crisis, which I address in Chapter 5. Because the goal of cooperation, in Harcourt's words, "is not to maximize the extraction of capital, but to support and maintain the stakeholders and distribute well-being, which depends on an ecologically healthy environment," it is less prone to economic and ecological crisis through over-consumption, largely facilitated by our easy access to credit.[178] In many respects, cooperatives outperform and outlast conventional publicly traded firms. They also often show themselves to be more resilient during economic downturns.[179] In 2018, in the Spanish region of Catalonia, the relatively modest bank Caixa d'Enginyers maintained a capital ratio of 14.24 percent (much higher than the financial sector average in Spain), increased its membership by 16.83 percent over 2017, and boasted the highest

Net Promoter Score (NPS) in Spain. In the US, for example, the median age of a mutual insurance company is about 120 years.

Existing cooperationist enterprises can be small. But they can "also be as large as multinationals" and "dominate the competition and be technological leaders in their field."[180] Let me refer to just two examples, which Harcourt mentions in his book. Founded in 1956, the Mondragón Cooperative Group headquartered in the Basque province of Gipuzkoa—a diversified enterprise manufacturing heavy and household equipment—employs over 74,000 workers in about sixty-five countries and brings in annual revenues in the billions of euros. It is the seventh largest and one of the most successful corporate groups in Spain. It also includes a credit union (Caja Laboral Popular Cooperativa de Crédito) and a university (Mondragon Unibertsitatea).[181] To single out another example, borrowed from the insurance industry: "half of the ten largest property and casualty insurance companies in the United States today are mutuals, and together those five mutual insurance companies serve 25 percent of the entire market (by contrast, the other five largest non-mutual insurance companies serve only 21 percent of the market)."[182] In Europe, the mutual/cooperative share in the insurance market has grown steadily since 2010 and was at 33.4 percent in 2022. It exceeds 50 percent in Sweden, Denmark, Slovakia, Austria, France, and the Netherlands, where it reaches 60.2 percent. The sector also proved remarkably resilient during the pandemic.[183]

To be sure, not all cooperatives are model organizations. Several suffer what are called de-cooperative phases. Some become mixed or hybrid as they grow, and resemble large shareholder companies, with power in effect concentrated in the hands of a few and rather opaque procedures (especially in matters of redistribution). But the cooperative model has been tried and tested. It provides an alternative to a mode of production based on accumulation and competition, and to the contradictions (and crises) generated by such a system. It is also more democratic and decentralized. Beyond the economic sphere, then, it can be seen as a model for the organization of society as a whole. In fact, one could argue that this model is real or basic communism, at least when defined by the principle "from each according to their abilities, to each according to their needs." What Graeber describes as "the need to share" is a constant of societies throughout history and geographies.[184] It is, Graeber claims, particularly acute in both the best of times and the worst of times: during famines, for example, but also during moments of extreme plenty.[185] To be sure, sharing is about morality and derives from a sense of obligation, however broadly defined. But it is also about pleasure. For most human beings, "the most pleasurable activities almost always involve sharing something: music, food, liquor, drugs, gossip, drama, beds."[186] In sharing a good, or the proceeds of a good, one's joy is increased, not decreased: a companion, after all, is someone with whom we share bread. It is only in a context in which the other member of the group is seen as a competitor struggling for the same good—food, money, recognition, love—that sharing is experienced as a punishment and is the source of sad passions, such as ambition, envy, humiliation, or resentment. What Graeber calls "baseline communism" is a default position of societies and a constant throughout history.

Conclusion

This chapter traced the origins of the articulation of crisis, critique, and revolution, and sketched the regime of crisis as contradiction. The examples I focused on—the general strike, the creation of a new hegemony, the cooperative movement following the (failed) struggles for recognition—can all be described as revolutionary, in that they seek to institute a new, alternative order through the creation of new norms. Of those, I believe the cooperative movement to be the most promising. The structure of scientific revolutions, inspired by Kuhn, which I analyzed in Chapter 1, is another example of a consensus forged following the pressure of contradictions, yet one that cannot easily be transposed to the political sphere. In the current (global and financial) regime of accumulation, however, the dominant forms of social contestation, especially since the financial crash of 2008, seem to be of a different kind: less concentrated, less organized, and less consensual—that is, less oriented toward the institution of a new normative order. This evolution is not a coincidence: the post-Fordist condition of workers in the global North is one of extreme atomization and dispersion; labor is constantly delocalized, outsourced, and precarious; the social body is fragmented. The current forms of social protest can be seen as morbid symptoms of a world in crisis in which one hegemony is contested but another has not yet emerged, and perhaps *cannot* emerge, so strong is the grip of capitalism on our social imagination. As Mark Fisher famously put it, "it's easier to imagine the end of the world than the end of capitalism."[187] Capitalism, not communism, is the unsurpassable horizon of our time.

In that respect, one of the most significant and exemplary forms of social unrest is the riot. As we saw in the French banlieues in 2005, 2009, and 2023; in London in the summer of 2011; in France again, with the yellow vest movement between late 2018 and 2020 (until the beginning of the lockdown); in Chile in 2019; or in the United States in the spring and summer of 2020, it is riots, and not strikes, which seem to embody today's discontent and *malaise*. For a long time, strikes constituted the dominant form of struggle against industrial, Fordist capitalism. They still take place and will perhaps continue to do so. But riots characterize the contemporary form of uprising against post-Fordist, consumption- and debt-driven capitalism, and against its managerial style of government, which has done much to erode the classical structure of labor movements by replacing disciplinary techniques with technologies of control. In light of the urban youth attacking the commercial symbols of capitalism, or the spontaneous blockade and occupation movements that have multiplied in the last few years and affect city centers as well as roads and roundabouts, one would need to supplement Benjamin's analysis with an analysis of a different kind. It would focus on the manner in which late, post-industrial, and financial capitalism intersects with new forms of bio- and sovereign power, and generates crises of a new kind. Joshua Clover describes them as crises of circulation, and distinguishes them from crises of production (and reproduction): "*crisis signals a shift of capital's center of gravity into circulation, both theoretically and practically, and riots is in the last instance to be understood as a circulation struggle, of which the price-setting struggle and the surplus rebellion are distinct, if related, forms.*"[188] According to Clover, industrialization in the nineteenth and twentieth centuries concentrated the workforce in shops and factories, and transformed the masses into wage laborers. The popular struggles that ensued were waged within the sphere of production and tended to focus on the price of labor power. By contrast, "phases led by circulation will see struggles in the marketplace, over the price of goods."[189] Whilst I don't think it is possible to claim that one form of uprising replaces another, and that the struggles inherent to the workplace will give way to struggles in the marketplace, it is useful to point to the specificity and increasing occurrence of the riot-form as a spontaneous, at times violent reaction to a process of exclusion and scarcity, rooted in indignation, frustration, and rage. The uprising in question, according to Clover, is not the crisis itself, but only its political, popular expression. The crisis—he speaks of a "Long Crisis"—goes back to the progressive deindustrialization and financialization of capitalism that began in 1973, and which shifted the interest of capital away from absorbing the masses into the labor market.

There are other examples of resistance to the current, neoliberal phase of capitalism. We see a proliferation of alternative autonomous political spaces and practices—movements of occupation of public spaces around the world, from Tahrir Square to Wall Street, to Gazi Park in Istanbul, to Syntagma Square, to the streets of Hong Kong, to the Place de la République in Paris—that amount to a kind of escape or flight from the political form of liberal democracy: they are not directed toward the state, they neither seek recognition from it, nor seek to seize state power, whether through democratic or revolutionary means. Rather, they embody a different type of desire—the sovereign desire for another type of life, one that is at once autonomous and sustainable, and which, following Rancière, we could call truly political or democratic, insofar as it reveals the demos as the literally anarchic principle simultaneously underpinning and exceeding the problematic of government (or, in Rancière's idiom, the "police").[190] While the latter is concerned with the theoretical principle or *arkhè* that justifies a clear distribution of positions and capacities, and grounds the distribution of power between those who rule and those who are ruled, the former expresses the paradox of a qualification to rule that is without qualification. To be sure, each qualification (birth, seniority, wisdom, expertise, strength, wealth, etc.) can lead to a specific form of government (aristocracy, gerontocracy, technocracy, plutocracy, etc.), the merits of which can be debated. But democracy is not the exercise or power of a qualification. Rather, it is the power of those that no *arkhè* entitles them to exercise. As such, it is neither a form of government nor a set of institutions, but the anarchic principle that must be presupposed for politics to exist at all, and which precludes the self-grounding of politics. This in turn means that, strictly speaking, the demos can never be in power, or seize power. It is the "inner" or "vanishing difference" of power, which "both legitimizes and de-legitimizes state institutions and practices of ruling."[191] Continually thwarted by the oligarchic running of those institutions, "the power of the people must be re-enacted ceaselessly by political subjects that challenge the police distribution of parts, places or competences, and that restage the anarchic foundation of the political."[192]

Finally, social struggles also take the simple form of indifference or non-participation. As Newman puts it, "not acting, or no longer acting in certain kinds of ways that reproduce submission—a kind of radical 'inaction'"[193]— can be just as effective as revolutionary action. One might think here of civil disobedience, or other forms of passive resistance, such as idleness, laziness, or the refusal to work and/or consume.[194] This is a perfectly legitimate strategy, especially in an age of ecological crisis. The lazy or idle person escapes the rationality of the market, the norm of competition, and the morality of work by refusing to lend them her body and desire. This, in essence, is what Russell tried to convey in a short piece, "In Praise of Idleness," which he wrote in 1932 with the hope of inducing "good young men to do nothing."[195] Critical of what he calls the "slave morality of work," he sees leisure (which he tends to identify with idleness) as "essential to civilization."[196] To be sure, he claims, "in former times leisure for the few was only rendered possible by the labors of the many. But their labors were valuable not because work is good, but because leisure is good."[197] The purpose of modern economics and good government, as a result, ought to be to "distribute leisure justly without injury to civilization."[198] This desirable outcome is unlikely, however, and Russell is prescient when he writes: "having taught the supreme virtue of hard work, it is difficult to see how the authorities can aim at a paradise in which there will be much leisure and little work. It seems more likely that they will find continually fresh schemes, by which present leisure is to be sacrificed for future productivity."[199] Indeed, the market principles of productivity, efficiency, and risk and cost calculation have been internalized as norms of life, thus turning the problem of life itself into one of investment and productivity, and blurring the very distinction between labor and leisure. If anything, leisure itself has become an industry, and is almost entirely absorbed within the regime of accumulation.

4

Deconstructing Crisis?

Before I turn to the fourth and final regime of crisis envisaged in this book, and to the ecological crisis as its current and most extreme expression, I would like to explore the objections and criticisms which, in a series of texts from the late 1980s and early 1990s—the period is relevant—Derrida formulated with respect to the concept, ideologeme, or philosopheme of crisis, and the then well-established connection between crisis, critique, and the demand to think who we are "today." Derrida's name has thus far come up on several occasions: in the introduction, alongside other skeptics of the notion of crisis; in the chapter on exception, to contrast his interpretation of *Hamlet* with that of Carl Schmitt; and in Chapter 3, in connection with Spivak's discussion of the voice of the subaltern. I believe Derrida's oblique but crucial critical remarks on crisis should be taken seriously, not only because they seek to replace it with other concepts, and to develop a kind of critique that is not attached to the concept of crisis, but also because they seek to engage with the range of problems—"crises"—I have thus far explored. This chapter is therefore both an exposition of Derrida's position and, ultimately, a further defense of the "crisology" for which I have been arguing.

Crisis, Derrida argues in substance, is not the only, or indeed the most useful and urgent concept to think the event (*l'événement*)—that is, what is happening or coming (*ce qui arrive, ce qui vient, ce qui advient*). That is because the event, especially in the form of the "promise" and the "aporia," exceeds and undermines the figure of crisis itself. He says it most explicitly in a short book devoted to the question of Europe.[1] But, as he recognizes himself in a footnote, what he has to say about crisis in that book, and indeed in *The Other Heading* as a whole, is itself the extension of another, very long footnote inserted *ex post* in the book version of another talk, given in 1987 at the Collège International de Philosophie and devoted to the fate of "spirit" (*Geist*) in Heidegger's thought, and more specifically to the place, role, and meaning of Heidegger's engagement in favor of National Socialism.[2] The theme of crisis as it's introduced is taken up and further developed in *Spectres of Marx*, published only two years after *The Other Heading*: that is, in the aftermath of the collapse of the Soviet empire and the context of the fate—the construction, reconstruction, and deconstruction—of "Europe." The fate of Spirit turns out to be also the fate of fate itself (*Schicksal*), of something like a European destiny (*Geschick*) and History (*Geschichte*).[3] The period of Derrida's work with which I shall be concerned, then, spans only five years (1987–1992). It is crucial in that it is defined by Derrida's attempt to take full stock of Heidegger's Nazism, the collapse of the communist bloc, the legacy of Marx, and the meaning of "Europe" and the European project. Much is at stake, therefore, in Derrida's brief, critical engagement with the idea of crisis, especially as it involves the greatest catastrophes and bloodshed ever perpetuated in Europe (and the world)—the greatest "crises" of its history, one would be tempted to say. In the end, Derrida seeks to expose the abyss that separates the philosophies of history bound to the schema of crisis and those bound to the structure of the promise; the eschatological and/or dialectical on the one hand, and the messianic on the other; the event as the site of the problematic and the event as the site of the aporetic; crisology and deconstruction. In that respect, Derrida's thought connects with Benjamin's historical messianism in "Theses on the Philosophy of History," and takes the form of a "messianicity without messianism."[4] It is also intimately bound up with the question of justice, as irreducible to both calculable and distributive justice—to the economy of right (*le droit*), the calculation of restitution, and the orthopedics of revenge and punishment, which seek to "set right" the time that is out of joint and restore the *nomos* of the social order—and the "purely" or "absolutely" political in the Schmittian sense, which decides on the state of exception and the suspension of the rule of law. And it is in connection with the question of justice that Derrida—like Levinas, to whom he is partly indebted—revisits tragedy, through the figure of the specter and the "hauntology" it reveals. But is the abyss ultimately as significant as Derrida suggests? Does he do away with crisis entirely, or simply give it a new name?

Rescuing "Europe" from Crisis

Earlier, I argued that whilst Heidegger does not use the notion of *Krise*, he does have recourse to the notion of *Not* (plight, distress, emergency). He also speaks of the *Entmachtung*—the "destitution" or "disempowerment" of Spirit[5]—to characterize the age of "machination" (*Machenschaft*) and the increasingly fragile and threatened place of Europe in the world. He is especially concerned with the fate of the German people, which he calls the most "metaphysical"[6] and "spiritual" (*geistig*)[7] people. Europe, Heidegger says, is caught between "America" and "Russia" as the two contemporary faces of the same nihilistic coin, the same will to dominate and unleash devastating industrial, military, and ideological power. But this difficult, distressing, and urgent situation is also that of "the great decision" (*die grosse Entscheidung*) and equally great "responsibility" that befall Europe in general, and Germany in particular. Only Germany, he claims, can generate "new historical spiritual forces from the Middle" (*neuer geschichtlich geistiger Kräfte aus der Mitte*).[8] Despite those similarities, which Derrida acknowledges in a series of "no doubt"[9] statements, Heidegger's discourse, he argues, "is not a discourse on crisis."[10] To which I would reply: *to be sure*, it is not a discourse on crisis in the Husserlian sense, and the nature of the crisis it addresses differs from Husserl's. To put it bluntly, "spirit" does not *mean* the same thing in Husserl and Heidegger: what Husserl calls spirit, and wants to rescue, is from Heidegger's perspective precisely a symptom of the decline or destitution of Spirit. Nor is the destitution of spirit in Heidegger's sense reducible to the spiritual crisis in Valéry's sense, despite some common elements. But it *is* crisis, *structurally*, as I argued in Chapter 1: it perpetuates a relatively classical construction of crisis, albeit under a different name, or set of names. In addition, I argued that the structures of Dasein and History—to the extent that they signal the possibility of a pivotal moment or turning (*Kehre*) within their own fate; to the extent that they indicate a shift from disowning to ownness, "inauthenticity" to "authenticity," or alienation to freedom—retain much of the classical conception of crisis as a turning point requiring the highest decision and determination. The latter, we saw, takes the form of an "either . . . or" which Derrida will replace with an "at the same time," indicative of an irreducible *undecidability* and an entirely different kind of *responsibility*, embodied in Hamlet's dilemma. Derrida does not claim that the space of decision is neutralized or rendered ineffective as a result of this undecidability. On the contrary, he claims that the latter opens up the former.

In his text on the question of European identity, Derrida speaks of a "contradictory" and even "impossible" task, which consists in making ourselves

> the guardians of an idea of Europe, *but* of a Europe that consists precisely in not closing itself off in its own identity and in advancing itself in an exemplary way toward what it is not, toward the other heading or the heading of the other, indeed—and this is perhaps something else altogether—toward the other *of* the heading, which would be the beyond of this modern tradition, another border structure, another shore.[11]

Put otherwise, this double bind and "double contradictory imperative" or refusal to limit Europe to its own geographical borders and declare it fixed or given once and for all, this invitation to hear, greet, and remain faithful to what comes or arrives (*ce qui vient, ce qui arrive*) from beyond its own frontiers is precisely what would define Europe, *here* and *now*. This "injunction" is one that is unfolding, in what amounts to an event that does not take place only once, but continues to take place, in a temporality that exceeds that of the present and mere chronology—an event in the form of a demand *and* a promise:

> I believe, rather, that this event takes place as that which comes, as that which seeks or promises itself today, in Europe, the today of a Europe whose borders are not given—no more than its name, Europe being here only a *paleonymic* appellation. I believe that if there is any event today, it is taking place here, in this act of memory that consists in betraying a certain order of capital to be faithful to the other heading and to the other of the heading.[12]

At precisely that point—that is, at the point where, somewhat abruptly, Derrida affirms the necessity to betray the order and logic of capital (I will return to this oblique reference), as well as the geopolitical order of borders, in the name of, and to remain faithful to, another *cap*, another direction— he introduces the notion of crisis. He introduces it in quotation marks—in reference to Valéry, who claims that the "spirit" and "capital" of Europe are "in peril"[13]—but only to dismiss it: "And this is happening at a moment for which the word *crisis*, the crisis of Europe or the crisis of spirit, is perhaps no longer appropriate."[14] If crisis is "no longer" appropriate, it is not in the sense in which it will have once been appropriate, and then somehow lost its efficiency or usefulness as a concept. "No longer," in this context, is to be understood not chronologically but logically: it signals the very limited sense in which "crisis" can do justice to the kind of event or "moment" we are faced with "today," one that has everything to do with justice itself, in excess of law. This injunction that happens and arrives (the French *arrive* means both) defines a present or "moment" that does not take place in time, alongside other events, which will eventually and inevitably replace it. Rather, it opens up time: the time of Europe as Idea, an ideal, and a "promise"—the time of a justice and democracy *to-come*.[15] It is a moment or present that does not so much exist, occur, and vanish as it insists, recurs, and never ceases to unfold. As such, it exceeds and suspends the very idea, concept, or philosopheme of crisis, and this means also the very philosophy of history or historiology rooted in the temporality or chronology of crisis:

> The coming to awareness . . . this moment of awakening, of sounding the alarm, has always been deployed in the tradition of modernity at the moment and as the very moment of what was called *crisis*. This is the moment of decision, the moment of *krinein*, the dramatic instant of a decision. . . . The crisis of Europe as the crisis of spirit.[16]

In his late talk on the legacy and future of the Enlightenment, Derrida said the following:

> Justice will never be reduced to law, to calculative reason, to lawful distribution, to the norms and rules that condition law. . . . [It] opens the free space of the relationship to the incalculable singularity of the other.[17]

Whilst "heterogeneous" to right, justice is not without relation to it: "there can be no justice without an appeal to juridical determinations, and to the force of law; and there can be no becoming, no transformation, history or perfectibility of law without an appeal to justice that will nonetheless always exceed it."[18] This difficult, even "impossible transaction between the conditional and the unconditional, calculation and the incalculable," is the very responsibility of reason, or what being reasonable means: "An always perilous transaction must thus invent, each time, in a singular situation, its own law and norm, that is, a maxim that welcomes each time the event to come."[19] This "exposition to the incalculable event" is our only protection against "the worst," a worse far worse than "what Kant thinks under the name radical evil."[20]

It is also within this space (and time), between the calculable and the incalculable, between what can and cannot be decided, that *decision* takes place. Decision, therefore, is reducible to neither calculation and arbitration nor sovereignty, understood as the decision regarding the state of exception: "it is thus no doubt necessary, in the name of reason, to call into question and to limit a logic of nation-state sovereignty," "to erode not only its principle of indivisibility but its right to the exception, its right to suspend rights and law."[21] The question of decision is displaced, wrenched or loosened not only from the juridical rule and game, from the rule of the juridical game, which applies the general rule to the particular case, but from the rule without rule of the state of exception. A double displacement and detachment, therefore, toward an excess or residue, which comes or arrives from beyond and before the law, yet enters with it in a certain kind of relation, summons it or exhorts it, carries it away; a displacement which upsets the autonomy—the freedom—of the subject of the law and exposes it to an older and irreducible heteronomy. The "undecidable"—this is how Derrida designates this experience—"haunts" every decision, in a way that is never overcome; it is, paradoxically, "essential":

> The experience of the undecidable . . . never passes away, is never overcome [*n'est jamais passée ou dépassée*]; it is not a moment that is overcome or

superseded (*aufgehoben*) in the decision. The undecidable remains caught, lodged, like a ghost at least, but an essential ghost, in every decision, in every event of decision.²²

Yet this undecidability, this justice that is both endless and always to-come, does not neutralize or paralyze decision. It makes it more *urgent*, and this urgency is the very temporality of justice: justice "cannot wait"; "a just decision is always required *immediately*, right away, as soon as possible."²³

To understand what is at stake in this event, the event of Europe, to understand the nature of the impossible tension or non-dialectical contradiction that defines Europe as such and makes us immediately realize that there is no such thing, there cannot be such a thing as Europe *as such*, we need precisely to let go of the word crisis, of the talk of the crisis of Europe, of "spirit," or of anything else that signals a turning point and a moment of great decision. Crisis is precisely not the paradigm with which to approach the question of European identity and history, precisely because the very idea of crisis presupposes that of its own overcoming or solution, the possibility of an after or beyond, as well as a before, the perspective of an old or new "normality" that we can return to or invent. The vocabulary of crisis is to be avoided because it obfuscates the nature of the event—the duty and responsibility—that defines "Europe," one that is couched in terms not of an either/or, such as the either/or of Heidegger's *Seynsgeschichte*, but of an (impossible, undecidable) and/and. *On the one hand*, Derrida insists, European cultural identity "cannot and must not be dispersed into a myriad of provinces, into a multiplicity of self-enclosed nationalisms, each one jealous and untranslatable. It cannot and must not renounce places of great circulation or heavy traffic, the great avenues or thoroughfares of translation and communication, and thus, of mediatization."²⁴ *On the other hand*, "it cannot and must not accept" the centralizing cultural mechanisms that ignore borders and margins; standardize and homogenize idioms, artistic discourses, philosophical or aesthetic norms; impose the pursuit of ratings and commercial profitability; in short, establish a hegemonic center. "If it is necessary to make sure that a centralizing hegemony (the capital) not be reconstituted," Derrida adds, it is also necessary not to multiply borders—

marches (*marches*) and margins (*marges*)—within Europe, or "cultivate for their own sake minority differences, untranslatable idiolects, national antagonisms."[25] "Neither monopoly nor dispersion," therefore.[26] There is an *aporia* here, constitutive of European identity and the construction of Europe as a united and unified space.[27] But, by virtue of being an aporia, or a "nondialectizable contradiction," it is irreducible and "interminable."[28] We must learn to live with it, and in it, rather than overcome it; and in doing so, we move further away from the historical schema or paradigm of crisis:

> I will even venture to say that ethics, politics, and responsibility, *if there are any*, will only ever have begun with the experience and the experiment of the aporia. . . . The condition of possibility of this thing called responsibility is a certain *experience of and experiment of the impossible: the testing of the aporia* from which one may invent the only *possible invention, the impossible invention*.[29]

It is not enough, and never will be enough, to designate this tension a crisis, precisely because it is a transcendental or quasi-transcendental condition of European identity, because it defines Europe as such:

> One must therefore try to *invent* gestures, discourses, politico-institutional practices that inscribe the alliance of these two imperatives, of these two promises or contracts: the capital and the a-capital, the other of the capital. That is not easy. It is even impossible. . . . But there is no responsibility that is not the experience and experiment of the impossible.[30]

The same aporia, the same impossible responsibility, is at work in our "*duty to respond to the call of European memory, to recall what has been promised under the name Europe, to re-identify Europe*," and our equally significant duty to open Europe "onto that which is not, never was, and never will be Europe."[31] The *same duty* also dictates that we welcome foreigners in order not only to integrate them but to recognize and accept their alterity—"two concepts of hospitality that today divide our European and national consciousness."[32] The "moment" is therefore *not* defined as a pivotal moment, as the moment at which one decides to follow one path and renounce the other. The moment—which defines us in that it calls upon us, summons us, and makes us responsible—opens up the space of ethics and politics:

> The *same duty* dictates assuming the European, and *uniquely* European, heritage of an idea of democracy, while also recognizing that this idea, like that of international law, is never simply given, that its status is not even that of a regulative ideal in the Kantian sense, but rather something that remains to be thought and *to come* [*à venir*]: not something that is certain to happen tomorrow, not the democracy (national or international, state or trans-state) of the *future*, but a democracy that must have the structure of a promise—and thus the memory of that which carries the future, the to-come, here and now.[33]

This is precisely the sense in which the contradiction or impossible demand with which Derrida associates the very idea of Europe differs from the dialectical conception of contradiction, whether idealist or materialist. The space of deconstruction, which is also that of justice and remembrance, of the fidelity toward another that one can only betray, is precisely the undecided and undecidable space of this double, contradictory demand, which is also the experience of the impossible and of the impossible decision. Elsewhere, Derrida explicitly defines deconstruction as an aporetic experience of the impossible.[34] This experience, this "nonpassive endurance of the aporia," he says, is "the condition of responsibility and of decision."[35] Aporia, rather than dialectical contradiction, then. But aporia, rather than antinomy, too. The word antinomy imposes itself "up to a certain point since, in terms of the law (*nomos*), contradictions or antagonisms among equally imperative laws" are at stake.[36] But since we are dealing with an *interminable* experience, rather than "an apparent or illusory antinomy," a "transcendental illusion" (or paralogism) in a Kantian sense, or a "contradiction in the Hegelian or Marxist sense," the antinomy here better deserves the name of aporia.[37] The experience of the aporetic, then, seems to exceed the schema of crisis as such, including in the various versions or regimes I have identified, including, that is, as anomaly, anomie, and antinomy.

Rescuing Marx from Crisis

How, then, could Derrida develop a critique of capitalism, including ofincluding its contradictions, without embracing Marx's critique of political economy, his philosophy of history, and his concept of crisis? This question guides a number of Derrida's texts from the early 1990s. In *L'Autre cap*, Derrida says that in order to address the question of European identity it is impossible not to address the role and place of capital, in Europe and elsewhere. This is especially urgent, given "the neo-capitalist exploitation of the breakdown of an anti-capitalist dogmatism in the states that had incorporated it," and the triumphant, unchallenged rhetoric of the liberal, market-driven version of the end-of-History, which I began by evoking in this book.[38] Now, Derrida insists, is the time to read or reread Marx's *Capital*, but from a non-dogmatic, and possibly non-Marxist perspective. Why? Because—this is now me speaking—by taking for granted the Marxist philosophy of history, based on the internal contradictions of capital, we are necessarily drawn back into the semantics, metaphysics, and politics of crisis, and therefore of another end-of-history, another eschatology. *The Other Heading* raises urgent questions in that regard, but leaves them unanswered: "Is it not necessary to have the courage and lucidity for a *new* critique of the *new* effects of capital (within unprecedented techno-social structures)? Is not this responsibility incumbent upon *us*, most particularly upon those who never gave in to a certain Marxist intimidation?"[39]

Specters of Marx, published three years after *The Other Heading*, returns to the question of another possible reading of, and fidelity to, Marx's text.[40] In fact, Derrida declares that deconstruction is and has always been an attempt to "radicalize" Marxism, that it "would have been impossible and unthinkable in a pre-Marxist space."[41] This somewhat theatrical declaration is hardly credible. It also raises the question of why Marxism needs to be "radicalized" in the first place, and why in the manner proposed by Derrida. A proper return to Marx, and our responsibility toward him, Derrida seems to imply, must take the form of deconstruction, and thus of a return to *a certain Marx*, which suspends his own concepts of critique and history:

It will always be a fault not to read and reread and discuss Marx—which is to say also a few others—and to go beyond scholarly "reading" and "discussion." It will be more and more a fault, a failing of theoretical, philosophical, political responsibility. When the dogma machine and the "Marxist" ideological apparatuses (states, parties, cells, unions, and other places of doctrinal production) are in the process of disappearing, we no longer have any excuses, only alibis, for turning away from this responsibility. There will be no future without, without the memory and the inheritance of Marx, of his genius, of at least one of his spirits.[42]

No future without Marx, then. Yet this return is precisely not a return to the *letter* of Marx's text, and especially not to the motif, semantics, and climate of crisis, contradiction, and the work of the negative. Crisis is "a very insufficient concept,"[43] and one we should *avoid*. It is a matter, then, of rescuing Marx from Marx, of providing a reading of Marx that bypasses its dialectical presuppositions and historical materialism, crystallized in the concept of crisis, and offering in its place another concept, another way of thinking the event, the present, and history more broadly. The question, which I leave open at this point, is this: is *Specters of Marx*, as Derrida claims, a new form of fidelity to Marx's text, to its genius and *spirit*, to everything spectral and haunting? Or is Derrida's avoidance of crisis an avoidance of Marx's text, by which I mean a distortion if not a betrayal of the *letter* of that text, in the name of its spirit(s)?

In *Specters of Marx*, Derrida's avoidance and neutralization of crisis as contradiction, and as the foundation of a philosophy of history rooted in the work of the negative, takes the form of a double, intertwined reading of *Hamlet* and of a few pages by Marx, the first framing, announcing, and preparing the second. Derrida refers again to *La Crise de l'esprit*, and mentions Valéry's evocation of "the European Hamlet" who, at the end of the war, "contemplates thousands of spectres" and picks randomly illustrious skulls: those of Leonardo, Leibniz ("who dreamt of universal peace"), and Kant ("*Kant qui genuit Hegel, qui genuit Marx, qui genuit . . .*").[44] Then, referring to some of his previous works, such as *Of Spirit* and *The Other Heading*, he posits that the question of Europe is identical with that of spirit, of the specter, and of Marx in particular. The specter is the figure through which Derrida challenges both Carl Schmitt's historicist and exceptionalist reading of *Hamlet* and the positivist, deterministic reading of Marx.⁴⁵ In both cases, what is at stake is the possibility of thinking history beyond or outside both the schema of crisis and that of the *eschaton*.

To my knowledge, Derrida refers to Schmitt's *Hamlet or Hecuba* only once, in a footnote and seemingly in passing (Derrida promises to return to that essay but never does).⁴⁶ The reference to Schmitt's essay occurs in the broader context of Derrida's long discussion of Schmitt's definition of the political as rooted in the "final" and "decisive" distinction between friend and enemy, and its manifestation in the always active *possibility* of either war or revolution (and nothing else).⁴⁷ War, whether between or within states, is "the most extreme consequence of enmity" and an unsurpassable horizon "so long as the concept of the enemy remains valid."⁴⁸ It is a limit-situation, analogous to the state of exception: "What always matters is the *possibility* of the *decisive* case taking place [*die Möglichkeit dieses entscheidenden Falles*], the real war [*des wirklichen Kampfes*], and the *decision* whether this situation has or has not arrived."⁴⁹ As Derrida himself puts it:

> The exception is the rule. . . . The exception is the rule of what takes place, the law of the event, the real possibility of its real possibility. The exception grounds [*fonde*] the decision regarding the case or the eventuality. . . . This exceptionality grounds (*begründet*) the eventuality of the event. An event is an event, and a decisive one, only if it is exceptional. An event as such is always exceptional. . . . That means that today war, the state of war, the eventuality of war or *casus belli* (*der Kriegsfall*), still remains the decisive ordeal, the serious thing, the main critical affair, the *krinein* of crisis, the very seriousness of the decision. . . . The serious decision is the *casus belli* [*le cas de guerre*], the absolute hostility which, therefore, always decides between the friend and the enemy.⁵⁰

In Chapter 2 I analyzed the connection Schmitt establishes between crisis and the state of exception, which, contrary to what Derrida seems to suggest in *Politics of Friendship*, is not limited to the case of war, or even civil war.

Derrida's footnote is preceded by a crucial emphasis on the empty (*leer*) and *spectral* (*gespenstisch*) nature of all characterizations of the political that are stripped of its conflictual, polemic, or antagonistic essence—stripped, that is, of the "real possibility of physical killing."[51] In the context of a definition of the political and its essence, which Schmitt is careful to distinguish from the "tactics and practices, competitions and intrigues, and the most peculiar dealings and manipulations" of politics, all distinctions and considerations that are not directly related to the friend-enemy grouping are mere abstractions: "political concepts, images, and terms have a polemical meaning. They are focused on a specific conflict and are bound to a *concrete* situation; the result (which manifests itself in war or revolution) is a friend-enemy grouping and they turn into *empty and ghostlike abstractions* [*werden zu leeren und gespenstischen Abstraktionen*] when this situation disappears."[52] It is precisely this series of distinctions—between the concrete and the abstract, the real and the spectral, the serious and the playful, the exception and the norm, the decisive and the merely important—with which Derrida takes issue. What he contests, however implicitly and obliquely at this stage, is the secondary, derivative, and abstract character of all determinations and practices of the political—beginning, of course, with the concept or philosopheme of friendship—that would not be rooted in the Schmittian distinction. To be more precise, Derrida sees what is "merely" secondary and derivative, unreal, or spectral, as constitutive of Schmitt's distinction, as well as of any distinction (and hierarchy) pitting an origin against its repetition or distortion, a real or actual (*wirkliche*) situation against an illusion, a ground against what it grounds. As a result, he questions the very primacy of the political, the exception, and the moment of decision, revealed and called for in a time of crisis.

How exactly? It is not entirely clear. Schmitt insists, "obsessively," on the fact that "only a *concrete, concretely determined* enemy can awaken the political; only a real enemy can shake the political out of its slumber and, as we recall, out of the abstract 'specularity' of its concept."[53] We saw a very similar logic orient Schmitt's conception of sovereignty as the decision regarding the state of exception, or the suspension of the legal *nomos*. But, Derrida adds, somewhat axiomatically, "there is the spectre, lodged within the political itself; the antithesis of the political dwells within, and politicizes, the political."[54] I say axiomatically because the haunting nature of this "antithesis" is not entirely clear. I take Derrida to be suggesting the following: if the *presence* of the political ultimately depends on war, whether as a possibility or a reality, and bearing in mind that Schmitt posits it as the condition of possibility of the political, then, insofar as it implies the death of the enemy, his physical disappearance and absence (as well as my own, for I am the enemy of my enemy), war presupposes the end or disappearance of the state and the political. In other words, the condition of possibility of the political and of the state is also its condition of impossibility, its evanescence, its vanishing. Similarly, and extending Derrida's remarks to the state of exception, one would arrive at the conclusion that the sovereign is only ever manifest as such in the moment of suspension of the legal nomos that guarantees its own existence.

Marx's Hauntology, or *Hamlet* Revisited

Specters of Marx grew out of a plenary address Derrida gave, in two parts, at a conference held at the University of California, Riverside, in April 1993. Held under the double auspices of Marx and Crisis (this seemingly inevitable yet, in relation to Derrida, problematic motif), "Whither Marxism: Global Crises in International Perspective" gathered thinkers and scholars from around the world.[55] Unsurprisingly, Derrida devotes much time and energy to avoiding the philosopheme—the all-too-metaphysical idea—of crisis, for which he substitutes (again) the related notions of spirit (*Geist, esprit*), specter (*Gespenst, spectre*), or ghost (*revenant*), all of which signal, albeit from afar, the event (*l'événement*) as what happens, comes, and returns (*ce qui advient, vient, revient*): "Repetition *and* first time: this is perhaps the question of the event as question of the ghost."[56] The temporality of *revenance*, the historicity of spectrality, the eventfulness of iterability and *différance* displace if not evacuate altogether the paradigm and structure of crisis. The contributors to the conference occasionally refer to specific crises, such as the crises internal to eastern Europe, the former Soviet Union, and (a certain) Marxism following the collapse of historical communism; or the crises of labor, rationality, subjectivity, and the environment. But they never feel the need to articulate a clear concept of crisis, or to problematize it. It is as if, once again, the *horizon* of crisis were self-evident, as if it were never *in question*. Where Derrida's omission is strategic, and the result of a careful, philosophically justified position—deconstruction, if such a thing exists, is also the deconstruction of crisis—the lack of engagement on the part of the remaining contributors is a manifestation of a certain pre-philosophical, average, and doxastic understanding of crisis, which as a result is never raised to the status of a genuine concept.

With a sleight of hand or contortionist trick, and through the figure and "economy" of the specter, Derrida attempts to dissociate Marx, or at least the "spirit" of Marx, from the eminently dialectical concept and labor of contradiction, and from crisis as its inevitable symptom. By invoking the specters of Marx, by which I mean a certain "return" or "*revenance*" of Marx in the specific context of the neoliberal consensus and "the end of history," as well as the "presence" (without presence) of the figure of the specter in Marx's text, Derrida hopes to wrest Marx—what this proper name stands for, or the event it designates—from an arche-teleological conception of history rooted in the work of the negative, contradiction, and crisis. In the name of another conception of critique and of the event, which he calls "justice," Derrida seeks to suspend the philosophy of history as a philosophy of crisis, if not the Philosophy of History *as such*, given its close and long-standing association with the figure, model, or philosopheme of crisis. He resists the narratives of both History (as intrinsically contradictory and as a succession of crises) and the End of History (as eschatology, or as the completion of history in a specific social, economic, and political form). In truth, the two narratives are one and the same, and the expression of a single metaphysical, arche-teleological schema. The horizon of history, Derrida claims, is not that of the reconciliation (*Versöhnung*) beyond and through its contradictions—its crises, jolts, convulsions, tremors, and eruptions. That, you will recall, was precisely the view of history that the young Hölderlin, Hegel, and Schelling derived from their interpretation of Greek tragedy. History—or, better said perhaps, the "logic" of the event which, by contrast, Derrida seeks to delineate—is the history of that which arrives, comes, or returns, but without ever having *actually* taken place, or *actually* taking place, *here and now* so to speak. What is coming or happening (*ce qui arrive, vient, advient*) will never quite arrive or reach its destination. It will never become incarnate in a full, radiating, triumphant, and sovereign presence. This excess or surplus, which is at the same time a dearth, this "trace" is precisely what Derrida means by "event." In rethinking the event along those lines, Derrida connects with and reveals another economy and theology, one that is messianic rather than eschatological, haunto-heterological rather than onto-tautological.

In the end, though, Derrida avoids not just speaking about crisis in relation to Marx; he also avoids *reading* Marx, or most of his text. His (limited) references are to the first page of the *Manifesto of the Communist Party*; a couple of pages from the 1841 dissertation, *The Difference in the Philosophy of Nature of Democritus and Epicurus*; a handful of pages from *The Eighteenth Brumaire of Louis Bonaparte*; another few pages from "Saint Max" in *The German Ideology*, and from the section on commodity fetishism in the first chapter of *Capital*. At times, one feels that by prefacing his text with such long preliminary remarks about how, by virtue of its spectrality (it always returns, comes back, *revient*), a return to Marx's text is inevitable, Derrida renders a proper *engagement* with it superfluous. His reading can appear as a cunning and formidable exercise in avoidance, most notably of Marx's analysis of labor and modes of production, class struggle, money, the state, or ideology. He reads Marx as a phenomenologist (he is not the only one), a phenomenologist of spirit, spirits, and spectrality, for whom "the phenomenal form of the world itself is spectral,"[57] that is, generates its own phantoms, illusions, deceiving appearances, fetishisms: *es spukt*. But this reading comes at a cost: Derrida simply suspends or filters out Marx's *materialist* critique of political economy and ideology, which I explored in some detail in Chapter 3. As we'll see, it is true that in Marx's view the material conditions of capitalist production mask those conditions and produce illusions. But does this mean that his thought as a whole is haunted as well as haunting—that is, animated by an ontology of spectrality?

To be sure, Derrida claims, "*the time is out of joint*" and "the world is going badly."[58] But this "wear and tear" is a matter of neither "crisis, nor even agony."[59] The event Derrida has in mind, and with which he associates the names of Marx and communism, is not one that happens *in* time, but *to* time itself; it is not "one more crisis," such as "a last crisis-of-Marxism, or a new crisis-of-capitalism."[60] Equally significant, and intimately related, is the fact that Derrida deploys his reading under the banner and authority of *Geist*, but this time understood as the world and experience of spectrality, spirits, ghosts, and revenants. Spirits are neither present nor absent, dead nor alive; they are always already there, yet always to come. Their ontological status is unstable and ungraspable, between presence and absence, and exceeds them. "Hauntology," if there can be such a thing, is irreducible to ontology. If it opens up the question of the event—particularly of justice, of communism, of the end of exploitation and subjugation—it does so in a way that remains forever irreducible to something that takes place once, and to which one can ascribe a date, and a place; it is irreducible to anything like the actual, historical form that communism took in the twentieth century, or might take in the future. Yet it never ceases to weigh in on the *here and now*, to define it, to subject it to an infinite, impossible demand, which will never be entirely fulfilled, or fulfilled *as such*, as if one could ever move on from its infinitely demanding call. This structure of the event, this event-hauntology, this philosophy of history, escapes the onto-logic of crisis as a turning point and a moment of decision. And the name of Marx, Derrida claims, is forever associated with such an event, which takes the form of a *promise*.

The return to Marx, to the *spirit* or *spirits* of Marx, takes the form of a return of Marx, and of a certain Marxian spectrality, if not of spectrality or *revenance* as the very form, or movement, of History *as such* (and this means precisely *not* that of *Wirklichkeit*, of actuality and rationality, of the real as rational, and the rational as real): "At a time when a new world disorder is attempting to install its neo-capitalism and neo-liberalism, no disavowal has managed to rid itself of Marx's ghosts. . . . Haunting belongs to the very structure of hegemony."[61] The *spirit* of Marx is an *insistent* one, and one that cannot be dismissed, not even by appealing to actual events and so-called empirical, historical evidence (the undeniable and catastrophic failures of the totalitarian police state of "real socialism"). The news of the death of Marxism, propagated by "a deafening consensus," is and will always be premature given the *promise* that it carries, given the spectral nature of its content.[62] The shadow or phantom of Marx continues to haunt us. The time marked by the triumph of free market economies and liberal democracies, and celebrated by Fukuyama as the end of regulative ideal or history, is also, and equally, the time (but a *different* time) of "a new Alliance" and a "new International" (the proximity of the messianic and the political, of the political as the promise of the international joining of forces in the name of the subjugated is not a coincidence, and is in fact *decisive*), "inspired by at least one of the spirits of Marx or of Marxism."[63] It takes the form "of a kind of counter-conjuration" and a renewed, radicalized "critique" of the new world order—of "the world-wide market" that "holds a mass of humanity under its yoke and in a new form of slavery"; of "that which links the State and international law to this market";[64] of "the laws of capital and the types of capital (financial and symbolic, and therefore spectral)";[65] of "the nation-State," "national sovereignty," and "citizenship"; of "the universal discourse of human rights."[66]

By privileging spectrality over crisis, Derrida is attempting to rescue another Marx, another view of history, of communism, and of democracy (as what is still and always to come, and not as "the end of history"). But he is also, he claims, following to the end the opening sentence and, he claims, the messianic logic of *The Communist Manifesto*: "A Specter [*ein Gespenst*] is haunting Europe—the Specter of communism." The spirit of Marx's text, which is also that of "Europe," contains "a certain emancipatory and *messianic* affirmation, a certain experience of the promise . . . open to the absolute future of what is coming,"[67] yet freed from dogmatism, positivism, and teleology, and carried out in the name of a radical, interminable critique (both theoretical and practical). The unconscious may be structured like a language. But history is structured like a promise and a trace; its signature is that of a ghost; and its experience is irreducibly aporetic.

Derrida develops his analyses of spectrality in yet a different direction, one that goes to the root of Marx's analysis of value and signals the self-deconstructive dimension of his text. The Marxist corpus, Derrida claims, is itself haunted, inhabited by the figure of spectrality, which Marx so desperately wants to dispel:

> Marx does not like ghosts any more than his adversaries do. He does not want to believe in them. But he thinks of nothing else. He believes rather in what is supposed to distinguish them from actual reality [*la réalité effective*], living actuality [*l'effectivité vivante*]. He believes he can oppose them, like life to death, like vain appearances of the simulacrum to real presence. He

believes enough in the dividing line of this opposition to want to denounce, chase away, or exorcise the specters but by means of critical analysis and not by some counter-magic. But how to distinguish between the analysis that denounces magic and the counter-magic that it still risks being?[68]

This is the dilemma, indeed the aporia that Plato faces in the *Sophist*. How, Plato asks, can we distinguish between the original and the simulacrum, and how stable can such a distinction be? How can we identify and expose those false appearances that escape and threaten the law of the original and the copy, those appearances that cannot be traced back to an original? How—with what means and methods—can we hunt down, expel, and exorcise the Sophist, whose tricks consist precisely in presenting appearances as reality, false images or simulacra (*phantasma*) as originals? Schmitt faced a similar problem with his distinction between the norm and the exception, the friend and the enemy, or tragedy (or myth) and mere play: at every point, those distinctions needed to be firmly in place for sovereignty and the political to exist, to be an actual thing. And yet, on Derrida's reading at least, they were always threatened, always unstable. Marx "too will have tried to conjure (away) [*conjurer*] the ghosts *like* the conspirators [*conjurés*] of old Europe on whom the *Manifesto* declares war . . . to *exorc-analyze* the spectrality of the specter."[69] He is a ghost hunter, intent on breaking the spell which relations of production and exchange cast on the world. Ideology, to begin with, whether in the form of religion or metaphysical idealism, is populated with phantoms and phantasms, which we believe in, and behave toward, as if they were real entities, when they are in fact mere shadows. Similarly, commodity fetishism, which is generated by the gap between use and exchange value, and conceals the real social relations that underpin it, produces objects of a very specific kind, imbued with supernatural powers that transcend their materiality. As soon as a mere table made of wood ceases to be defined by its use value and becomes an object attached to a more abstract exchange value (money), it becomes a "ghostly objectivity" (*eine gespenstige Gegenständlichkeit*), a "mystical" thing, both sensible and supersensible, "sensuously supersensible" (*ein sinnlich übersinnliches Ding*).[70] Marx mentions "the whole mysticism of the world of commodities, all the magic and necromancy [*all der Zauber und Spuk*] that surrounds the products of labour on the basis of commodity production,"[71] in a way that reminds one of the critique of the *phantasma*, or simulacra, he inherits from Epicurus and Greek atomism. It is not a matter of an existence that hovers between life and death, presence and absence, and has the structure of *revenance*. It is more a matter of the material conditions of production, reproduction, and consumption, as well as the specific organization of labor--which are required for us to invest (economically, libidinally) and believe in the *existence* or *value* of the commodity. The commodity form transforms physiological labor relations between producers, and "the expenditure of human brain, nerves, muscles and sense organs,"[72] into a relation between objects, which takes on an existence of its own, detached from the producers. Furthermore, the objects themselves acquire subjective qualities, as if they were living, spiritual entities. They conceal their material, human origins, rooted in labor relations, and reveal a different, dematerialized, and autonomous form of existence. The aura that surrounds the commodity is a smokescreen, an illusion, sustained by a new form of magical thinking, a new idolatry or superstition. The world stands on its head. Everything is topsy-turvy. The spiritual is both an effect and an occultation of the material. The "event" Marx describes is a process of abstraction, whereby labor is—magically, miraculously—transformed, reified, and disguised as exchange value.

But, Derrida wants to argue, "spirit," whether in the form of ideology discourse or commodity, is always more than a mere effect. Spirit is also and above all *spectrality*. As such, its ontological (or "hauntological") constitution, its spatiality and temporality, is that of *revanance*, of an originary presence-absence, of an *arch-trace*, "older" than presence itself. Derrida's claim is clear: Marx's philosophy of history and his implicit ontology—a "critical" yet "pre-deconstructive" ontology of "presence as actuality [*Wirklichkeit*] and objectivity [*Gegenständlichkeit*]" (p. 214)—are underpinned and at the same time undermined by a *hauntology*, which functions as their condition of possibility *and* impossibility. His political economy presupposes an economy of a different kind: what Marx denounces as a mysterious, magical process, through which something appears to be something else, is actually a function and effect not of a simple illusion, but of an economy and ontology of spectrality, supplementarity, and iterability—in short, of *différance*. And this, Derrida implies, is why critique is best understood and practiced as deconstruction, why it can and should never rely on an original or primordial form (whether linguistic, conceptual, historical, or economic), why the idea of use value is itself a fiction. In that respect, and should one want to retain the motif of crisis *in the end*, one would have to define it as the crisis of origin, identity, or presence itself. Spectrality would be the name and haunting figure of that crisis, its only possible (and never completed or full) manifestation, its necessarily insufficient schematization. To be more precise: spectrality would be one of the many names of crisis, alongside supplement, *différance*, and (more explicitly still) aporia.

This is something Derrida himself established very early on. The connection between crisis and deconstruction is one that *Of Grammatology* emphasizes explicitly, albeit only in passing, by exploring the logic and economy of the supplement in Rousseau's writings on writing. Writing, Rousseau claims, is a "dangerous supplement" to living speech, insofar as it introduces a distance and separates the subject from itself. Writing represents speech, which represents thought. In *living* speech, the word is at once closer to the subject (to their voice and thought) and to the thing itself (the phenomenon). At the same time—and this is the second sense of the noun *supplément* and the verb *suppléer*—writing is an evil we cannot do without: it is this exteriority that, in principle, language should do without, yet in fact cannot. Rousseau therefore condemns writing as the destruction of presence and the malady of speech, whilst constantly recognizing the necessity of its mark or trace. To be sure, Rousseau uses the expression "dangerous supplement" to define not writing as such, but masturbation.[73] But Derrida insists on the pertinence of the parallel between the danger of writing and that of onanism: the supplement that, in Rousseau's own words, "cheats" maternal "nature" operates as writing, and is dangerous to life as writing: "Just as writing opens the *crisis* of the living speech in terms of its 'image,' its painting or its representation, so onanism announces the *ruin* of vitality in terms of imaginary seductions."[74] The crisis is therefore the crisis of nature itself, which, from the start, points beyond itself to a culture that is its realization and, at the same time, its betrayal. But this crisis—a crisis in the form of supplement rather than contradiction—can and does take many forms, in addition to writing (in relation to living speech) and autoeroticism (in relation to procreation). It can take the form of art, technics, education, the law, or representation in the political, democratic sense, which Rousseau opposes to direct democracy, in which the will of the Sovereign (the people) is ideally and immediately expressed, yet impossible to realize.[75] As a supplement, representation is always unsatisfactory: representative democracy fills a gap—the gap left by the impossibility of direct representation—and coincides with a state of permanent tension, or crisis, between the people *qua* sovereign, its representatives, and government. Like the state of nature, direct democracy is a (possibly useful) fiction, generated *ex post* by the logic of the supplement: the origin is secondary, produced as an effect of *différance*.

But it can also take the form of economic value, and of money in particular. Indeed, the logic of supplementarity also underpins (and equally undermines) Marx's distinction between use and exchange value, the economy of the latter having in fact (and in the capitalist mode of production) always and already begun to affect the former, the auto-affection of the former having always and already been exposed to the heteronomous force of the latter. What Marx criticizes in the system of capitalism is precisely the translation, alteration, and alienation of one value in another, the disappearance of nature—of human nature and natural relations—into an abstraction, an artificial construct in which a natural force, labor, and the class that assumes it, are presupposed and rendered invisible at the same time: exchange value, then, as a *dangerous* supplement, or "something accidental and purely relative."[76] Like Rousseau, Marx sees in supplementarity the very form of "the negativity of evil" and the origin of the crises of capitalism, or capitalism *as* crisis. For both, evil is precisely heteronomy: what is "exterior to nature, to what is by nature innocent and good. It supervenes upon nature [*Il survient à la nature*]. But always by way of compensation for [*sous l'espèce de la suppléance*] what *ought* to lack nothing at all in itself."[77] But if that is the case, all the crises Marx speaks of and accounts for as *contradictions* inherent to the modern mode of production known as capitalism presuppose crisis in that other, more primordial sense: the "original" and "founding" (in quotation marks, or under erasure) crisis is the crisis of origin, that is, the impossibility of origin, of something like a self-present, self-identical moment or state, one that would not be engaged in the process of its own reiteration, displacement, difference, contamination *from the very start*. Whether as voice, speech, or use value, "nature" is always and from the start marked by an Other, which it always seeks but fails to reduce and neutralize, in what amounts to the promise of a reunified world, a moment of final closure, an eschatology. And it is in the *aporetic* space (and time) of that impossible closure, that irreducible fissure or *brisure*, that everything is played out, at once decided and suspended: that conflicts are born, decisions are made, and justice is revealed as an infinite task. The structure in question is defined by an irreducible openness and indeterminacy, an unassimilable difference, such that the moment of the universal, of hegemony and closure, can never *actually* take place: the space of crisis is originary and ineliminable.

On the question of the distinction between use and exchange value, my response to Derrida would be the following. Derrida is right to say that the exchange-value "haunts" the use-value and has left its mark on it *from the start* ("The commodity haunts the thing, its specter is at work in use-value"—p. 189); that the use-value is always already encroached upon, eroded, or supplemented by the exchange-value; that the latter has left its mark on the former *from the very start*; that the founding distinction of Marx's analysis of the commodity form is unstable, and that the "original" form of the thing of use is characterized by a structure of iterability, supplementarity, and exchangeability; that Marx appears as an exorcist whose task is to chase away the ghosts that populate our world and conjure the spell under which we have fallen. But use-value is perhaps nothing other than a fiction that is necessary or at least useful to think the commodity form, rather than an actual state of affairs (past or present). In that respect, it is equivalent to the fiction of the state of nature in Rousseau. But a fiction is not an illusion, a phantasm or simulacrum. It can be read as a strategic device to analyze critically a state of affairs, and specifically the genesis of labor as the social form that generates exchange value. Were the commodity form to disappear, and depending on what would replace it, the use-value could also disappear. Commodity fetishism is thus characterized only in the context of the capitalist relations of production and labor. One can imagine a different, say, symbolic economy, or an economy of the gift, which would recognize exchangeability as intrinsic to the said economy, yet would not take the commodity form and would also not be reducible to mere use-value. Should the process of abstraction, through which labor is transformed into ever more ethereal forms of value (money, credit, and obscure financial instruments), be overturned, would social relations still be governed and *haunted* by a logic of iterability and supplementarity, of *différance* and spectrality?

Conclusion

I turned to Derrida's text as an objection, and indeed the most extreme form of objection, to the crisology I am attempting to develop. In the end, however, I see Derrida as rejecting a certain view and concept of crisis—crisis as contradiction and antinomy, crisis as exception and suspension—but only to deploy it in a new direction and context, to displace it and give it a new meaning: crisis as aporia, that is, as an inescapable structure or quasi-transcendental schema within which all the other senses and regimes of crisis unfold. Far from merely rejecting crisis, then, Derrida turns it into a condition of possibility of history, responsibility, and action. He sees it as opening up the space of decision, one that is always and necessarily insufficient and unsatisfactory: every decision is a bad decision, a compromise, and it is through this failure that history enters the realm of the real. That is what distinguishes crisis in a deconstructive sense from crisis as exception or contradiction, suspension or revolution.

But I am also skeptical of the Derridean paradigm as such, or its universalist transcendental claim. Is it the case that all decisions take place against the backdrop of an irreducible undecidability, that the space of decisiveness and decision-making is necessarily aporetic? Is it the case that there is only one kind of ethical-political demand, and that is the impossible demand, or the demand of the impossible? Is the "here and now" really opened up and at the same time limited by the promise—of a justice, a democracy, a Europe, an Other to-come? In other words, is messianism, understood as a certain experience of the promise, the only alternative to eschatology, teleology, and the end or progress of history? By emphasizing the logic and economy of spectrality over that of actual, material processes, and by unveiling the ghosts of hauntology behind the world of phenomena and events, does Derrida not end up chasing phantoms?

In that respect, I agree with Spivak's objection, which I presented earlier: the epistemic violence of the science of writing of modernity, rooted in Eurocentric phonocentrism and the metaphysics of presence, downplays if not marginalizes the capitalist imperialist project, rooted in the division of labor and the expansionist logic of market economies. Derrida is entirely aware of the risks of depoliticization and dilution involved in a return to Marx. This is what he writes toward the beginning of the book, and to clarify what he means by such a return:

> What risks happening is that one will try to play Marx off against Marxism so as to neutralize, or at any rate muffle the political imperative in the untroubled exegesis of a now canonical work [*une œuvre classée*]. One can sense a coming fashion or indulgence and affectation [*on sent venir une mode ou une coquetterie*] in this regard in the culture and more precisely in the university. . . . This recent stereotype would be destined, whether one wishes it or not, to depoliticize the Marxist reference, to do its best, by putting on a tolerant face, to neutralize a potential force, primarily by enervating a *corpus*, by silencing the *revolt* it contains [the return is acceptable provided that the *revolt*, which initially inspired uprising, indignation, insurrection, revolutionary momentum, does not come back]. People would be ready to accept the return of Marx or the return to Marx, on the condition that a silence is maintained about Marx's injunction not just to decipher but to act and to make the deciphering (the interpretation) into a transformation that "changes the world." . . . It is something altogether other that I wish to attempt here as I turn or return to Marx.[78]

How successful was he? In the end, it is difficult to see how he escapes the charges he himself formulates, how he avoids emptying Marx's text of what is most urgent and critical in it: a critique of political economy, of the role and function of money as abstraction, of the world-market and the endless exploitation of resources, of exploitation and other processes of subjectivization, of the common destiny of capital and technics. It is difficult to see how his quasi-transcendental reading of Marx is much more than a *coquetterie* of the kind he denounces. Furthermore, isn't crisis—the word, of course, but more importantly the combination of critical diagnosis, affectivity, and call for action it contains—precisely what makes a praxis-oriented reading and appreciation of Marx possible? By refusing to embrace crisis, or by reconfiguring it as a quasi-transcendental, does Derrida not fall prey to the very danger he identifies, and deprive himself of a critical-normative tool, the range of which, as I have tried to demonstrate, is significant? In Chapter 5, the final chapter, I want to show how the schema of crisis can be extended to the ecological emergency, yet only on the condition that we recognize its singularity, its specific *modus operandi* or regime.

5

Crises of Extinction, or Gaia in Peril

Let me take a step back. Following our intuitive, pre-theoretical understanding of "crisis," I began by identifying two types of crises. The first, "weak" type signals a deviation from an established norm. Following either a natural evolution or a series of targeted measures, we expect it to be followed by a return to its normal state. In the second, "strong" type, the norms of a given system come under greater pressure and can even be threatened. As a result, the system can require the invention of new norms. But I quickly refined that initial picture and adopted a threefold distinction, which also led me to speak of "regimes" of crisis. I spoke of crises of deviation, exception, and contradiction, which I associated with specific techniques of government (management, suspension, and revolution in the broad sense). The latter two are crises in the strong sense, whereas the former amounts to a weak form of crisis. Naturally, there is always room for dispute around the type of crisis we are confronted with, and therefore the kind of response it calls for. Much of today's politics—of politics *tout court*—revolves around such disputes; and I provided explanations for, and criticisms of, the contemporary resurgence and frequent use of the state of exception in response to a range of real or perceived crises. I also insisted on the intrinsically conservative nature of the technologies of management and suspension corresponding to crises of deviation and exception, and the potentially (or normatively) creative nature of crises of contradiction.

In this final chapter, I want to explore yet another (and final) regime of crisis, which I will define as *catastrophic*. The latter sense is illustrated (at least partly) by the current ecological crisis.[1] It is particularly complex, not least because it concerns the fate of complex systems, life being the most complex of all. But it is also complex because it can be seen from two different perspectives. On the one hand, it appears to be a crisis of contradiction of the severest kind: our phenomenal capacity to produce and innovate in the realms of science and technology has gone hand in hand with a no less formidable capacity to destroy natural environments and species and to modify the climate. Our omnipotence has turned out to be our own undoing. Yes, *Homo sapiens* became a Titan, and Prometheus a reality. However, our punishment for our hubris and foolishness comes not from the gods, but from the effects of our actions on the earth: our utopian project has hit a *physical* wall, one it can no longer push back or pretend does not exist. At the same time, and for reasons that will become clear, the environmental crisis is not simply or exclusively a crisis of contradiction. It is also a crisis of *extinction*. Not every crisis of contradiction leads to extinction. And not every extinction is the result of a crisis of contradiction. Naturally, in the context of the ecological crisis, extinction refers to the sixth great extinction of species on earth.[2] But it also refers to the threat of extinction of humanity itself.[3] Finally, and most importantly, it refers to the threat and possibly extinction facing not the norms, but the very normativity of the biosphere, by which I mean its ability to generate new norms in the face of the considerable problems and challenges it is currently facing. The ecological crisis, then, is a singular event insofar as it affects not, or not only, specific forms of life, but the very *conditions* of life, including our own. Although this chapter focuses on the ecological crisis, it is important to note from the outset that crises of collapse or extinction can also happen at the individual, existential level (in the case, say, of a deep and chronic depression), as well as at the political level. I have already referred to the situation—the genocidal war—in Palestine following the attacks of October 7, 2023. The evidence regarding the indiscriminate and widespread killing of over 50,000 innocent men, women, and children in Gaza, the forced displacement and concentration of 2 million Palestinians, the orchestration of famine, and the systematic destruction of Gaza's natural resources, farmland, water, electricity, and general infrastructure, is now overwhelming and indisputable.⁴ We can speak of a crisis of collapse, which affects not only Palestinian lives and bodies, but their material conditions of existence, by which I mean the possibility of survival. And in the case of what Said has called "the question of Palestine," the latest escalation of violence can be traced back to the founding *contradiction* of the Zionist project, for which Palestine is a land without a people, destined to be converted into a Jewish state, "without making it possible for the world to take seriously (or even later to know about) the natives' protests" and realize "the systematic repression of the Arab reality."⁵ This contradiction applies even to the "socialist" kibbutzim, which "were and are established on land confiscated from Arabs."⁶

From the start, I have argued that the concept of crisis involves a practical as well as a theoretical aspect. That is why I distinguished between forms of action corresponding to different types of crises. I spoke of practices of management, suspension, and uprising. In the context of the ecological crisis, the question of praxis is made more complex by the fact that human action is at the root of a problem of normativity affecting the conditions of life. The ecological crisis therefore requires that we act differently at the level not of a specific area of human life or experience—economic, political, legal—but of the conditions of life itself. It requires that we concern ourselves with, and care for, the transcendental-physical ground of human experience. Yet this form of action, I will argue, cannot happen without something like a conversion, by which I mean a profound transformation of our way of being, our attitude toward the world, the earth, and life on earth. Here, I suggest that we distinguish between revolution and conversion, if only to single out the specific form of response adequate to the crisis of extinction and the threat of collapse we are currently facing. I want to mobilize the no doubt historically and specifically religiously loaded notion of conversion to single out the attitude required to lift the hold we currently have on the normativity of the biosphere and on the earth's ecosystems. I suggest we understand the notion of conversion in its etymological sense—that is, as a change of direction or course, a turning or pivoting away from a voluntaristic and conquering attitude, a will to control and subjugate, and toward a letting-be. We need to let go of our stranglehold on the earth. Instead of governing nature, as we have done for so long, we need to learn to govern ourselves *with* it, seal a new alliance with nature, or establish what Michel Serres called a "natural contract," based on the ideas of symbiosis and reciprocity between the human world and nature.[7] Far from encouraging passivity, this new covenant with nature signals a different kind of engagement, which can manifest itself in political and legal action, in acts of resistance, and in simpler, more disengaged forms of life. *Gelassenheit*, to use the old mystical term, is a good strategy for inhabiting the world differently and beginning to affect the norms of life positively.

Facing the Catastrophe

For millennia, human beings assumed the permanence of the earth and the everlasting nature of the elemental, most elegantly expressed by Percy Bysshe Shelley two hundred years ago:

> The everlasting universe of things
> Flows through the mind, and rolls its rapid waves,
> Now dark—now glittering—now reflecting gloom—
> Now lending splendour, where from secret springs
> The Source of human thoughts its tributes brings
> Of waters—with a sound but half its own,
> Such as a feeble brook will oft assume,
> In the wild woods, among the mountains lone,
> Where waterfalls around it leap for ever,
> Where woods and winds contend, and a vast river
> Over its rocks ceaselessly bursts and raves.[8]

Today we can only read those lines with a certain nostalgia. The world they describe is under threat: our fresh waters are polluted and sometimes dying; the waterfalls do not "leap forever," and we can no longer take for granted the "everlasting" universe of things.[9]

Now contrast Shelley's lines with Professor Challenger's earth experiments in Conan Doyle's *When the World Screamed*, written a century after *Mont Blanc*.[10] By having his two assistants insert an electrified iron dart into its "sensory cortex" (p. 613) or "nerve ganglion" (p. 614), Professor Challenger, a "bullying megalomaniac" (p. 597) and alpha male who wants to force the earth to acknowledge his existence and power (p. 593), also endangers the earth's offspring. This is how the professor's assistant narrates the episode:

> At the same time our ears were assailed by the most horrible yell that ever yet was heard. Who is there of all the hundreds who have attempted it who has ever yet described adequately that terrible cry? It was a howl in which pain, anger, menace, and the outraged majesty of Nature all blended into one hideous shriek. For a full minute it lasted, a thousand sirens in one, paralysing all the great multitude with its fierce insistence, and floating way through the still summer air until it went echoing along the whole South Coast and even reached our French neighbours across the Channel. No sound in history has ever equalled the cry of the injured Earth.

In retrospect, Professor Challenger's experiment can be read as a metaphor for the rape and agony—the vocabulary of penetration runs deep in the story—to which the earth has been subjected for over two hundred years. Conan Doyle represents "Mother Earth" as a kind of sea urchin, which means as a living body, but of a particular kind: on the one hand, it is a body without organs; on the other hand, it is the matrix for the emergence of all other life-forms. The professor appears as a Promethean figure, or a fictitious rendering of Francis Bacon, for whom Man (and not Woman) is the measure of all things. Drunk on his own will to power, Challenger is determined to carry out the Western technoscientific project. We recoil in horror when we read Conan Doyle's fiction, because we see it as the tale of a rationality gone mad and a warning not heard.

Specialists agree that the economic activity of human beings, especially under capitalism, has become the main driver of climate change and the rate of extinction of species. Ours is a world in which the demand for pointless goods and services, and the equally pointless jobs that help produce them, comes at a staggering and, we now realize, unaffordable ecological cost. Somewhere between the Anthropocene and the Capitalocene, things started to go terribly wrong.[11] There came a point when "Man" began affecting its own conditions of existence and habitability, when it began growing into a "significant and morphological force."[12] There came a point when human history and geological time became intertwined, when human history affected the biosphere itself, and therefore the conditions of life on earth. When did it all start? A very long time ago, with the appearance of *Homo faber*? A long time ago, with the beginning of agriculture in Mesopotamia, some 12,000 years ago?[13] Or perhaps more recently, with the industrial revolution and the patenting of the steam engine, which Marx hailed as the driver of industrial capitalism?[14] Or as late as 1945, when the spike in the processes unleashed by fossil fuel burning became so vividly apparent?[15] Finally, some, like Timothy Morton, seem to include several or all of them, whilst singling out "agrologistics," or the "agrologistic axiom" of the Fertile Crescent, as the main culprit, and the defining feature of our present.[16] We are all Mesopotamians, he claims.[17] This lack of clarity and agreement alone could militate in favor of calling the phenomenon in question not the Anthropocene—as it is not *anthropos* as such or as a whole, but a moment of its history, which is at stake—but the the *agrocene*, or the *capitalocene*.[18] Or perhaps the *androcene*, as ecofeminists suggest.[19] While those terms are all legitimate, insofar as they help us understand the nature of the catastrophic event we are currently experiencing, I will prefer to speak of the *Technocene*. The climatic and environmental catastrophe, I argue, is attributable to the emergence and history of a global, predatory, resource-hungry, shortsighted, ultra-productivist and consumerist, technology-driven—and yes, essentially masculine—humanity.

Though a natural phenomenon, climate change has accelerated as a result of human systems of production and consumption, combined with rapid population growth.[20] Soil erosion and land degradation,[21] the rise of global temperatures due to the increase of CO_2 in the atmosphere,[22] and the increased rapidity, number, and intensity of extreme meteorological events are some of the consequences of the current techno-capitalist scheme, which threatens life on Earth as we know it. Capitalism, we saw, is a system full of contradictions, the most patent of which is arguably its relation to the environment: capitalism relies on nature, which it uses as a sink—an endlessly exploitable reserve of resources—as well as a depository in which it dumps its waste. To secure its growth and expansion, capitalism extracts raw materials, mostly from developing countries, and creates new markets. In the process, it disrupts social relations of production and exchange by securing access to cheap labor, privileging large companies over small local firms, and encouraging long circuits of production over short ones;[23] by promoting intensive, industrialized agriculture—monoculture practices with a massive use of fertilizers and pesticides, which, after an initial and remarkable burst of productivity, destroy biodiversity and lead to soil degradation;[24] by disrupting the lives and ways of life of local communities;[25] by introducing a vicious circle between climate change, droughts, land degradation, and migration.[26] Our economy and the rationality that underpins it are basically at war with our ecosystem. As the now often-quoted complex systems engineer Brad Werner said ten years ago, global capitalism "has made the depletion of resources so rapid, convenient and barrier-free that 'earth-human systems' are becoming dangerously unstable in response."[27] Or, as Jason W. Moore puts it, capitalism can be seen as "a 'world-ecology' in which the endless accumulation of capital, the pursuit of power, and the coproduction of nature form an organic whole."[28] Moore also notes how, throughout its history, capitalism has been able to overcome the natural limits of its own ecosystem by locating, producing, and dominating low-cost natural areas from outside its own system.[29]

This intensive, hyper-productivist, and polluting model is one that was also adopted by communist regimes around the world, which sought (and ultimately failed) to compete with capitalist societies. As it turned out, Stakhanov "the hero of socialist labor" and Andrew Carnegie "the self-made man" were two sides of the same coin, two faces of the same Titanic project.[30] Both were heroes of competing epics of productivity, expressions of the triumph of technology in the form of "total mobilization."[31] This is a reality that Walter Benjamin understood very early on. In his "Theses on the Philosophy of History" (1935), already mentioned, he notes the infatuation of the German working class with technological developments and the "illusion" of technological progress as a political achievement.[32] In that attitude, he sees a secularized form of the old Protestant work ethic. He mentions the Gotha Congress of 1875, which united the two German Socialist parties, one led by Ferdinand Lassalle, the other by Karl Marx and Wilhelm Liebknecht. The program, drafted by Lassalle and Liebknecht, was severely and famously attacked by Marx in London.[33] Benjamin is also critical of the program's "vulgar-Marxist" definition of labor as "the source of all wealth and all culture." He quotes Josef Dietzgen's subsequent proclamation, according to which "the savior of modern times is called work." The problem with this "conformist" view of labor is that it reinforces rather than questions that of Social Democracy: progress, it claims, resides in the mastery of nature. To that extent, and more importantly still, "it already displays the technocratic features later encountered in Fascism." Unlike the Socialist utopias that inspired the revolution of 1848, the "new" conception of labor "amounts to the exploitation of nature, which with naïve complacency is contrasted with the exploitation of the proletariat." It is as if one form of exploitation could redeem another. The view, expressed by Dietzgen, according to which nature "exists gratis" is "a complement to the corrupted conception of labor." Of course, one could reverse the proposition and claim that the corrupted, "Gotha" vision of labor is itself the complement of a technocentric view of nature. Benjamin contrasts this "positivistic conception" of labor with Fourier's utopian "fantasies," so often the object of ridicule, yet ultimately "surprisingly sound." Fourier's *cooperative* vision of labor, which I mentioned in Chapter 3, "illustrates a kind of labor which, far from exploiting nature, is capable of delivering her of the creations which lie dormant in her womb as potentials." In the *thesis* I just quoted, Benjamin identifies a common element in the Social Democratic, Socialist, and Fascist view regarding the nature of labor and its relation to nature as pure resource and sink. Without using the term, he points to what I call the Technocene.

The Technocene is currently experiencing its own end, or completion, in the form of a formidable force that has turned against the humanity that generated it. We have created a largely autonomous dynamic—a Monster—that threatens the material conditions of human life, and of many other forms of life. As Günther Anders put it over forty years ago, our technological age is one in which "we tirelessly pursue the production of our own destruction [*die Produktion unseres eigenen Unterganges pausenlos betreiben*]."[34] It is as if, starting with the industrial revolution, yet unbeknownst to us, we had placed a ticking time bomb under the seat of our system of production—a bomb composed principally of carbon dioxide, nitrogen oxides, and methane, and which is now detonating, its conflagration affecting every corner of our planet. The writing has been on the wall for quite some time. Confused and terrified, we look at this monster and mutter: "What have we done?" This is where the other side or sense of crisis comes into play, where the crisis of contradiction morphs into a crisis of extinction. However serious and whatever their domain, the crises of contradiction I have analyzed thus far did not exclude the possibility of another normality, another set of norms, another paradigm or consensus. On the contrary: the crises in question, be they economic, political, scientific, aesthetic, or existential, called for the creation of new norms and the emergence of new forms of life. As we saw, revolution in the broadest sense seeks not merely to destroy a given order, but to replace it with a better one. In the case of the ecological crisis, we face a different and hitherto unknown experience. As Françoise d'Eaubonne, the French mother of "ecofeminism," once claimed, we have reached the point when we need to "change the world not to better it [*l'améliorer*], but *so that there might still be a world*."[35] The question of praxis—of what we can and must do—is now and for the first time oriented toward the world as such and as a whole.

In the 1983 preface to the English edition of *The Imperative of Responsibility*, Hans Jonas warns his reader in very similar terms against the deleterious effects of the Technocene on the biosphere. I quote him at length to emphasize the lucidity of his diagnosis, including the positive feedback loop of technological power on nature:

> Modern technology, informed by an ever-deeper penetration of nature and propelled by the forces of market and politics, has enhanced human power beyond anything known or even dreamed of before. It is a power over matter, over life on earth, and over man himself; and it keeps growing at an *accelerated pace*. Its unfettered exercise for about two centuries now has raised the material estate of its wielders and main beneficiaries, the industrial "West," to heights equally unknown in the history of mankind. Not even the ravages of two world wars—themselves children of that overbrimming power—could slow the upward surge for long; it even gained from the spin-off of the technological war effort in its aftermath. . . . But lately, the other side of the triumphal advance has begun to show its face. . . . Not counting the insanity of a sudden, suicidal atomic holocaust, which *sane fear can avoid with relative ease*, it is the slow, long-term, cumulative—the peaceful and constructive use of worldwide technological

> power, a use in which all of us collaborate as captive beneficiaries, through rising production, consumption, and sheer population growth—that poses threats much harder to counter. The net total of these threats is the *overtaxing of nature*, environmental and (perhaps) human as well. *Thresholds may be reached* in one direction or another, *points of no return*, where processes initiated by us will run away from us on their own momentum—and toward disaster.[36]

Jonas also speaks of "the so-called greenhouse effect of continued immoderate burning of fossil fuels," of "the catastrophic climatic changes [that] could be caused by the heating up of the atmosphere, with melting of the polar ice caps." Thus, he concludes, "the happy-go-lucky feast of a few industrial centuries could be paid for with millennia of altered terrestrial nature."[37]

The climate and environmental crisis that defines our time is unusual and extreme in that it affects not just our ability, but the ability of the biosphere itself, to do what it has done for billions of years: namely, to meet pressures and challenges of all kinds by creating new norms. It is a crisis not of norms, but of normativity. When I say crisis, I do not mean that the biosphere, and life more specifically, have lost entirely their ability to generate new norms, to adapt to the changing and increasingly challenging circumstances to which they are subjected. As we'll see, the biosphere is a highly resilient and resourceful system, entirely indifferent to the survival of the human species; and it will, until the time of its programmed death from overheating in about one billion years, continue to adapt to the increasing pressures thrown at her: a large portion of the earth's organisms are "extremophiles," such as lichens and bacteria, which can endure and indeed thrive under almost unimaginable conditions. This is how Merlin Sheldrake puts it: "Recent finding from the Deep Carbon Observatory report that more than half of all Earth's bacteria and archaea—so-called 'infra-terrestrials'—exist kilometres below the planet's surface, where they live under intense pressure and extreme heat. . . . Lichens are no less impressive. In the hottest, driest parts of the earth's deserts, you'll find lichens prospering as crusts on the scorched ground."[38] Similarly, and in the words of George Monbiot, "the self-organized, adaptive world that microbes, plants and animals build to suit themselves helps to explain soil's extraordinary resilience in the face of droughts and floods: it survives crises that would otherwise reduce it to amorphous powder."[39] Yet the biosphere's ability to generate new norms is being *eroded* and *tested* because of human activity. This erosion translates into an unprecedented rate of extinction and increase of constraints and pressures on the remaining species, including the human species, with the physiological, social, and political consequences we already recognize. The pressures and challenges are in themselves or in their nature nothing new: as climate and environmental negationists rightly claim, climate has always gone through dramatic changes, and species have always gone extinct (whilst other species appear). But that is not the issue: the (twofold) issue is the speed at which this phenomenon takes place, or the rate of acceleration of those transformations, as well as the (now unquestionable) human factor in this acceleration. Extinction is indeed the horizon, as the rate of reproduction and mutation of species continues to fall behind the rate of extinction: the conditions of emergence and sustainability of life are increasingly negatively affected. In this instance, crisis affects the very conditions of normativity itself. But it does so as a result of the earth and the biosphere having become sensitive to the actions of a single species, our own. The "human" factor, and its until recently unimaginable disruptive power, is what's at stake. This, I believe, is what Greta Thunberg has in mind when she writes:

> "This is the new normal" is a phrase we often hear when the rapid changes in our daily weather patterns—wildfires, hurricanes, heatwaves, floods, storms, droughts and so on—are being discussed. . . . But this is not "the new normal." What we are seeing now is only the very beginning of a climate change, caused by human emissions of greenhouse emissions. Until now, Earth's natural systems have been acting as a natural shock absorber, smoothing out the dramatic transformations that are taking place. But the planetary resilience that has been so vital to us will not last forever, and the evidence seems to suggest more and more clearly that we are entering a new era of more dramatic change.

> Climate change has become a crisis sooner than expected. . . . The climate and ecological crisis is not happening in some faraway future. It's happening right here and right now.[40]

I call this ultimate level of crisis *catastrophic*. It corresponds to the crossing of a negative *and* irreversible critical threshold, which signals the system's imminent *collapse*. A complex system collapses when the conditions under which it finds itself are such that its self-organizing properties, which up until that critical point had secured its stability, now have the opposite effect: pushed toward a threshold, the system behaves increasingly chaotically, and eventually collapses, often also triggering the collapse of other systems with which it interacts. This is what began to happen to the financial system in 2008: had it not been for the global bailout amounting to trillions of dollars, which brought the system back into a safer, more stable state, the chain reaction that affected the financial institutions, strongly linked to each other by a similar aggressive risk model based around securitization and derivatives trading, would have precipitated the system into the abyss. But this is also what happens today to ecosystems around the world, from glaciers to the Gulf Stream and the Amazon forest. And it happens because of human activity. In the last fifty years, the world's soy production, three-quarters of which is fed to farm animals, has increased at an extraordinary rate.[41] This has resulted in the destruction of the remarkably rich and varied ecosystems of the *cerrado* (savannah) of central Brazil, and of the Gran Chaco forests in Paraguay and Argentina.[42] This is how Monbiot describes the critical threshold those vast areas are approaching:

> When trees are felled, their long roots no longer draw water from the aquifers and release it into the air. As water vapour reduces while temperatures rise, dew, which is essential to the survival of many wild plants and animals, stops forming. This triggers a cycle of collapse that might lead to the tipping and entire hysteresis of the entire ecosystem by the middle of the century, to be replaced by desert.[43]

A collapsing world is the new reality we face. But under no circumstance can we call it "the new normal."

The Facts

On July 25, 2019, in the midst of a major heat wave and record temperatures in Europe, the media reported on the most authoritative global warming study thus far.[44] Three studies published in *Nature* and *Nature Geoscience* used extensive historical data to show there has never been a period in the last 2,000 years when temperature changes have been as fast and extensive as in recent decades. According to the lead author of the study, scientific consensus that humans are causing global warming is likely to exceed 99 percent. In other words, global warming is a certainty, and human responsibility in the manufacturing of this crisis is also a certainty. The summer of 2021 was worse: records were broken in northern and southern Europe (34°C in Finland, 48°C in Sicily), North America (49.6°C in Lytton, Canada, and 46.1°C in Portland, Oregon), and Siberia.[45] And the late spring and summer of 2022 in the northern hemisphere were even worse, with temperatures hitting 40°C in Britain, 42°C in southwest France, 46°C in Spain and Portugal, and over 50°C in several cities in Pakistan. 2023 was the hottest year ever recorded, until the record was broken the following year. The world is on fire. Literally. From the northwest to the southwest of the American continent, from Greece to Siberia, fires are raging everywhere, destroying hundreds of millions of hectares. At the same time, the world is subject to extraordinary and devastating floods. The summer of 2021 saw torrential rains flood Germany, Belgium, the Netherlands, and Luxembourg. India, Pakistan, Bangladesh, South Africa, and eastern Australia suffered terrible floods in the spring and summer of 2022. The case of Pakistan is particularly striking: as a result of an exceptionally violent monsoon season and melting glaciers (Pakistan has the second largest amount of glaciers in the world), a third of the country was under water by September 2022. Fifteen hundred people had died—nearly half of them children—and more than 33 million people had been displaced. In April and May 2022, Iraq and other neighboring countries suffered repeated and extreme sandstorms, due to soil degradation, intense droughts, deforestation, overgrazing, and overuse of river water. Thousands were hospitalized after experiencing respiratory problems. Schools, public buildings, and airports shut down. In October 2024, following three years of drought and water restrictions, southeastern Spain suffered an intense cold drop which resulted in severe flooding and 230 deaths.

The sixth report of the French Groupe d'Experts Intergouvernmental sur l'Évolution du Climat (GIEC), which covered the period between 2015 and 2023, estimated that the +1.5°C threshold in relation to pre-industrial times (1850–1900), and one of the climate "tipping points," would be crossed in the 2030s.[46] In fact, it was crossed in the summer of 2024. In addition, the current trajectory of emissions would bring us to +3°C this century, and as early as 2050. Even if all countries were to achieve their 2015 Paris Agreement targets, average global temperatures are on track to rise 2.7 degrees Celsius by the end of the century—1.2 degrees over the goal. Finally, reports highlight the irreversibility of certain phenomena, such as the rise of sea levels and the melting of icebergs. As a result of climate change and widespread deforestation, the Amazon is also close to a tipping point. It is losing its ability to recover from disturbances like droughts, and fast approaching a critical threshold beyond which much of it will be replaced by grassland, with severe *further* consequences for global climate change, in what amounts to positive feedback. Losing the rainforest could add up to 90 billion tons of carbon dioxide to the atmosphere—the equivalent of several years' worth of global emissions.[47] All this evidence is corroborated by, and summarized in, the 2021 "Summary for Policymakers" of the Report of the IPCC (Intergovernmental Panel on Climate Change).[48] The report begins by stating the "unequivocal" human responsibility for global warming and the "widespread and rapid changes in the atmosphere, ocean, cryosphere and biosphere" caused by human action (A.1). The *scale* of such changes across the climate system as a whole and the present state of many aspects of the climate are unprecedented over many centuries to many thousands of years (A.2). For example (A.2.1), in 2019, atmospheric CO_2 concentrations were higher than at any time in at least 2 million years (*high confidence*), and concentrations of CH_4 (methane) and N_2O (nitrous oxide) were higher than at any time in at least 800,000 years (*very high confidence*). In addition, since 1750, increases in CO_2 (47 percent) and CH_4 (156 percent) concentrations far exceed the natural multi-millennial changes observed between glacial and interglacial periods over at least the last 800,000 years (*very high confidence*). Major disruptions to weather patterns (heatwaves, heavy rains, droughts, tropical cyclones) due to human activity, already noted in the previous report (2014), have intensified.[49]

The destruction of biodiversity is also sobering. In October 2022, it was announced that Earth's wildlife populations have plunged by an average of 69 percent between 1970 and 2018 (in 2014, the figure stood at 60 percent).[50] Latin America and the Caribbean region, including the Amazon, have seen the steepest decline in average wildlife population size, with a 94 percent drop in forty-eight years. The rate of extinction of species in the last one hundred years has been multiplied by one hundred. The current, so-called sixth mass extinction is largely due to the impact of human activity on soils, land, forests, air quality, and climate: for the first time in the history of our planet, a single species, representing 0.01 percent of existing species, threatens the stability and viability of this shared ecosystem.[51] In her unsettling book, *The Sixth Extinction: An Unnatural History*, Elizabeth Kolbert establishes the following damning record:

> Today, amphibians enjoy the dubious distinction of being the world's most endangered class of animals; it's been calculated that the group's extinction rate could be as much as forty-five thousand times higher than the background rate. But extinction rates among many other groups are approaching amphibian levels. It is estimated that one-third of all reef building corals, a third of all freshwater mollusks, a third of sharks and rays, a quarter of all mammals, a fifth of all reptiles, and a sixth of all birds are headed toward oblivion. The losses are occurring all over: in the South Pacific and in the North Atlantic, in the Artic and the Sahel, in lakes and on islands, on mountaintops and in valleys. If you know how to look, you can probably find signs of the current extinction event in your own backyard.[52]

In the face of such facts, the very notion of "ecological crisis" seems like an understatement. Some, like Bill McGuire, who is emeritus professor of geophysical and climate hazards at University College London, prefer to speak of an all-pervasive climate *breakdown*: we have passed the point of no return and nothing we can do today has a realistic chance of keeping the rise of global temperatures to 1.5°C.[53] According to McGuire, a rise of 2°C will trigger increasingly lethal heatwaves in many parts of the world, extreme drought, devastating floods, reduced crop yields, rapidly melting ice sheets, and surging sea levels, as well as increasingly acidic oceans. As such, it is a serious threat to the global world order.[54] Bruno Latour, whom I already mentioned, holds a similar view: we are, he claims, past the point of crisis. The current *catastrophic* situation makes us nostalgic not only for Shelley's romantic experience of nature, but for crisis itself: "If only it were just a crisis! If only it had been just a crisis!"[55] Because we have "crossed a series of thresholds" and "lived through" disaster and devastation without even experiencing it, the vocabulary of crisis is no longer adequate to describe, define, and come to grips with the event we are facing.[56] It is more, I would say, a matter of a *hubris* that could end, Oedipus-style, in an act of self-inflicted blindness, so utterly useless has our vision turned out to be, so unable we have been to *see* what we were doing. Latour suggests that we speak instead of an "ecological mutation" and "profound alteration of our relation to the world."[57] This signals a significant departure from his earlier work, in which he embraced the notion of crisis, if only to define the current ecological crises not as crises of "nature" or "natural objects" (which he also defines as "modern" or "without risk," with clear essences and borders) but as crises of "objectivity," by which he means crises of objects to which a risk factor is attached systematically, and which need not be "natural."[58] His recent skepticism toward the notion of crisis as applied to the ecological disaster reflects the rate at which the latter is accelerating. And it confirms the analogy Lovelock draws between crossing a threshold of climate change, such as the melting of Arctic ice, and "the imagined experience of an astronaut unlucky enough to fall into a massive black hole." The astronaut passing through its point of no return, known as the event horizon, where gravity is so strong that not even light can escape, would be entirely unaware of what is happening. Similarly, "when we pass the threshold of climate change there may be nothing perceptible nothing to mark this crucial step, nothing to warn us that there is no returning."[59] Tipping points don't call attention to themselves.

Key Epistemic Concepts: Normativity, Plasticity, Symbiosis

Gaia Under Pressure

To be sure, because the sun, which heats Gaia, burns hotter as it ages, and does so by virtue of the accumulation of residual energy emitted by its core thermonuclear fusion reactions, there will come a time when the earth will no longer be hospitable to life. But until then, Gaia will do what she has done for over three billion years: namely, regulate its temperature to sustain habitability for whatever life-forms happen to be inhabiting it.[60]

However, doing so will be increasingly difficult for it, given the effects of human activity on the climate and the complex ecosystems that evolved to keep it relatively stable: "our adding carbon dioxide to the air and soon doubling its abundance is seriously destabilizing an Earth system already struggling to maintain the desired temperature."[61] But we don't only add greenhouse gases—carbon dioxide, methane, water vapor, ozone—to the air. We also replace natural ecosystems like forests with farmland, thus making the problem worse: we turn up the heat and at the same time remove the natural systems that help to regulate it. For that is what vegetation, clouds, and polar ice do: they bring the temperature down, keep Earth cool, and thus maximize the occupancy of its ecological niches. They are essential cooling mechanisms in the self-regulation of this dynamic, homeostatic system we call Earth, which includes physical, chemical, biological, and human components. Without them, and given its relative proximity to the sun (comparable to that of Venus), its surface temperature would be much higher (around 475°C) and therefore uninhabitable. But Earth's air conditioning is under threat. Consider the state of our oceans: the vast ecosystems, mostly algae, "which used to pump down carbon dioxide from the air, can no longer do so because the ocean turns to desert as it warms and grows more acidic."[62] Algae, Lovelock explains, "are unusually influential in Earth's climate: in addition to removing carbon dioxide, they are the source of the gas dimethyl sulphide, which oxidizes in the air to become the tiny nuclei that seed the droplets of clouds."[63] Marine heatwaves are increasingly frequent, resulting in the destruction of large canopy macroalgae and the increase of turf-forming macroalgae (seaweeds), thus contributing to the decrease of carbon burial and the rise of global temperatures.[64] Our forests are suffering an identical fate: whether through systematic deforestation or regular and ever-increasing wildfires, their ability to regulate the climate, store carbon, and provide a home to roughly 80 percent of the world's biodiversity is threatened.[65]

Each separate increase adds heat, and the sum of these increases *amplifies* the warming we cause. It is crucial to understand the physical reality behind this amplification process. All dynamic self-regulating systems will, "if sufficiently stressed, change from stabilizing negative feedback to destabilizing positive feedback. When this happens, they become amplifiers of change" and behave *chaotically*.[66] As Stuart Kauffman explains, "in the chaotic regime, similar initial states tend to become progressively more dissimilar, and hence to *diverge* farther and farther in state space, as each passes along its trajectory."[67] This is known as the butterfly effect, or sensitivity to initial conditions: small perturbations amplify with time. By contrast, Kauffman argues, in the ordered regime similar initial states become increasingly similar, converge, in what amounts to an expression of *homeostasis*. Concretely, and to return to the warming of the atmosphere, this means that, at a critical threshold of carbon dioxide in the atmosphere, a small increase of heat or carbon dioxide translates into a dangerous rise in temperature.[68] Put another way, such systems are not linear: the mathematical term "nonlinear," Lovelock explains, "implies that properties such as temperature are not directly proportional to others, such as carbon dioxide concentration, but are linked in ways that change with change."[69] This nonlinearity is what causes the transition from negative to positive feedback: at a certain critical point the sensitivity to initial conditions is no longer constant, but begins to fluctuate, thus calling into question the linear equations of most large climate models.

To be sure, far-from-equilibrium (or highly ordered) states tend toward (entropic) equilibrium *in the long run*. But this should not be interpreted as a goal, or even a "normal" outcome for systems that are far from equilibrium. As Kauffman explains, the increase in entropy in equilibrium systems— those closed to the exchange of matter and energy with their environment— stems from the statistical tendency of the system to pass through all possible arrangements (the so-called "ergodic" hypothesis) and eventually settle for a uniform distribution.[70] This is what we witness when we watch a drop of milk slowly and inevitably diffuse in a cup of tea, and never revert to its initial state: the molecules that move about entirely randomly in the cup will only move in the same direction accidentally, and in a way that is statistically insignificant. The consequence of the second law of thermodynamics is that, "in equilibrium systems, order—the most unlikely of the arrangements—tends to disappear."[71] Because entropy increases *irreversibly* in closed systems, we tend to think of the collapse of order as the natural outcome of any system. But the truth of the matter is that most natural (or cultural) systems are not closed, but open, not *at* but *far from* equilibrium: they unfold at the edge of chaos. At a (sometimes considerable) energetic cost, order can be, and in fact is, constantly generated *from* disorder.

Arguably the most obvious and spectacular examples of self-organized physical-chemical systems are living organisms, for which the environment is not a binary principle of conservation and/or elimination, but a disruptive force that drives life to adapt, diverge, and evolve. Following Stuart Kauffman's terminology, we can say that life unfolds "at the edge of chaos"—that is, in the *critical* region between supra- and subcriticality, or order and chaos. Today this region is under pressure, threatening the emergence of complexity and divergence.[72] With the climate and environmental crisis, we reach a threshold beyond which the biosphere's ability spontaneously to create order out of chaos is threatened, a threshold which imperils the supracritical behavior of the biosphere. If complexity theory is the search for the laws that govern the explosion of molecular diversity and complexity of the biosphere, collapse theory, as I understand it, analyzes the conditions under which, and pressure points at which, this explosion is threatened. It is concerned with the crossing of critical thresholds not from sub- to supracritical behaviors, but from supra- to subcritical.

Is Gaia Alive?

Unlike Professor Challenger, Lovelock stops short of categorizing Gaia as an actual organism. We know that the earth is not an organism, that it does not "live" in a biological sense. Yet we need to "imagine it as the largest living thing in the solar system," since it behaves "as if it were alive, at least to the extent that it regulates its climate and chemistry."[73] Lovelock is unapologetic about his use of images borrowed from the world of living things to help us understand it: Gaia is "a kind of living organism," a "superorganism composed of all life coupled with the air, the oceans, and the surface rocks."[74] Elsewhere, he compares "Mother Earth" to an old lady in declining health, an aging body which, like our own, and within limits, is able to regulate its own temperature and stay close to the right chemical composition for life.[75] He also compares it to an animal, and a camel in particular, which is able to regulate its body temperature at two different but stable states (at 40°C during daytime, when it is extremely hot in the desert, and at 34°C at night, when it gets very cold). As such, Gaia is perhaps best viewed as a giant body without organs, as the body that contains all living bodies, from bacteria to human beings, and generates the conditions of their emergence. Others agree: Coccia, for example, defines the earth "as a body formed of the bodies of all species, each of which lives off the life of others, and all of which are inseparable."[76]

However, neither the earth nor the biosphere can be referred to as organisms; and they need to be clearly distinguished from one another.[77] The earth provides the complex, self-organized system we call the biosphere with its material conditions of existence. The biosphere is a thermodynamic system, with the sun as its source of heat. To be more specific, it is a complex, open, dissipative system. Not all open systems are dissipative. A crystal, for example, is an open system, which contains within itself the ability to transform itself, through a process known as crystallization. Crystallization involves phase transitions of the first order, or the crossing of critical points, at which the order of the structure changes. And this process takes place as a result of the relation between the system and its environment. Yet this potential for self-transformation is not identical with, or sufficient to understand, evolution in the biological sense. To understand evolution and, more broadly, the emergence and mode of operation of the biosphere, we need to introduce the notion of dissipation. Yet, as Miquel emphasizes, even dissipation will not be sufficient to account for the specificity of the biosphere as a thermodynamic system.[78] Consider, Miquel says, the example of a dissipative structure, such as a flame: under certain circumstances, a thermodynamic system generates a specific, teardrop- or tongue-like form, which is that of the flame. But if the circumstances change—if, for example, the gas flow rate in a burner increases—the shape of the flame changes; it moves from a laminar to a turbulent flow. And if it rains, or if, through the activation of a fire extinguisher, carbon dioxide is sprayed on the flame, the flame disappears altogether. A Rayleigh-Bénard convection is yet another form spontaneously generated by specific dissipative systems, in which a plane layer of fluid is heated from below and cooled from above. At a certain point, the fluid develops a regular pattern, and continues to do so as long as the differential conditions remain within certain values. Convections of this kind are a major feature of the dynamics of the oceans and the atmosphere, as well as of the interior of stars and planets. As I've already indicated, the oceans and the atmosphere are distinctive features of Gaia which play a key role in its self-regulation. Without them, there would be no life. Yet they are not living organisms. In the case of both the flame and the Rayleigh-Bénard convection, we're dealing with critical points and thresholds, but of a different kind from those involved in crystallization: an entropic value is attached to the systems in question, and to the shapes they generate. Heat and heat exchange ("dissipation") are the defining dynamic elements. Yet those examples of open, dissipative systems are not sufficient to understand the singularity of the biosphere as a system, namely of evolution. The laminar or turbulent flows of the flame, the convections of oceans and the atmosphere can and do undergo changes. But they don't *evolve* in the biological sense of the term. To be sure, they are temporal phenomena, in that time is constitutive of what they are. But their temporality does not take the form of history, memory, or heredity. For that to happen, something quite different needs to take place. The dissipative system in question needs to transform itself, to alter its own liminal conditions; and those transformations, in turn, need to affect its dissipation, thus increasing its irreversibility. In other words, the system needs to become *creative*. And it becomes creative by increasing its plasticity and generating new constraints or norms.[79]

The biosphere presupposes the specific sun-earth assemblage, from which the oceans and the atmosphere emerged that keep it (for how long?) within a critical range of temperatures. As a result, it is subjected to certain *internal* constraints that define it as an open system and maintain it within a state of permanent dissipation and irreversibility. It is open not at the edges or the periphery, like a crystal or even a flame, but internally, and entirely. It is made up not of isolated critical points, corresponding to phase transitions, but of a critical space, or a space of criticality. It is *everywhere* critical, which means that its critical points are distributed across an entire field. Simondon defines this space as a "theatre," Deleuze as an "egg," and Coccia as a "cocoon" or "postnatal egg." The biosphere is constrained by feedback from the non-living environment. It is subjected to environmental constraints such as the composition of the atmosphere and the oceans, as well as the climate. Stuart Kauffmann, you will recall, puts it like this: life naturally *evolves* toward a regime that is poised *between* order and chaos, or between sub- and supra-criticality. Evolution unfolds *at the edge of chaos*, or in "the transitional region" (also referred to as a "phase transition") between those two states: "Just between, just near this phase transition, just at the edge of chaos, the most complex behaviors can occur—orderly enough to ensure stability, yet full of flexibility and surprise. Indeed, this is what we mean by complexity."[80] And the reason why complex systems unfold at the edge of chaos is because of the survival advantage that evolution represents.[81] Evolution is an inexhaustible source of variety and heterogeneity, a creative tension between contradictory points of view, which is never resolved. To be more precise: its resolution is always deferred, and this deferral is itself creative.

This is why, in biology, there isn't a state space (a set of all possible states) that would be given in advance, and within which we could trace evolutionary trajectories. No such space can be drawn in advance. No such trajectories can be predicted. This is what distinguishes life from, say, weather systems, which follow complex patterns that are increasingly well predicted. What there is, instead, is a virtual space, a reservoir of *plasticity* constantly fueled by the elements that compose the biosphere, and of which flowers and insects, with their power to transform any one form into another, are prime examples. Because it is able constantly to delay the conditions of its own individuation, through divergence and the internalization of its forces of dissipation, the biosphere never dies (until, that is, the sun becomes too hot for there to be any form of life). It does not even age. In some cases, it even does the opposite.

Turritopsis dohrii (or *Turritopsis nutricula*), a jellyfish capable of reversing its developmental cycle even after sexual reproduction, is a case in point.[82] When confronted by environmental adversity or stresses, *Turritopsis* can regress to its asexual, polyp state. The organism destroys a part of its body to take on another form. A twofold process takes place. On the one hand, the differentiated somatic cells of the sexual—"medusa"—stage degenerate, while the production of polyp cells is activated "by a set of undifferentiated reserve cells that were previously not irreversibly committed."[83] At the same time, it would appear that the already differentiated somatic cells of the medusa "transdifferentiate," or "change their commitment and gene expression or revert to undifferentiated cells."[84] This transformation, the scientists write, amounts to a true "ontogeny reversal" triggered in response to stress conditions or senescence. It is not, therefore, a matter of mere transformation, or metamorphosis. It is a matter of reversibility and rejuvenation. But this process of rejuvenation also takes place, and most evidently, through reproduction—that is, "through the constitution of a numerically different and autonomous body."[85] What rejuvenates is not the *form* that life takes at any point, but life as such. The future that life promises, but for which no trajectory can be drawn in advance, is "more than the logical or historical consequence of what has been."[86]

Structurally incomplete, always postponing the moment of its actualization, the biosphere's identity is through and through *virtual*. For that reason, at any given moment and unlike an engine or a chair, it is not more but less than the sum of its *actual* parts.

We saw how, to understand the singularity of the biosphere, we needed to introduce the notions of dissipation and evolution; and further to understand the singularity of evolution, and the mode of being of the biosphere, I introduced the notions of plasticity and normativity. Let me try and bring these key notions together. I mentioned that the biosphere is open not just to the outside and on its periphery, but to the core, through and through. This openness of the biosphere explains why it is constantly generating new forms of organization, which further increase its openness, in what amounts to a virtuous circle or regulative feedback loop. The internalization of the constraints of openness generates new constraints, which in turn generate further internalization. This, in turn, means that, unlike the flame, for example, what changes as a result of the dissipation of the biosphere is not simply its shape, but its norms. As a result of the internalization of dissipation, the biosphere constantly renews its norms. As a direct consequence of its permanent and specific mode of openness, it is able to invent new norms: autocatalysis,[87] cross-catalysis, membrane invagination, stocking of hereditary information in molecules, replication, respiration, photosynthesis, or technocratic. It is in a permanent critical state, or a state of extended criticality, which accompanies it at all times and provides it with the conditions of its own normativity—that is, of the renewal of its norms. The greater the plasticity of the biosphere, the greater its normativity. This is because evolution, through the process of natural selection, produces not convergence but divergence. Life selects not actual individuals—that is, fully individuated organisms—but specific characteristics or traits, which individuals carry. Those traits are more than the individuals in which they are embodied. They have a virtual existence, a future, outside of their particular individuation: their virtuality exceeds the field of complex, at times chaotic possibilities that govern nonlinear systems such as weather patterns, and which can be predicted. The individualized existence of life-forms does not exhaust their being. Natural selection, coupled with the principle of hereditary variation, maximizes the emergence of new norms. It is the greatest normative machine conceivable, the most ingenious generator of difference.

Symbiosis

In addition to the organisms that populate it and are defined by the hereditary variations they carry, the biosphere is constituted by relations of cooperation. In fact, cooperation is key to the normativity of the biosphere, or its ability to *invent* new norms. This dimension is emphasized in the literature on symbiosis, which explores the close relationships that form between unrelated organisms and often questions the epistemological framework of self-interest, zero-sum games, and winner-take-all competitions in evolutionary biology.[88] Before I give a few examples of symbiosis, it is worth noting that the idea of "symbiosis" is not new. It was coined in 1877 by the German botanist Albert Frank to describe the "living together" of fungal and algal partners in lichens.[89] That revolutionary and controversial idea was introduced in 1869 in a paper by the Swiss botanist Simon Schwendener. Lichens, he claimed, were not a single organism, but the *convergence* of two organisms, fungus and algae. The idea was met with fierce opposition on the part of the community of lichenologists and mycologists because, following Darwin's theory of evolution by natural selection, first published in 1859, it was assumed that species emerged by *diverging* from one another. According to Sheldrake, Schwendener's "dual hypothesis" challenged this view by claiming that, within lichens, "branches of the tree of life that had been diverging for hundreds of millions of years" were in fact "*converging*."[90] Soon after the publication of Frank's paper, another German botanist, mycologist, and plant pathologist, Heinrich Anton de Bary, adopted and generalized the term "symbiosis" "to refer to the full spectrum of interactions between different types of organism, from parasitism at one end to mutually beneficial relationships at the other."[91] He also forged the term "symbiont" to define the "living together of unlike organisms." Lichens became "a gateway organism to the idea of symbiosis," which soon included fungi, algae living inside coral and sponges, and even viruses within bacteria.[92] All of this is to say that the symbiotic turn, if not revolution, which began to take place in the late 1960s with the work of the American biologist Lynn Margulis and is today in full swing, is in fact the return of an idea that emerged a century before, and was repressed as a result of a rigid and narrow interpretation of Darwin's idea of evolution through natural selection, one that privileged competition and conflict over collaboration. Collaboration does not exclude competition, and should not be mistaken for moral, anthropocentric values such as altruism or disinterestedness: every living thing is *interested* in living on, and living better. It is the tendency to live better, be healthier, or increase its own power, which pushes life to pursue certain connections and seek assemblages. In emphasizing those interactions, I am therefore not introducing anthropocentric, and specifically moral categories in biological life. But, following a Spinozist line, I am claiming that certain kinds of cooperation or assemblages between species can be mutually beneficial, can translate into an increase in health and flourishing, in the same way that cooperatives are beneficial to workers and society.

In 1967, Margulis argued that "some of the most important moments in evolution had resulted from the coming together—and staying together—of different organisms."[93] Eukaryotes, or multicellular organisms, she claims, are the product of such a process: they arose "when a single-celled organism absorbed a bacterium, which continued to live symbiotically within it."[94] This means that all multicellular organisms, from plants to animals and fungi, arose from this case of indigestion. Mitochondria, which are the structures where the energy required by the cell is produced, were the descendants of these bacteria. And chloroplasts, which are the equivalent structure in plants, and where photosynthesis happens, were the descendants of photosynthetic bacteria that had been absorbed by an early eukaryotic cell. In the early 1950s, Lederberg and his graduate student Zinder demonstrated that bacteria can acquire genes horizontally (they called it "transduction").[95] Margulis set out to show that single-celled organisms had acquired entire bacteria. Evolution, she suggested, happens not simply vertically and through many generations, but horizontally and symbiotically, which also means (in evolutionary time) rather suddenly.[96] Margulis's basic idea—the endosymbiotic theory, as it came to be known—was vigorously opposed, and at times viciously attacked.[97] Today it is acclaimed as "one of the great achievements of twentieth-century evolutionary biology" and "one of the most beautiful ideas ever encountered."[98]

As it turns out, symbiosis is everywhere. Life as we know it is divided into three domains: eukarya, bacteria, and archaea. Like bacteria, archaea are single-celled microbes. Together, they are referred to as prokaryotes. Eukaryote-prokaryote symbioses with animals, particularly insects, are already well documented: the cells of some insects are inhabited by bacteria that themselves contain bacteria. Assemblages of a host and the many other species living in and around it are known as "holobionts" (as well as "symbionts"). The flagellate *Mixotricha paradoxa*, which lives in the gut of an Australian termite, *Mastotermes darwiniensis*, is one such (and often discussed) holobiont.[99] Symbioses in the microbial world have also been receiving a lot of attention lately. Again Lynn Margulis was a pioneer: today's molecular tools for the study of microbial communities confirm her now decades-old intuition about the mutualistic interactions in ecology and evolution.[100] Symbiotic relations between bacteria and plants, or bacteria and marine animals, are particularly worth mentioning.

The microbial communities that inhabit sponges and constitute a third of their biomass are able to fix carbon and contain proteins that mediate interactions between microbes and their host. Similar interactions take place in coral-reef ecosystems, populated by highly diverse and truly mutualist microbial communities, now under threat as a result of climate-change-induced ocean acidification and warming. Other examples include the diminutive Hawaiian bobtail squid, *Euprymna scalopes*, and its bacterial symbionts, *Vibrio fischeri*. Following the research of the marine invertebrate biologist and biochemist McFall-Ngai, Haraway describes the symbionts as "essential for the squid's constructing its ventral pouch that houses luminescing bacteria, so that the hunting squid can look like a starry sky to its prey below on dark nights, or appear not to cast a shadow on moonlit nights."[101]

Recently, the idea of the "biological individual," on which genetics, immunology, evolution, development, anatomy, and physiology have relied for decades, has come under criticism. Recent developments in nucleic acid analysis reveal the magnitude of symbiotic events and the extent to which such interactions blur the boundaries that heretofore had characterized the biological individual.[102] Gilbert, Sapp, and Tauber dispute the legitimacy of that notion at every level—anatomical, developmental, physiological, genetic, immunological, evolutionary. For example, referring to the Australian termite, *Mastotermes darwiniensis*, already mentioned, they write:

> How can a worker termite be considered an individual when it is the hive that is the reproductive unit of the species, and the worker cannot even digest cellulose without its gut symbiont, *Mixotricha paradoxa*, which is itself a genetic composite of at least five other species? Neither humans, nor any other organism, can be regarded as individuals by *anatomical* criteria. To capture this complexity, the term "holobiont" has been introduced as the anatomical term that describes the integrated organism comprised of both host elements and persistent populations of symbionts. (Rosenberg et al. 2007)[103]

Or, turning now to *developmental* individuality, and to the example of the newborn of the squid *Euprymna scalopes*, which lacks a light organ yet develops one in cooperation with the luminescent bacteria *Vibrio fischeri*, also already mentioned, the authors remark that "without the bacteria, the organ does not develop."[104] Development, they claim, is largely "a matter of interspecies communication."[105] In addition, the classical *physiological* view of animal individuality as an organism made of parts corresponding to a strict division of labor, which cooperate for the good of the whole, is challenged by a growing body of evidence. This "physiological division of labor," as Gilbert, Sapp and Tauber call it, is also performed by different species living together, as we have already seen in the case of various symbioses involving fungi, lichen, bacteria, or algae. The classical view of the immune individual or "self" as a system of defense against a hostile exterior world or pathogenic agents (worms, protists, fungi, bacteria, and viruses) is also radically questioned by recent studies showing that "an individual's immune system is in part created by the resident microbiome."[106] Finally, and perhaps most importantly, symbiotic associations force evolutionary biology to consider the idea of not individual but group selection, "so abhorrent to neo-Darwinian sensibilities, and so denigrated by sociobiologists' conceptions based on game theory."[107] Darwinists normally consider genes or monogenomic associations to be the object of natural selection. This is what, for them, counts as an individual. But we saw how organisms are multigenomic and multispecies complexes. Is it possible, Gilbert, Sapp and Tauber ask, "that organisms are *selected* as multigenomic associations? Is the fittest in life's struggle the multispecies group, and not an individual of a single species in that group?"[108] Drawing on the most recent literature, the authors show that in a number of cases, involving insects, squid, and mammals, "the coevolution of host and symbiont" enables the immune system—a clear marker for evolutionary advantage—"to facilitate the endosymbiotic relationship."[109] In other words, "Immunity does not merely guard the body against other hostile organisms in the environment; it also mediates the body's participation in a community of 'others' that contribute to its welfare. . . . The immune system has learned through evolution which organisms to exclude and kill, and which organisms to encourage, allow entry, and support."[110] Immunity requires that we acknowledge the socializing and unifying force of the whole, or the holobiont, in evolution. If it is an "individual" or "self," it is a dynamic and context-dependent one.

The mycosphere provides another remarkable illustration of symbiosis at work. It designates a specific region of this complex, self-organized, spatially and temporally finely differentiated system known as soil. It is estimated that over 80 percent of plants establish symbiosis with specific fungi, "which provide them with nutrients from the soil, such as nitrogen or phosphorous," as well as zinc and copper, "in exchange for energy-giving sugar and lipids produced in photosynthesis—the process by which plants eat light and carbon dioxide from the air."[111] Fungi also provide plants "with water and help them survive drought."[112] This is a trading relationship, in which different needs are negotiated; neither plant nor fungus dictates the terms of the relationship. Commenting on the research of Toby Kiers, a professor at Vrije Universiteit Amsterdam who investigates how plants and fungi maintain their "balance of power," Sheldrake notes that "between them, they are able to strike compromises, resolve trade-offs and deploy sophisticated trading strategies."[113] This is what we would call a partnership.

Plants don't only interact with fungi. They also interact with one another *through* fungi, or, more precisely, through what's known as the "mycelium," which is also referred to as the "mycorrhizal network," the "Earth's natural internet" (Paul Stamets), or the "Wood Wide Web" (German forester Peter Wohlleben).[114] The mycelium is a vast, underground fungal superhighway that connects the roots of individual plants, and allows substances (energy-rich carbon compounds, nitrogen, phosphorus, and water) to pass between them. Sheldrake describes this transport and communication network as "ecological connective tissue, the living seam by which much of the world is stitched together."[115] It does many things: it is the glue that holds soils together; it increases the volume of water the soil can absorb; it supports intricate food webs by allowing carbon to flow through its channels; depending on the ecological "fit," it *can* increase the quality of a harvest and make crops less susceptible to drought and heat; it sustains the life of an unimaginable quantity of bacteria, protists, insects, and arthropods contained in just a teaspoon of healthy soil.[116] But it can also be used in many different ways: first, its appetite is such that it decomposes just about anything, including highly toxic pollutants, which no other life-form is able to break down (this is known as "mycoremediation"); but it is also, and increasingly, a clean and sustainable alternative to a range of building materials, from plastics (especially polystyrene) to leather, brick, concrete, and particle board ("mycrifabrication").[117]

At every level, in every region, soil reveals examples of symbiosis and mechanisms of cooperation aimed at maintaining its equilibrium. Soil is not a homogeneous, undifferentiated mass, but, in the words of Monbiot, "a cosmopolitan city of zones and structures, in which distinct cultures inhabit adjacent parishes," each performing specific functions and responding to the needs and calls of its neighbors.[118] I have already mentioned the rhizosphere, which consists of the narrow wards surrounding the roots of plants. The rhizosphere, Monbiot writes, "lies outside the plant, but it is as essential to its health and survival as the plant's own tissues."[119] Scientists see it as the plant's external gut.[120] Like the human gut, the rhizosphere's microbes break down organic material into the simpler compounds the plant can absorb. But it also helps to protect the plant from disease by creating a defensive ring around the root and attacking invading pathogens through the multiplication of beneficial bacterial species. Other critical regions of soil include the myrmecosphere, or the ant borough, and the drilosphere, or the earthworm zone. The burrows of earthworms aerate the soil and help water to trickle through it. They limit and even halve the rate of soil erosion. But, in reversed conditions, they can make the soil less porous by bringing loose soil to the surface. They can pull down into their burrows almost all the leaves and stems and twigs that fall on the ground. The bacteria that live in their guts help digest them, and some species then excrete everything they can't absorb onto the surface of the soil, in the form of casts. Because of the organic material they eat, their casts are much richer in minerals than the rest of the soil. By grinding up dead plants, they make their nutrients available to bacteria and fungi, which in turn make them available to living plants.[121] Earthworms also "release plant growth hormones," and "make plants more resistant to parasitic nematodes and sucking insects, either by unlocking nutrients or by triggering their immune system with chemical signals. In turn, plants might use their chemicals to control the behaviour of worms."[122] Soil is thus a multiplicity of worlds folded into one another, a vast cosmopolis populated by earthworms, roots, and fungi. Together, Monbiot writes, they create "clumps of soil, glued together with the fibers and sticky chemicals they make, called aggregates"; and "within these aggregates, tiny animals like mites and springtails create smaller clumps"; and within them, "bacteria and their microscopic predators such as tardigrades, ciliates, and amoebas form still smaller aggregates."[123] Worlds within worlds within worlds. By creating these aggregates, microbes "stabilize the soil and assemble habitats for themselves. Over time, this process builds an ever more complex architecture: pores and passages through which water, oxygen, and nutrients can pass."[124] In other words, "soil organizes itself spontaneously into a multiplicity of coherent worlds," and this self-organized cooperation between microbes, plants, and worms "helps to explain soil's astonishing structural resilience in the face of droughts and floods," its ability to survive "crises that would otherwise reduce it to amorphous powder."[125]

Monbiot's point, which I translate into my own conceptual framework, is that soil—but the same can be said of the biosphere more generally—is remarkably resilient in the face of natural crises. This, as I have argued, is a function of evolution—of its plasticity, normativity, and virtual resources. Now it is precisely this remarkable architecture that is threatened when artificial chemicals are massively and systematically introduced in the soil:

> When farmers or gardeners apply nitrogen fertilizer under certain conditions, the microbes in the soil respond by burning through the carbon in the soil, much of which is stored in or by the microbes that build the catacombs. Without cement, the structures—and the system—begin to disintegrate. The pores cave in. The passages collapse. Oxygen and water can no longer permeate.[126]

We have reached the *critical* point at which this bio-normativity is called into question. This is what we mean when we talk about the ecological crisis: namely, a crisis not just of norms, but of normativity itself, of the biosphere's ability to continue to do what it has done for three billion years. Through their action, and therefore their own normativity, human beings have endangered the biosphere's capacity to generate its own constraints, and have thereby threatened the vital space of criticality itself. We, one critical point within the biosphere, have brought about the crisis of bio-criticality. We thought we were the invisible hand of progress, the instrument of the kingdom of ends, the chosen creature in a hidden theodicy. We thought of ourselves as the clever species. But the tragic joke is on us: with all the CO_2 and CH_4 we've been spewing into the atmosphere, with all the forests and savannas we've decimated to raise and feed cattle, with all the insecticides and pesticides with which we've been spraying our fields and crops, and the staggering volumes of water and fertilizers we've had to use to sustain our hybrid, intensive, yet increasingly unproductive agriculture, with all the polymers that end up in our oceans, we were just pulling the rug out from under our own feet, and the feet of a staggering number of other species. We, the *stupid* species (Homo stultus). One species, *Homo sapiens*, is currently limiting life's capacity to renew its norms.

Eco-critical Affects

One key element of crisis, I have argued, is its subjective, experiential, and specifically affective dimension. So long as we don't *feel* the crisis, in our bones as it were, crisis remains abstract, and cannot be acted on. So long as we don't experience it or feel directly threatened by it, whether through extreme heat, fire, drought, or flooding, information alone—no matter how convincing and indisputable—will never be sufficient to move us into action. For decades now, scientists have accumulated and presented solid, even indisputable evidence, which was largely ignored. Today, the evidence can no longer be ignored, and is in fact recognized by most. Yet the mere fact of knowing does not seem sufficient to trigger action. The problem is not an epistemic one. We *know*. But we *only* know. We say: "I know, I know," in the secret hope that the problem will vanish, miraculously as it were. In other words, we know without really *understanding*. For change to happen and for us truly to understand the event we're faced with, emotions need to kick in. But what emotions could possibly correspond to such an extreme, monstrous event? The problem is further complicated by the fact that we might and in fact do feel the crisis in a way that leads not to action, but to paralysis.

According to Latour, with whom I agree up to a point, the dominant affects in the current ecological catastrophe are anxiety and boredom. They are extremes, and somewhat contradictory: we are anxious about the state of the world, and at the same time bored by the constant, relentless information we receive on the subject. Morton agrees:

> Who hasn't become 'bored' in this way by ecological discourse? Who really wants to know where their toilet waste goes all the time? And who really wants to know that in a world where we know exactly where it goes, there is no 'away' to flush it to absolutely, so that our toilet waste phenomenologically sticks to us, even when we have flushed it?[127]

As for *anxiety*, it can be described as "the feeling that things have lost their seemingly original significance, the feeling that something creepy is happening, close to home."[128] A recent survey by a team of psychologists confirms the significance of eco-anxiety experienced by 10,000 young people aged sixteen to twenty-five from countries in the global South and North.[129] According to the survey, seventy-seven percent say "the future is frightening," 68 percent feel sad, and 63 percent feel anxious. Even more significantly perhaps, 39 percent feel "hesitant to have children." Almost two decades ago another psychologist, Elke Weber, noted that "it is only the potentially catastrophic nature of (rapid) climate change" and the global dimension of what she calls "adverse affects," rooted in personal experience, rather than abstract and statistical data coming from science, "which have the potential for raising a visceral reaction to the risk."[130] At the time, Weber thought it was difficult to engage the affective system in the case of climate change because "personal experience with noticeable and serious consequences of global warming is still rare in many regions of the world."[131] Obviously, Weber's view needs to be revised, on two counts at least. First, today only a few and increasingly rare regions of the earth are spared the experiences of the kind Weber mentioned. Second, the affects that are experienced as a result of climate change do provoke a "visceral reaction to the risk," but not one that is or can immediately be translated into a form of action. We have reached the "catastrophic" threshold she mentions. But it is one that, translated into anxiety, leads to paralysis and inaction.

What boredom and anxiety have in common—as Heidegger makes amply clear in his work from the late 1920s—is their paralyzing effect. *Machenschaft* has come full circle: from the unleashing of the will to power to a mix of anxiety and *ennui*, which takes the form of a profound disengagement from, and lack of interest in, politics and the political class, institutions, work, the news, education, and even procreation. From a feeling of omnipotence, or of an absolute power of control and destruction over things and beings, we have moved to a feeling of anxiety and terror, which reveals itself when we realize the ecological cost, hitherto unknown or ignored, of this total hold on the world: the ground beneath our feet gives and reveals a vertiginous abyss. No wonder we feel lost, anxious, and disengaged. Eco-anxiety and eco-depression are different from the fear of war, nuclear annihilation, or terrorism. They undermine the very possibility of action. As such, they would seem to call into question the claim I have been making concerning the necessary yet implicit connection between theory and praxis when referring to crisis.

The fundamental question, then, is whether and how we can overcome those paralyzing affects and develop new ones that are more conducive to action. Do those alternative affects already exist, or do they need to be generated? Such a question might seem strange, as we are used to thinking about the range of human emotions as given once and for all, and consider them to belong to a fixed human nature and therefore not as a product of history. My contention is that the singular nature of the crisis we are facing calls for a new kind of affectivity. This claim echoes both Heidegger's reflections on the fundamental "attunement" (*Grundstimmung*) corresponding to *Machenschaft* and *Technik* as historical epochs, as well as Anders's work on the "Promethean gap" between our ability to represent and produce the means of destruction of humanity as a whole and our ability to experience it at an emotional level.[132]

How, in other words, can our own affectivity rise to the occasion and correspond to this disproportionate, even monstrous event, which our reason facilitated? How can our sensibility and our imagination catch up with the catastrophe that our will to power and instrumental reason generated? And how can this newly found affectivity allow us to react and act differently? Ideally, the emotions in question would be joyful, and would involve generosity, hope, love, solidarity, or compassion. But they need not be joyful: fear, anger, indignation, and shame are also powerful emotions that can translate into action. In his critique of technology, especially as embodied in the atomic weapon, Günther Anders speaks of the "Promethean shame" (*die prometheische Scham*) human beings feel when they realize the "humiliating or shameful [*beschämend*] quality of the things they have themselves produced."[133] The same, I believe, can be said of the ecological catastrophe: for decades now, "we" (and I am fully aware that the "we" in question concerns the "West" and the "North" more than the "global South") have been complicit in it, doing our bit and playing our small part in carrying out its grand design. We did not actively promote it, or really know what we were doing. But we were not merely passive either. We were neither active nor passive: we went along with it. We were *collaborators*. "It" could not have happened without our participation. Yet by acting as mere collaborators in the catastrophe, rather than as agents, we were somehow avoiding responsibility, and therefore remained shielded from the negative or sad passions, such as shame, I just mentioned. The frustration, anger, or shame we experience *today* are themselves indications of a moment of awareness, and the beginning of a possibility of change. Yet are they sufficient?[134]

Anders also and above all speaks of the need to educate ourselves into a new sensibility—that is, "to educate our moral imagination [*Ausbildung der moralischen Phantasie*]," "to adjust the capacity and elasticity of our imagination [*Vorstellens*] and our sentiment [*Fühlens*] to the disproportionate character of our own products and to the unpredictable character of the catastrophes we can provoke."[135] The crucial point here is that the unprecedented event with which we are faced, and which, once again, revealed itself only too late, requires the creation of new feelings and emotions, the stretching or self-overcoming of our sensibility. The task of the moralist today, Anders concludes, is to carry out "*moral stretching exercises [moralische Streckübungen]*," to "transcend" the normal boundaries of our imagination and feelings.[136] Today's spiritual exercises involve the ability to overcome the "normal" regime of sensibility and include an experience, similar in kind, to that of the gigantic Kant spoke of in his analysis of the natural and mathematical sublime. In the *Critique of Judgment*, Kant claims that, unlike our experience of the beautiful, which is defined by a certain agreement or harmony between our faculty of imagination and our faculty of cognition, the sublime is characterized by a certain conflict between those two faculties, which results in a different, expanded regime of the imagination, one hitherto unsuspected, and a different synthesis, between the imagination and reason not in a cognitive but a moral sense. It is not this specific synthesis that either Anders or I have in mind in relation to the ecological crisis. But it is one that recognizes another crisis of the faculties, and calls for a different accord between our sensibility, our imagination, and our moral responsibility. In addition, the morality that is in question here is not a function of our nature as rational agents, bound to the universality of the moral law. It is itself a function of a certain history, and of the role, and indeed the crisis, of Western rationality understood as technology within it. Anders's point, which I embrace, is that what stops us from truly understanding the "apocalyptic situation" in which we find ourselves is a *moral* deficiency brought about by a specific historical event, which he refers to as "technology." The factors responsible for our lucidity (*Sehenkönnen*) or blindness (*Blindheit*) in the face of the apocalypse are themselves moral.[137] Whether we understand the severity of the situation depends on the moral situation in which we find ourselves. Our understanding of it—to return to the question I began by broaching—is not primarily an epistemic matter, or a matter for a new or revised theory of knowledge. For before we can know it, we need to be concerned by it, to care about it. The crisis needs to become an object of concern and ultimately of *care*. Then and only then does everything we can and need to *know* about it become relevant, and even urgent. Then and only then can we begin to act. But I would add that those conditions of understanding, and not simply of knowledge, are also political in the broadest sense. For their historical, social, economic, and political circumstances of various kinds decide whether I am in a position to be concerned in the first place, to care about the situation. For example, the extreme division of labor and the precarious working conditions affecting many, the power of pressure groups, large corporations, political parties, governments, the media (whether traditional or social), or the entertainment industry can all hinder and harm our ability to educate ourselves morally. In other words, and although the ecological crisis is decisive, it is not simply a matter of an individual decision. It is a matter of a historical turning or shift, and a transformation of culture. By the same token, it is an opportunity to bring about a new hegemony or consensus.

In *The Imperative of Responsibility*, Hans Jonas picks up the argument where Anders left it.[138] He too, as we saw, speaks of the permanent crisis caused by the Promethean (and Faustian) trajectory of the Western, technologically driven subject.[139] But he locates the greatest danger and power of destruction of *modern* technology not in the atomic weapon, but in ecological devastation. That event, he claims, calls for a new theory of ethical responsibility, and a new philosophy of nature, in which human beings have a place, but not as master and commander of the natural world. A new theory of ethical responsibility, Jonas claims, is required to address the singular nature of the event of *modern* technology.[140] Born of danger, of the threat to the conditions of human life on Earth and to the whole of nature, this responsibility takes the form of an ethics not of "progress and perfection," as the Enlightenment and utopian traditions believed, but of "preservation and prevention."[141] Given the magnitude of the power humanity has attained in the pursuit of technical progress, both humanity and nature now need protection *from* power. Understandably, Jonas's theory leads to a prophecy not of "bliss," but of "doom," and to a fundamental mood of fear rather than hope.[142] Fear, not hope, is the affect corresponding to the "exhaustion," "pollution," and "desolation" of the planet, which Jonas attributes to the "unintended dynamics" of our technological age.[143] "For many," he writes, most likely with Anders in mind, "the apocalyptic potential of our technology is concentrated in the atom bomb."[144] To be sure, the threat of nuclear annihilation was real, and possibly at its peak, when Jonas was writing his book. And it remains a threat today. Yet Jonas's primary claim is that the greater threat of apocalypse comes from our systematic and abusive exploitation of the planet's resources. Contrary to the threat of nuclear weapons, the threat of ecological ruin is the result of a long process, which cannot be reversed. It is a weapon of mass destruction that was detonated slowly and without a big bang, its noise covered up by the clamors of excitement of a humanity enamored with its Promethean destiny and fantasy of total sovereignty, fascinated by its ability to tame, exploit, and plunder nature: to turn it into a mere thing. The specific temporality of the Technocene is of the essence, and revealed in the future anterior, in a strange discrepancy or asynchronicity between our enjoyment (in the present) and the exorbitant price that, in the end, we will have had to pay. This is another aspect of the Promethean gap. As it turns out, nothing is for free in the biosphere, especially for a human population of eight billion bent on organizing scarcity within abundance and promoting a sense of lack within a hyper-productivist model: for centuries now, and increasingly, if not frenetically, we lived on borrowed time.

As a result, the "heuristics of fear" proposed by Jonas constitutes a sound and "extremely useful first word" in our attempt to address the ecological crisis.[145] But what kind of fear is at issue here? And how does it differ from the (paralyzing) anxiety I was referring to earlier? It is, Jonas argues, a singular, *spiritual* or *ethical* kind, one that is motivated not by our own feeling or interest, but by the fate of future generations—a fear that is not immediate and pathological, but the result of an *education* of the soul. Jonas's position echoes that of Anders:

> The fear in question then cannot be, as in Hobbes, of the "pathological" sort (to use Kant's term), which compulsively overcomes us in the face of its object, but rather a *spiritual* sort of fear which is, in a sense, the work of our own *deliberate attitude*. Such an attitude must be *cultivated*: we must *educate* our soul to a willingness to *let* itself be affected by the mere thought of possible fortunes and calamities of future generations, so that the projections of futurology will not remain mere food for idle curiosity or equally idle pessimism. Therefore, bringing ourselves to this *emotional readiness*, developing an attitude open to the stirrings of fear in the face of merely conjectural and distant forecasts concerning man's destiny—a new kind of *éducation sentimentale*—is the second, preliminary duty of the ethic we are seeking, subsequent to the first duty to bring about that mere thought itself. Informed by this thinking, we are obliged to lay ourselves open to the appropriate fear.[146]

Today, as we are increasingly forced directly to experience the effects of the ecological catastrophe, our fear has become perhaps less ethical and more pathological. Still, it requires an ethical leap to be transformed into action, both immediate and in the name of future generations. Where I believe the fear in question ceases to be straightforwardly pathological, and becomes ethical, is if it leads to a new form of solicitude or care for the well-being of future generations, and for the earth as providing the necessary material conditions of that well-being. Clean water, air, and soil become moral objectives. In becoming moral objectives, they cease to be mere things or commodities, and are given a form of sacred or sanctuaried subjectivity, if not a legal existence. Haraway makes a similar claim in her recent work. In "disturbing times, mixed-up times, troubling and turbid times," she claims, we need to "stir up" a response adequate to the "devastating events" with which we're faced. But this means "staying with the trouble," tarrying with the negative and the pain it causes, educating ourselves in new forms of affectivity, a mix of pain *and* joy that avoids falling into the trap of a paradise lost and of apocalypse, of blind technological optimism *or* pessimism. We need to find the right mood to confront the "scandals" and "horrors" of the Anthropocene and the Capitalocene, to learn to live (and die) on a "damaged earth," and, eventually, to "rebuild quiet places."[147]

But those new affects, in turn, require a profound modification of our attitude toward not just human beings, but all forms of life: animals other than human, soils, algae, lichen, fungi. The transformation of affects presupposes a profound transformation of our way of being, of how we understand ourselves and the world around us. This, I will argue, requires a renewed and rigorous concept and practice of *care*. If we fail to take care of Earth and to recognize its declining health, Lovelock writes, "it surely will take care of itself by making us no longer welcome."[148]

What Can Be Done? Resistance, Innovation, Conversion

I began this chapter by noting that our economy and our ecology are at odds. The question is: how can they be aligned? More to the point: how can our modes of production and consumption, and our economic credo, not exceed the means of the planet? How can human life, by which I mean the human mind and body, the human socius, and the human sense of place and belonging, find its place within Gaia's living systems?

In what follows, I consider various answers to those questions, many of which are already being discussed, and some of which are already in place. Something like a global awareness of the climate crisis is underway. It is driven by scientific research and development, a minority of farmers and companies, the media (or at least some media), environmental activists and campaigns, lawsuits, and (increasingly) governmental interventions. An ecological conscience is emerging; a new conception of citizenship, based on the idea of Earth as a common good, is on the horizon. For the first time in humanity's history, a communism of the earth, or gaiapolitanism, is being contemplated.[149] Naturally, it is still facing huge obstacles, coming from powerful industrial lobbies, economic interests and dogmas, political ideologies, long-standing habits (including on the part of governments), and the conditioning of the (mostly Western) mind over several centuries. Much remains to be done. For the current crisis calls for regime or system change: "To avert systemic environmental collapse, we need systemic economic and social change. Our lives must depend on triggering what scientists call a cascading regime shift, a flip from one equilibrium to another, followed by a beneficial hysteresis: in other words, permanent system change."[150]

Legal Action

The struggle against climate change is beginning to find a crucial ally in legal action, and climate justice is a major evolution of the last few years. Currently, there are between 1,500 and 2,000 environmental legal actions against states or corporations. The Supreme Court of the Netherlands was the first to strike: in December 2019, it ordered the Dutch state to reduce its emissions in the name of "the rights of Dutch citizens." In 2020, the French Conseil d'État ruled against the state, and in favor of the town of Grande-Synthe, which was suing the state for "climatic inaction." In Germany, the Constitutional Court, the highest court of the land, ruled that the climate law of the Merkel government was not lawful and was contrary to the fundamental rights of its citizens, since it shifted the bulk of responsibility for reduction of emissions to future generations. Under pressure, the government had to revise and raise its targets (a drop of 65 percent of emissions, rather than 55 percent, by 2030). In Portugal, Cláudia Agostinho, a nurse, along with her siblings and cousins, was engaged in a legal battle against thirty-two European countries, which they accused of inadequate and insufficient climate policies. On April 9, 2024, the Court declared the application inadmissible.[151] Businesses and corporations are also affected: in 2021, a tribunal in The Hague forced Shell to halve its CO_2 emissions by 2030. The green transition is becoming a right as well as an obligation.

Earth law, which is based on the idea that ecosystems have the right to exist, thrive, and evolve, is also making strides in some countries, including at the constitutional level. On March 25, 2022, the plenary body of Chile's Constitutional Convention formally approved the Rights of Nature within its proposed constitutional text.[152] On September 4, 2022, a majority of Chilean citizens voted against the text that would have made them the second country in the world (after Ecuador) to recognize rights of nature constitutionally. The Rights of Nature recognized in Article 4 would have included the right to have its existence protected and respected, to regeneration, and to the maintenance and restoration of its functions and dynamic balances, which include natural cycles, ecosystems, and biodiversity. Article 26 identifies environmental principles as those necessary for the protection of nature and the environment. They include the principles of progressiveness (*progresividad*), precaution (*precautorio*), prevention (*preventivo*), environmental justice, intergenerational solidarity, responsibility, and just climate action. Rights of Nature laws were also passed in Panama (2022), Bolivia (2011), and Uganda (2021). Bolivia is faced with ecological devastation and the prospect of becoming a desert in one hundred years. The Law of Mother Earth, which establishes eleven new rights for nature, is inspired by indigenous spirituality and philosophy. It places the environment and the earth deity known as the Pachamama at the center of all life. Humans are considered equal to other beings. Speaking of the Ecuadorian case, Ricardo Rozzi writes:

> This constitution is innovative because it incorporates the normative determination of nature as a subject with rights and is the first in the world to assign this legal category to nature. The legal dogmatism of positive law has been based on paradigms that serve the unlimited exploitation of the earth. If we change the paradigm to conceive it as Mother Earth, *Pacha Mama*, or *Gaia*, then law must foster a communal sense of reciprocity, complementarity, and relationality.[153]

This worldview is expressed in Article 71 of the Constitution of Ecuador: "Nature, or Pacha Mama, where life is reproduced and occurs, has the right to integral respect for its existence and for the maintenance and regeneration of its life cycles, structure, functions and evolutionary processes." Article 14 recognizes the right of the population to have access to a healthy environment and a good way of living: "The right of the population to live in a healthy and ecologically balanced environment that guarantees sustainability and the good way of living, Sumak Kawsay, is recognized." *Sumak Kawsay* means harmonious life within and among human beings, as well as between human beings and the earth. It is perhaps best translated as "plentiful life." Key here is the idea of the good life as intrinsically relational and harmonious, and involving human as well as nonhuman beings, including rivers, oceans, and the air. It is also future-oriented, in that it involves a sense of responsibility toward the generations to come, and *their* right to live well. Most importantly, and despite its integration within the constitutions of Ecuador and Bolivia, it is not a state- but a community-generated, place-based concept, formed in the struggle against persistent colonial power structures, and the state structure in particular.[154]

In 2021, the state of Oaxaca, Mexico, passed a similar state constitutional amendment recognizing the following Rights of Nature: the right to preservation, the right to protection of its elements, the rights to exercise its natural and vital cycles and its ecological functions, the right to integral restoration of its balance, and the right to be legally represented.[155] Oaxaca joined other states of the republic, such as Colima, Guerrero, and Mexico City, in recognizing the Rights of Nature. In 2020, the Nez Perce tribe General Council recognized the rights of the Snake River, which flows through their traditional territory, currently corresponding to central Idaho and parts of southeastern Washington and northeastern Oregon. In November 2024, Spain's highest court upheld the legality of a previous law, which granted legal personhood to the Mar Menor lagoon.[156] This was a European first and historic victory for earth law. A few months later, a landmark decision from Lewes District Council recognized the Rights of the River Ouse.[157] In Switzerland and France, the Appel du Rhône movement seeks to give legal right to the Rhône River.[158] The Earth Law Center, together with Pakistan Fisherfolk Forum, is seeking to obtain legal rights for the Pakistani portion of the Indus River.[159] Similar efforts are underway to recognize and protect the rights of oceans. The Earth Law Center, together with The Ocean Race and Nature's Rights (amongst others), is currently lobbying world leaders and change-makers to obtain a Universal Declaration of Ocean Rights by 2030. Others, such as the Institut de Recherche pour le Développement (IRD), together with representatives of Pacific Island Nations, seek to establish the Pacific Ocean as a legal entity, which will allow lawsuits to be filed on behalf of ecosystems.[160] The current legal framework, animated by a logic of state sovereignty and territoriality, does not consider the ocean as one, but divides it into zones and layers of varying degrees of protection. In addition to guaranteeing the rights of the Pacific Ocean as a single entity, the new proposal would also be consistent with the traditional views of those island cultures for which the Ocean is a person, a God, a mother.

Those initiatives and laws resonate strongly with the ancient Greek view of nature as organic, nurturing, benevolent, and female. According to Merchant, mining was prohibited in antiquity because it was thought to be "mining the earth's womb."[161] Only with the technoscientific revolution, when the historical gaze shifts and nature is seen as inert, dead, and mechanistic, does the exploitation of the earth become possible, if not inevitable.

Resistance

Litigation, legal action, and legislation are certainly a useful tool and a means of resistance. But there are others. Bottom-up pressures, campaigns, and ecological resistance movements, some of which can be illegal, are also effective means of bringing about change. In the summer of 2022, members of Ultima Generazione glued themselves to the glass protecting Botticelli's *Primavera* at the Uffizi in Florence. On October 14, 2022, the climate change protest group Just Stop Oil dumped two cans of tomato soup on Van Gogh's *Sunflowers* at London's National Gallery, before gluing their hands to the museum's walls. Similar protests quickly sprang up around Europe. In Germany, Letzte Generation activists threw mashed potatoes on Monet's *Haystacks* at the Barberini Museum in Potsdam. In 2021, the same movement staged a hunger strike outside the Reichstag building in Berlin to protest the lack of political action on the climate emergency. In 2022, they glued themselves to some of Germany's busiest motorways. In Italy activists threw pea soup at Van Gogh's *The Sower*. None of the paintings, which are protected by glass, were damaged. Like Insulate Britain and Just Stop Oil, Ultima Generazione has received funding from the US-based Climate Emergency Fund, a philanthropic fund set up to channel money to direct action groups. Examples include "public actions of civil disobedience and nonviolent direct action, such as guerrilla garden creation, public demonstration of techniques in alter-globalization oppositional events, and 'seedbombing.'"[162] Even acts of care, Puig de la Bellacasa argues, drawing on the work of Singleton and Law, can be considered as a kind of resistance "in contexts of managerial control that underestimate care's value and even penalize its practice."[163]

Technology

A technological revolution is also underway. It involves the development of green energy—solar and wind, as well as fourth-generation nuclear reactors—to power our economies; the search for, and production of, alternative, less energy-hungry and non-polluting building materials; widespread recycling; cheap hydrogen to fuel cell batteries; and alternative, "farm-free" food sources.[164] Some of those technologies are promising. Others appear fanciful. Recently, a group of astrophysicists published a study in which they suggest that the amount of earthbound sunlight could be reduced by 1–2 percent if we were to launch massive quantities of dust from the moon, which would remain in a stable orbit between the sun and Earth and create a sunshade.[165] Less fanciful but arguably more problematic are negative emissions technologies (NETs).[166] Their objective is to remove carbon dioxide from the atmosphere and store it in stable forms that will prevent it from reverting to its gaseous form in the middle to long term. They "range from natural climate solutions, including afforestation and soil carbon sequestration, to more human-driven interventions, such as bioenergy with carbon capture and storage (BECCS) and direct air capture with carbon storage (DACCS)."[167]

Technology alone, however advanced, cannot save us. Only from within the Technocene can we think it can. But the Technocene and its crisis-management attitude is precisely what's in question, the horizon we need to extricate ourselves from and overcome.

The Ontological Conversion

The most fundamental transformation that needs to take place is *ontological*. Our *way of being* is the problem. *We* are the catastrophe: we—Western humans—have poisoned the air and waters, and increased the occurrence and scale of tornadoes, hurricanes, and droughts. By standing and asserting ourselves *against* the earth, we have set ourselves on a path of self-destruction. Paradoxically, by conquering and plundering the earth, we have deprived ourselves of the possibility of relating to it as a place of *dwelling*. Our hostility toward it has made it inhospitable. This homelessness is yet more fundamental and radical than statelessness. The two phenomena are linked: the climate crisis already forces many (the poor and powerless especially) to flee, sometimes beyond their own borders, and seek a new "home." But what happens when entire states become uninhabitable, flooded, or dried up? What happens when the earth has become a site of *total* crisis? How can philosophy be part of the solution?

Initially, perhaps, by recognizing that the earth is on the verge of becoming uninhabitable not only, or even primarily, because of the environmental and ecological crisis, but because we have lost sight of the earth as our place of sojourn, and of *habitability* as a way of being *with* the earth, *with* other species and the stuff they are made of, which is also the stuff *we* are made of. Between them and us, there is continuity and mutual dependence, a de facto intertwining and solidarity that only an extraordinary yet highly effective abstraction and implicit ontology have managed to render unthinkable. This is the ontology of subjects and objects, mind and body, spirit and matter, activity and passivity, mastery and submission, freedom and necessity, being and nothingness. But it is also the ontology of ends. It is the teleology of life—think here of Kant's geography, anthropology, and natural history—according to which everything on Earth, every life-form, is *for* something, and ultimately for *us*, the human species, the chosen species, which is itself made for the conquest, transformation, and shaping of its own environment, the realization of higher ends, of "reason" and "freedom." This is the reductionist yet imperialistic ontology that led to the interpretation of the world, and everything in it, including other human types, as endlessly (or so we thought) exploitable resources, as value to be extracted, irrespective of the consequences.

Ultimately, we need an alternative ontology. It is, as I have already suggested, the *with*-ontology, the ontology of interconnectedness. Whether implicitly or explicitly, the ontology in question is a distinctive feature of deep ecology. For Arne Naess, the father of deep ecology, "everything hangs together, everything is interrelated."[168] The same emphasis on relationality can be found in Aldo Leopold's "land ethic," first formulated in 1949.[169] In his essay, Leopold puts forward a notion of the self as a relational, ecological being who is a member of the larger biotic (living, organic, ecological) community. Drawing on both deep ecology and Leopold's work, ecofeminist philosophers have also emphasized the relational ethics and ontology I wish to promote.[170]

But I also want to draw on the resources available in Heidegger's existential analytic. *Mitsein*, or "being-with," Heidegger claims in *Being and Time*, is a constitutive and irreducible feature of who we are. To be sure, he restricts the term to us as *existing* rather than *living* beings, as *Dasein* rather than *lebenden Seienden*.[171] But we can and need to extend this category to living beings as a whole. In the process, we need to transform the analytic of *Dasein* into an analytic of life, rethink our place and role on Earth as a *living* entity, and open human experience to beings other than human. In fact, this is exactly what Heidegger came close to doing in his later work: we are not simply *in* the world, navigating its limits and opportunities, shaping it in our own image and interest, projecting ourselves against a horizon of possibilities. We are also *on* and, more importantly, *of* the earth as the dimension that escapes and exceeds our worldly, practical concerns, as the hidden ground that sustains us and to which we remain indebted. We need to inject a dose of materialism and science in Heidegger's concept of the earth; we need to allow it to become synonymous with *soil*. In doing so, however, we must be careful not to fall prey to a romanticized view of "nature," in which we would advocate a return to and a protection of "nature," or, worse, to a micro- or ecofascism, enamored with the idea of a motherly nature and the fantasy of a pristine, native soil—an *Urlandschaft*, to use the term coined by the German environmentalist (and Nazi supporter) Walther Schoenichen.[172] Soil needs to be understood not as *Blut und Boden*, but as the organic system that includes "biota"—that is, organisms ranging from microbial to invertebrate fauna (such as earthworms), and, of course, plants, roots, lichen, and fungi.[173] Equally, we need to connect Heidegger's Earth to the biosphere as I have tried to define it. But we also need to retain Heidegger's core idea, that of a *ground* that precedes us and with which we are entrusted, of a place of dwelling, rather than occupation and appropriation, a horizon of habitability rather than ownership. What we treasure most is not something we possess. This is the paradox of ontology: our "ownmost," that with which we are entrusted, is not our own. The earth: the most precious, and yet not a possession. Equally, we need to supplement the Heideggerian intuition regarding ecstatic temporality as the meaning or "ground" of the human *being* with a more complex, differentiated temporality: the temporality, and even temporalities, of the biosphere.

Let me expand.

An ontology worthy of our time, provoked by the current ecological catastrophe and inspired by recent research in ecology and evolutionary biology, emphasizes circulation and loops, intertwinings and meshes, complex assemblages; it is a symbiotic ontology of interconnectedness and absolute immanence, in which no being, human or otherwise, can be singled out as more significant or worthy than any other. To return to the way things are ("to the things themselves"), rather than how we wish them to be, and to live accordingly, a radical decentering of "Man" and a questioning of competition as a universal norm, or the key mechanism to evolution, innovation, and "progress," needs to take place. Following Bernard Harcourt's recent work, I already presented the case for a cooperative model for our economy and society. But this model needs to be expanded to include the place of the human in Gaia. To be sure, this is yet another iteration of what Freud called the narcissistic wound of "Man," its fourth and hopefully fatal wound, after those inflicted by Copernicus (astronomy), Darwin (evolution), and Freud himself (metapsychology). The problem with the previous wounds is that they remained too abstract, too distant, too *academic*. We don't experience the roundness and rotation of the earth, the duration of evolution, the reality of the unconscious. But we all experience heatwaves, droughts and wildfires, floods and hurricanes, the increasing fury of the elements. What's wounded is the Narcissus in us—the anthropo-phallogocentric being with which we have learned to identify. What is left? The self that is not narcissistic, yet not without self-love; the self that is not individual, for never fully individuated, but relational, or transindividual; the self that is not an enclosed self, ontologically distinct from the reality around it, but in a constantly evolving assemblage with it; the self that is traversed by, and host to, flows of matter and information; the self that carries others—other selves and other material bodies, from atoms to molecules, strands of DNA, cells, bacteria, or technocratic—within it: the *dividual* self.

A proper ecosophy, then, requires that we de-individualize subjectivity, that we recognize that "I" am not—or at least not necessarily, inevitably, or only—an individual, but a relay, a point of passage or transience, a critical field inhabited by physical, molecular, and biological (but also social, technological, aesthetic) bodies, which have congregated there, established a provisional residence in me. As Sheldrake puts it, our gut, ears, toes, mouth, skin, and every surface, passage, cavity we possess teem with microbes, bacteria, and fungi.[174] "I" is a fragile and haphazard concatenation of physical-chemical components, in no way reducible to the stretch of time that extends between "my" birth and death. For the components in question preceded my birth and will continue to live, in other human or nonhuman bodies, long after "my" death. We, like all things on earth, are only passing through; we are only ever in transit. "There have never been individuals. We are all lichens."[175] Or fungi. Or coral. We are all Gregor Samsa. Infected ants (in the case of *Ophiocordyceps*) stop behaving like ants and *become* fungus. Fungi can't move or fly. But some find hosts in the form of insects (ants, flies, cicadas), which they use and even hijack. Once inside the body of the insect, they control and manipulate its behavior. Eventually, they find the optimal place and time to disperse their spores and reproduce. Some carry around a certain type of virus that infects insects, not fungi. They use the virus to target, weaken, and eventually rupture specific parts of the insect's body, from which they're able to spread their spores. This is not a metaphor, but a real process of transformation, a behavioral, physiological, and evolutionary metamorphosis. Whether as subjects or groups, individuals or collective bodies, we are all flows—material, semiotic, social flows—that constantly pass through, and intersect with, other flows. We each host hundreds of billions of atoms that were once in everyone else's bodies, but also in the bodies of dinosaurs that lived millions of years ago. As I write these words, my lungs probably contain one atom of the last breath of *Tyrannosaurus Rex*, Julius Caesar, and Marie Curie. Yet 90 percent of the atoms in my body are replaced every year, assembled into new molecules and cells.[176] All sorts of living and nonliving entities, from the food we eat to the air we breathe, pass through our bodies and eventually end up in the bodies of other human beings and organisms, through our breath and sweat, the matter we secrete or excrete. Nothing is wasted. The air we breathe, with its 21 percent oxygen content, is a by-product of plant life; it is the waste produced by the existence of plants.[177] The tens of trillions of bacterial cells that thrive in our digestive tract are part of our own inner landscape, and an essential component of our immune and digestive systems; but they are also organisms in their own right, which connect with other organisms in symbiotic relations. Even bacteria have viruses within them. Even viruses have smaller viruses within them. Organisms within organisms within organisms. And when it's finally over, when I "die," my body becomes an opportunity for other organisms: it is broken down, turned into nutrients, recycled. As Coccia puts it, "the breath of life will not expire in our corpse; it will go on to feed those for whom we will become a festive Last Supper."[178] There is no such thing as death (if by death we mean the end of life). There are only states of matter and "metamorphic thresholds."[179] *Life goes on*.

An ontology worthy of our time can only be a trans-ontology: an ontology of transience, transversality, and trans-individuality. It requires that we think life, and more generally matter, horizontally rather than vertically; rhizomatically rather than arborescently; symbiotically rather than antibiotically; as what happens in between rather than at the extremities; as becoming rather than being. Even Darwin's tree needs to be read differently, set on its side, its branches now visible as roots that cross over one another, intertwine, and move in multiple directions at once—like the neural networks of the brain, the digital networks of the World Wide Web, or the chemical rhizome of the mycelium.

But the ontological revolution also requires that we think *time* differently. An ontology worthy of our time of ecological crisis is one that includes the relation between different kinds of temporalities, human and nonhuman. To be sure, we need to include the time of human, lived experience, with its horizon of projection, its concerns and priorities, its needs and aspirations, its life expectancy, but also its historical dimension, which involves the complex cultural process of sedimentation *and* construction we usually refer to as collective memory. This includes the economic, short-term temporality of value production and extraction, and the political temporality of election-based governments, which also privileges short-term decisions and gains over long-term vision and plans. This short-term horizon also influences our view of the past, our reading of history. And we need to include the time of care, the time of the biosphere, which itself includes the long, slow time of geological processes (the formation and breaking down of rocks, the formation, evolution, and movement of continents); the equally long, slow time of evolution; the relatively shorter time cycle of climate change; and the even shorter time cycle of life and ecology, through which soils are renewed. Human temporality, geological time, soil time, the time of evolution, and of climate all intertwine to constitute a complex fabric, which we necessarily live *with*, yet can learn to live with *better*.

As we know, human temporality has had a disproportionate effect on at least two of the temporalities mentioned: that of the climate, and that of soil renewal. Assuming that global warming is a current trend overlaid on a cyclical, natural pattern, human economic activity, through intensive agriculture and industrial output, has worked as a formidable accelerator and aggravator of such a trend by dramatically raising the levels of CO_2, methane, nitrous oxide, and carbon dioxide in the atmosphere. But the same activity has also altered the time of soils.[180] Soil, Puig de la Bellacasa reminds us, is created through the long, slow time of geological processes; but it is also constituted by "relatively shorter ecological cycles by which organisms and plants, as well as humans growing food, decompose materials that contribute to renew the topsoil."[181] The problem is that human agriculture has exhausted soils across the world. According to the UN, since 1900 the world's crops have lost 70 percent of their genetic diversity.[182] This process, which saw the depletion of soils and the search for fertile grounds, started well before the industrial revolution.[183] Today we know that the current productionist model is unsustainable: we are running out of land, and know that extensive forest clearing for the purpose of extending is driving factor of climate change. "Peak soil" is as real a phenomenon as "peak oil," and one that signals a greater crisis.[184] This is how Puig de la Bellacasa formulates the conflicting, if not contradictory, temporal logic with which soils are now confronted:

> The future of soils appears to be pulled forward by an accelerated timeline toward a gloomy environmental future, while the time left for action in the present is compressed by urgency. And so the temporal pace required by soil's ecological care as a slow renewable resource might again be at odds with these conditions of emergency, running against the accelerated linear rhythm of intervention characteristic of technoscientific futuristic response, traditionally straddled to a productionist pace.[185]

This tension is reflected in soil science itself, which, according to the American soil scientist Dick Arnold, "operates simultaneously in the realms of ecology and of economics, each of which marks time by different clocks"— the first driven by a short-term logic of exploitation and an acceleration of technological solutions, the second by a long-term logic of sustainability and the acknowledgment of soil as a slowly renewable entity.[186]

Crises themselves have different temporalities, which can conflict with one another. For example, a public health crisis, with its very short-term horizon, can conflict with (and possibly aggravate) an already existing economic crisis. Crisis management is then a delicate exercise in establishing levels of urgency and arriving at an equilibrium. But those crises take place within, or are an expression of, human temporality. More seriously still, we need to recognize that a clash between different temporalities, human and nonhuman, can be the very origin of crises. For example, faced with exponential growth, the world population needs to negotiate the tension between the intensification of agricultural methods in the global South, which will further exhaust soils, and the risk of starvation. This is how human temporality, with its small scale and limited horizon, conflicts with the temporality of the biosphere (from soil renewal to climate change and the evolution of species). But it need not be that way. To be sure, it will always be very difficult for human beings to extract themselves from their own finite temporality, their limited ability to project themselves into the future, and remember the past. Yet historical and geographical differences—different ways of organizing social relations, modes of production, and consumption—have taught us that human activity can be more or less divorced from natural cycles and care for the earth, more or less aligned with the complexity, rhythms, and fragile equilibrium of the biosphere. And we know that technoscientific thinking, with its anthropocentric and predatory worldview, is at the root of the current ecological crisis. The ontological revolution is therefore also a temporal one; the narcissistic wound is also a chronic one. We need to think of how, instead of presiding over the destiny of the planet as a whole, human temporality can find its place within the order of a differentiated, nonhuman temporality. This requires knowledge: a familiarity with the earth, life and soil sciences, thermodynamics, and complexity theory, which, taken together, question and provide alternatives to the technoscientific, progressive, productivist paradigm. But it also requires the transformation of one's habits, one's view of one's place in the world, one's relation to future generations, human and nonhuman. To care is to devote time to someone or something. But to care for the earth is to devote one's human time to other temporalities, to allow one's own temporal horizon to be transformed by other, nonhuman horizons. It is to be expanded and stretched—through understanding and learning, but also through imagination, sensibility, and affectivity. This is how humanity lived for much of its history. Until the advent of the Technocene, it knew itself to be a part of Gaia, and understood Gaia to be an organic, relational totality. To be sure, this knowledge was pre-theoretical. But it was deep, and it was wise, because it was the fruit of an experience accumulated over centuries.

The New Responsibility

Because, through our actions rather than through the mere mechanisms of evolution, it is in our power to affect the very conditions of this reality, we are responsible for it. This responsibility is the result of a specific history, that of the Technocene. This ontological reality implies also, and from the start, an ethics, which I have begun to explore from the perspective of intergenerational justice and the emotional readiness and education that are required to *become* responsible.

Once again, Jonas hit the nail on the head when, forty years ago, he raised the question of the "rights" of nature. What if, as a result of an historical development (the Technocene), the question of ethics extended beyond the human, and the anthropocentric confinement of former ethics no longer held? What if a new imperative, or the duty to preserve the conditions for the permanence of the biosphere, emerged from human beings' capacity to imperil those very conditions? This is the question toward which I have been moving, and have formulated in terms of the biosphere's normativity and the necessity on our part to align our own social, economic, political, and ethical norms with those of the biosphere. This is how Jonas formulates the question:

> It is at least not senseless anymore to ask whether the condition of extrahuman nature, the biosphere as a whole and in its parts, now subject to our power, has become a human *trust* and has something of a moral claim on us *not only for our ulterior sake* but for its own and in its own right. If this were the case it would require *quite some rethinking in basic principles of ethics*. It would mean to seek not only the human good but also the good of things *extrahuman*, that is, to extend the recognition of "ends in themselves" beyond the sphere of man and make the human good include the care for them. No previous ethics (outside of religion) has prepared us for such a role of stewardship.[187]

It is important to emphasize that Jonas's main interlocutor and source of inspiration in developing his ethics for an age of ecological crisis is Kant. He adopts Kant's moral principles as *formal* obligations, or imperatives, and adapts them to the present context. To be more specific: he reinscribes the formalism of Kant's ethics in a historical context which, he claims (rightly, in my view), radically transforms the meaning of ethics. In other words, he includes nonhuman, nonrational entities in the kingdom or dignity of ends (rather than means), thereby reducing the onto-ethical gap between free rational agents and those governed purely mechanically, that is, according to the laws of nature. But he does so only indirectly—that is, in the name of humanity itself, or, more precisely still, in the name of future generations. The new imperative thus takes the following form: "Act so that the effects of your action are compatible with the permanence of genuine human life"; or expressed negatively: "Act so that the effects of your action are not destructive of the future possibility of such life"; or simply: "Do not compromise the conditions for an indefinite continuation of humanity on earth."[188] The new imperative says that "we may risk our own life, but not that of humanity"; that "we do not have the right to choose, or even risk, nonexistence for future generations on account of a better life for the present one."[189] It does not go so far as to include nonhuman entities in the formulation of the imperative. But it does include them as conditions necessary for the fulfillment of the new obligation, and to ensure the *quality* of life of future generations. Our primary duty, then, is toward the future of humanity as such, or futurity—that is, toward the possibility that there be a future. The first and most fundamental imperative is *that there be a humanity*. It is not a *hypothetical* imperative, which would stipulate something like "*if* there are human beings in the future—which depends on our procreation—then such and such duties are to be observed by us toward them in advance." It is a *categorical* or unconditional imperative, which commands "*that* there be *human beings*."[190] In turn, this care for the future of humanity includes "care for the future of all nature on this planet as a necessary condition of man's own"; since the long-term interest of humanity coincides with that of the biosphere as its "worldly home in the most sublime sense of the word," the new responsibility applies equally to the future generations and the biosphere.[191]

Without wanting to delve too deeply into current debates on intergenerational justice, let me introduce Lukas Meyer's "sufficientarian" take on the question, which is a useful complement to Jonas's Kant-inspired imperative of responsibility. It involves a commitment to a "threshold notion of harm" according to which "an action harms a person only if, as a consequence of that action, the then existing person falls below a normatively defined threshold."[192] In addition, it involves the *specification* of the threshold notion of harm in terms of well-being: future people must have *sufficiently* good lives or lives worth living. We should do what is necessary to allow future people to live, or continue to live, not simply under just institutions, as Rawls's contract doctrine claims, but according to a minimally good life, as defined by basic needs,[193] central capabilities,[194] or personal or cultural preferences.[195] The Rawlsian principle of "just savings," understood as "an understanding between generations to carry their fair share of the burden of realizing and preserving a just society," provides an argument for the present generation's duty not to violate the rights of future generations.[196] What obligations, if any, besides rights-based obligations, might we have in relation to future people, especially in a time of ecological crisis? To answer this question, Meyer introduces the Kantian idea of respect. Yet unlike Kant, who limited it to our duty toward reasonable, moral agents, Meyer extends it to material goods and cultural values inherited from previous generations. This also broadens the idea of the minimally good life:

> Those currently alive owe respect to highly valuable goods that their predecessors bequeathed to them as well as to more remote future people, and they also owe respect to the highly valuable future-oriented projects of their contemporaries. Owing such respect gives rise to a general obligation, namely that current people should not willfully destroy the inherited goods and the condition that are constitutive of persons' pursuit of future-oriented projects.[197]

My claim is that this is precisely what we have failed to do: the current ecological crisis is a flagrant case of disrespect of the most fundamental good bequeathed to us, and of future generations. By threatening the material, elemental conditions of life, and the cultural heritage with which they are often associated, we have robbed future people of their own futurity (their "projects") and therefore their being. This, I believe, is how the ecological crisis both aggravates and transforms the question of our responsibility toward future generations.

Our responsibility *today*, I want to claim, is first and foremost toward the transcendental-physical ground on which we tread, and which we share with other species. It is not simply toward other human beings as rational agents, or even toward other living beings as sentient beings. It is toward the *conditions of life* on Earth. This is not something we could have anticipated. This realization is retrospective, and stems from the recognition that a particular articulation of knowledge and power, of the place of the human on Earth and a mode of production, has led to the deterioration of those conditions to such an extent that, paradoxically, they have become visible. As a result of our technological, power-driven agenda, they had been made invisible, or made visible only as resource. The ecological crisis is precisely the return of their visibility, but in the form of their erosion and fragilization, their near collapse. The Promethean project, bent on the domination and invisibilization of the ground, has backfired: the ground manifests itself, but in the form of a nature out of joint, increasingly unstable and unpredictable, full of sound and fury. Our new responsibility, born of a historical event—the Technocene—that was long in the making, is toward nature as a mesh and a continuum, as a finite substance generating a quasi-infinite number of modes. The human species is one such mode. Its *responsibility* toward the other modes and toward their ground stems entirely from its ability to alter the ground—that is, to affect the normativity of the biosphere. We are responsible for those conditions—not de jure, but de facto, as a result of an historical event of epic proportions.

I call this specific responsibility "care."

Daring to Care

What I have said thus far points in the direction of a sense of responsibility for which there is no difference *in kind*, ontological or ethical, between the human good and the good of nonhuman entities, between ethics and natural right, between how we ought to comport ourselves and live—that is, by maximizing our power (*potentia*) to think and act, and a proper understanding of how nature works, or the sort of substance that it is. This is why I began by laying out the basic mechanisms of the biosphere as an open, dissipative, nonlinear system of which we are the expression, or a mode, and whose existence is intimately and irreducibly bound up with all the other modes of nature. By learning to compose our nature with that of the beings around us, human and nonhuman, present and future, and thus living in harmony with them, we may not increase our *imperium* over them, but we increase our *potentia*. We learn to live in *solidarity* with them. I understand solidarity in a double sense: descriptive and prescriptive, ontological and ethical. Solidarity is first and foremost an ontological concept: the image here is of a dry wall the stones of which are held together not by mortar or cement, but by the very way they are disposed and assembled. But solidarity is also and at the same time an ethical principle, born of the realization on the part of the human species of its ability to harm the conditions of emergence and evolution of this complex assemblage or web of interactions and to limit the divergence potential of life itself. Ultimately, the ontological and the ethical are indistinguishable, precisely because the ontology is relational and specifically loopy, and because ethics raises the question of the conditions under which the relationality in question can be increased, expanded, maximized, thus leading to greater, more powerful (*potentia*) assemblages or greater clusters (networks) of *potentia*. The ethical question is that of the specific interactions that are most conducive to a life worth living, of the construction or creation of assemblages that enhance life: not just my life, but the life of those around me, beneath me and above my head. It's those processes—Deleuze and Guattari call them "becomings"—that matter. The question, then, is of the kind of assemblages we are currently caught up in—an individualized subject interacting with an infinity of partial objects, itself connected to an infinite flow of circulation of goods, capital, and desire, which cover the entire surface of the earth and facilitate its destruction; and the kind of assemblages we are able to construct instead, the kind of intensities we are able to create. But it is not a matter of turning one's back on science and technology, of reversing the clock. Rather, it is a matter of using them differently. It is, to borrow Haraway's formulation, a matter of "passionate constructions," in scientific as well as ecological and political communities.[198]

This coming together of reason and passion, of intelligence and emotions, is a distinctive feature of ecofeminist philosophy. In her work, Karren Warren promotes "ecological spiritualities" and "emotional intelligence" as a way of healing the wounds the patriarchal order has inflicted on women and nature. In response to those who, like Janet Biehl, call ecofeminism "a force for irrationalism," or, like Baird Callicot, see it as anti-scientific and anti-rational, Warren understands "emotional intelligence" and, more broadly, the care-sensitive, *situated* (rather than transcendent and universal) ethics she promotes as a genuine, coherent, and pluralistic theory.[199] For her, "spiritualities are a way to show that emotions need not be reduced to the denigrated side of the reason/emotion dichotomy, but rather, that one can reflect upon feelings, and feel strongly about reasoned convictions."[200] The reason that is under scrutiny and criticized is dualistic, instrumental, and objectifying. But there are other uses of reason, other forms of rationality, which science and philosophy promote, or can promote.

Consider the example of permaculture as experienced and theorized by Puig de la Bellacasa. Permaculture is a global movement informed by techniques and practices "shared with and/or borrowed from agroecology, biodynamical agriculture, indigenous modes of land care (more on the latter later), and more."[201] It promotes "technologies that foster ecological living (urban and rural) through alternative systems of local food production, waste management, alternative energies, and radical democratic forms of organization."[202] But permaculture is much more than a technique, or a set of techniques. It is also and above all an ethics of care—of the earth and of people—rooted in everyday "doings," such as composting and soil-caring, inscribed in concrete mundane relations that are more than human.[203] This, in turn, means that humans are not the sole origin of care, that they are themselves recipients of care. It means that the object of care is relationality itself. Permaculture and other soil foodweb communities "are not only about knowing the soil better so that we can extract more efficiently from it but about another way of relating, about the thicker, haptic, involvements and embodied traffics in a more than human community of soil makers."[204] For it is indeed a matter of caring by *growing soil*, that is, by "returning the surplus" in order to continue to make soil as much as to consume it.

Care is crucial for several reasons: First, because it is an emotion, or disposition, and thus an alternative to the anxiety, boredom, or even spiritual fear I began by mentioning. We say that we care or are concerned *about* someone, their physical or mental health, their general well-being. Second, care is a form of action rooted in love or compassion: we care *for* or look after ourselves and others. As a virtue, care is a form of benevolent vigilance directed toward others or oneself. Finally, care is a mode of thinking, or at least an intelligent emotion: it is not purely immediate, but oriented toward deliberation and action. We need to be cautious here and not fall into essentializing care along gender lines. We must avoid identifying or venerating care as a "feminine" value, to be opposed to the aggressive and even destructive "nature" of men.[205] Everyone—women especially—knows how utterly consuming caring can be, how care can devour their lives. Feminist thinkers have shown the extent to which affective labor is often an undervalued, unrecognized, yet socially and economically crucial form of labor.[206] In capitalist societies, care is largely devalued as "unproductive" or "merely" reproductive—that is, excluded from the social and political sphere of production and recognized labor, and relegated to that of biological life. At the same time, and for that reason, the labor of care is often outsourced and commodified, while receiving among the lowest wages. It cannot be, therefore, a matter of idealizing care and reinforcing a gender divide, which is also an economic and political divide between the private or domestic and the public, between "bare" life and "political" life. Understandably, Beauvoir saw in the equation of ecology and feminism, and in the idea of care especially, a "renewed attempt to pin women down to their traditional role."[207] But the care Warren, Haraway, Puig de la Bellacasa, and other feminists have in mind is of a different kind. Ecofeminist spiritualities, Warren notes, are often explicitly earth-based. But this does not reinforce the identification of women with nature. Instead, it questions the opposition between the human and nature, or between male rationality and female naturality: "earth" here functions as a deconstructive term *and* an ethical injunction, like the one Nietzsche encouraged through the figure of Zarathustra.[208] Warren's "spiritualities" do not aim to reduce women to their traditional role as caretakers (and thus to their place within the reproduction of capital), or to the sphere of natural needs. Rather, they aim to include men (and the non- or differently gendered) in processes of care *and* expand the sphere of care to nonhuman beings. Care becomes a matter for all, a way of being as much as a function. It is a collective and equally shared good. For that reason, it avoids "affective and material burnout—including burnout of nonhumans subjugated in relations of ecological 'service' and humans bound to the logics of productivist exploitation of nature."[209] Drawing on the work of Joan Tronto,[210] Puig de la Bellacasa defines care as everything that *is done*, rather than everything that *we* do, to maintain and repair the world, so that *all* can live in it as well as possible. What the "all" includes remains contingent on "specific ecologies and human-nonhuman entanglements."[211] They involve what Haraway calls "interspecies intimacies" or "interspecies relationalities." They manifest themselves as affective relations with human and nonhuman beings.[212] Then and only then can care become synonymous not with labor and burden, but with a joyful affect.

The ethics of ecological care, whether expressed in permaculture or in other practices, avoids the usual distinction between self and other, between care of the self and care of the other, between the personal and the collective, between a utilitarian and an altruistic relation to nature. Why? Because we're dealing with a world that is intrinsically relational, entangled, where individuals are co- or mutually dependent on one another: not in- but interdependence is the starting point. Everything happens *between* points. Care, then, becomes care for the relationality itself, for the multiplicity of relations. I care for myself by caring for others (humans and nonhumans). Caring for others is caring for oneself. It is a matter not of altruism, but of affirming a pluralistic world, of cultivating habits, gestures, and practices that will not reduce but increase the normativity of life, of deriving one's norms of life from the normativity of life itself.

Non-Western Wisdom

The practice of care thus understood has been known to many (mostly non-Western) cultures for centuries. As one commentator puts it, "those who in the past put down as being primitive the reverence and affection original indigenous people express for the Mother Earth . . . now find support for their viewpoints in these same 'primitive' people."[213]

When Hernán Cortés and his troops arrived in Tenochtitlán in 1521, they discovered not only what was then one of the most populated and beautiful cities in the world, built on islands surrounded by lakes and volcanoes, but also a highly sophisticated, efficient, and sustainable system of agriculture, made of small plots of land delimited by hundreds of small, medium, and large canals. The *chinampas*, as they are known, consist of a combination of lower areas for deep water, rich in minerals and nutrients, and raised islands made of vegetation and mud for cultivation, delineated by trees that act as water pumps. Historically, similar raised fields could be found in South America,

Asia, Oceania, and parts of Africa. The *chinampas* used to feed a population of over 200,000 people, every day of the year, and yielded up to seven harvests in a year. Unfortunately, the Spaniards abandoned the *chinampas* and cut them off from Mexico City by draining the lakes, leaving only a portion of them intact. Today the *chinampas* are being revived and are considered as among the most fertile and productive soils anywhere in the world. The soil is black, which indicates its richness in volcanic, fertile residue. It produces food all year round without intensifying agricultural yields, and yet is never exhausted. Naturally, given their very limited surface and the current population of greater Mexico City (roughly 22 million), they cannot fulfill the role they once played. But they provide hope for the future by pointing to alternative farming methods.

I have already referred to the key Quichua interpretations of the earth (*Pachamama*), the good life (*Sumak Kawsay*), and their intimate connection. Traditional Hawaiian culture also has a concept of the good life (*pono*), which implies a kinship with all living beings. *Pono* indicates a harmony that is reached through social and ecological practices of care of the land that provide well-being and health.[214] Rozzi puts it like this:

> The intimate coupling between ecological and social orders supports, and is sustained by, habits of life that are consistent with the Hawaiian concept that humans are not landowners, but rather administrators or caretakers of the land or habitat. The concept of *pono* requires establishing relationships of reciprocity between humans and the land. Reciprocity is based on *ecological concepts* of the amount of energy that can be withdrawn from ecosystems and on *social concepts* of governance that indicate the amount of energy that must be returned to ecosystems. Reciprocity is implemented through practices of care of the land and supervision of the social structures destined to the common welfare.[215]

Economies of care, whether applied to soils or to other human/nonhuman entities, are circular gift economies, and thus a clear alternative to the one-way, predatory and ultimately counterproductive economy of the global food system.

Reciprocity is also a key feature of Aymara culture.[216] According to Xavier Albó, for Aymara people as well as many other native peoples around the world "nature itself must be cared for and respected as a valuable part of the community." The land should not be owned, but valued and protected.[217] *Qamaña* means to inhabit, to live in a specific place or environment, and to dwell. *Qamasiña* means "to live with someone." "*Qamaña* also is the name that is given to a sheltered place, protected against the wind, constructed in a semicircle of stones, as a resting place for shepherds while they relax or attend their flocks."[218] As such, *qamaña* evokes the idea of being as dwelling, living with, caring, and sheltering. To live *well* is to live in such a way that those various dimensions are fully integrated in one's life. This idea is further expressed in the word *qamasa*, which means "character and shape of being," as well as "bravery, audacity, valor, and courage." As such, it designates a way of being or disposition, as well as a virtue. Applied to places rather than human beings, it designates a force or a vital energy, which one can absorb through specific gestures and rituals. One can simply live. The Aymara people call it *jakaña*. But to live well—that is, to live "in peace," "joyously and pleasurably"— one needs *qamaña*. *Qamaña* is not an economic, quantifiable concept, but a qualitative, ecological one. Here I use ecology in the broadest sense, as involving a profound sense of the solidarity and reciprocity between human beings, as well as between human beings and the biosphere as the relational whole in which all things find their place. At the same time, quantifiable economic scores cannot be ignored, especially in situations of poverty that force populations to struggle merely to survive. In this respect, and still according to Albó, economic instruments that seek to identify thresholds of survival (*jakaña*), such as the unsatisfied basic need index or the vulnerability index, can prove helpful and even decisive in identifying the minimum conditions for the pursuit of "the good life." Following Amartya Sen's suggestion, the world is progressively moving away from a "per capita income" model of development, which measures averages of income in which the very rich and the very poor are thrown together, to a Human Development Index (HDI), which includes many of the features I have just discussed, such as the quality of social relations and of relations to the environment.

The concept of *qamaña* resonates strongly with concepts across history and geographies. It certainly resonates with Guattari's own concept of ecology, which includes three dimensions: the quality of the environment and our relation to it, the quality of social and specifically labor relations, and the quality of our mental states and emotional life. But I would like also to stress the obvious proximity between *qamaña* and Heidegger's idea of the earth as the dimension we inhabit rather than appropriate; in which we dwell and find shelter rather than simply reside; of which we are the custodians rather than the possessors. To be sure, Heidegger claims, the world is (for the most part and normally) a familiar, ordered place, in which beings, human and nonhuman, have a place and a function. It is a place in which we orient ourselves freely, a place we navigate with a degree of expertise and control, and with certain practical aims in mind. Although Heidegger doesn't say it explicitly, it is also the place of economy in the broadest sense, from the organization of the domestic sphere to that of the modes of production at the level of an entire society. For those reasons, it is also a place of power relations, structures, and struggles—of politics in the broadest sense. But the earth is something different: namely, the ground that simultaneously sustains and escapes us, the "shelter" in which we find refuge yet which we can never possess. It is the place and environment, at once everywhere and nowhere, that provides the conditions of possibility of survival in the biological sense, but also of the "authentic" or "caring" mode of life. It is material as well as ethical.

Conclusion

Whilst no doubt dominant, and virtually unchallenged, technological thinking is not inevitable. Critical thinking pivots around the crisis of instrumental reason and machinic thinking, which have precipitated the event of extinction. Critique, and eco-criticism more specifically, emerges from within the threat of extinction, and as a response to it. It does so by envisaging the earth as what has been entrusted to us and what needs to be kept *safe*—not, therefore, as empowerment, but as endowment. Not availability, but habitability defines our relation to the earth and those living on it. This, in turn, orients our modes of production not toward growth (i.e., accumulation and consumption), but toward sustainability. As Rexroth puts it: we need to learn to live according to the principles of "mutual aid and respect for life, awareness of one's place in the community of creatures."²¹⁹ Things begin to change when we think of the earth as what we *share* with other living entities and self-organized, complex ecosystems, such as soil. A different, original sense of community begins to emerge. An eco-solidarity or communism of the earth becomes not only possible, but desirable. Science itself is deployed anew, not as an instrument of power and domination, but *for* the earth, and with a view to establishing our place on it, rather than our dominion over it: our *humanity*. *Humanus*, after all, has its etymological and ontological roots in *humus*, in the ground and soil of the earth. And if an old or new form of animism, and a new mythology, are required to establish this new covenant and federate desires, so be it. The science and the philosophy behind it are sound.

Conclusion

The time has come to take stock of the ground covered in this book, draw a few conclusions, and look toward the future.

The book was an attempt to construct a philosophy—more specifically, a critique—of crisis. It should by now be clear that this was meant in at least two different senses, which reveal (on my part at least) a certain ambivalence toward the vocabulary and schemas of crisis. First, it was meant in the sense of a philosophical, especially critical reflection on the *discourse* of crisis: on the ubiquity of the notion, and on the risks and dangers associated with its use. The diagnosis of crisis is never neutral: it is always formulated from a certain discursive position and almost always within a specific power dispositive. It is also often used as, or produces the effect of, a performative utterance: by saying "this is a crisis," I set in motion a process, or at least indicate a path, both theoretical and practical, the various historical origins and developments of which I have tried to analyze. If the diagnosis of crisis is a warning of some kind, a critique of crisis is also a warning against the dispositive of crisis and its potential practical—social, economic, and political—implications. When told of a crisis, we should exercise caution and not rush to the sort of action or solution we are often told is preferable or, worse, inevitable. We should bear in mind the origins and lineages of the schemas of crisis with which we are presented. And when told, whether by the political class, the media, or the experts, that everything is in crisis, or that crisis has become the general, permanent state of the world, we should be even more cautious: first because such a diagnosis can lead to a total and possibly totalitarian solution, and second because by including everything under the diagnosis of crisis, we run the risk of making crisis itself meaningless, no longer associated with the unusual, the exceptional, and the urgent. In the age of total and polycrisis, we risk crisis *fatigue* and developing a kind of indifference in response—one that is especially risky, given the growing authoritarian and "exceptionalist" solutions to crises that are currently adopted. "Crisis" always signals a danger. But it also harbors its own dangers: the capacity to create new forms of hegemony, or power, or to strengthen existing ones. In other words, one must remain vigilant, if not skeptical, toward the rhetoric, hermeneutics, and normativity of crisis.

At the same time, the critique of crisis developed in this book was meant as a contribution to the understanding of our present as a time of crisis. In that respect, it found itself in conversation with a tradition, or a range of traditions, in and outside philosophy, for which the present day appears *in* and *as* crisis. For such a tradition, the phenomenality of history is bound up with the *experience* of crisis. That experience involves at least three dimensions of our subjectivity, or three of our faculties. First, it is indissociable from a certain affectivity or emotional state, some of which are paralyzing (anxiety, depression, boredom), others more conducive to action (fear, indignation, anger). Second, it requires that we make sense of the situation, and therefore make use of our faculty of understanding and critical analysis. Third, it is also a call to act, to modify the conditions of one's existence, or transform those of the system in question. In that respect, it also implicates our faculty of desire, or action. Although crises can't be reduced to crises of subjectivity, subjectivity (especially in relation to the play of faculties) is necessarily implicated and shaken in times of crisis.

The other main goal of the book was to clarify what we mean when we say that a person, a situation, or a system is in a critical state, or is going through a crisis. That operation of clarification turned out to be complicated, for at least two reasons. First, the aim was never simply semantic. It was not to provide a blanket definition of crisis, which could be applied to all crises, past and present. It was not to identify a core, general meaning of crisis and subsume all cases of crisis under it. I was therefore concerned less with the semantics of crisis (although I did draw on its etymology) than with its architecture and mechanics. Crisis does not *mean* as much as it *functions*. Revealing the structure of crisis required identifying its distinctive features. Crisis, I argued, is a distinctive concept, in that it is at once theoretical and practical, descriptive and prescriptive. In addition, crisis is binary: sooner or later, inevitably, it takes the form of an either/or, of a "before" and "after." It signals a bifurcation and a moment of decision, whether personal (or existential), collective, or systemic in the broadest sense. A bifurcation forces one to decide and exclude: one cannot go down two or more separate roads at the same time. That possibility is open only to subatomic particles. The binary structure of crisis is precisely why Derrida, of whose critique I am ultimately skeptical, rejects crisis as a concept adequate to think the eventfulness or discontinuity of history. Revealing the mechanics of crisis, or how it works, also and above all required that we distinguish between its various regimes. To be sure, I argued, it is possible to distinguish between crisis in a weak and a strong sense, or between crises that are mere deviations from the norm and crises that affect the norm, force us to question it, and eventually replace it with new norms. Initially useful, that typology turned out to be too coarse. Instead, drawing on a literature ranging across disciplines and centuries, as well as on current situations and events, I suggested that we distinguish between four regimes of crisis, without claiming that there are or could only ever be four. As the regimes in question are intimately bound up with concrete and historically defined situations, their number cannot be defined *a priori*. There is something irreducibly empirical about the philosophy of crisis. Furthermore, there are, and always will be, disputes about the nature of the crisis we are facing. Is it a crisis of deviation or contradiction? Of exception or extinction? Or of all these types? These questions are not merely academic, as their answers define solutions and courses of action. The very nature of our politics, and particularly of our democratic politics, is at stake in such a dissensus. A consensus or agreement of some kind, which is always preferable, requires the dispute and deliberation about the nature of the crisis we are dealing with, and whether what we are dealing with is even a crisis in the first place. What we have, instead and too often, is a cacophony in which every voice is forced to shout increasingly short, loud, and reductive slogans.

Revealing the mechanics of crisis also helps us raise the question of what to do, by way of either counter-conducts or counterproposals. One does not engage with a crisis of deviation, either by finding a solution within the limits of its regime or by questioning the managerial response to which it is subjected, in the same way that one engages with, or responds to, a crisis of contradiction. And as we saw, there is much at stake politically in a possible disagreement about the nature of the crisis one is facing, and whether one is indeed faced with a crisis. Crises require analytical or epistemic tools to be deciphered. Those, in turn, open up the realm of tactical responses: counter-conducts and counterproposals, which might involve movements of resistance, the creation of new norms and ways of life, but also, at times, simple adjustments. Not every crisis is a crisis of contradiction, requiring the overhaul of the system as a whole. In Chapter 2, for example, I analyzed the circumstances in which the exceptionalist regime of crisis can be legitimately activated, while pointing to the authoritarian and anti-democratic tendencies at work in such a regime, and very much in vogue today. To be sure, the migrant or detainee camp, and the border more broadly, is a contemporary *topos* of the exceptionalist diagnosis and treatment of contemporary crises. As such, "crisis" operates not as a problem to be solved, but as a dispositive—that is, as a technique of government and control. At the same time, the exceptional measures introduced by most countries during the Covid-19 pandemic were justified, so long as they were not prolonged indefinitely or used to constrain the democratic space in the long term. And migration flows can be regulated without activating a dispositive of crisis. Similarly, we need to educate ourselves to see and respond adequately to crises affecting the norms of the system under consideration, rather than seeing them as crises of deviation that can be "fixed" or "tweaked." What Kuhn says about the scientific community is even truer of societies: we are creatures of habit and tend to replicate a paradigm, or find solutions within its boundaries, for as long as we can. Only repeated shocks, sustained misery, or deep frustration will force us out of this dogmatic slumber. But even then, denial and paralysis, in place of lucidity and action, can overwhelm us when we are faced with the magnitude of the crisis in question. In any event, I cannot imagine a crisis that does not include a certain violence, whether in the way it is experienced or the measures that are introduced in response to it: insofar as it coincides with the suspension of the rule of law, the state of exception is a state of violence; similarly, revolution, whether in the social, aesthetic, or scientific realms, also involves a kind of violence toward established norms and habits. This is why, in the table provided in the introduction, I included a category on "violence."

This, I believe, is where we are now in relation to the ecological crisis. We have had to reach the domain of "shock and awe" to realize the severity of the situation. We have had to wait for the time bomb we placed in the belly of the biosphere to detonate fully to acknowledge its presence and confront its consequences. In the case of the biosphere and the ecological crisis, however, the shock is perhaps greater than with any other crisis, since it involves the recognition that we may have damaged it to such an extent that its normativity is itself affected. In other words, the blast is less a warning than the terrifying sign of an event that has already taken place and is irreversible. And because the event in question affects the transcendental-physical ground on which we stand, it could be considered as a founding or archaic event, were it not for the fact that it is an event of collapse, in which life as we know it *zu Grunde geht*. It is a founding, epoch-making event. But it is also an ungrounding, or *collapse*. The normativity of the biosphere, altered and threatened as an intended result of human action, far exceeds the normative capabilities of human beings. There is a radical and disturbing asymmetry here, which increases our feeling of crisis. On the one hand, human action has altered the balance of the biosphere. On the other, human action is limited in what it can do in the face of the dynamic of thresholds and tipping points it has unleashed. Human beings are both a cause of the transformation of the behavior of the system they inhabit, one that had remained at equilibrium for millennia, and a very limited part of the solution. That, we saw, is a function of the nonlinear thermodynamic system in question, one defined by its irreversibility: the glaciers will not unmelt, global temperatures will not return to their pre-industrial levels. Human subjectivity—its temporality, affectivity, and sense of self—is shaken to the core, and reveals, but only *ex post* and terrifyingly, the extent to which its destiny is bound up with that of the earth, the climate, and *all* living things. In other words, crisis has reached its chronic and total state.

Does this mean we should do nothing? That question is itself the wrong one, since much is now being done, or set in motion, at least in certain parts of the world. More, as we saw, can and should be done, especially by way of a transformation of our relation to, or being-in, the world. A new education of the self is required, one that is far from the liberal, neoliberal, disciplinary, controlling, or digital techniques of the self promoted in the last two hundred years. This ontological conversion, as I call it, also presupposes a kind of violence, but toward oneself. Yet this doing violence to oneself is radically, ontologically different from the violence of the Technocene. Ultimately, it is a turn away from our predatory, extractive, and exploitative habits, and toward a symbiotic assemblage. Such is the reason why, even where and when it is animated by the best intentions, I am skeptical of capitalism's ability to reform itself and be part of the solution. Its very nature is to extract value—from the earth, human beings, and nonhumans—and to do so through a generalized system of competition. I have tried to show how cooperation, solidarity, and sustainability, whether in the bio- or the socioeconomic sphere, are ultimately less crises-generating than the norms of competition, value-extraction, and resource-exploitation under which our system of production and consumption has been operating for the last two hundred years. Whether we like it or not, a new form of cosmopolitanism is forced upon us. Let us call it gaiapolitanism. I believe it is inevitable. Yet—I want to say once again—the world is pulled in two different directions. One is taking us closer to the international cooperation necessary to tackle the magnitude of the crisis we face. The other, fueled by the fear of experiencing yet another "global" movement, the most visible face of which is that of the migrant, is taking us in the opposite direction, toward ultra-nationalism, the securing of borders, and the erection of walls to keep the threat at arm's length. The fear is understandable: it is born of the disenchantment with globalized capitalism, with the flows of capital it facilitates and the movements of population it provokes, as well as with a profound sense of loss of identity and community. But the sovereignist-territorial answer is an illusion; it is the wrong answer to a badly posed problem. This is where we need to distinguish gaiapolitanism from globalized capitalism, the mechanisms of solidarity and cooperation of the former from the values of competition, productivity, and growth that characterize the latter.

The ecological crisis is also the most severe because of its temporality. As we saw, it is one that combines two very different temporalities, or durations. The temporality of the biosphere is slow: its evolution and cycles are calculated in tens or even hundreds of thousands of years. As such, it is largely invisible to the human eye and can only be perceived and measured using the tools of science—unless and until, as is currently the case, it is experiencing an extraordinary, highly unusual period of acceleration. Human temporality, by contrast, is marked by finitude. It is overwhelmingly determined by the proximity of human events, the life and death of ourselves and those immediately around us. An extraordinary effort of imagination is required to expand our temporality to include that of other, future generations, of often invisible life-forms, and, even more so, of the biosphere. But it is an effort that is now also forced upon us, in the most unpleasant manner, through droughts and floods, heatwaves, and wildfires of biblical proportions. However unpleasant, this stretching of the imagination and (to use a Kantian vocabulary) the conflict of the faculties to which it gives rise is a sign or a call to action that we cannot ignore. We realize that we cannot be moved into action without this internal crisis of the faculties, without the disorder or tension we experience between our faculties of perception, understanding, reason, and imagination. A hitherto unsuspected assemblage of the faculties has been set in motion. It is at once akin to, yet fundamentally different from, the experience of the sublime Kant describes in the *Critique of Judgment*. The *horror*, *disgust*, and *shame* we experience are the conditions for a new ethics, a new way of being-in-the-world and dwelling-on-the-earth. Only through the articulation of a different kind of subjectivity, a constantly mutating socius, and a new relation to the environment, Guattari argued, "will we escape from the major crises of our era." The most significant crises explored in this book, along with the regimes to which they correspond, all situate themselves at the juncture of those "three ecologies," and lead to suggestions regarding how we might overcome them.

Notes

Introduction

1 Francis Fukuyama, "The End of History?," *The National Interest* 16 (1989): 3–18; Fukuyama, *The End of History and the Last Man* (New York: Macmillan, 1992), xiii. See also Alexandre Kojève, *Le Concept, le temps et le discours* (Paris: Gallimard, 1991).

2 See José Luis Villacañas, "Crisis: ensayo de definición," *Vínculos de Historia* 2 (2013): 122–4.

3 Isaak Iselin, *Philosophische Mutmaßungen über die Geschichte der Menschheit*, 5th ed., vol. 2 [1764/1770] (Basel, 1876), 380. Cited in Reinhart Koselleck, *Crisis*, trans. Michaela W. Richter, *Journal of the History of Ideas* 67, no. 2 (April 2006): 377. For a more recent edition, see Isaak Iselin, *Gesammelte Schiften*, vol. 4, *Geschichte der Menscheit*, ed. Sundar Henny, in collaboration with Isabelle Wienand (Basel: Schwabe, 2018).

4 Félix Guattari, *The Three Ecologies*, trans. Ian Pindar and Paul Sutton (London: The Athlone Press, 2000).

5 Many studies emphasize the mental health crisis currently affecting Western societies, and in particular the increase in serious mental health illness. The situation in the US is especially dire. On the one hand, suicidal ideation and depression have been going up every year since 2010 (see https://mhanational.org/issues/state-mental-health-america). On the other, recent decreases in the number of psychiatric hospitals and beds have given rise to a substantial increase of individuals with serious illness who are confined in correctional facilities. The percentage of people with serious mental illness in prisons rose from 0.7 percent in 1880 to 21 percent in 2005—see Samantha Raphelson, "How the Loss of US Psychiatric Hospitals Led to a Mental Health Crisis," *Here & Now*, November 30, 2017, https://tinyurl.com/5n6rs8rx. The securitization of mental illness further aggravates the problem. In Canada, a recent study from the Centre for Addiction and Mental Health reports that "in any given year, 1 in 5 Canadians experiences a mental illness or addiction problem," and "by the time Canadians reach forty years of age, 1 in 2 have—or have had—a mental illness"; see "Mental Illness and Addiction: Facts and Statistics," Centre for Addiction and Mental Health, accessed February 3, 2021, https://tinyurl.com/yffkh27d. The latest data from the UK are also alarming, with significant increases in the rates of common and

severe mental illness, and a dramatic rise in self-harm and suicidal thoughts—see "Mental Health Facts and Statistics," *Mind*, June 2020, https://tinyurl.com/2yje579v. Unsurprisingly, all reports emphasize the close connections between the mental and social ecologies: a very high percentage of those suffering from serious mental illness experience or have experienced economic hardship, exclusion or discrimination based on their race or gender, war and/or forced exile, or some contact with the justice system. To this connection, we should add the growing number of people affected by climate and eco-anxiety, a term (not yet a condition) made official by the American Psychological Association. See Sarah Jaquette Ray, *A Field Guide to Climate Anxiety: How to Keep Your Cool on a Warming Planet* (Berkeley, CA: University of California Press, 2016); Anouchka Grose, *A Guide to Eco-Anxiety: How to Protect the Planet and Your Mental Health* (London: Watkins, 2020). I return to eco-anxiety, and eco-affectivity more broadly, in Chapter 5.

6 Guattari, *The Three Ecologies*, 33. On algorithmic governmentality, see Antoinette Rouvroy, "Technology, Virtuality, and Utopia: Governmentality in an Age of Autonomic Computing," in *Law, Human Agency and Autonomic Computing: The Philosophy of Law Meet the Philosophy of Technology*, ed. Mireille Hildenbrandt and Katja DeVries (Abingdon: Routledge, 2011); "The End(s) of Critique: Data Behaviourism Versus Due Process," in *Privacy, Due Process and the Computational Turn: The Philosophy of Law Meet the Philosophy of Technology*, ed. Mireille Hildenbrandt and Katja DeVries (Abingdon: Routledge, 2012); Antoinette Rouvroy and Thomas Berns, "Le Nouveau pouvoir statistique," *Multitudes* 40 (February 2010): 88–103; Stephen Shapiro, "Foucault, Neoliberalism, Algorithmic Governmentality, and the Loss of Liberal Culture," in *Neoliberalism and Contemporary American Literature*, ed. Liam Kennedy and Stephen Shapiro (Hanover, NH: Dartmouth College Press, 2019).

7 Guattari, *The Three Ecologies*, 23.

8 Facebook would be a good case study: the algorithms it generates systematically reward hatred and division over generosity and solidarity, simply because (as Spinoza would have it) hatred, especially in the form of indignation, fascinates and federates more easily than love. It is a machine that plugs into, feeds off of, and capitalizes on our (it seems infinite) capacity for hatred. It is itself governed by, and pulled between, two poles: one, the "social responsibility" arm of the company, aims to identify, rectify, and minimize the polarizing tendencies of algorithms; the other, more powerful, aims to increase Facebook's client base and capture as much of their time and data as possible. It is therefore a good example of a specific assemblage, which is at once technological, capitalistic, political, and affective. It may have started with the assumption that human beings aspire to "communicate" and "share" experiences with one another, but it soon found ways of capitalizing on the *jouissance* we find in envy, spite, scorn, division, and humiliation. In an effort to counter the toxicity and harm social media causes to the mental health of young Australians, the Australian parliament introduced the first social media ban (for under-16) in November 2024.

9 Guattari, *The Three Ecologies*, 28.

10 Barack Obama, interview with Jeffrey Goldberg, "Why Obama Fears for Our Democracy," *The Atlantic*, November 16, 2020, https://www.theatlantic.com/ideas/archive/2020/11/why-obama-fears-for-our-democracy/617087/. At the same time, I can only agree with Paul Preciado when he wonders how we might expect American society to embrace "truth" when it has itself constructed its political and cultural hegemony on "colonial fictions, capitalist tales, and audio-visual and numerical myths (from Hollywood to Facebook)." See Paul Preciado, *Dysphoria mundi* (Paris: Grasset, 2022), 308. Preciado's claim is that we are not experiencing an epic battle between truth and error, reality and fiction, or reliable versus "fake" news, but a profound transformation of our "regime of truth." What is currently at stake is a dispute over the procedures through which we distinguish between what is true and what is false. To be sure, the "truths" of the American (and European) "petro-sexo-racial" order are currently in dispute and challenged by what Deleuze and Guattari would describe as a "minority-knowledge" (*savoir minoritaire*). It is also the case, however, that a world of "alternative facts," otherwise known as lies or half-truths, is growing behind the back of verifiable facts and is increasingly presented as legitimate.

11 "Remarks by President Biden at the Virtual Leaders on Climate Opening Session," The White House, April 22, 2021, https://tinyurl.com/47at9e56.

12 See Jonathan Weisman, "For Republicans, 'Crisis' Is the Message as the Outrage Machine Ramps Up," *New York Times*, June 17, 2021, https://tinyurl.com/2xdysbk3.

13 See Adam Tooze, "Chartbook #130 Defining Polycrisis—From Crisis Pictures to the Crisis Matrix," *Chartbook*, June 24, 2022, https://tinyurl.com/2v82bxvw.

14 This is a turn of events Fukuyama himself recognizes when, in the subtitle to a recent book, he speaks of "the crisis of democracy." See Fukuyama, "Against Identity Politics: The New Tribalism and the Crisis of Democracy," *Foreign Affairs*, September/October 2018; "Trump and the Crisis of Liberalism," *Foreign Affairs Interview*, November 21, 2024, https://tinyurl.com/du6v9v4c. The question, of course, is one of knowing what causes this crisis of democracy, and especially liberal democracy. See also Marcel Gauchet's, *Le Nœud démocratique. Aux origines de la crise néolibérale* (Paris: Gallimard, 2024), which follows from his four volumes devoted to *The Advent of Democracy* (2007–2017).

15 If I may say once again, it is because Europe, and Germany especially, went through a long period of crisis-thinking in response to the Great War, which generated a literature, culture, and *zeitgeist* of collapse and apocalypse. See Rudolf Pannwitz, *Die Krisis der europäischen Kultur* (Nuremberg: Carl, 1917); Paul Ernst, *Der Zusammenbruch des deutschen Idealismus* (Munich: G. Muller, 1918); Oswald Spengler, *The Decline of the West*, trans. C. F. Atkinson (New York: Knopf, 1926); Arthur Liebert, *Die geistige Krisis der Gegenwart* (Berlin: Pan-Verlag Rolf Heise, 1924).

16 E. Morin, "Pour une crisologie," *Communications* 25 (1976): 149.

17 Janet Roitman, *Anti-Crisis* (Durham, NC and London: Duke University Press, 2014), 127n30. See also Arjen Boin, Paul t'Hart, and Alan McConnell, "Crisis Exploitation: Political and Policy Impacts of Framing Contests," *Journal of European Public Policy* 16, no. 1 (2009): 81–106, https://doi.org/10.1081/13501760802543221.

18 Roitman, *Anti-Crisis*, 39.

19 Rodrigo Cordero, "Crisis and Critique in Jürgen Habermas' Social Theory," *European Journal of social Theory* 17, no. 4 (2014): 497–515, https://doi.org/10.1177/1368431013520387.

20 See Ulrich Beck, *Risk Society: Toward a New Modernity* (London: Sage, 1992); "World Risk Society as Cosmopolitan Society? Ecological Questions in a Framework of Manufactured Uncertainties," *Theory, Culture and Society* 13, no. 4 (1996): 1–32; Ulrich Beck and Christopher Lau, "Second Modernity as a Research Agenda: Theoretical and Empirical Explorations in the 'Meta-Change' of Modern Society," *British Journal of Sociology* 56, no. 4 (2005): 525–55.

21 See Jean Baudrillard, *Symbolic Exchange and Death*, trans. Iain Hamilton Grant (London: Sage, 1993); Baudrillard, *Simulacra and Simulation*, trans. Sheila Faria Glaser (Ann Arbor, MI: University of Michigan Press, 1994).

22 See Niklas Luhmann, *Die Wissenschaft der Gesellschaft* (Frankfurt am Main: Suhrkamp, 2011), 311; Luhmann, *Soziale Systeme* (Frankfurt am Main: Suhrkamp, 1984), 587. See also "The Self-Description of Society: Crisis Fashion and Sociological Theory," *International Journal of Sociology* 25, no. 1–2 (1984): 59–71.

23 See Michel Foucault, "On the Ways of Writing History," in *Essential Works 1954–1984*, vol. 2, ed. James Faubion, trans. Robert Hurley (London: Penguin Books, 2000), 282; Foucault, "How Much Does It Cost for Reason to Tell the Truth," in *Foucault Live: Collected Interviews, 1961–1984*, ed. Sylvère Lotringer (New York: Semiotext[e], 1996), 359. For a nuanced assessment and ultimately a defense of Foucault's (actually) complex take on crisis, especially beyond its mode of operation within the neoliberal technology of government, see Rodrigo Cordero, *Crisis and Critique: On the Fragile Foundations of Social Life* (London and New York: Routledge, 2017), Chapter 6 ("Making Things More Fragile: The Persistence of Crisis and the Neoliberal Disorder of Things—Michel Foucault"). I will offer a qualified defense of the Marxist and post-Marxist view of crisis in Chapter 3.

24 See Koselleck, *Crisis,* 397. Koselleck's article was originally published in a German dictionary of concepts comprising eight volumes and 122 entries. See R. Koselleck, "Krise," in *Geschichtliche Grundbegriffe: Historisches Lexicon zur politisch-sozialen Sprache in Deutschland,* ed. Otto Brunner, Werner Conze, and Reinhart Koselleck, vol. 3 (Stuttgart: Klett-Cotta, 1982), 617–50.

25 Koselleck, *Crisis,* 398.

26 See Peter Collier and David Horowitz, *The Rockefellers: An American Dynasty* (New York: Henry Colt & Co, 1976); Robert T. Rich Kiyosaki, *Dad Poor Dad: What the Rich*

Teach Their Kids About Money That the Poor and Middle Class Do Not! (Scottsdale, AZ: Plata Publishing, 1997).

27 See Joseph A. Schumpeter, *Das Wesen und der Hauptinhalt der theoretischen Nationalökonomie* (Berlin: Duncker & Humblot, 1908), 618.

28 See Roland Barthes, *La Préparation du roman* (Paris: Les Éditions du Seuil, 2015), 589–92; Évelyne Grossman, *La Créativité de la crise* (Paris: Les Éditions de Minuit, 2021), 21–49.

29 Contemporary equivalents of the Castex and Surer manual would include Alain de Botton, *How Proust Can Change Your Life* (London: Picador, 2006) and John Armstrong, *Life Lessons from Nietzsche* (London: Macmillan, 2013).

30 See Georges Canguilhem, *The Normal and the Pathological*, trans. Carolyn R. Fawcett and Robert S. Cohen, intro. Michel Foucault (New York: Zone Books, 1991).

31 Roitman, *Anti-Crisis*, 13.

32 See Brian Milstein, "Thinking Politically about Crisis: A Pragmatist Perspective," *European Journal of Political Theory* 14, no. 2 (2015): 141–60, https://doi.org/10.1177/1474885114546138.

33 It would be reductive, and in some cases misleading, to identify what is normal with an average. This is particularly true of the human body: what is normal for a given individual—say, to sleep four or five hours a day, or have a heart rate of 40—does not correspond to the human average.

34 Cordero, *Crisis and Critique*, 129. I return to the broadly liberal framing of crisis as an object of management in Chapter 1.

35 Michel Foucault, *Lectures on the Will to Know: Lectures at the Collège de France 1970–1971 and Oedipal Knowledge*, ed. Daniel Defert, François Ewald, and Alessandro Fontana, trans. Graham Burchell (London: Palgrave, 2013), 194. See also Foucault, *The Archaeology of Knowledge*, trans. A. M. Sheridan Smith (London: Routledge, 2002), 26–30.

36 Stéphane Mallarmé's famous "Crise de vers" would be a good example of a revolutionary moment in poetry, and (given the superior place he assigns to that genre) in art more broadly. See Stéphane Mallarmé, "Crisis of Verse," in *Divagations*, trans. Barbara Johnson (Cambridge, MA: Harvard University Press, 2007), 201–11. Subsequent references are to S. Mallarmé, *Œuvres complètes*, vol. 2, ed. Bertrand Marchal (Paris: Gallimard Pléiade, 2003). After the death of the French literary giant Victor Hugo, who brought the classical *alexandrin* verse to a state of perfection, the question of poetry's future became vital. A new way forward was required. Mallarmé celebrates the loosening of the *alexandrin* in some of his immediate predecessors and contemporaries, and the advent of what came to be known as the *vers libre* or free verse. He speaks of the "exquisite and fundamental crisis" (p. 201) or "disjunction" to which literature is subjected (pp. 299, also 305). The crisis of the *alexandrin* and *disparition* of Victor Hugo are the condition for the emergence of "the pure work," one

in which individual idioms (*les langues*) would lose their contingency and reach the "absolute" or "truth" of "*la langue*" (pp. 329–30). I will not deal with aesthetic crises in any detail. However, I will argue that tragedy provided a powerful schema through which modern philosophy envisaged its own present as a site of historical crisis.

37 F. Guattari, *Qu'est-ce que l'écosophie?* (Paris: Éditions Lignes, 2013), 528.

38 Guattari, *The Three Ecologies*, 47.

39 For a phenomenology of the political affects associated with crisis, see Ruth Rebecca Tietjen, "Feeling and Performing 'the Crisis': On the Affective Phenomenology and Politics of the Corona Crisis," *Phenomenology and the Cognitive Sciences* (2023): esp. section 3.2, https://doi.org/10.1007/s11097-022-09877-9.

Chapter 1

1 See Reinhart Koselleck, *Kritik und Krise. Eine Studie zur Pathogenese der bürgerlichen Welt* (Munich: Verlag Karl Alber, 1959). Translated by the author as *Critique and Crisis: Enlightenment and the Pathogenesis of Modern Society* (Cambridge, MA: The MIT Press, 1988). See also Koselleck, *Crisis*, op. cit. Other useful sources include André Béjin and Edgar Morin, "La notion de crise," *Communications* 25 (1976); Nelly Tsouyopoulos, "Krise" II, in *Historisches Wörterbuch der Philosophie*, ed. Joachim Ritter, Karlfried Gründer, and Gottfried Gabriel, vol. 4 (Basel and Stuttgart: Schwabe, 1976), 1240ff.; Gerhard Masur, "Crisis in History," in *Dictionary of the History of Ideas: Selected Study of Pivotal Ideas*, ed. Philip P. Wiener, vol. 1 (New York: Macmillan, 1973), 589ff.

2 Koselleck, *Crisis*, 358, 371.

3 See "κρίσις," *Logeion*, accessed July 24, 2022, https://logeion.uchicago.edu/κρίσις. Examples from Greek literature would include Aeschylus, *Agamemnon*, in *Oresteia*, trans. with intro. and notes by Christopher Collard (Oxford: Oxford University Press, 2002), 1285–94; Sophocles, *Oedipus Tyrannus*, in *The Complete Plays of Sophocles*, trans. Robert Bagg (New York: HarperCollins, 2011), 498–506; Sophocles, *Electra*, in *The Complete Plays of Sophocles*, trans. Robert Bagg (New York: HarperCollins, 2011), 681–5. See also Koselleck, *Crisis*, 358–60.

4 See Jean Bodin, *Les six livres de la République*, book 1 (1583; repr. Paris: Le livre de poche, 1993), chapter 10; Samuel von Pufendorf, *De jure naturae et gentium*, vol. 2, trans. C. H. Oldfather and W. A. Oldfather (1934; repr. Buffalo, NY: Hein, 1995), book 7; Gabriel Naudé, *Considérations politiques sur les coups d'État, preceded by Louis Marin, Pour une théorie baroque de l'action politique* (Paris: Les Éditions de Paris, 1988). The 1639 original edition consisted of only twelve copies (see Marin, *Pour une théorie baroque de l'action politique*, 10, 12; Naudé, *Considérations politiques sur les coups d'État*, 104). The second, posthumous edition (1667), was more widely

discussed and followed by another, edited by Louis du May, under the title *Sciences des Princes* (see Marin, *Pour une théorie baroque de l'action politique*, 10).

5 Carl Schmitt, *Political Theology: Four Chapters on the Concept of Sovereignty*, trans. George Schwab (1922; repr. Chicago, IL: The University of Chicago Press, 2005), 13, translation modified.

6 Schmitt, *Political Theology*, 12.

7 See Pierre Judet de La Combe, "Catastrophe et crise: de l'épopée à la tragédie (grecques)," *Critique* 8, no. 783–4 (2012): 642–52.

8 See Michel Foucault, *Lectures on the Will to Know: Lectures at the Collège de France 1970–1971 and Oedipal Knowledge*, ed. Daniel Defert, François Ewald, and Alessandro Fontana, trans. Graham Burchell (London: Palgrave, 2013), March 17, 1971; Louis Moulinier, *Le pur et l'impur dans la pensée des Grecs d'Homère à Aristote* (Paris: Klincksieck, 1952); Fabian Meinel, *Pollution and Crisis in Greek Tragedy* (Cambridge: Cambridge University Press, 2015).

9 Meinel, *Pollution and Crisis in Greek Tragedy*, 9.

10 See Édouard Will, *Le monde grec et l'orient*, vol. 1, *Le V° siècle (510–403)* (Paris: PUF, 1972), 522–5. See also Foucault, *Lectures on the Will to Know*, 200n7.

11 Meinel, *Pollution and Crisis in Greek Tragedy*, 9.

12 On the connection between Greek medicine and tragedy, see Jacques Jouanna, "Hippocratic Medicine and Greek Tragedy," in *Greek Medicine from Hippocrates to Galen*, trans. Neil Allies, Studies in Ancient Medicine 40 (Boston, MA and Leiden: Brill, 2012), 55–79.

13 Shakespeare's knowledge of medicine is now well documented. References to diseases, doctors, and treatments occur in almost every play, most often metaphorically. But his knowledge exceeded that of the layman. Shakespeare was aware of the circulation of the blood, long before William Harvey formulated his model in 1628. He also shows evidence of following Paracelsus, "the Father of Pharmacology," who relied on distillations of herbs and minerals, rather than the bloodletting and purges the College of Physicians recommended. See John Charles Bucknill, *The Medical Knowledge of Shakespeare* (London: Longman, 1860); R. R. Simpson, *Shakespeare and Medicine* (Edinburgh: Livingstone, 1959); Aubrey C. Kail, *The Medical Mind of Shakespeare* (Balgowlah: Williams & Wilkins, 1986); Frank M. Davis, MD, "Shakespeare's Medical Knowledge: How Did He Acquire It?," *The Oxfordian* 3 (2000): 45–58.

14 Paul Kottman, "Disinheriting the Globe: On Hamlet's Fate," in "SHAKESPEARE: Philosophical Aspects," special issue, *Revue Internationale de Philosophie* 63, no. 247.1 (2009): 20.

15 I will return to *Hamlet*. At this point, I am interested only in pointing out the play's connection with ancient tragedy, and with the sense of crisis as pollution. But I am

not claiming that *Hamlet* is reducible to that regime of crisis. As a *modern* tragedy, perhaps best revealed in Hamlet's delay in carrying out his duty, and therefore in the possible limits of the duty in question, *Hamlet* transcends the confines of pollution and the revenge drama.

16 The corpus in question comprises eleven volumes in the Loeb Classical Library and is known as the W. H. S. Jones edition. See *Hippocrates* (Cambridge, MA: Harvard University Press, 1868–2018).

17 There are over 120 volumes by Galen, although experts estimate this is only a third of what he wrote. In the early sixth century, the priest and physician Sergios of Raʾs al-ʿAin (d. AD 536), also known as Sergius of Reshaina, translated thirty-two works by Galen into Syriac. They were the first translations of Greek medical work into a Semitic language. In the ninth century, during the Abbasid Caliphate, the Nestorian Christian translator, scholar, physician, and scientist Ḥunayn ibn Isḥāq al-'Ibādī relied heavily on Sergius' translations in his own translations of works by Galen—including *On Crises*, *On Critical Days*, and *On the Difference of Fevers*—into Arabic. According to Dols and Immisch, "Ḥunayn ibn Isḥāq and his colleagues usually translated or retranslated Greek scientific and philosophic texts into Syriac and, then, into Arabic because the latter did not possess a technical vocabulary for such complicated Greek texts." See Michael W. Dols and Diana E. Immisch, "Galen Into Arabic," in *Majnūn: The Madman in Medieval Islamic Society* (Oxford: Oxford University Press, 1992; online ed., Oxford Academic, October 3 2011), 40, accessed February 8, 2023, https://tinyurl.com/5bvduepy. The first Latin translations of Galen appeared in the eleventh century. They were the work of two monks, both linked in different ways to Montecassino: Alfano, a monk at the abbey and later Archbishop of Salerno, and Constantine the African. Later translators drew either directly on Galen or on existing Syriac and Arabic translations. See Anna Maria Urso, "Translating Galen in the Medieval West: The Greek-Latin Translations," in *Brill's Companion to the Reception of Galen*, ed. Petros Bouras-Vallianatos and Barbara Zipser (Leiden: Brill, 2019), 359–80, accessed February 8, 2023, https://tinyurl.com/36h3d6wx.

18 See Thomas Sydenham (1624–1689), known as "the English Hippocrates" and the author of *Observationes medicae circa morborum acutorum historiam et curationem. Methodus curandi febres, propiis observationibus superstructa* (London: Kettilby, 1676); *Medical Observations Concerning the History and Cure of Acute Diseases*, trans. R. G. Latham, in *The Works of Thomas Sydenham, M.D.*, vol. 1 (London: The Sydenham Society, 1848). Hermann Boerhaave (1668–1738), a Dutch physician and professor of medicine, wrote textbooks that were widely used during and after his lifetime. See H. Boerhaave, *Institutiones Medicae* [Medical Principles] (Leiden, 1708), and *Aphorisimi de Cognoscendis et Curandis Morbis* [Aphorisms on the Recognition and Treatment of Diseases] (Leiden, 1709); B. Aymen, *Dissertation [sur] les jours critiques* (Paris: Rault, 1752). The article "Crise" in the *Encyclopédie ou Dictionnaire raisonné des sciences, des arts et des métiers* of D'Alembert and Diderot, vol. 4 (Lausanne: Société typographique) was written by the French physician Théophile de Bordeu (1722–1776), and fills eighteen folio pages. See also M. Foucault,

Psychiatric Power: Lectures at the Collège de France, 1973–74, trans. Graham Burchell (Basingstoke and New York: Palgrave Macmillan, 2006), January 23, 1974, esp. notes 258–59n23 and 24.

19 Hippocrates, *Affections* VIII, in *Hippocrates*, vol. 5, trans. Paul Potter (Cambridge, MA: Loeb Classical Library, 1988).

20 Helen King, *Greek and Roman Medicine* (Bristol: Bristol Classical Press), 13.

21 *Galenos Peri Kriseon: Überlieferung und Text*, ed. and trans. Bengt Alexanderson, Studia Graeca et Latina Gotheburgensia 23 (Gothenburg: Elanders Boktryckeri Aktiebolag, 1967). No English translation available.

22 Galen, *Prognostic and Epidemics I: Prognostic*, chapter 20; *Epidemics* I, chapter 26. Available from the Perseus Digital Library, https://tinyurl.com/2k7xbmwn. Galen considered a critical day to occur every four days. Based on his and others' observation of malaria, he concluded that the most important critical days were the seventh, fourteenth, and twentieth. See Galen, *Galenos Peri Kriseon*, and *On the Critical Days*, in *Medieval Prognosis and Astrology: A Working Edition of the* Aggregationes de crisi et criticis diebus *with Introduction and English Summary*, ed. Cornelius O'Boyle (Cambridge: Wellcome Unit for the History of Medicine, 1991).

23 King, *Greek and Roman Medicine*, 18.

24 See Fielding H. Garrison, *An Introduction to the History of Medicine* (Philadelphia, PA: W. B. Sanders Company, 1966), chapter 4.

25 See "Hippocratic Oath," Perseus Digital Library, https://tinyurl.com/587shp8s.

26 See Glen M. Cooper, "Numbers, Prognosis, and Healing: Galen on Medical Theory," *Journal of the Washington Academy of Sciences* 90, no. 2 (2004): 47.

27 Abu 'Ali al-Husayn Ibn (Avicenna), *Cantica Avicennae*, Ia pars, 3, v. 366. Avicenna's *Poem on Medicine* was translated several times in Latin between the thirteenth and seventeenth century, and widely read. See *Cantica Avicennae*, or *Poème de la médecine*, Latin trans. Armengaud de Blaise (thirteenth century), French ed. and trans. Henri Jahier and Abdelkader Noureddine (Paris: Les Belles Lettres, 1956).

28 Avicenna, *Cantica Avicennae*, v. 489.

29 "This is the Crysis of Parliaments; we shall know by this if Parliaments live or die." Cited in Koselleck, *Crisis*, 362.

30 *Journal et mémoires du Marquis d'Argenson*, vol. 2 (Paris: Mme Ve Jules Renouard, 1859), 335 (from December 1739); vol. 7 (Paris: Mme Ve Jules Renouard, 1865), 221 (from May 6, 1752).

31 See Koselleck, *Crisis*, 368.

32 John Hicks, "Keynes' Theory of Employment," *The Economic Journal* 46, no. 182 (June 1936): 239.

33 Simon Clarke, *Marx's Theory of Crisis* (Basingstoke: The Macmillan Press, 1994), 3.

34 James Meadway, "We're Living in an Age of Permanent Crisis—Let's Stop Planning for a 'Return to Normal,'" *The Guardian*, July 22, 2022.

35 Peter Barnes, "Economics for the Anthropocene," ed. Hildegarde Hannum, Schumacher Center Lecture, American Institute for Economic Research, Great Barrington, MA, July 2014, https://centerforneweconomics.org/publications/economics-for-the-anthropocene/.

36 *The Economist* mentions Minsky in thirty articles between 2007 and 2016, but in only one (and in passing) prior to that.

37 See Hyman Minsky, *Stabilizing an Unstable Economy* (New Haven, CT: Yale University Press, 1990).

38 Clarke, 4. In §3 of his 1857 *General Introduction to the Critique of Political Economy*, Marx announces a plan in five parts, the fifth of which was to be devoted to "the world market and crises." This topic and the connection between those two phenomena appear again in *Capital*, vol. 4, Part II, chapter 17: "Ricardo's Theory of Accumulation and a Critique of It. (The Very Nature of Capital Leads to Crises)," especially §§ 6–15. In the early 1840s, Engels published articles on the *critical* economic situation in England, which he attributed to its inherent contradictions. See F. Engels, "The English View of the Internal Crises," *Rheinische Zeitung* 342 (December 8, 1842); "The Internal Crises," *Rheinische Zeitung* 343 (December 9, 1842). Both are available in *Marx and Engels Collected Works*, vol. 2. (London: Lawrence Wishart, 1975).

39 Max Horkheimer, *Critical Theory: Selected Essays*, trans. Matthew J. O'Connell and others (New York: Continuum, 1992), 227.

40 Wilhelm Röpke, *The Social Crisis of Our Time*, trans. Annette Peter Schiffer Jacobsohn (Chicago, IL: The University of Chicago Press, 1950). In 1943, Röpke published an article in which he described the Beveridge Plan, then in place in the United Kingdom and inspired by Keynes, as paving the road to authoritarian rule and tyranny. See W. Röpke, "Das Beveridgeplan," *Schweizer Monatshefte für Politik und Kultur*, June–July 1943. Röpke reiterated his critique a year later in *Civitas Humana* (1944), translated by Cyril Spencer Fox as *Civitas Humana: A Humane Order of Society* (London: William Hodge, 1948), 142–9. In 1944, the Labor Party was elected in the UK in a landslide that brought about the implementation of the 1944 Education Act and the creation of the National Health Service, together with the provision of universal entitlements for pensions and unemployment. But Röpke's ideas, and those of neoliberalism more generally, resurfaced in 1975, when Margaret Thatcher held up Hayek's work as the new bible and proceeded to turn it into policy in the early 1980s.

41 Michel Foucault, *The Birth of Biopolitics: Lectures at the Collège de France, 1978–1979*, trans. Graham Burchell (New York: Palgrave Macmillan, 2008), 104.

42 Röpke, *The Social Crisis of Our Time*, 23.

43 Röpke, *The Social Crisis of Our Time*, iii.

44 Michel Foucault, *"Society Must Be Defended." Lectures at the Collège de France, 1975–1976*, trans. David Macey (London: Penguin Books, 2004), March 17, 1976; *Security, Territory, Population: Lectures at the Collège de France, 1977–1978*, trans. Graham Burchell (New York: Picador, 2004), January 11 and 25, 1978.

45 Foucault, *Psychiatric Power*, 265.

46 G. Canguilhem, "Health: Popular Concept and Philosophical Question," in *Writings on Medicine*, trans. S. Geroulanos and Todd Meyers (New York: Fordham University Press, 2012), 48.

47 Foucault, *Security, Territory, Population*, 88–90.

48 Foucault, *Security, Territory, Population*, 88.

49 Foucault, *Security, Territory, Population*, 88–9.

50 Foucault, *Security, Territory, Population*, 89.

51 Foucault, *Security, Territory, Population*, 89–90.

52 Rodrigo Cordero, *Crisis and Critique: On the Fragile Foundations of Social Life* (London and New York: Routledge, 2017), 141.

53 See Foucault, *The Birth of Biopolitics*, 116.

54 The Draft Statement of Aims is reproduced in *The Road from Mont Pèlerin: The Making of the Neoliberal Thought Collective*, ed. Philip Mirowski and Dieter Plehwe (Cambridge, MA: Harvard University Press, 2009), 22–4.

55 Mirowski and Plehwe, *The Road from Mont Pèlerin*, 22–3.

56 Mirowski and Plehwe, *The Road from Mont Pèlerin*, 22–3, emphasis added.

57 Philip Mirowski, "Postface: Defining Neoliberalism," in Mirowski and Plehwe, *The Road from Mont Pèlerin*, 437.

58 Rob Van Horn and Philip Mirowski, "The Rise of the Chicago School of Economics," in Mirowski and Plehwe, *The Road from Mont Pèlerin*, 161–2.

59 David Hume, *An Enquiry Concerning Human Understanding*, ed. Stephen Buckle (Cambridge: Cambridge University Press, 2007 [1748]), Section VIII, Part I, 65.

60 See M. Foucault, *Qu'est-ce que la critique? suivi de La culture de soi*, ed. Henri-Paul Fruchaud and Daniele Lorenzini (Paris: Vrin, 2015), 81–4. See also Foucault's 1978 "Introduction" to the American translation of Georges Canguilhem's *The Normal and the Pathological*, trans. Carolyn R. Fawcett in collaboration with Robert S. Cohen (New York: Zone Books, 1991), 5, 10.

61 Foucault, *Psychiatric Power*, 239–47.

62 Aristotle, *On Interpretation*, in *The Basic Works of Aristotle*, ed. Richard McKeon, trans. E. M. Edghill (New York: Random House, 1941), 17a1–3.

63 Mendelssohn's response to the question "*Was ist Aufklärung?*" ("What Is Enlightenment?") was originally published in the *Berlinische Monatsschrift* 4 (1784): 193–200. Reprinted in Moses Mendelssohn, *Gesammelte Schriften Jubilaümsausgabe*, vol. 6/1 (Stuttgart-Bad Cannstatt: Frommann-Holzboog, 1981), 115–19. Kant's response, which was written before its author had a chance to read Mendelssohn's piece, was published in the same journal in December 1784. See I. Kant, "Beantwortung der Frage: Was ist Aufklärung?," *Berlinische Monatsschrift* 12 (1784): 481–94; I. Kant, "An Answer to the Question: What Is Enlightenment?" in Kant, *Practical Philosophy*, trans. and ed. Mary J. Gregor (Cambridge: Cambridge University Press, 1999), 11–22. For Foucault's assessment of those texts, see Michel Foucault, *The Government of Self and Others: Lectures at the Collège de France, 1982–83*, trans. Graham Burchell (New York: Palgrave Macmillan, 2010), January 5, 1983.

64 Foucault, *The Government of Self and Others*, 184.

65 Foucault, *The Government of Self and Others*, 106.

66 M. Foucault, *The Courage of Truth (The Government of Self and Others II): Lectures at the Collège de France 1983–1984*, trans. Graham Burchell (New York: Palgrave Macmillan, 2011), 19.

67 Foucault, *The Government of Self and Others*, 47.

68 Foucault, *The Government of Self and Others*, 229.

69 Foucault, *The Government of Self and Others*, 196.

70 Foucault, *The Government of Self and Others*, 232.

71 Foucault, 214–19, 227–31.

72 Plato, letter VII, 330c-d, cited in Foucault, *The Government of Self and Others*, 231. See Plato, *The Collected Dialogues*, ed. Edith Hamilton and Huntington Cairns, trans. L. A. Post (Princeton, NJ: Princeton University Press, 1961), 1579: "One who advises a sick man, living in a way to injure his health, must first effect a reform in his way of living. Must he not? And if the patient consents to such a reform, then he may admonish him on other points? If, however, the patient refuses, in my opinion it would be the act of a real man and a good physician to keep clear of advising such a man."

73 Foucault, *The Government of Self and Others*, 231.

74 Foucault, *The Government of Self and Others*, 231.

75 Foucault, *The Government of Self and Others*, 232.

76 Foucault, *The Government of Self and Others*, 232.

77 Foucault, *The Government of Self and Others*, 232, emphasis added.

78 Foucault, *The Government of Self and Others*, 233.

79 Foucault, *The Government of Self and Others*, 66.

80 Cordero, *Crisis and Critique*, 135.

81 Foucault, *The Courage of Truth*, 183–6. I analyze the logic of revolution in Chapter 3.

82 Michel Foucault, "Interview between Michel Foucault and Claude Bonnefoy, 1968," in *Speech Begins After Death: In Conversation with Claude Bonnefoy*, ed. Philippe Artières, trans. Roberto Bononno (Minneapolis, MN: University of Minnesota Press, 2013), 35.

83 Koselleck, *Critique and Crisis*, 102n11. To be sure, in book 2 of *Émile ou de l'Éducation* (1761) Rousseau announced an age of "crisis" and "revolution": "You reckon on the present order of society, without considering that this order is itself subject to inscrutable changes, and that you can neither foresee nor provide against the revolution which may affect your children. The great become small, the rich poor, the king a commoner. Does fate strike so seldom that you can count on immunity from her blows? The crisis is approaching, and we are on the edge of a revolution." See Jean-Jacques Rousseau, *Émile*, trans. Barbara Foxley (New York: Barnes and Noble, 2005), 77. A few years after the publication of *Émile*, Thomas Payne chose the title *The Crisis* for his periodical, in which he commented on the American War of Independence between 1776 and 1783, a civil war he described as a moral crisis and a struggle between virtue and vice, or Freedom and Tyranny. Still, crisis is not a fundamental concept in Rousseau, and remained marginal throughout the eighteenth century.

84 Marsilius of Padua, *The Defender of the Peace*, ed. and trans. Annabel Brett (Cambridge: Cambridge University Press, 2005), discourse 1, chapter 1, §3; Alexander Aichele, "Heart and Soul of the State: Some Remarks Concerning Aristotelian Ontology and Medieval Theory of Medicine in Marsilius of Padua's *Defensor pacis*," in *The World of Marsilius of Padua*, ed. Gerson Moreno-Rieño (Turnhout: Brepols, 2006), 163–86; Takashi Shogimen, "Medicine and the Body Politic in Marsilius' *Defensor Pacis*," in *A Companion to Marsilius of Padua*, ed. Gerson Moreno-Rieño and Cary J. Nederman (Leiden: Brill, 2011), 71–115.

85 On the question of the influence of Marsilius on Machiavelli, see Antonio Toscano, *Marsilio da Padova e Niccolò Machiavelli* (Ravenna: Longo editore, 1981). See also Laurent Gerbier, *Histoire, médecine et politique. Les figures du temps dans le Prince et les Discours de Machiavel* (Doctoral thesis, Université François-Rabelais de Tours, December 20, 1999), 274–82. My thanks to Laurent Gerbier for sharing his thesis with me. On the presence and significance of the medical paradigm in Machiavelli, see Anthony Parel, *The Machiavellian Cosmos* (Princeton, NJ: Princeton University Press, 1992) and Gerbier, *Histoire, médecine et politique*, part 3 ("Les Figures médicales du temps"). Much of the following draws on chapters 7 and 8 of Gerbier's thesis.

86 Niccolò Machiavelli, *The Prince*, trans. Harvey C. Mansfield, 2nd ed. (Chicago, IL: The University of Chicago Press, 1998).

87 Niccolò Machiavelli, *Discourses on Livy*, trans. Harvey C. Mansfield and Nathan Tarcov (Chicago, IL: The University of Chicago Press, 1996).

88 Niccolò Machiavelli, *Florentine Histories*, trans. Laura F. Banfield and Harvey C. Mansfield (Princeton, NJ: Princeton University Press, 1988).

89 On the role and meaning of "humors" in Machiavelli's thought, see Marie Gaille-Nikodimov, "A la recherche d'une définition des institutions de la liberté. La médecine, langage du politique chez Machiavel," *Astérion* 1 (2003), https://doi.org/10.4000/asterion.14. See also Gerbier, *Histoire, médecine et politique*, 287–94.

90 Machiavelli, *The Prince*, 39. See also *Discourses*, I, 4. In *The Prince*, chapter 19, Machiavelli also includes the army as a humor.

91 Machiavelli, *Discourses*, I, 17.

92 Machiavelli, *Discourses*, I, 2, §7.

93 Filippo Del Lucchese, "Crisis and Power: Economics, Politics and Conflict in Machiavelli's Thought," *History of Political Thought* 30, no. 1 (Spring 2009): 76.

94 Machiavelli, *Discourses*, I, 18, §4.

95 Machiavelli, *Discourses*, I, 9, §2.

96 Del Lucchese, "Crisis and Power," 95–6.

97 Del Lucchese, "Crisis and Power," 81.

98 Machiavelli, *Florentine Histories*, II, 12.

99 Machiavelli, *Florentine Histories*, II, 17.

100 There is much debate around how to read and interpret the speech, especially around the question of whether it reflects Machiavelli's own view (at least in part), or if he presents it as a cautionary tale. On this question, see Yves Winter, "Plebeian Politics: Machiavelli and the Ciompi Uprising," *Political Theory* 4, no. 6 (December 2012): 736–66. In any event, Machiavelli is clear about the fact that the history of Florence is one in which certain groups—the *popolo minuto* and the *pleba infima* in particular—were profoundly dissatisfied as a result of a deeply entrenched inequality of wealth and power between groups.

101 See Machiavelli, *Florentine Histories*, preface.

102 See Machiavelli, *The Prince*, chapter 3.

103 See Machiavelli, *Discourses*, I, 7.

104 See Koselleck, *Crisis*, 372–6, 387.

105 I will focus on Hölderlin, Schelling, and Hegel. For an account of Schiller's views on tragedy, see Joshua Billings, *Genealogy of the Tragic: Greek Tragedy and German Philosophy* (Princeton, NJ: Princeton University Press, 2014), 88–97, 113–23. In his book, and in addition to the figures I mentioned, Billings also discusses A. W. Schlegel, Friedrich Schlegel, and Gottfried Hermann.

106 Billings, *Genealogy of the Tragic*, 132.

107 Billings, *Genealogy of the Tragic*, 135.

108 In Chapter 2, I analyze Carl Schmitt's reading of *Hamlet* as a response to Walter Benjamin's *The Origin of the German Tragic Drama* and as a way of illustrating his own theory of sovereignty as the decision regarding the state of exception.

109 Immanuel Kant, *Critique of Pure Reason*, trans. and ed. Paul Guyer and Allen W. Wood (Cambridge: Cambridge University Press, 1998), A840/B868.

110 See Françoise Dastur, "Tragedy and Speculation," in *Philosophy and Tragedy*, ed. Miguel de Beistegui and Simon Sparks (London: Routledge, 2000), 77.

111 Friedrich Hölderlin, *Essays and Letters on Theory*, ed. Thomas Pfau (Albany, NY: SUNY Press, 1988), 84.

112 Hölderlin makes this clear in a letter to his friend Niethammer, dated February 24, 1796. See Hölderlin, *Essays and Letters*, 131.

113 Friedrich Wilhelm Joseph Schelling, *Philosophische Briefe über Dogmatismus und Kriticismus* in *Schellings sämmtliche Werke*, ed. K. F. A. Schelling, vol. 01.1.1 (Stuttgart: Cotta, 1856). See Peter Szondi, "The Notion of the Tragic in Schelling, Hölderlin and Hegel," in *On Textual Understanding and Other Essays*, trans. Harvey Mendelsohn (Minneapolis, MN: University of Minnesota Press, 1986), 43–55; and the chapter devoted to Schelling's poetics of genre in Szondi's *Poetik und Geschichtsphilosophie II* (Frankfurt am Main: Suhrkamp, 1974). See also Dastur, "Tragedy and Speculation," 78–9.

114 Friedrich Joseph Wilhelm von Schelling, *The Philosophy of Art*, trans. Douglas W. Stott (Minneapolis, MN: University of Minnesota Press, 1989), 249. Cited in Jean-François Courtine, "Of Tragic Metaphor," in *Philosophy and Tragedy*, ed. Miguel de Beistegui and Simon Sparks (London: Routledge, 2000), 58.

115 Dastur, "Tragedy and Speculation," 79.

116 Billings, *Genealogy of the Tragic*, 127.

117 Hölderlin, *Essays and Letters*, 85.

118 Hölderlin, *Essays and Letters*, 37.

119 Hölderlin, *Essays and Letters*, 71.

120 See Hölderlin, "Remarks on 'Antigone,'" in *Essays and Letters*, 113–14. The latter possibility, Dastur argues, appears in the figure of the adversary in the third version of Hölderlin's *Antigone*.

121 G. W. F. Hegel, *Natural Law*, trans. T. M. Knox (Philadelphia, PA: University of Pennsylvania Press, 1975).

122 Hegel, *Natural Law*, 104.

123 Hegel, *Aesthetics: Lectures on Fine Art*, trans. T. M. Knox, 2 vols. (Oxford: Oxford University Press, 1975).

124 Hegel, *Aesthetics*, 2.1198.

125 Hegel, *Natural Law*, 104.

126 More recently and in the specific context of the ecological crisis, Stephen M. Gardiner has adopted the motif of tragedy to characterize the ethical conflict, or "perfect moral storm," with which we are currently confronted. It is one that pits the interests and well-being of this generation against those of future generations. Climate change, he argues, is an instance of "intergenerational ethics" and the most obvious and serious example of "intergenerational buck-passing." See Stephen M. Gardiner, *A Perfect Moral Storm: The Ethical Tragedy of Climate Change* (Oxford: Oxford University Press, 2011). While Gardiner doesn't understand tragedy in a dialectical sense, he does equate crisis in the strong sense with tragedy, and tragedy with a profound ethical conflict (a "perfect moral storm") involving, in addition to intergenerational conflict, the asymmetrical relation of power between rich and poor, and the vulnerability of "nature" in the face of human activity. In my discussion of the ecological crisis, I too will retain the idea of a duty to future generations, and to the earth, as a crucial principle of environmental ethics. But I am most skeptical of Gardiner's separation of ethics and politics, and his avoidance of what I take to be a necessary *critique* of the long-term and far-reaching material processes—capitalism and technology in particular—that led to the crisis in question. Instead, Gardiner constructs a "fairy tale," a "pure scenario" or de-historicized "hypothetical case" and "paradigm" (pp. 149, 150, 164), against which he examines the question of our moral obligation toward future generations, and the data available from the Intergovernmental Panel on Climate Change (IPCC). I want to include the "impurity" of material processes, of history, of power structures, and of human passions and desires in my own assessment of the ecological crisis, indeed of crisis in general, and in the kind of ethics this time of crisis might call for.

127 G. W. F. Hegel, *Logik*, vol. 2, 563/835. References are to the edition in two volumes published by Suhrkamp as volumes 5 and 6 of G. W. F. Hegel, *Werke in zwanzig Bänden* (Frankfurt am Main: Suhrkamp, 1969), followed by references to A. V. Miller's translation, *Hegel's Science of Logic* (Atlantic Highlands, NJ: Humanities Press, 1969), which I modify.

128 Hegel, *Logik*, 75/439–40, emphasis added.

129 Hegel, *Logik*, 78/442.

130 Hegel, *Logik*, 75/439.

131 Jürgen Habermas, *Zur Verfassung Europas. Ein Essay* (Berlin: Suhrkamp Verlag, 2011).

132 Roberto Esposito, *Da Fuori. Una filosofia per l'Europa* (Turin: Einaudi, 2016).

133 Frédéric Worms, *Les maladies chroniques de la démocratie* (Paris: Desclée de Brouwer, 2017).

134 Bernard E. Harcourt, *Critique & Praxis* (New York: Columbia University Press, 2020), 22.

135 Paul Valéry, "La Crise de l'esprit," in *Essais quasi politiques, Œuvres*, vol. 1, ed. Gallimard (Paris: Bibliothèque de la Pléiade, 1957), 988–1014. The two "Letters from France" were originally published in *The Athenaeum: A Journal of English and Foreign Literature, Science, The Fine Arts, Music, and the Drama* 4641 (April 11, 1919): 182–84, and *The Athenaeum* 4644 (May 2, 1919): 279–80.

136 Edmund Husserl, *The Crisis of European Sciences and Transcendental Phenomenology*, trans. David Carr (Evanston, IL: Northwestern University Press, 1970). As a Jew, Husserl was denied any public platform and had to publish his text outside Germany, through a publisher in Belgrade. Karl Jaspers develops a similar argument in *Man and the Modern Age*, trans. Eden Paul and Cedar Paul (Garden City, NY: Doubleday, 1957). The crisis of science, he writes, "really depends upon the human beings who are effected by the scientific situation" (p. 147).

137 Jacques Derrida, "The 'World' of the Enlightenment to Come (Exception, Calculation, Sovereignty)," trans. Pascale-Anne Brault and Michael Naas, *Research In Phenomenology* 33 (2003): 19.

138 Husserl, *Crisis of European Sciences*, 290.

139 Husserl, *Crisis of European Sciences*, 299.

140 Husserl, *Crisis of European Sciences*, 299.

141 Friedrich Meinecke, *Historism: The Rise of a New Historical Outlook*, trans. J. E. Anderson (London: Routledge and Kegan Paul, 1972). On Heidegger's critique of historicism and, more broadly, the crisis of historicism as a narrative about progress, meaning, and rationality in Germany between 1880 and 1930, see Charles R. Bambach, *Heidegger, Dilthey and the Crisis of Historicism* (Ithaca, NY: Cornell University Press, 1995). I agree with Bambach's claim that Heidegger's work represents "a genuine philosophy *of* crisis" (p. 14), albeit one that is never presented as such. Heidegger's specific crisis-philosophy is also incomprehensible outside the general "crisis-consciousness" of the time, reflected in the themes of loss, destruction, apocalypse, catastrophe (especially that of 1918), and decline found in the works of Spengler, Barth, Weber, Bloch, Meinecke, Troelsch, and others (p. 14), as well as in the crisis affecting philosophy itself, torn as it was between the positivism of

neo-Kantian *Erkenntnistheorie* and the "world-view" philosophy that stressed the lived, relative, and historical character of truth. Heidegger's philosophy of crisis is therefore a response to the cultural and "spiritual" crisis of the time, as well as to the internalization of crisis as a defining schema of existence and history.

142 M. Heidegger, *Gesamtausgabe 60: Phänomenologie des religiösen Lebens*, ed. Matthias Jung, Thomas Regehly, and Claudius Strube (Frankfurt am Main: Vittorio Klostermann, 1995), hereafter cited as *GA 60*; M. Heidegger, *Sein und Zeit* (Tübingen: Max Niemeyer, 1927), hereafter cited as *SZ*.

143 See *GA 60*, §12.

144 *GA 60*, 244, 254, 266.

145 *GA 60*, 268.

146 *SZ*, §§ 54–60.

147 M. Heidegger, *Gesamtausgabe 65: Beiträge zur Philosophie (Vom Ereignis)*, ed. Friedrich-Wilhelm von Herrmann (Frankfurt am Main: Vittorio Klostermann, 1989), 98. I return to this question, and to what I call the Technocene, in the final chapter of this book.

148 M. Heidegger, *Nietzsche*, vol. 4, trans. David Farrell Krell (New York: Harper & Row, 1982), 241.

149 See Heidegger, *Gesamtausgabe 65: Beiträge zur Philosophie*, §§ 44–9.

150 M. Heidegger, *Gesamtausgabe 71: Das Ereignis*, ed. Friedrich-Wilhelm von Herrmann (Frankfurt am Main: Vittorio Klostermann, 2009), §§ 111, 131–38, 280, 354.

151 M. Heidegger, *Gesamtausgabe 69: Die Geschichte des Seyns*, ed. Peter Trawny (Frankfurt am Main: Vittorio Klostermann, 1998), §§ 59–60, hereafter cited as *GA 69*.

152 *GA 69*, §§ 99–100, 195; M. Heidegger, *Gesamtausgabe 94: Überlegungen II-VI (Schwarze Hefte 1931–1938)*, ed. Peter Trawny (Frankfurt am Main: Vittorio Klostermann, 2014), 362; M. Heidegger, *Gesamtausgabe 96: Überlegungen VII–XV (Schwarze Hefte 1938–1941)*, ed. Peter Trawny (Frankfurt am Main: Vittorio Klostermann, 2014), 17.

153 Hannah Arendt, "The Crisis in Education" and "The Crisis in Culture: Its Social and Its Political Significance," in *Between Past and Future* (New York: The Viking Press, 1968).

154 Hannah Arendt, *Crises of the Republic* (San Diego, CA, New York, and London: HBJ Book, 1972). The volume includes a famous—and still topical—essay on "Lying in Politics."

155 Arendt, *Between Past and Future*, 175, emphasis added.

156 Arendt, *Between Past and Future*, 185.

157 Arendt, *Between Past and Future*, 205.

158 Arendt, *Between Past and Future*, 189–94, 208–9.

159 Arendt, *Between Past and Future*, 178.

160 Arendt, *Between Past and Future*, 174.

161 Thomas S. Kuhn, *The Structure of Scientific Revolutions* (Chicago, IL: The University of Chicago Press, 1962).

162 Kuhn, *Structure of Scientific Revolutions*, 96.

163 Kuhn, *Structure of Scientific Revolutions*, 24.

164 Kuhn, *Structure of Scientific Revolutions*, 24.

165 Kuhn, *Structure of Scientific Revolutions*, 52, 96.

166 Kuhn, *Structure of Scientific Revolutions*, 53.

167 Kuhn, *Structure of Scientific Revolutions*, 53.

168 Alan Musgrave and Charles Pigden, "Imre Lakatos," in *Stanford Encyclopedia of Philosophy*, Fall 2020 edition, https://plato.stanford.edu/entries/lakatos/.

169 Musgrave and Pigden, "Imre Lakatos."

170 Imre Lakatos, *The Methodology of Scientific Research Programmes: Philosophical Papers 1*, ed. John Worrall and Gregory Currie (Cambridge: Cambridge University Press, 1978), 6.

171 Lakatos, *Methodology of Scientific Research Programmes*, 34.

172 Musgrave and Pigden, "Imre Lakatos."

173 Kuhn, *Structure of Scientific Revolutions*, 97.

174 Kuhn, *Structure of Scientific Revolutions*, 97.

175 "Luminiferous aether"—a "material substance" with a "state of motion"—was thought to be the medium for the propagation of light.

176 Kuhn, *Structure of Scientific Revolutions*, 68.

177 Kuhn, *Structure of Scientific Revolutions*, 109.

178 Kuhn, *Structure of Scientific Revolutions*, 93.

179 Kuhn, *Structure of Scientific Revolutions*, 121.

180 Kuhn, *Structure of Scientific Revolutions*, 121.

181 Kuhn, *Structure of Scientific Revolutions*, 122.

182 Kuhn, *Structure of Scientific Revolutions*, 111.

183 Kuhn, *Structure of Scientific Revolutions*, 111.

184 Kuhn, *Structure of Scientific Revolutions*, 112.

185 Kuhn, *Structure of Scientific Revolutions*, 119.

186 Kuhn, *Structure of Scientific Revolutions*, 109. See also p. 148. Kuhn provides several examples. One, which I already mentioned, is that opposing Aristotelians and Galileo in the early seventeenth century. Another is the dispute between the two French chemists Proust and Berthollet: "The first claimed that all chemical reactions occurred in fixed proportions, the latter that they did not. Each collected impressive experimental evidence for his view. Nevertheless, the two men necessarily talked through each other, and their debate was entirely inconclusive" (p. 132). It was even aporetic. It is only when John Dalton, who was not a chemist and was not even interested in chemistry, but a meteorologist investigating the (for him) physical problems of the absorption of gases by water and of water by the atmosphere, came up with his famous theory of chemical atomic theory that the aporia was lifted. Only by adopting another paradigm, one in which forces of affinity played no role, was he able to account for the observable homogeneity of solutions and reveal the law of constant proportion as a tautology. "A law that experiment could not have established before Dalton's work, became, once that work was accepted, a constitutive principle that no single set of chemical measurements could have upset" (p. 133). If this particular case study is such a good example of a scientific revolution, it is because "the same chemical manipulations assumed a relationship to chemical generalization very different from the one they had had before" (p. 133). A new way of practicing chemistry had been introduced.

187 Kuhn, *Structure of Scientific Revolutions*, 148.

188 Kuhn, *Structure of Scientific Revolutions*, 148.

189 Kuhn, *Structure of Scientific Revolutions*, 149.

190 Kuhn, *Structure of Scientific Revolutions*, 149.

191 Kuhn, *Structure of Scientific Revolutions*, 157.

192 Kuhn, *Structure of Scientific Revolutions*, 94, emphasis added.

193 Kuhn, *Structure of Scientific Revolutions*, 158, emphasis added.

194 Kuhn, *Structure of Scientific Revolutions*, 150.

195 Kuhn, *Structure of Scientific Revolutions*, 94.

196 Kuhn, *Structure of Scientific Revolutions*, 94.

197 Kuhn, *Structure of Scientific Revolutions*, 94.

198 Kuhn, *Structure of Scientific Revolutions*, 94.

199 Kuhn, *Structure of Scientific Revolutions*, 158.

200 Kuhn, *Structure of Scientific Revolutions*, 93.

201 See Lázló Ropolyi, "Lakatos and Lukács," in *Appraising Lakatos: Mathematics, Methodology and the Man*, ed. G. Kampis, L. Kvasz, and M. Stöltzner (Dordrecht: Kluwer Academic Publishers, 2002): 303–37.

202 Georg Lukács, *History and Class Consciousness*, trans. Rodney Livinsgtone (Cambridge, MA: The MIT Press, 1968), 10.

203 Lukács, *History and Class Consciousness*, 10.

204 Lukács, *History and Class Consciousness*, 10.

205 Lukács, *History and Class Consciousness*, 10.

206 Lukács, *History and Class Consciousness*, 11.

Chapter 2

1 See G. Agamben, *State of Exception*, trans. Kevin Attell (Chicago, IL: The University of Chicago Press, 2005), Chapter 3. On the connection between crisis and the state of exception in Roman times, see A. Bowman, A. Cameron, and P. Garnsey, eds., *The Cambridge Ancient History 12: The Crisis of Empire, A.D. 193–337*, 2nd ed. (Cambridge: Cambridge University Press, 2005 [second edition]); Arthur M. Eckstein, *Mediterranean Anarchy, Interstate War, and the Rise of Rome* (Berkeley and Los Angeles, CA: University of California Press, 2006), 1–36; Olivia Hekster, Gerda de Kleijn, and Daniëlle Slootjes, eds., *Crises and the Roman Empire: Proceedings of the Seventh Workshop of the International Network Impact of Empire* (Leiden: Brill, 2007); Gregory K. Holden, *Crisis Management during the Roman Empire* (Cambridge: Cambridge University Press, 2013).

2 Adolf Berger and Andrew Lintott, "*Iustitium*," in *Oxford Classical Dictionary*, ed. Simon Hornblower, Antony Spawforth, and Esther Eidinow (Oxford: Oxford University Press, 2020).

3 Holden, *Crisis Management during the Roman Empire*, 87.

4 Marin, *Pour une théorie baroque de l'action politique*, 27.

5 Marin, *Pour une théorie baroque de l'action politique*, 27–8.

6 Marin, *Pour une théorie baroque de l'action politique*, 28.

7 Gabriel Naudé, cited in Foucault, *Security, Territory, Population: Lectures at the Collège de France, 1977–1978*, 261. The passage Foucault refers to is the following: "*marcher sous la même définition que nous avons déjà donnée aux maximes et à la raison d'État, qu'elles sont un excès du droit commun, à cause du bien public,* ou pour m'étendre un peu davantage en français, *des actions hardies et extraordinaires que les*

princes sont contraints d'exécuter aux affaires difficiles et comme désespérées, contre le droit commun, sans garder même aucun ordre ni forme de justice, hasardant l'intérêt du particulier, pour le bien du public" (Naudé, p. 156). To illustrate his theory, Naudé refers to various examples, such as the expulsion of the Moriscos and Marranos from Spain, the execution of 40,000 Romans in one day by Mithridates, or the Sicilian Vespers. But he singles out the mass killing of Protestants by Catholics on 24 August 1572, known as the massacre of Saint Bartholomew, as the boldest and finest *coup d'état* ever perpetrated in France (188). He also finds it entirely justified and necessary, yet incomplete (p. 191). Interestingly, the language he uses in his assessment of a job only half done is borrowed from the medicine of humors and crisis: "*Il fallait imiter les chirurgiens experts, qui pendant que la veine est ouverte, tirent du sang jusques aux défaillances, pour nettoyer les corps cacochymes de leurs mauvaises humeurs . . .*" (p. 189). See Yves-Charles Zarka, "Raison d'État, maximes d'État et coups d'"État chez Gabriel Naudé," in *Raison et déraison d État. Théoriciens et théories de la raison d État aux XVIe et XVIIe siècles*, ed. Yves-Charles Zarka (Paris: PUF, 1994), 151–69.

8 Cardin Le Bret, *De la souveraineté du roi, de son domaine et de sa couronne* (Paris, 1632), cited in M. Foucault, *Security, Territory, Population*, 263.

9 Foucault, *Security, Territory, Population*, 262.

10 I will return to some of those examples. For a survey of Carl Schmitt post-9/11, see William E. Scheuerman, "States of Emergency," in *The Oxford Handbook of Carl Schmitt*, ed. Hens Meierhenrich and Oliver Simons (Oxford: Oxford University Press, 2016), 560–5. See also Scott Horton, "The Return of Carl Schmitt," *Balkanization* (blog), November 7, 2005, https://tinyurl.com/3ke23vd4; William E. Scheuerman, "Carl Schmitt and the Road to Abu Ghraib," *Constellations* 13 (2006): 108–24. A recent collection of essays, *States of Exception: Law, History, Theory*, ed. Cosmin Cercel, Gian Giacomo Fusco, and Simon Lavis (Abingdon and New York: Routledge, 2021), engages at length and in different ways with the state of exception as formulated by Carl Schmitt, Walter Benjamin, and Giorgio Agamben.

11 Michael Hoelzl and Graham Ward, "Introduction," in *Dictatorship: From the Origin of the Modern Concept of Sovereignty to Proletarian Class Struggle*, ed. Carl Schmitt (1921, 1928; Cambridge: Polity Press, 2014), xi. The second edition (1928) appeared with a long appendix, "The Dictatorship of the President of the Reich According to Article 48 of the Weimar Constitution," which was originally delivered in April 1924 in Jena at the meeting of the German Constitutional Jurists.

12 Hoelzl and Ward, "Introduction," xi.

13 Scheuerman, "States of Emergency," 549.

14 Hoelzl and Ward, "Introduction," xi.

15 Carl Schmitt, "Diktatur," in *Staatslexikon im Auftrage der Görresgesellschaft*, vol. 1 (Freiburg: Herder, 1926), 1448. Cited in Hoelzl and Ward, xxiii, emphasis added.

16 Carl Schmitt, *Political Theology: Four Chapters on the Concept of Sovereignty*, trans. George Schwab (1922; repr. Chicago, IL: The University of Chicago Press, 2005), 9.

17 Schmitt, *Political Theology*, 12.

18 Schmitt, *Political Theology*, 13, 6.

19 Schmitt, *Political Theology*, 15, emphasis added.

20 Schmitt, *Political Theology*, 12.

21 Schmitt, *Political Theology*, 12.

22 Schmitt, *Political Theology*, 36.

23 Schmitt, *Political Theology*, 5.

24 Carl Schmitt, *Hamlet or Hecuba: The Intrusion of the Time into the Play*, trans. D. Pan and J. R. Rust (1956; repr. New York: Telos Press, 2009). Schmitt's interest in Shakespeare, and specifically *Hamlet*, belongs in a German tradition that dates back to Herder's *Shakespeare* (1773). See Johann Gottfried Herder, *Shakespeare*, ed. and trans. Gregory Moore (Princeton, NJ: Princeton University Press, 2008). Of particular significance for Schmitt's reading is Herder's historicist approach, for which the value of cultural artifacts consists in their ability to respond to their own historical context. For my discussion of Schmitt on *Hamlet* and, more broadly, tragedy, I have relied on the following three sources: David Pan, "Tragedy as Exception in Carl Schmitt's Hamlet or Hecuba," in Meierhenrich and Simons, *The Oxford Handbook of Carl Schmitt*, 731–50; Jennifer R. Rust and Julia Reinhard Lupton, "Introduction: Schmitt and Shakespeare," in Schmitt, *Hamlet or Hecuba*, xv–li; Victoria Kahn, "Hamlet or Hecuba: Carl Schmitt's Decision," *Representations* 83, no. 1 (Summer 2003): 67–96, https://tinyurl.com/3ph3m8x5.

25 See Walter Benjamin, *The Origin of German Tragic Drama*, trans. John Osborne (London: Verso Books, 1998).

26 Jacques Derrida, *Specters of Marx: The State of the Debt, the Work of Mourning and the New International*, trans. Peggy Kamuf, with intro. by Bernd Magnus and Stephen Cullenberg (1992; New York and London: Routledge, 1994).

27 Kahn, "Hamlet or Hecuba," 81–2.

28 Schmitt, *Hamlet or Hecuba*, 45.

29 Schmitt, *Hamlet or Hecuba*, 43.

30 Joshua Billings, "Margins of Genre: Walter Benjamin and the Idea of Tragedy," in *Tragedy and the Idea of Modernity*, ed. Joshua Billings and Miriam Leonard (New York: Oxford University Press, 2015), 269–70.

31 Benjamin, *Origin of German Tragic Drama*, 62.

32 Benjamin, *Origin of German Tragic Drama*, 53.

33 Rust and Lupton, "Introduction: Schmitt and Shakespeare," xxxvi.

34 This proximity is especially visible in the first two drafts of the essay. See Johann Gottfried Herder, *Shakespeare*, in *Schriften zur Asthetik und Literatur, 1767–1781*, ed. Günter E. Grimm, vol. 2 of Johann Gottfried Herder, *Werke* (Frankfurt am Main: Deutscher Klassiker Verlag, 1993), 524--5, 542, 548. For the history of the reception of Shakespeare in Germany, see Roger Paulin, *The Critical Reception of Shakespeare in Germany, 1682 1914* (Hildesheim: Olms, 2003). For an account of Herder's essay in its historical context, its opposition to an (essentially French) imitation of Greek tragedy, and its emphasis on the specific historical circumstances behind Shakespeare's dramas, see Billings, *Genealogy of the Tragic*, 55–9.

35 Schmitt, *Hamlet or Hecuba*, 48.

36 Carl Schmitt, *The Concept of the Political*, trans. George Schwab, foreword by Tracy Strong (Chicago, IL: The University of Chicago Press, 1996), 101, 103.

37 Søren Kierkegaard, *Fear and Trembling*, ed. and trans. with intro. and notes by Howard V. Hong and Edna H. Hong (Princeton, NJ: Princeton University Press, 1983), 83.

38 Søren Kierkegaard, *Either/Or*, vol. 1, trans. David F. Swenson and Lillian Marvin Swenson, with revisions and a foreword by Howard A. Johnson (Princeton, NJ: Princeton University Press, 1959), 285.

39 This strategy is paradigmatically illustrated by the anonymous author of "The Rotation Method: An Essay in the Theory of Social Prudence," as well as by Johannes in "Diary of a Seducer." See Kierkegaard, *Either/Or*, vol. 1, 281–7, 337–8, 341–2, 361–3.

40 In *Political Theology*, Schmitt praises Kierkegaard and draws on his conception of the "teleological suspension of the ethical"—his notion that faith demands an existential decision that cannot be conceptualized in terms of preexisting ethical or aesthetic categories—in formulating his conception of the political. However, by regarding the state of exception as "analogous" to the miracle in theology, Schmitt brings the religious and the political together in a way that Kierkegaard does not. This difference is reflected in Kierkegaard's own view of the tragic, which belongs in the ethical-political sphere, but not the religious one. Abraham, who epitomizes the religious stage of life, or the knight of faith, is precisely not a tragic character. See Kierkegaard, "The Tragic in Ancient Drama Reflected in the Tragic in Modern Drama," in *Either/Or*, vol. 1, and *Fear and Trembling*, especially Problema I ("Is There a Teleological Suspension of the Ethical?") and Problema III ("Was It Ethically Defensible for Abraham to Conceal His Undertaking from Sarah, from Eliezer, and from Isaac?").

41 Kahn, "Hamlet or Hecuba," 88; Kierkegaard, *Either/Or*, 141, 139–40.

42 Kahn, "Hamlet or Hecuba," 89

43 Kierkegaard, *Either/Or*, 141.

44 Schmitt, *Hamlet or Hecuba*, 40.

45 Schmitt, *Hamlet or Hecuba*, 41.

46 Schmitt, *Hamlet or Hecuba*, 41.

47 Schmitt, *Hamlet or Hecuba*, 41.

48 Marin, *Pour une théorie baroque de l'action politique*, 29.

49 As evidence, Marin mentions Corneille's *The Death of Pompey* (1642). See Marin, *Pour une théorie baroque de l'action politique*, 42 n.18. The tragedy begins with a deliberation between King Ptolemy XIII and his entourage (Act I, sc. 2, v. 43–8): should he order the assassination of Pompey, who is seeking refuge in Egypt after his defeat at the Battle of Pharsalus? "... *jamais potentat/N'eut à délibérer d'un si grand coup d'État.*" Marin also cites Racine's "Discours prononcé à l'Académie française à la reception de MM. de Corneille et de Bergeret, le deuxième Janvier 1685," in Jean Racine, *Œuvres complètes*, vol. 2 (Paris: Pléiade, 1966), 350. See Marin, *Pour une théorie baroque de l'action politique*, 43–4n28.

50 Benjamin, *The Origin of German Tragic Drama*, 62.

51 Benjamin, *The Origin of German Tragic Drama*, 65; see also Samuel Weber, "Taking Exception to Decision: Walter Benjamin and Carl Schmitt," *Diacritics* 22, no. 2.4 (1992): 6–7.

52 Schmitt, *Hamlet or Hecuba*, 41.

53 Schmitt, *Hamlet or Hecuba*.

54 See Schmitt, *Hamlet or Hecuba*, "Appendix Two: On the Barbaric Character of Shakespearean Drama: A Response to Walter Benjamin's *The Origin of German Tragic Drama*," 59–65.

55 Benjamin, *The Origin of German Tragic Drama*, 65. In late 1930, Benjamin wrote a letter to Schmitt in which he announces the imminent arrival of *The Origin of German Tragic Drama* and expresses both his debt to Schmitt's theory of sovereignty in the seventeenth century and his proximity to Schmitt's philosophy of the state as expressed in *Die Diktatur*. See Benjamin to Schmitt, December 9, 1930, in Walter Benjamin, *Gesammelte Schriften*, ed. R. Tiedemann and H. Schweppenhäuser (Frankfurt am Main: Suhrkamp, 1974–1989), vol. 1 (3), 887. Gershom Sholem, who was closest to Benjamin, spoke of the "deep admiration" his friend had for Schmitt (cited in C. Schmidt, *Der häretische Imperativ: Überlegungen sur theologischen Dialektik der Kulturwissenschaft in Deutschland* [Tübingen: Niemeyer, 2000], 157n2). And Benjamin himself, in his short curriculum vitae of 1928, confirms that his *Trauerspiel* book was methodologically influenced by both the art historian Alois Riegl and Carl Schmitt. For a detailed account of Benjamin's appreciation of Schmitt, see Horst Bredekamp, "Walter Benjamin's Esteem for Carl Schmitt," in Meierhenrich and Simons, *The Oxford Handbook of Carl Schmitt*, 679–704.

56 Kahn, "Hamlet or Hecuba," 82.

57 Benjamin, *The Origin of German Tragic Drama*, 88.

58 Benjamin, *The Origin of German Tragic Drama*, 88.

59 Benjamin, *The Origin of German Tragic Drama*, 95–6.

60 Bredekamp, "Walter Benjamin's Esteem for Carl Schmitt," 686.

61 Benjamin, *The Origin of German Tragic Drama*, 65.

62 Bredekamp, "Walter Benjamin's Esteem for Carl Schmitt," 692.

63 See Harold Bloom, *Hamlet* (New York: Riverhead Books, 2003), 19. See also Ann Thompson and Neil Taylor London, "Introduction," in *Hamlet*, ed. Ann Thompson and Neil Taylor London (London: The Arden Shakespeare, 2006), 57. However, "the first performance of *Hamlet* of which we have a specific record took place, bizarrely, on board a ship anchored off the coast of Africa in 1607" (Thompson and Taylor, "Introduction," 53).

64 Schmitt, *Hamlet or Hecuba*, 52.

65 In their Introduction (section 4), Rust and Lupton show how, in response to Weber, Schmitt sees the Catholic Church as the only authentic "power of representation" in the modern, capitalist world. The Church stands as a public, "visible institution," in contrast to the "privatized" religion of the tolerant modern state, which is the product of the "inner-worldly" Protestant ethic. In addition, the Catholic Church derives its representational authority "from above," in contrast to modern parliamentary representation, which derives its authority from the people below. See Carl Schmitt, *Roman Catholicism and Political Form*, trans. G. L. Ulmen (1923, Westport, CT: Greenwood Press, 1996), 25–6.

66 Schmitt, *Hamlet or Hecuba*, 30, 27.

67 Schmitt, *Hamlet or Hecuba*, 61.

68 Schmitt, *Hamlet or Hecuba*, 59.

69 Schmitt, *Hamlet or Hecuba*, 62.

70 Schmitt, *Hamlet or Hecuba*, 61.

71 Schmitt, *The Leviathan in the State Theory of Thomas Hobbes: Meaning and Failure of a Political Symbol*, trans. George Schwab and Erna Hilfstein (1938, Westport, CT: Greenwood Press, 1996), 33.

72 Schmitt, *Hamlet or Hecuba*, 30.

73 Miriam Leonard, "Carl Schmitt: Tragedy and the Intrusion of History," in *Tragedy and Modernity*, 201.

74 Schmitt, *The Leviathan in the State Theory of Thomas Hobbes*, 24.

75 See Roberto Navarette Alonso, "Soberanía, dictadura y barroco. En torno a Walter Benjamin y Carl Schmitt," *Ingenium. Revista Electrónica de Pensamiento Moderno*

y Metodología de las Ideas 14 (2021): 48, https://doi.org/10.5209/inge.78435. The following remarks on the figure of the leviathan follow closely Navarette's.

76 Schmitt, *The Leviathan in the State Theory of Thomas Hobbes*, 79. The difference between these two forms of power (English and continental, or absolute) is reflected in French dramas of the seventeenth century (see note 86), and in Corneille's early tragedies in particular. See *Le Cid*, Act II, sc. 1, and *Horace*, Act V. sc. 3, v. 1759–63, in Corneille, *Œuvres complètes*, ed. Georges Couton (Paris: Bibliothèque de la Pléiade, 1980). See also Franziska Sick, "Pouvoir politique et politique du pouvoir dans le théâtre de Corneille," in *Pratiques de Corneille*, ed. Myriam Dufour-Maître (Mont-Saint-Aignan: Presses Universitaires de Rouen et du Havre, 2012), https://doi.org/10.4000/books.purh.10440.

77 Schmitt, *The Leviathan in the State Theory of Thomas Hobbes*, 79.

78 Schmitt, *The Leviathan in the State Theory of Thomas Hobbes*, 80.

79 Schmitt, *The Leviathan in the State Theory of Thomas Hobbes*, 80.

80 Schmitt, *Hamlet or Hecuba*, 44.

81 Schmitt, *Hamlet or Hecuba*, 45 (emphasis added).

82 Schmitt, *Hamlet or Hecuba*, 45.

83 Schmitt, *Hamlet or Hecuba*, 45.

84 Bloom, *Hamlet*, 25.

85 Rust and Lupton, "Introduction: Schmitt and Shakespeare," xxxiii.

86 Schmitt, *Hamlet or Hecuba*, 43–4.

87 Schmitt, *Hamlet or Hecuba*, 52.

88 Kahn, "Hamlet or Hecuba," 85.

89 Kahn, "Hamlet or Hecuba," 83.

90 Karl Löwitt, "The Occasional Decisionism of Carl Schmitt," in *Martin Heidegger and European Nihilism*, ed. Richard Wolin, trans. Gary Steiner (New York: Columbia University Press, 1995), 146.

91 Schmitt, *Political Theology*, 62, 63.

92 Schmitt, *Political Theology*, 65. See also C. Schmitt, *The Crisis of Parliamentary Democracy*, trans. Ellen Kennedy (1923, 1926; Cambridge, MA: MIT Press, 1988). The crisis of contemporary parliamentarism, Schmitt writes, "springs from the consequences of modern mass democracy and in the final analysis from the contradictions of a liberal individualism burdened by moral pathos and a democratic sentiment governed essentially by political ideals. A century of historical alliance and common struggle against royal absolutism has obscured the awareness of this contradiction. But the crisis unfolds today ever more strikingly, and no cosmopolitan

rhetoric can prevent or eliminate it. It is, in its depths, the inescapable contradiction of liberal individualism and democratic homogeneity" (p. 17). It is worth observing that Schmitt locates the origins of the crisis of parliamentarism in contradictions inherent to the liberal order, without feeling committed to the Marxist view, which he also criticizes. The conclusion I draw is that the notion of contradiction does not necessarily commit one to a dialectical view of history.

93 Schmitt, *Political Theology*, 65.

94 Schmitt, *Political Theology*, 65.

95 Miguel de Beistegui, *The Government of Desire: A Genealogy of the Liberal Subject* (Chicago, IL: The University of Chicago Press).

96 Clinton L. Rossiter, *Constitutional Dictatorship: Crisis Government in the Modern Democracies* (Chicago, IL: The University of Chicago Press, 1948), 5.

97 Article 1 of the Constitution provides for the suspension of the writ of habeas corpus in cases of rebellion or invasion: "The privilege of the Writ of Habeas Corpus shall not be suspended, unless when in Cases of Rebellion or Invasion the public Safety may require it."

98 Rossiter, *Constitutional Dictatorship*, 313.

99 John C. Yoo, "Unitary, Executive, or Both?," *The University of Chicago Law Review* 76 (2009): 1965–6, emphasis added. Yoo's article is a review of Steven G. Calabresi and Christopher S. Yoo, *The Unitary Executive: Presidential Power from Washington to Bush* (New Haven, CT: Yale University Press, 2008). John C. Yoo develops his argument in greater detail in *Crisis and Command: A History of Executive Power from George Washington to George W. Bush* (New York: Kaplan, 2010).

100 Yoo, "Unitary, Executive, or Both?," 1999. Locke defines prerogative power thus: "This power to act according to discretion, for the public good, without the prescription of the law, and sometimes even against it, is that which is called prerogative: for since in some governments the lawmaking power is not always in being, and is usually too numerous, and so too slow, for the dispatch requisite to execution; and because also it is impossible to foresee, and so by laws to provide for, all accidents and necessities that may concern the public, or to make such laws as will do no harm, if they are executed with an inflexible rigour, on all occasions, and upon all persons that may come in their way; therefore there is a latitude left to the executive power, to do many things of choice which the laws do not prescribe."

101 Yoo, "Unitary, Executive, or Both?," 2018.

102 See Scott Horton, "The Return of Carl Schmitt," *Balkinization* (blog), November 7, 2005, https://tinyurl.com/3ke23vd4.

103 See David Linker, "Carl Schmitt and the American Right," *The New Republic*, March 3, 2009, https://newrepublic.com/article/48178/carl-schmitt-and-the-american-right.

104 Achille Mbembe, *Necropolitics*, trans. Steven Corcoran (Durham, NC and London: Duke University Press, 2019), 60.

105 Giorgio Agamben, *Sovereign Power and Bare Life: Homo Sacer 1* (Stanford, CA: Stanford University Press, 1998), 170.

106 Agamben, *State of Exception*, 73.

107 Michel Agier, *Managing the Undesirables: Refugee Camps and Humanitarian Government* (Cambridge: Polity Press, 2011), 45.

108 "Australia's Immigration Detention Policy and Practice," Australian Human Rights Commission, accessed December 10, 2023, https://tinyurl.com/2k2tsyyz.

109 "In the Freezer: Abusive Conditions for Women and Children in US Immigration Holding Cells," *Human Rights Watch*, February 28, 2018, https://www.hrw.org/report/2018/02/28/freezer/abusive-conditions-women-and-children-us-immigration-holding-cells.

110 Amanda Holpuch, "'This Is Literally an Industry': Drome Images Give Rare Look at For-Profit ICE Detention Centers," *The Guardian*, January 29, 2021, https://tinyurl.com/4ajwuspr.

111 Adam Serwer, "A Crime by Any Name," *The Atlantic*, July 3, 2019, https://tinyurl.com/y99pnext.

112 On the fantasy and illusion of "Fortress Europe," and the necessary permeability of its borders to migrants, see Vassilis Tsianos and Sehrat Karakayali, "Transnational Migration and the Emergence of the European Border Regime: An Ethnographic Analysis," *European Journal of Social Theory* 13, no. 3 (2010): 373–87, accessed July 1, 2022, https://tinyurl.com/2965hymf. Thomas Nail makes a similar and compelling case in relation to the United States—see Thomas Nail, *Theory of the Border* (New York: Oxford University Press, 2016).

113 "Mediterranean Update—Migrant Deaths Rise to 3,329 in 2015," International Organization for Migration, http://www.iom.int/news/mediterranean-update-migrant-deaths-rise-3329-2015.

114 The literature on the government of migrants and borders in Europe through the state of exception is now vast. Examples include Daria Davitti, "Biopolitical Borders and the State of Exception in the European Migration Crisis," *European Journal of International Law* 29, no. 4 (2018): 1173–96; Birgit Spengler, Lea Espinoza Garrido, Sylvia Mieszkowski, and Julia Wewior, "Introduction: Migrant Lives in a State of Exception," *Parallax* 27, no. 2 (2021): 115–58; Nick Vaughan-Williams, "The Generalised Bio-Political Border? Re-conceptualising the Limits of Sovereign Power," *Review of International Studies* 35 (2009): 729–49. For a useful and more critical (although now more than a decade old) survey of the literature on migration and the state of exception, see Carl Levy, "Refugees, Europe, Camp/State of Exception: 'Into the Zone,' The European Union and Extraterritorial Processing of Migrants,

Refugees, and Asylum-Seekers (Theories and Practice)," *Refugee Survey Quarterly* 29, no. 1 (2010): 92–119, https://www.jstor.org/stable/45074228.

115 Katie Hopkins, "Rescue Boats? I'd Use Gunships to Stop Migrants," *The Sun*, April 17, 2015, https://tinyurl.com/y74a5eyj.

116 Silvia Carta, "Beyond Closed Ports: The New Italian Decree-Law on Immigration and Security," *Odysseus Network*, October 31, 2018, https://tinyurl.com/35xxsnzz.

117 Javier de Lucas, *Mediterráneo, el naufragio de Europa* (Valencia: Tirant lo Blanch, 2015); Donatella Di Cesare, *Stranieri residenti. Una filosofia della migrazione* (Turin: Bollati Boringhieri, 2017), chapter 2 ("Fine dell'ospitalità?") and 223–30; Fabienne Brugère and Guillaume Le Blanc, *La fin de l'hospitalité. L'Europe, terre d'asile?* (Paris: Flammarion, 2017).

118 Achille Mbembé, "Necropolitics," trans. Libby Meintjes, *Public Culture* 15, no. 1 (2003): 11–40; and *Necropolitics*, 97–104.

119 María Díaz Crego and Silvia Kotanidis, "States of Emergency in Response to the Coronavirus Crisis: Normative Response and Parliamentary Oversight in EU Member States during the First Wave of the Pandemic," *European Parliamentary Research Service* (2020), https://doi.org/10.2861/892605.

120 France, where the idea of the state of *état de siège* originated during the Revolution, has a long history of declaring such states. See Agamben, *State of Exception*, 11–14.

121 See Stéphanie Hennette Vauchez, *La démocratie en état d'urgence. Quand l'exception devient permanente* (Paris: Seuil, 2022).

122 See Jucier Gonçalves Júnior, Jair Paulino de Sales, Marcial Moreno Moreira, Woneska Rodrigues Pinheiro, Carlos Kennedy Tavares Lima, and Modesto Leite Rolim Neto, "A Crisis within the Crisis: The Mental Health Situation of Refugees in the World during the 2019 Coronavirus (2019-NCoV) Outbreak," *Psychiatry Research* 288 (June 2020), https://tinyurl.com/s5a5ducy; G. Lourdes Velázquez, "The Role of Philosophy in the Pandemic Era," *Bioethics Update* 6, no. 2 (July 1, 2020): 92–100; Daniele Lorenzini, "Biopolitics in the Time of Coronavirus," *Critical Inquiry* 47, no. 2 (January 2021): 40–5; Ferdinand C. Mukumbang, "Are Asylum Seekers, Refugees and Foreign Migrants Considered in the COVID-19 Vaccine Discourse?," *BMJ Global Health* 5, no. 11 (November 2020); Emmanuel Raju and Sonja Ayeb-Karlsson, "COVID-19: How Do You Self-Isolate in a Refugee Camp?," *International Journal of Public Health* 65, no. 5 (June 1, 2020): 515–17; Jessica Saifee, Carlos Franco-Paredes, and Steven R. Lowenstein, "Refugee Health During COVID-19 and Future Pandemics," *Current Tropical Medicine Reports* 8, no. 3 (2021): 1–4.

123 Isabelle Niu, Emily Rhyne, and Aaron Byrd, "How ICE's Mishandling of Covid-19 Fueled Outbreaks Around the Country," *New York Times*, April 25, 2021, https://tinyurl.com/3bh3dfxy.

124 Gábor Mészáros, "How Misuse of Emergency Powers Dismantled the Rule of Law in Hungary," *Israel Law Review* 57, no. 2 (2024): 289, https://tinyurl.com/38mxnr5a.

Following Alan Greene's, *Permanent States of Emergency and the Rule of Law: Constitutions in an Age of Crisis* (London: Hart Publishing, 2018), Mészáros claims that the state of exception has become permanent when "the so-called exception has become the norm and temporary powers endure" (p. 289).

125 See Toni Skorić, "Is the State of Emergency in Hungary Really Over?," *Friedrich Naumann Foundation for Freedom*, June 29, 2020, https://tinyurl.com/4ecpemat.

126 Mészáros, "How Misuse of Emergency Powers Dismantled the Rule of Law in Hungary," 288.

127 Mészáros, "How Misuse of Emergency Powers Dismantled the Rule of Law in Hungary," 293. To put things in perspective, in 2023, according to Eurydice, an official website of the European Union, the share of foreign citizens in Hungary amounted to 2.35 percent, one of the lowest rates in Europe, and one that is significantly below the European average of 8 percent. https://tinyurl.com/3zzfu5d7.

128 Mészáros, "How Misuse of Emergency Powers Dismantled the Rule of Law in Hungary," 302.

129 See Viktor Orbán, "The World is on the Brink of Economic Crises," *Radio Free Europe/Radio Liberty*, May 24, 2022, https://tinyurl.com/4wb39x2v.

130 See John Quigley, "Israel's Forty-Five Year Emergency: Are There Limits to Derogations from Human Rights Obligations," *Michigan Journal of International Law* 15, no. 2 (1994): 491–518, https://tinyurl.com/3anjj8zc. The same state of emergency has allowed Israel to react quickly and decisively to the Covid-19 pandemic: between March and June 2020 (a period covering the height of the pandemic *and* a constitutional crisis), the caretaker government (introduced after three inconclusive rounds of elections) issued more than one hundred Emergency Regulations. See Aeyal Gross and Nir Kosti, "The Paradox of Israel's Coronavirus Law," *Verfassungsblog*, January 8, 2021, https://tinyurl.com/bdep6h5f.

131 Yoav Mehozay, "The Fluid Jursiprudence of Israel's Emergency Powers: Legal Patchwork as a Governing Norm," *Law & Society Review* 46, no. 1 (2012): 137, https://www.jstor.org/stable/41475256.

132 Mehozay, "The Fluid Jursiprudence of Israel's Emergency Powers," 138.

133 See Nasser Hussain, *The Jurisprudence of Emergency: Colonialism and the Rule of Law* (Ann Arbor, MI: The University of Michigan Press, 2003). See also Mbembe, "Necropolitics," 22–30. Mbembe draws an explicit parallel between the plantation system in the Americas, early modern colonial occupation, and the regimes of apartheid in South Africa (yesterday) or Palestine (today). They all required the creation of zones of exception.

134 B'Tselem, "Defense (Emergency) Regulations," https://tinyurl.com/47a46fzc.

135 Edward W. Said, *The Question of Palestine* [1979] (London: Fitzcarraldo Editions, 2024), 80.

136 Said, *The Question of Palestine*, 80.

137 Said, *The Question of Palestine*, 80.

Chapter 3

1 Étienne Balibar, "Critique in the 21st Century: Political Economy Still, and Religion Again," *Radical Philosophy* 200 (November/December 2016).

2 It is worth remembering that the close association between crisis and revolution is not exclusive to Marxist and post-Marxist thought. I already mentioned Kuhn's conception of the structure of scientific revolutions. But, despite his anti-Hegelian and anti-Marxist positions, one could also mention Jacob Burckhardt's strong conception of crisis in the formation of historical epochs. See J. Burckhardt, "Weltgeschichtliche Betrachtungen. Über geschichtliches Studium," in *Gesammelte Werke*, vol. 4 [1870] (Basel and Stuttgart: Schwabe & Co., 1970); and Theodor Schieder, "Die historischen Krisen im Geschichtsdenken Jacob Burckhardts," in *Begegnungen mit der Geschichte* [1950] (Göttingen: Vandenhoeck & Ruprecht, 1962), 129–62. Although Burckhardt recognizes "war as international crisis," he draws most of his examples from revolutionary processes, which he understands in a rather restricted sense ("Weltgeschichtliche Betrachtungen," 117). "Real crises," he claims, "are rare" (pp. 122, 138). Most crises are terminated before they can reach their final endpoint, which for Burckhardt means the transformation of social relations. Thus, not even the German Reformation, the English Revolution, or the French Revolution were crises in the "true" sense.

3 Simon Clarke, *Marx's Theory of Crisis* (Basingstoke: Macmillan, 1994), 74. See also David Harvey, *Seventeen Contradictions and the End of Capitalism* (London: Profile Books Ltd., 2014).

4 See Haslan Islatince, "Marxist Crisis Theories," *Journal of Current Researches on Social Science* 13, no. 3 (2023), https://doi.org/10.26579/jocress.13.3.2; Lea Ypi, "Rosa Luxemburg," in *The Stanford Encyclopedia of Philosophy* (Summer 2024 Edition), https://plato.stanford.edu/archives/sum2024/entries/luxemburg/; Ghassan Dibeh, "Time Delays and Business Cycles: Hilferding's Model Revisited," *Review of Political Economy* 13, no. 3 (2001): 329–41, https://doi.org/10.1080/09538250120055177. I discuss Marx's theory of the tendency of the rate of profit to fall and Gramsci's theory of crisis below.

5 Karl Marx, "Ricardo's Theory of Accumulation and a Critique of It. (The Very Nature of Capital Leads to Crises)," in *Theories of Surplus-Value, Capital*, vol. 4, part 2, chapter 17 (esp. §§ 8–11), https://www.marxists.org/archive/marx/works/1863/theories-surplus-value/ch17.htm. See also K. Marx, *Grundrisse* (1857–61), or *Foundations of the Critique of Political Economy* (Rough Draft), trans. Martin Nicolaus (London: Penguin Books in association with *New Left Review*, 1973),

146–52 (on the contradictions inherent to money), 401–10 (on the contradictions inherent to the circulation of capital), 745–52 (on the law of the tendency of the rate of profit to fall, and the crises that ensue).

6 Marx, *Grundrisse*, 408, translation modified.

7 Marx, *Grundrisse*, 424.

8 In his recent bestseller, Kohei Saito argues that Marx's late unpublished manuscripts reveal a more ecologically minded philosopher, whose thoughts on the management of "commons"—or goods that are essential for our daily lives, such as water, electricity, education, and medical care—in pre-capitalist societies yield precious lessons for a sustainable and socially equal world. See Kohei Saito, *Karl Marx's Ecosocialism: Capital, Nature, and the Unfinished Critique of Political Economy* (New York: Monthly Review Press, 2017).

9 Marx, *Grundrisse*, 409. I return to discussing the intertwining of the capitalocene and the Technocene in Chapter 5.

10 Marx, *Grundrisse*, 409.

11 Heidegger's position is very close to that of Marx, and his assessment of the project of modernity as bound up with what he calls the "scientific projection of nature" echoes the Marxist critique. Unlike Marx, however, Heidegger attributes this tendency and epochal shift not to capitalism *per se*, but to an inflection point within the history of being, the roots of which, he claims, can be found in the covering up and forgetting of the *essence* of being as concealment and sheltering. Capitalism and communism, he claims, are in this respect two sides of the same coin—that is, of the will to subjugate nature and unleash the human will to power. See M. Heidegger, *Gesamtausgabe 65: Beiträge zur Philosophie (Vom Ereignis)*, ed. Friedrich-Wilhelm von Herrmann (Frankfurt am Main: Vittorio Klostermann, 1989), §§ 50–80; *Gesamtausgabe 67: Metaphysik und Nihilismus* (Frankfurt am Main: Vittorio Klostermann, 1999), ed. Hans-Joachim Friedrich, §§ 131–42; *Gesamtausgabe 69: Die Geschichte des Seyns*, ed. Peter Trawny (Frankfurt am Main: Vittorio Klostermann, 1998), §§ 37–68; "Die Frage nach der Technik" and "Wissenschaft und Besinnung," in *Gesamtausgabe 7: Vorträge und Aufsätze*, ed. Friedrich-Wilhelm von Herrmann (Frankfurt am Main: Vittorio Klostermann, 2000).

12 Marx, *Grundrisse*, 409.

13 Marx, *Grundrisse*, 409.

14 Marx, *Grundrisse*, 409.

15 Marx, *Grundrisse*, 409. I have explored capitalist fetishization as a modern and specifically economic form of superstition in *Thought Under Threat: On Superstition, Spite, and Stupidity* (Chicago, IL: The University of Chicago Press, 2021), 110–30.

16 Marx, *Grundrisse*, 409, translation modified.

17 See John Bellamy Foster, "The Epochal Crisis: Converging Economic and Ecological Contradictions," *Monthly Review* 65, no. 5 (October 2013). See also Jason W. Moore, *Capitalism in the Web of Life: Ecology and the Accumulation of Capital* (New York: Verso Books, 2015), 125–40, 297–305.

18 Karl Marx, *Capital*, vol. 1 (New York: Penguin Books, 1976), 637.

19 Moore calls it "Cheap Nature." See *Capitalism in the Web of Life*, Chapters 9 and 10.

20 See Marx, *Grundrisse*, 745–58; *Capital*, vol. 3 (London: Penguin Books, 1991), 317–75. Focusing on the performance of the US economy between 1948 and 2007, and developing a specific econometric approach to assess the validity of Marx's "law," Basu and Manolakos find evidence of a weak but tangible downward trend in its general rate of profit. See Deepankar Basu and Panayiotis T. Manolakos, "Is There a Tendency of the Rate of Profit to Fall? Econometric Evidence for the US Economy, 1948–2007," *Review of Radical Political Economics* 45, no. 1 (2013): 76–95, https://tinyurl.com/47957a9j. The authors also provide extended references to, and a critical engagement with, the now vast literature on this controversial topic, beginning with Okishio's claim to have disproved the "law." See Nuobo Okishio, "Technical Change and the Rate of Profit," *Kobe University Economic Review* 7 (1961): 85–99. Prominent scholars agreeing with Okishio include J. E. Roemer, *Analytical Foundations of Marxian Economic Theory* (Cambridge: Cambridge University Press, 1981). Scholars who reject the so-called Okishio Theorem and maintain the validity of the TRPF include Shaikh and Rosdolsky. See, by A. Shaikh: "Political Economy and Capitalism: Notes on Dobbs's Theory of Crisis," *Cambridge Journal of Economics* 2, no. 2 (1978): 233–51; "The Falling Rate of Profit and the Economic Crisis in the U.S.," in *The Imperiled Economy, Book I: Macroeconomics from a Left Perspective*, ed. R. Cherry (New York: Union for Radical Political Economy and Monthly Review Press, 1987); and "The Falling Rate of Profit as the Cause of Long Waves: Theory and Empirical Evidence," in *New Findings in Long Wave Research*, ed. A. Kleinknecht (London: Macmillan, 1992). By R. Rosdolsky, see *The Making of Marx's Capital* (London: Pluto Press, 1977). A third group falls somewhere in between, arguing that neither a secular tendency for the rate of profit to fall nor a secular tendency for the rate of profit to increase can be a priori associated with capitalist development. See D. K. Foley, *Understanding Capital: Marx's Economic Theory* (Cambridge, MA: Harvard University Press, 1986); T. Michl, "The Two-Stage Decline in US Nonfinancial Corporate Profitability, 1948–1986," *Review of Radical Political Economics* 20, no. 2 (1988): 1–22; and Fred Moseley, *The Falling Rate of Profit in the Postwar United States Economy* (New York: St. Martin's Press, 1991). By G. Duménil and D. Lévy, see *The Economics of the Profit Rate: Competition, Crises and Historical Tendencies in Capitalism* (Aldershot: Edward Elgar, 1993); "The Profit Rate: Where and How Much Did It Fall? Did It Recover? USA 1948–2000," *Review of Radical Political Economics* 34, no. 4 (2002): 437–61; and "Technology and Distribution: Historical Trajectories à la Marx," *Journal of Economic Behaviour and Organization* 52 (2003): 201–33. See also D. K. Foley and T. Michl, *Growth and Distribution* (Cambridge, MA: Harvard University Press, 1999). I tend to agree with the latter category of scholars, as I am

deeply suspicious of any attempt to extract so-called "laws"—with their necessary and universal implications—from an economic system, whatever its nature. Norms are not laws. The same suspicion applies to the "laws" discovered by classical and neoclassical economists.

21 Geoffrey M. Hodgson, *After Marx and Sraffa: Essays in Political Economy* (New York: Palgrave Macmillan, 1991), 28.

22 Stephen Cullenberg, *The Falling Rate of Profit: Recasting the Marxian Debate* (New York: Pluto Press, 1994), 1.

23 Marx, *Grundrisse*, 748.

24 Marx, *Grundrisse*, 749, emphasis added.

25 Marx, *Grundrisse*, 749.

26 Marx, *Grundrisse*, 749.

27 Marx, *Grundrisse*, 750.

28 Marx, *Grundrisse*, 750–1.

29 Marx, *Capital*, vol. 3 (London: Penguin Books, 1981), 339ff.

30 Nancy Fraser, "Legitimation Crisis? On the Political Contradictions of Financialized Capitalism," *Critical Historical Studies* 2, no. 2 (2015): 163.

31 Marx, *Grundrisse*, 750.

32 Fraser, "Legitimation Crisis?," 166.

33 Fraser, "Legitimation Crisis?," 167.

34 Fraser, "Legitimation Crisis?," 167n13.

35 Fraser, "Legitimation Crisis?," 167.

36 Fraser, "Legitimation Crisis?," 167.

37 W. Benjamin and B. Brecht, cited in Erdmut Wizisla, *Walter Benjamin and Bertold Brecht: The Story of a Friendship*, trans. Christine Shuttleworth (New Haven, CT: Yale University Press, 2009), 190.

38 W. Benjamin, "Critique of Violence," trans. E. Jephcott, in Benjamin, *Selected Writings*, vol. 1, ed. M. Bullock and M. W. Jennings (Cambridge, MA: Harvard University Press, 1996). "Zur Kritik der Gewalt" was originally published in *Archiv für Sozialwissenschaften und Sozialpolitik* 47 (1921) and is now in Walter Benjamin, *Gesammelte Schtiften*, vol. 2.1, ed. R. Tiedemann and H. Schweppenhäuser (Frankfurt am Main: Suhrkamp, 1991).

39 Benjamin, "Critique of Violence," 246, emphasis added.

40 Benjamin, "Critique of Violence," 246.

41 Benjamin, "Critique of Violence," 248.

42 Benjamin, "Critique of Violence," 240.

43 Benjamin, "Critique of Violence," 240.

44 Benjamin, "Critique of Violence," 246.

45 Benjamin, "Critique of Violence," 246.

46 Carl Schmitt, *Political Theology: Four Chapters on the Concept of Sovereignty*, trans. George Schwab (1922; Chicago, IL: The University of Chicago Press, 2005), 12.

47 Benjamin, "Critique of Violence," 252.

48 Benjamin, "Critique of Violence," 252 and 248.

49 C. Schmitt, "Dictatorship," in *Staat, Großraum, Nomos: Arbeiten aus den Jahren 1916–1969*, ed. Günther Maschke (Berlin: Duncker & Humblot, 1995), 35. Cited in Carl Schmitt, *Dictatorship: From the Origin of the Modern Concept of Sovereignty to Proletarian Class Struggle* (1921, 1928; Cambridge: Polity Press, 2014), "Translator's Introduction," xxiv.

50 William E. Scheuerman, "States of Emergency," in *The Oxford Handbook of Carl Schmitt*, ed. Hans Meierhenrich and Oliver Simons (Oxford: Oxford University Press, 2016), 554.

51 G. Agamben, *State of Exception*, trans. Kevin Attell (Chicago, IL: The University of Chicago Press, 2005), 52.

52 Agamben, *State of Exception*, 54.

53 C. Schmitt, *Die Diktatur. Von den Anfängen des Modernen Souveränitätsgedankens bis zum Proletarischen Klassenkampf* (1921; Munich and Leipzig: Duncker and Humblot, 1928); English version, *Dictatorship: From the Origin of the Modern Concept of Sovereignty to the Proletarian Class Struggle*, trans. Michael Hoelzl and Graham Ward (Cambridge: Polity Press, 2014).

54 Agamben, *State of Exception*, 54.

55 W. Benjamin, *Ursprung des deutschen Trauerspiels*, in *Gesammelte Schriften*, vol. 1, pt. 1, ed. R. Tiedemann and H. Schweppenhäuser (Frankfurt am Main: Suhrkamp, 1974), 245. Translated by John Osborne as *The Origin of German Tragic Drama* (1928; London: Verso Books, 1998), 65.

56 W. Benjamin, "Theses on the Philosophy of History," in *Essays and Reflections*, ed. with intro. Hannah Arendt, trans. Harry Zorn (New York: Schocken Books, 1969), 253–64.

57 Agamben, *State of Exception*, 58.

58 Agamben, *State of Exception*, 59–60.

59 G. Agamben, "A Jurist Confronting Himself: Carl Schmitt's Jurisprudential Thought," trans. Leland de la Durantaye, in *The Oxford Handbook of Carl Schmitt*, 458.

60 Schmitt, "Preliminary Remarks to the First Edition," in *Dictatorship*, xli.

61 Schmitt, "Preliminary Remarks to the First Edition," in *Dictatorship*, xl.

62 See Rafal Manko, "'Our Fatherland Has Found Itself on the Verge of an Abyss': Poland's 1981 Martial Law, or the Unexpected Appearance of the State of Exception under Actually Existing Socialism," in Agamben, *States of Exception*, 140–66.

63 Manko, "'Our Fatherland Has Found Itself on the Verge of an Abyss,'" 147–8.

64 Jan Sowa, cited in Manko, "'Our Fatherland Has Found Itself on the Verge of an Abyss,'" 147.

65 Manko, "'Our Fatherland Has Found Itself on the Verge of an Abyss,'" 163–4.

66 Antonio Gramsci, "Notes on the Southern Question," in *Selections from Political Writings 1921–1926*, ed. and trans. Q. Hoare (New York: International Publishers, 1978).

67 Gramsci, "Notes on the Southern Question," 443.

68 See Ernesto Laclau and Chantal Mouffe, *Hegemony and Socialist Strategy: Towards a Radical Democratic Politics*, trans. Winston Moore and Paul Cammack (London: Verso Books, 2001 [1985]), 66.

69 Antonio Gramsci, *Quaderini del carcere*, four volumes, ed. Valentino Gerratana (Turin: Einaudi, 1975). The Gerratana complete edition contains twenty-nine notebooks. *Prison Notebooks*, 3 vols., ed. and trans. Joseph A. Buttigieg (New York: Columbia University Press, 1992–), covers notebooks 1 to 8. Throughout, I will reference the original notebook, paragraph, and page numbers, followed wherever possible by the volume and page number from the translation. Numerals indicate the number Tatiana Schucht assigned to the notebook in the cataloging system she devised when organizing Gramsci's papers soon after his death.

70 Laclau and Mouffe, *Hegemony and Socialist Strategy*, 67.

71 Gramsci, *Quaderni* 14, §48, 1707.

72 See Gramsci, *Quaderni* 12, §1, 1518–19.

73 Gramsci, *Quaderni* 8, §213, 1071; *Prison Notebooks* 3, 360.

74 *Quaderni* 11, §16. See A. Gramsci, *Subaltern Social Groups: A Critical Edition of Prison Notebook 25*, ed. and trans. Joseph A. Buttigieg and Marcus E. Green (New York: Columbia University Press, 2021), 94. In addition to the translation of Notebook 25, this volume also contains translations of sections from various notebooks related to subaltern social groups.

75 See *Quaderni* 8, §204, §213, §220; *Quaderni* 10, §12; *Quaderni* 11, §12.

76 See *Quaderni* 4, §15, §20, and §22; *Quaderni* 8, §220; *Quaderni* 10, Part II, §§ 41 (I) and (XII) (also in *Subaltern Social Groups*, 69–72); *Quaderni* 11, §12 (also in *Subaltern Social Groups*, 73–89).

77 Gramsci, *Quaderni* 10, Part II, § 41 (XII), 1319; *Subaltern Social Groups*, 70.

78 *Quaderni* 10, Part II, § 41 (XII), 1319–20; *Subaltern Social Groups*, 70.

79 Jürgen Habermas, *Legitimation Crisis*, trans. Thomas McCarthy (1973; London: Heinemann, 1976). While the word crisis (*Krise*) does not appear in the original German title, *Legitimationsprobleme im Spätkapitalismus* (Frankfurt am Main: Suhrkamp Verlag, 1973), it does in virtually every part and section of the book.

80 Habermas, *Legitimation Crisis*, 2, 3.

81 Fraser, "Legitimation Crisis?," 169.

82 Fraser, "Legitimation Crisis?," 170.

83 Habermas, *Legitimation Crisis*, 46.

84 Habermas, *Legitimation Crisis*, 46.

85 Habermas, *Legitimation Crisis*, 47.

86 Habermas, *Legitimation Crisis*, 75.

87 Habermas, *Legitimation Crisis*, 48.

88 Habermas, *Legitimation Crisis*, 52.

89 Habermas, *Legitimation Crisis*, 51.

90 Habermas, *Legitimation Crisis*, 52.

91 Habermas, *Legitimation Crisis*, 62.

92 Fraser, "Legitimation Crisis?," 170.

93 Fraser, "Legitimation Crisis?," 171.

94 Habermas, *Legitimation Crisis*, 75.

95 Fraser, "Legitimation Crisis?," 171.

96 Fraser, "Legitimation Crisis?," 171.

97 Fraser, "Legitimation Crisis?," 171.

98 *Quaderni* 10, Part Two, § 41 (XII), 1319–20; *Subaltern Social Groups*, 70.

99 *Quaderni* 8, §220, 1080; *Prison Notebooks* 3, 369.

100 *Quaderni* 11, §12, 1378–79; *Subaltern Social Groups*, 76.

101 Gramsci embraces the view presented by Albert Mathiez in *La Révolution française*, vol. 1 (Paris: Colin, 1922).

102 *Quaderni* 4, §69, 513; *Prison Notebooks* 2, 241, emphasis added.

103 *Quaderni* 4, §69, 513; *Prison Notebooks* 2, 241–2.

104 *Quaderni* 4, §69, 513; *Prison Notebooks* 2, 241–2.

105 *Quaderni* 7, §77, 910; *Prison Notebooks* 3, 209.

106 *Quaderni* 13, §23, 1602–3; *Subaltern Social Groups*, 103.

107 *Quaderni* 13, §23, 1603; *Subaltern Social Groups*, 103, emphasis added.

108 *Quaderni* 13, §23, 1604–5; *Subaltern Social Groups*, 104.

109 *Quaderni* 3, §34, 311; *Prison Notebooks* 2, 32–3.

110 Milan Babic, "Let's Talk about the Interregnum: Gramsci and the Crisis of the Liberal World Order," *International Affairs* 96, no. 3 (2020): 773.

111 Gramsci, *Quaderni* 9, §68, 1139; *Subaltern Social Groups*, 67.

112 Gramsci, *Quaderni* 13, §23, 1604, and *Quaderni* 14, §34, 1692; *Subaltern Social Groups*, 104 and 114.

113 Gilbert Achcar, "Morbid Symptoms: What Did Gramsci Really Mean?," *Notebooks: The Journal for Studies on Power* 1, no. 2 (2021): 379–87. See also A. Agosti, "The Italian Communist Party and the Third Period," in *In Search of Revolution: International Communist Parties in the Third Period*, ed. M. Worley (London: I. B. Tauris, 2004), 97–8.

114 See Achcar, "Morbid Symptoms," 382n7.

115 K. Marx, *The Civil War in France* (1871), in *Karl Marx Frederick Engels Collected Works*, vol. 22 (New York: Lawrence & Wishart, 1986), 330, emphasis added.

116 Gramsci, *Quaderni* 15, §5, 1755–9.

117 Laclau and Mouffe are more explicit about, and double down on, their diagnosis in their preface to the second edition of *Hegemony and Socialist Strategy*: far from leading to a regeneration of the Left, the anti-democratic neoliberal hegemony has forced socialism into a crisis of its own, branded as a "third way" beyond the traditional Right-Left divide.

118 Laclau and Mouffe, *Hegemony and Socialist Strategy*, preface, xix.

119 Laclau and Mouffe, *Hegemony and Socialist Strategy*, 57

120 Laclau and Mouffe, *Hegemony and Socialist Strategy*, 56–7. Lukács' *History and Class Consciousness* is exemplary of the view Laclau and Mouffe criticize. The move from bourgeois or liberal thought to critique, Lukács argues, requires that one adopt the standpoint of the proletariat, for it is only from its vantage point that the crises of capitalism appear as inevitable and as a *necessary* aspect of this mode of production. See Georg Lukács, *History and Class Consciousness*, trans. Rodney Livingstone (Cambridge, MA: MIT Press, 1968), 243–4. But this standpoint

is achieved only when the proletariat acquires "a true understanding of its class situation and a true class consciousness" (Lukács, *History and Class Consciousness*, 76). This, Lukács explains, corresponds to the "active" and "practical" side of class consciousness, which can only happen "when an acute crisis in the economy drives [the proletariat] to action" (Lukács, *History and Class Consciousness*, 40). The "latent" and "theoretical" side of class consciousness, by contrast, corresponds to the "permanent" yet "latent" crisis of capitalism. But there is more: the emergence of the proletariat's self-consciousness coincides with "the discovery of dialectics in history itself," that is to say, with its "logical manifestation" in and as history (Lukács, *History and Class Consciousness*, 177). In other words, with class consciousness, history becomes self-conscious, or conscious of its own dialectical, contradictory logic and necessity. Finally, revolution—and the violence it entails—is the practical outcome of class consciousness, that is, of the realization that crisis is structural, rather than accidental, that acute crises in the economy are driven by contradictions inherent to the capitalist mode of production, and that the belief according to which the so-called laws of economics can lead us out of a crisis just as they lead us into it is nothing but a delusion (Lukács, *History and Class Consciousness*, 244). If the proletariat "can do no more than negate some aspects of capitalism, if it cannot at least aspire to a critique of the whole" and "understand the crisis fully," its mode of existence, defined by its "inhumanity" and "reification," will remain unchanged (Lukács, *History and Class Consciousness*, 76). This, in effect, means that the central problem for the dialectical method and the critique of political economy—for theory, then—is "to change reality" (Lukács, *History and Class Consciousness*, 3).

121 Laclau and Mouffe, *Hegemony and Socialist Strategy*, 69.

122 For illuminating observations on the Gramscian use and concept of philology, see Joseph A. Buttigieg's Introduction to Gramsci's *Prison Notebooks* 1, 59–64.

123 Gramsci, *Quaderni* 7, §6, 856–57; *Prison Notebooks* 3, 159.

124 Laclau and Mouffe, *Hegemony and Socialist Strategy*, 2nd ed., preface, xiii.

125 Gayatri Chakravorty Spivak, "Can the Subaltern Speak?," in *Colonial Discourse and Post-Colonial Theory: A Reader*, ed. Patrick Williams and Laura Chrisman (1988; New York: Columbia University Press, 1994). I will return to Derrida, and specifically to his strong reservations regarding the idea and semantics of crisis in Chapter 4.

126 G. Deleuze and M. Foucault, "Les intellectuels et le pouvoir," *L'Arc* 49 (1972): 3–10.

127 Is it worth recalling that Spivak is the translator of Derrida's 1967 *Of Grammatology*, the third chapter of which she uses to develop her argument? See J. Derrida, *Of Grammatology*, trans. Gayatri Chakravorty Spivak (Baltimore, MD and London: The Johns Hopkins University Press, 1974).

128 This is what Derrida shows in his critical reading of Lévi-Strauss and of the latter's study of the Nambikwara in particular in the chapter in *Of Grammatology* titled "The Violence of the Letter: From Lévi-Strauss to Rousseau." See *Of Grammatology*, 101–40.

129 Spivak, "Can the Subaltern Speak?," 89. Spivak's essay antedates Derrida's *Specters of Marx* by a few years. See Jacques Derrida, *Specters of Marx: The State of the Debt, the Work of Mourning, and the New International*, trans. Peggy Kamuf, intro. Bernd Magnus and Stephen Cullenberg (1993; New York and London: Routledge, 1994). In Chapter 4, I will argue that, far from disproving Spivak's critique, Derrida's book on Marx confirms it.

130 W. E. B. Du Bois, *Black Reconstruction in America 1860–1880* (1935; New York: The Free Press, 1998), 3.

131 Du Bois, *Black Reconstruction in America*, 11.

132 The penultimate chapter of *Black Reconstruction in America* bears the unequivocal title "Back toward Slavery."

133 W. E. B. Du Bois, "An Open Letter to Woodrow Wilson" (March 1913), in *Writings* (New York: The Library of America, 1986), 1142.

134 W. E. B. Du Bois, "An Open Letter to Woodrow Wilson" (September 1913), in *Writings*, 1145.

135 Du Bois, "An Open Letter to Woodrow Wilson" (September 1913), 1145.

136 Du Bois, "An Open Letter to Woodrow Wilson" (September 1913), 1145.

137 Du Bois, "An Open Letter to Woodrow Wilson" (September 1913), 1146.

138 Du Bois, "The Crisis" (November 1910), in *Writings*, 1131.

139 Du Bois, *Black Reconstruction in America*, 703.

140 Du Bois, *Black Reconstruction in America*, 703.

141 W. E. B. Du Bois, "I Am Resolved," in "Articles from *The Crisis*," in *Writings*, 1137.

142 Du Bois, "I Am Resolved," 1137–8.

143 W. E. B. Du Bois, "Dusk of Dawn: An Essay Toward an Autobiography of a Race Concept" [1940], in *Writings*, 531.

144 Du Bois, "Dusk of Dawn," 760.

145 Du Bois, "Dusk of Dawn," 761.

146 Du Bois, "Dusk of Dawn," 762.

147 Du Bois, "Dusk of Dawn," 762.

148 Du Bois, "Dusk of Dawn," 763.

149 Du Bois, "Dusk of Dawn," 765–6.

150 Nelson Mandela, *The Struggle Is My Life*, 3rd ed. (New York: Pathfinder, 1990), 176.

151 Mandela, *The Struggle Is My Life*, 175.

152 Mandela, *The Struggle Is My Life*, 175.

153 Mandela, *The Struggle Is My Life*, 149, 175.

154 Mandela, *The Struggle Is My Life*, 149–50.

155 See Thabo Mbeki, "'Two Nations' Speech to Parliament," *Umrabulo* 5, no. 3 (1998), accessed December 10, 2023, https://tinyurl.com/yckc2cht.

156 Du Bois, "Dusk of Dawn," 770.

157 Du Bois, "Dusk of Dawn," 770.

158 In *The Government of Desire*, op. cit., I argue that the norms of liberal governmentality apply to the economic as well as the libidinal sphere, to the eighteenth- and early nineteenth-century sciences of political economy and psychopathology. In a subsequent book, *Lacan: A Genealogy* (London: Bloomsbury, 2021), I show how, early on and throughout his life, Lacan criticized what he called the "liberal" or "utilitarian" view of desire, based on the principles of self-interest and pleasure.

159 De Beistegui, *Government of Desire*, 770–1.

160 See Wilhelm Reich, *The Mass Psychology of Fascism*, trans. Theodore P. Wolfe (1933; New York: Orgone Institute Press, 1946); Herbert Marcuse, *Eros and Civilization: A Philosophical Inquiry into Freud* (1956; New York: Routledge, 1998).

161 Du Bois, "Dusk of Dawn," 775.

162 Du Bois, "Dusk of Dawn," 774.

163 Du Bois, "Dusk of Dawn," 774.

164 Du Bois, "Dusk of Dawn," 775.

165 Du Bois, *Black Reconstruction in America*, 700 and 701; see also 21, 29.

166 Du Bois, "A Negro Nation Within the Nation," *Current History* 42, no. 3 (June 1935): 265.

167 Du Bois, "A Negro Nation Within the Nation," 265–6.

168 Du Bois, "A Negro Nation Within the Nation," 267.

169 Du Bois recounts the painful circumstances of his resignation in "Dusk of Dawn," 782–4.

170 Bernard E. Harcourt, "The Abolition of Capital: An Introduction," *Abolition 13/13*, December 12, 2020, https://tinyurl.com/2fw2cph4.

171 Du Bois, "A Negro Nation Within the Nation," 270.

172 Bernard E. Harcourt, *Cooperation: A Political, Economic, and Social Theory* (New York: Columbia University Press, 2023), 85.

173 Du Bois, "A Negro Nation Within the Nation," 265.

174 See Harcourt, *Cooperation*, 83. Harcourt mentions the influence of Peter Kropotkin's *Mutual Aid: A Factor of Evolution* (New York: Dover Publications, 2006), the Cooperative League of the United States of America, and other cooperative movements.

175 See Harcourt, *Cooperation*, 75. These visionaries, Harcourt claims, wanted to reorganize the forms of economic production for the benefit of workers and their families, limit the hours of labor, improve living conditions, and promote education (Harcourt, *Cooperation*, 75). To this list, one could add the names of the French geographer, proto-ecologist, and anarchist Elysée Reclus (1830–1905), as well as the American writer, philosopher, social reformer, and feminist utopian Charlotte Perkins Gilman (1860–1935).

176 Existing models of cooperation permeate the economy in North America, South America, Europe, Asia, and Africa. Worldwide, cooperatives have approximately 800 million members in over one hundred countries. They also secure 100 million jobs. In Germany, where cooperatives are the economic form with the most members, 7,500 cooperatives have more than 20 million members. In Canada, every third citizen is a cooperative member. In Japan, 91 percent of farmers are organized in cooperatives. In Bolivia, cooperatives manage a quarter of all national savings ("Creating Values Together," *Deutschland.de*, July 5, 2018, https://www.deutschland.de/en/topic/business/cooperatives-examples-from-germany-and-around-the-world). In the United States, Isthmus Engineering and Manufacturing in Madison, Cooperative Home Care in the Bronx, King Arthur Flour in Vermont, and AK Press in California are worker cooperatives. Land O'Lakes, Sunkist, and Ocean Spray are producer cooperatives. REI is a consumer cooperative, and Ace Hardware is a retailer cooperative. The Navy Federal Credit Union, with over $125 billion in assets and 8 million members, is a member credit union. See Lynn Pitman, "History of Cooperatives in the United States: An Overview," University of Wisconsin-Madison Center for Cooperatives, December 2018, https://tinyurl.com/y58kxjtr.

177 Harcourt, *Cooperation*, 22.

178 Harcourt, *Cooperation*, 24.

179 Brian Van Slyke, "Pandemic Crash Shows Worker Co-Ops Are More Resilient Than Traditional Businesses," *Truthout*, May 8, 2020, https://tinyurl.com/2hbtrxcm.

180 Harcourt, *Cooperation*, 17.

181 "About Us," Mondragon Corporation, accessed September 5, 2020, https://tinyurl.com/bdfkc4xw. See also Xabier Barandiaran and Javier Lezaun, "The Mondragón Experience," in *The Oxford Handbook of Mutual, Co-operative, and Co-owned Business*, ed. Jonathan Michie, Joseph R. Blasi, and Carlo Borzaga (Oxford: Oxford University Press, 2017); Sharryn Kasmir, *The Myth of Mondragón: Cooperatives, Politics, and Working-Class Life in a Basque Town* (Albany, NY: State University of New York Press, 1996). Harcourt also mentions Swann-Morton, a worker cooperative

in Sheffield, England, which produces and sells surgical blades and scalpels and exports to over 100 countries around the globe (Harcourt, *Cooperation*, 17). "Swann-Morton History," Swann-Morton Ltd., accessed September 5, 2020, https://tinyurl.com/2s3b5hps. Estimated revenues from "Swann-Morton's Competitors, Revenue, Number of Employees, Funding and Acquisitions," *Owler*, accessed September 5, 2020, https://www.owler.com/company/swann-morton.

182 Harcourt, *Cooperation*, 16. "About Mutual Insurance," National Association of Mutual Insurance Companies, accessed August 7, 2021, https://www.namic.org/about/mutuals.

183 See "European Market Share 2022," a report by the International Cooperative and Mutual Insurance Federation, accessed February 6, 2023, https://tinyurl.com/yc43b27t.

184 David Graeber, *Debt: The First 5,000 Years* (New York: Melville House, 2011), 95–102.

185 Graeber, *Debt*, 98.

186 Graeber, *Debt*, 99.

187 This is the title of the first chapter of Mark Fisher's *Capitalist Realism: Is There No Alternative?* (London: Zero Books, 2009).

188 Joshua Clover, *Riot. Strike. Riot: The New Era of Uprisings* (New York: Verso, 2016), 126.

189 Clover, *Riot*, 21.

190 See Jacques Rancière, "Does Democracy Mean Something?," in *Dissensus: On Politics and Aesthetics*, ed. and trans. Steven Corcoran (London: Continuum, 2010), 45–61.

191 Rancière, "Does Democracy Mean Something?," 54.

192 Rancière, "Does Democracy Mean Something?," 54.

193 Saul Newman, *Postanarchism* (Cambridge: Polity, 2016), 128.

194 On civil disobedience and, more generally, on the art of being governed less, see Henry David Thoreau's essay "Resistance to Civil Government" (1849), also known as "Civil Disobedience," in Henry David Thoreau, *Walden and Civil Disobedience* (London and New York: Penguin Books, 1983). On the history of laziness, idleness, and the various forms of resistance to the capitalist *ethos*, see Michel Foucault, *The Punitive Society: Lectures at the Collège de France 1972–1973*, trans. Graham Burchell (London: Palgrave Macmillan, 2015), 186–200. The political-economical, and specifically liberal, condemnation of laziness and idleness is to be related to, yet distinguished from, its moral and religious counterpart, which, in the seventeenth century, saw in laziness an anti-Christian attitude, and especially a rejection of the human condition as essentially fallen, sinful, and bound to the necessity of work. On that particular condemnation, see Michel Foucault, *History of Madness*, trans. Jonathan Murphy and Jean Khalfa (London: Routledge, 2006), part 1, chapter 2, esp.

69–72. See also the famous opus by the communist (and son-in-law of Karl Marx) Paul Lafargue, *The Right to be Lazy* [1883], ed. Bernard Marszalek (London: AK Press, 2011), as well as David Price, *Laziness Does Not Exist* (New York: Simon & Schuster, 2022). On the "anti-work" movement, see Kathi Weeks, *The Problem with Work: Feminism, Marxism, Antiwork Politics, and Postwork Imaginaries* (Durham, NC and London: Duke University Press, 2011); David Frayne, *The Refusal of Work: The Resistance and Practice of Resistance to Work* (London: Zed Books, 2015).

195 Bertrand Russell, *In Praise of Idleness* (1935; London: Routledge, 2003), 2.

196 Russell, *In Praise of Idleness*, 5.

197 Russell, *In Praise of Idleness*, 5.

198 Russell, *In Praise of Idleness*, 5.

199 Russell, *In Praise of Idleness*, 10.

Chapter 4

1 Jacques Derrida, *The Other Heading: Reflections on Today's Europe*, trans. Pascale-Anne Brault and Michael B. Naas (1990; Bloomington and Indianapolis, IN: Indiana University Press, 1992). "The Other Heading" was the title of a talk Derrida gave at a colloquium on "European Cultural Identity" in Turin in May 1990. An abridged version of the talk was subsequently published simultaneously in four languages and four major European newspapers in 1990.

2 Jacques Derrida, *Of Spirit: Heidegger and the Question*, trans. Geoffrey Bennington and Rachel Bowlby (Chicago, IL: The University of Chicago University Press, 1987).

3 Derrida, *Of Spirit*, 122–4.

4 Jacques Derrida, "The 'World' of the Enlightenment to Come (Exception, Calculation, Sovereignty)," trans. Pascale-Anne Brault and Michael Nass, *Research in Phenomenology* 33 (2003): 44.

5 M. Heidegger, *Einführung in die Metaphysik* (Tübingen: Max Niemeyer Verlag, 1953), 34.

6 Heidegger, *Einführung in die Metaphysik*, cited in Derrida, *Of Spirit*, 45.

7 M. Heidegger, *Die Selbstbehauptung der deutschen Universität*, ed. Hermann Heidegger (1933; Frankfurt am Main: Vittorio Klostermann, 1983). Cited in Derrida, *Of Spirit*, 33.

8 Heidegger, *Einführung in die Metaphysik*, 36. Cited in Derrida, *Of Spirit*, 45. I leave aside here the question of Heidegger's utter blindness and delusion regarding *Nazi* Germany, of his profound ignorance of both "America" and "Russia," and of his deep

Euro- and Germano-centrism, to say nothing of his anti-Semitism. The literature on those aspects of Heidegger's thought is now vast and growing, especially after the publication of the so-called *Black Notebooks*, which began in 2014. Those private manuscripts, which Heidegger wrote between 1931 and 1970, are edited by Peter Trawny and consist of nine volumes. The first three volumes, which cover the period between 1931 and 1941, are the most relevant. See Martin Heidegger, *Gesamtausgabe 94: Überlegungen II-VI (Schwarze Hefte 1931–1941)*, ed. Peter Trawny (Frankfurt am Main: Vittorio Klostermann, 2014); *Gesamtausgabe 95: Überlegungen VIII-XI (Schwarze Hefte 1931–1941)*, ed. Peter Trawny (Frankfurt am Main: Vittorio Klostermann, 2014); *Gesamtausgabe 96: Überlegungen XII-XV (Schwarze Hefte 1931–1941)*, ed. Peter Trawny (Frankfurt am Main: Vittorio Klostermann, 2014). I made my position clear in de Beistegui, *Heidegger and the Political* (London: Routledge, 1998).

9. Derrida, *Of Spirit*, 60.
10. Derrida, *Of Spirit*, 60.
11. Derrida, *The Other Heading*, 29.
12. Derrida, *The Other Heading*, 30–1. A paleonym is the deliberate retention of an old word after new meanings have been added to it.
13. P. Valéry, *Essais quasi politiques, Œuvres* (Paris: Gallimard Bibliothèque de la Pléiade, 1957), vol. 2, 1090.
14. Derrida, *The Other Heading*, 31.
15. Derrida, *The Other Heading*, 78.
16. Derrida, *The Other Heading*, 31–2.
17. Derrida, "The 'World' of the Enlightenment to Come," 41.
18. Derrida, "The 'World' of the Enlightenment to Come," 41.
19. Derrida, "The 'World' of the Enlightenment to Come," 42.
20. Derrida, "The 'World' of the Enlightenment to Come," 44.
21. Derrida, "The 'World' of the Enlightenment to Come," 48.
22. Derrida, *Force de loi* (Paris: Galilée, 1994), 54.
23. Derrida, *Force de loi*, 57.
24. Derrida, *The Other Heading*, 39.
25. Derrida, *The Other Heading*, 44.
26. Derrida, *The Other Heading*, 41.
27. See Jacques Derrida, *Aporias*, trans. Thomas Dutoit (Stanford, CA: Stanford University Press, 1993), esp. 12–21.
28. Jacques Derrida, *Parages* (Paris: Galilée, 1986), 72, and *The Other Heading*, 79.

29 Derrida, *The Other Heading*, 41.

30 Derrida, *The Other Heading*, 44–5.

31 Derrida, *The Other Heading*, 76 and 77. Derrida deploys the same argument and logic in his tribute to Nelson Mandela. He emphasizes Mandela's repeated admiration for the European (and North American) liberal order, parliamentary democracy, the separation of powers, or technocratic. But he also emphasizes Mandela's admiration for the economically and socially egalitarian structure and organization of early African societies, which put into perspective, if not radically into question, the Western liberal order. See J. Derrida, "Admiration of Nelson Mandela, or The Laws of Reflection," *Law and Literature* 26, no. 1 (Spring 2014): 9–30.

32 Derrida, *The Other Heading*, 77.

33 Derrida, *The Other Heading*, 78.

34 J. Derrida, *Psyché: Inventions de l'autre* (Paris: Galilée, 1983), 27.

35 Derrida, *Aporias*, 16.

36 Derrida, *The Other Heading*, 79, and *Aporias*, 16.

37 Derrida, *Aporias*, 16.

38 Derrida, *The Other Heading*, 57.

39 Derrida, *The Other Heading*, 56–7.

40 Jacques Derrida, *Specters of Marx: The State of the Debt, the Work of Mourning and the New International*, trans. Peggy Kamuf, intro. Bernd Magnus and Stephen Cullenberg (1993; New York and London: Routledge, 1994). Since its original publication in 1993, *Specters of Marx* has sparked critical responses from some of the most prominent figures in Marxist and post-Marxist cultural theory, including Aijaz Ahmad (1994), Fredric Jameson (1995), Gayatri Spivak (1995), Pierre Macherey (1995), and Ernesto Laclau (1995). Those responses, along with others and a response by Derrida, were subsequently collected in a volume titled *Ghostly Demarcations*, ed. and intro. Michael Sprinker (London: Verso, 1999). See also Richard Halpern, "An Impure History of Ghosts: Derrida, Marx, Shakespeare," in *Marxist Shakespeares*, ed. Jean E. Howard and Scott Cutler Shershow (London and New York: Routledge, 2001), 31–52.

41 Derrida, *Specters of Marx*, 115.

42 Derrida, *Specters of Marx*, 14.

43 Derrida, *Specters of Marx*, 97.

44 Derrida, *Specters of Marx*, 4.

45 Derrida is not alone in this endeavour. In 1946–1947, Levinas gave a series of four lectures at Jean Wahl's *Collège Philosophique*. The lectures were published in 1978 under the title *Time and the Other*. In the third lecture, Levinas famously (and somewhat enigmatically) claims that "the whole of philosophy is only a meditation

on Shakespeare." See Emmanuel Levinas, *Time and the Other*, trans. Richard A. Cohen (Pittsburgh, PA: Duquesne University Press, 1987), 72. The modern tragic hero, Levinas claims, triumphs over fatality by retaining his or her power to die, to choose death. But Hamlet is different: by realizing that death is not the solution, he "is beyond tragedy or the tragedy of tragedy" (Levinas, *Time and the Other*, 50). Levinas also identifies the figure of the ghost, whether in *Hamlet* or *Macbeth*, with that of the murdered and haunting Other, whose silenced voice and powerlessness traumatizes and suspends the sound and fury of power, as well as the enjoyment and mastery of those who are still living and view their own death as an expression of their freedom. See E. Levinas, *De l'existence à l'existant* (1947; Paris: Vrin, 1990), 86/100. See also Howard Caygill, "Levinas and Shakespeare," in *The Routledge Companion to Shakespeare and Philosophy*, ed. Craig Bourne and Emily Caddick Bourne (London and New York: Routledge, 2019), 145–51.

46 See Jacques Derrida, *The Politics of Friendship*, trans. George Collins (1994; London: Verso Books, 1997), 156 and 169n32. The footnote on *Hamlet or Hecuba* occurs in the context not of the ghostly figure of the king in *Hamlet*, on which Derrida focuses, but in that of a more limited claim regarding the lack of women, female figures, and sexual difference in Schmitt. As if objecting to his own claim, Derrida recognizes Schmitt's own recognition of the role of the queen and Hamlet's sister in *Hamlet*, but only to dismiss it as irrelevant: ultimately, the play is a matter of a struggle to the death between brothers. Schmitt, he concludes, perpetuates and reformulates a very Western form of androcentrism, or a logo-phallo-polemocentrism.

47 Carl Schmitt, *The Concept of the Political*, trans. George Schwab, foreword by Tracy Strong (Chicago, IL: The University of Chicago Press, 1996), chapters 2 and 3.

48 Schmitt, *The Concept of the Political*, 33.

49 Schmitt, *The Concept of the Political*, 35, emphasis added.

50 Derrida, *The Politics of Friendship*, 127–8, translation modified.

51 Schmitt, *The Concept of the Political*, 33.

52 Schmitt, *The Concept of the Political*, 30, emphasis added.

53 Derrida, *The Politics of Friendship*, 138.

54 Derrida, *The Politics of Friendship*, 138.

55 Bernd Magnus and Stephen Cullenberg, eds., *Whither Marxism: Global Crises in International Perspective* (New York and London: Routledge, 1995).

56 Derrida, *Specters of Marx*, 10.

57 Derrida, *Specters of Marx*, 169.

58 Derrida, *Specters of Marx*, 96.

59 Derrida, *Specters of Marx*, 96.

60 Derrida, *Specters of Marx*, 97.

61 Derrida, *Specters of Marx*, 45–6.

62 Derrida, *Specters of Marx*, 120.

63 Derrida, *Specters of Marx*, 107.

64 Derrida, *Specters of Marx*, 117.

65 Derrida, *Specters of Marx*, 108.

66 Derrida, *Specters of Marx*, 117.

67 Derrida, *Specters of Marx*, 111–12.

68 Derrida, *Specters of Marx*, 58.

69 Derrida, *Specters of Marx*, 58.

70 Karl Marx, *Capital*, vol. 1 (London: Penguin Books, 1976), 165.

71 Marx, *Capital*, 169.

72 Marx, *Capital*, 164.

73 See Jean-Jacques Rousseau, *The Confessions*, trans. with intro. J. M. Cohen (New York: Penguin Books, 1953), and *Emile, or On Education*, trans. Allan Bloom (New York: Basic Books, 1979), book 4. Cited in Derrida, *Of Grammatology*, 150.

74 Derrida, *Of Grammatology*, 151, emphasis added.

75 The latter, specifically the political problem, is at the heart of part 3 of *The Social Contract*, in *The Social Contract and Other Political Writings*, trans. Quentin Hoare and ed. Christopher Bertram (London: Penguin Books, 2012), as well as part 7 of *Considérations sur le gouvernement de Pologne et sur sa réformation projetée*, in *Œuvres complètes*, vol. 3, ed. Bernard Gagnebin and Marcel Raymond (Paris: Gallimard, 1964).

76 Marx, *Capital*, vol. 1, 126.

77 Derrida, *Of Grammatology*, 145.

78 Derrida, *Specters of Marx*, 38–9, translation modified.

Chapter 5

1 Many recognize the exceptional nature of the ecological crisis, calling it a "curious crisis," "unlike the crises of inequality, racism, or even the Covid-19 pandemic." See Daniel Aldana Cohen and David Bond, "Toward a Theory of Climate Praxis: Confronting Climate Change in a World of Struggle," in *Crisis under Critique: How*

People Assess, Transform, and Respond to Critical Situations, ed. Didier Fassin and Axel Honneth (New York: Columbia University Press, 2022), 274. Most often, and as with previous forms of crises, "crisis" functions as a transcendental or loose condition of possibility for the critical assessment of the phenomenon in question. My goal in this chapter will be to identify the specific nature of the ecological crisis.

2 Elizabeth Kolbert, *The Sixth Extinction: An Unnatural History* (New York: Henry Holt and Company, 2014).

3 Over half a century ago, the US West Coast anarchist poet Kenneth Rexroth published an essay, "Facing Extinction," in which he described the prospect of human extinction as the most significant issue facing the counterculture. See Kenneth Rexroth, "Facing Extinction," in *The Alternative Society: Essays from the Other World* (New York: Herder and Herder, 1970), 183–96. I am indebted to Jason Wirth for the discovery of Rexroth's work. See Jason Wirth, "Extinction Event," *PhilosophyX*, accessed August 17, 2019, https://tinyurl.com/57ah4nue.

4 According to Al Jazeera, the official figure of 50,026 deaths and 113,274 wounded, communicated by Gaza's Ministry of Health, does not include the many others who were buried without being registered or have gone missing since October 2023. See Al Jazeera, "Israel's War on Gaza has Killed 50,000 Palestinians since October 2023," accessed May 20, 2025, https://www.aljazeera.com/news/2025/3/23/israeli-offensive-in-gaza-has-killed-50000-palestinians-since-october-2023#flips-#:0. A recent report by Amnesty International concluded that "Israel Is Committing Genocide in Gaza," accessed December 15, 2024, https://tinyurl.com/yc28cy52. On January 26, 2024, the International Court of Justice provided an interim ruling, which granted it the legal right to proceed with the case concerning the crime of genocide in Gaza, https://tinyurl.com/bdzcswsf. See also Forensic Architecture's meticulous cartography of the genocide and ecocide in Gaza since 2023, accessed December 12, 2024, https://tinyurl.com/4px6adf3, https://tinyurl.com/ytb2ba4x; Didier Fassin, *Une étrange défaite. Sur le consentement à l'écrasement de Gaza* (Paris: La Découverte, 2024); Omer Bartov, "What I Believe as a Historian of Genocide," *The New York Times*, November 10, 2023; Neve Gordon and Mouna Haddad, "The Road to Famine in Gaza," *The New York Review of Books*, April 18, 2024; Raz Segal, "A Textbook Case of Genocide," *Jewish Currents*, October 13, 2023; Amos Goldberg, "Yes, It Is a Genocide," *The Palestine Project*, April 18, 2024.

5 Said, *The Question of Palestine*, 61–2.

6 Said, *The Question of Palestine*, 62.

7 Michel Serres, *Le contrat naturel* (Paris: Éditions Le Pommier, 2018).

8 Percy Bysshe Shelley, "Mont Blanc. Lines Written in the Vale of Chamouni" (1817), in *The Complete Poetry of Percy Bysshe Shelley*, vol. 3, ed. Neil Fraistat and Nora Crook (Baltimore, MD: Johns Hopkins University Press, 2001), 79.

9 Industry has, of course, played a major role in this process. But agriculture, and livestock farms in particular, are also part of the problem. See George Monbiot,

Regenesis: Feeding the World Without Devouring the Planet (London: Allen Lane, 2022), 60–4, 256–7, and notes 26–34. Monbiot refers to studies carried out in Wales, Ireland, New Zealand, Germany, and China. The studies reveal the extent to which cow and pig manure is responsible for lake and river death. Toxic enough when "pure," the manure is often contaminated with high levels of metal salts (mercury, copper, zinc, arsenic, chromium, and manganese) and antibiotics.

10 Sir Arthur Conan Doyle, "When the World Screamed," in *Professor Challenger: Complete Edition of the Five Novels*, Open Access, printed in Poland. Conan Doyle's science fiction short story was first published in *Liberty* magazine, from February 25 to March 3, 1928.

11 Coined by the American ecologist Eugene Stoermer and the Dutch Nobel Prize-winning atmospheric chemist Paul Crutzen, the term refers to the beginning of a new epoch of the earth following the Holocene, which dated from the end of the last ice age, or the end of the Pleistocene, about twelve thousand years ago, and during which the earth remained stable, indifferent to human history. The Anthropocene designates the eruption of the human onto the geological scene, and the disruption of the latter by the former. See Paul J. Crutzen and Eugene F. Stoermer, "The Anthropocene," *Global Change Newsletter* 41 (2000): 17–18; see also Colin N. Waters, Jan Zalaciewicz et al., "The Anthropocene Is Functionally and Stratigraphically Distinct from the Holocene," *Science* 851 (January 8, 2016): 1203–7. For a broader discussion of the Anthropocene, see Christophe Bonneuil and Jean-Baptiste Fressoz, eds., *The Shock of the Anthropocene: The Earth, History, and Us*, trans. David Fernbach (London: Verso Books, 2016).

12 Crutzen and Stoermer, "The Anthropocene," 17.

13 Jared Diamond calls Fertile Crescent Agriculture "the worst mistake in the history of the human race." See Jared Diamond, "The Worst Mistake in the History of the Human Race," *Discover Magazine*, May 1987, 64–6. See also Mark Nathan Cohen and George J. Armelagos, *Paleopathology at the Origins of Agriculture* (Gainesville, FL: University Press of Florida, 2013).

14 This is the view held by Crutzen and Stoermer. See also Andreas Malm, *Fossil Capital: The Rise of Steam Power and the Roots of Global Warming* (London: Verso Books, 2016), and Tim di Nunzio, *Carbon Capitalism: Energy, Social Reproduction, and World Order* (New York and London: Rowman and Litllefield, 2015).

15 Jan Zalaciewicz, Mike Walter, Phil Gibbard, and John Lowe, "When Did the Anthropocene Begin? A Mid-Twentieth-Century Boundary Is Stratigraphically Optimal," *Quaternary International* 383 (2015): 196–203. For a sociological history of fossil fuels, especially in relation to the "Great Acceleration" post-1945, see Peter Wagner, *Carbon Societies: The Social Logic of Fossil Fuels* (Cambridge: Polity, 2024).

16 For a defense of the use of the term "Anthropocene," and a detailed response to objections regarding its use, see Timothy Morton, *Dark Ecology: For a Logic of Future Coexistence* (New York: Columbia University Press, 2016), 14–24. Ultimately,

he claims, what matters is not the name itself but the recognition that humans are a geophysical force responsible for the devastation of the planet. Human beings—not jellyfish, cows, or computers—began to wreck the planet around 1790 by emitting carbon dioxide and related gases. To which I would reply that one needs to investigate the historical—material *and* epistemic—conditions under which this process began. We need to consider and account for this nonlinear event, or this historical caesura. Critique must deploy the necessary tools to rise to the social, political, and ethical challenge posed by this event.

17 Morton, *Dark Ecology*, 8, 38–40, 61–9. For Morton, the Anthropocene is "temporally fuzzy" yet not "absolutely indeterminate": it did not originate a million years ago (p. 76).

18 For a critique of the Anthropocene as a historical argument aimed at understanding the nature of the current ecological crisis, and a defense instead of the Capitalocene as a concept best able critically to explore its origins in the rise of capitalist strategies of "global conquest, endless commodification, and relentless rationalization," see Jason W. Moore, *Capitalism in the Web of Life* (London: Verso Books, 2015), 169–92. See also Donna J. Haraway, *Staying with the Trouble: Making Kin in the Chthulucene* (Durham, NC and London: Duke University Press, 2016), 47–51.

19 One of the key criticisms ecofeminists have leveled at some ecological movements, deep ecology in particular, is their emphasis on anthropocentrism and their failure to address the problem of androcentrism. The domination of women and the domination of nature, they claim, are intimately connected, and mutually reinforcing. See Ariel Kay Salleh, "Deeper than Deep Ecology: The Ecofeminist Connection," *Environmental Ethics* 6 (1984): 339–45; Janet Biehl, "It's Deep, But Is It Broad? An Ecofeminist Looks at Deep Ecology," *Kick It Over*, Special Supplement (1987): 2A; Val Plumwood, *Feminism and the Mastery of Nature* (London and New York: Routledge, 1993), Chapter 7 ("Deep Ecology and the Denial of Difference"). For a response to those criticisms, see Deborah Slicer, "Is There an Ecofeminist—Deep Ecology 'Debate'?" *Environmental Ethics* 17, no. 2 (1995): 151–69; and Christian Diehm, "Arne Naess, Val Plumwood, and Deep Ecological Subjectivity: A Contribution to the 'Deep Ecology-Ecofeminism Debate,'" *Ethics and the Environment* 7, no. 1 (2002): 24–38. On the specific connection between carbon capitalism and masculinity, see Cara Daggett, "Petro-Masculinity: Fossil Fuels and Authoritarian Desire," *Millennium: Journal of International Studies* 47, no. 1 (2018): 25–44, https://tinyurl.com/yfpzwdrk.

20 Christophe Bonneuil and Jean-Baptiste Fressoz, *The Shock of the Anthropocene: The Earth, History, and Us* (London: Verso, 2017), 99–121, 148–69.

21 Piers M. Blaikie, *The Political Economy of Soil Erosion in Developing Countries*, Longman Development Studies (New York: Longman, 1985): 1–11, 117–24. For a more current explanation related not to agriculture but to the effects of war and the argument on the "Environmentalism of the Poor," see Chapters 6 (Thanatocene) and 8 (Polemocene) of Bonneuil and Fressoz's *The Shock of the Anthropocene*, 122–47 and

170–97, respectively. For a more detailed account of the latter, see Isabel Anguelovski and Joan Martínez Alier, "The 'Environmentalist of the Poor' Revised: Territory and Place in Disconnected Global Struggles," *Ecological Economies* 102 (2014): 167–76.

22 Bonneuil and Fressoz, *The Shock of the Anthropocene*, 99–121. For a more specific and mathematical approach to the impact of CO_2, see Martin Hänsel, Moritz Drupp, Daniel Johannson, et al., "Climate Economics Support for the UN Climate Targets," *Nature Climate Change* (2020): 2–15 and 30.

23 John Pickles and Adrian Smith, "Delocalization and Persistence in the European Clothing Industry: The Reconfiguration of Trade and Production Networks," *Regional Studies* 45, no. 2 (2011): 167–85; Peter J. Buckley and Roger Strange, "The Governance of the Global Factory: Location and Control of World Economic Activity," *Academy of Management Perspectives* 29, no. 2 (2015): 237–49.

24 According to the UN Food and Agriculture Organization, at current rates of soil degradation the world on average has sixty more years of harvests. See Chris Arsenault, "Only 60 Years of Farming Left if Soil Degradation Continues," *Scientific American*, December 6, 2014. As for the collapse of insect life in the last few decades, and its effect on bird diversity, that phenomenon is now well documented. For a review of the scientific evidence, see Monbiot, *Regenesis*, 263–5, notes 101–14.

25 Blaikie, "Erosion," 117–24.

26 Kathleen Hermans and Robert McLeman, "Climate Change, Drought, Land Degradation and Migration: Exploring the Linkages," *Current Opinion on Environmental Sustainability* 50 (2021): 236–44.

27 Cited in Naomi Klein, "How Science Is Telling Us All to Revolt," *The New Statesman*, October 29, 2013, updated September 27, 2015, https://tinyurl.com/34r2y9b9. See also Haraway, *Staying with the Trouble*, 49.

28 Jason W. Moore, "Cheap Food and Bad Climate: From Surplus Value to Negative Value in the Capitalist World-Ecology," *Critical Historical Studies* 2 (Spring 2015): 8.

29 Moore, "Cheap Food," 5.

30 This "Promethean arrogance," Jonas claims, is equally at work in both the capitalist and the Marxist cults of technology and industrialization. See Hans Jonas, *The Imperative of Responsibility: In Search of an Ethics for the Technological Age*, trans. Hans Jonas with David Herr (1979; Chicago, IL: The University of Chicago Press, 1984), 143, 189, and chapters 5 and 6 more generally.

31 See Ernst Jünger, *Total Mobilization* [1930], trans. Joel Golb and Richard Wolin, in *The Heidegger Controversy: A Critical Reader*, ed. Richard Wolin (Cambridge, MA: MIT Press, 1992), 119–39; and Jünger, *The Worker: Dominion and Form* [1932], trans. Bogdan Costea and Laurence Paul Hemming (Evanston, IL: Northwestern University Press, 2017).

32 See W. Benjamin, thesis 11 of "'Theses on the Philosophy of History," in *Illuminations*, trans. Harry Zohn (New York: Schocken Books, 1969), 258–60.

33 See Karl Marx, "Critique of the Gotha Program," trans. Kevin B. Anderson and Karel Ludenhoff (Binghamton, NY: PM Press/Spectre, 2022).

34 Günther Anders, *Die Antiquiertheit des Menschen*, vol. 2., *Über die Zerstörung des Lebens im Zeitalter der dritten industriellen Revolution* (Munich: C. H. Beck, 1980), 20. In the wake of the explosion of the atomic bombs in Hiroshima and Nagasaki, Günther (Stern) Anders—Arendt's first husband, a friend of Hans Jonas, and like them a student of Husserl and Heidegger in Freiburg in the early 1920s—developed a sustained critique of technology. The first volume of *Die Antiquertheit des Menschen*, *Über die Seele im Zeitalter der zweiten industriellen Revolution*, came out in 1956 (Munich: C. H. Beck). In between, Anders published *Endzeit und Zeitenende. Gedanken über die atomare Situation* (Munich: C. H. Beck, 1972). To be sure, when writing the two volumes of *The Obsolescence of the Human*, Anders had in mind the advent of technology and its culmination in the atomic bomb. But his analysis of "the three industrial revolutions" applies equally, I would argue, to the threat of extinction or "obsolescence" of the biosphere.

35 Françoise d'Eaubonne, *Le féminisme ou la mort* [1974] (Paris: le passage clandestin, 2020), 316.

36 Jonas, *The Imperative of Responsibility*, ix, emphasis added.

37 Jonas, *The Imperative of Responsibility*, 190.

38 Merlin Sheldrake, *Entangled Life: How Fungi Make Our Worlds, Change Our Minds, and Shape Our Futures* (London: Vintage Books, 2020), 95.

39 Monbiot, *Regenesis*, 24.

40 Greta Thunberg, "We've Been Greenwashed Out of Our Senses. It's Time to Stand Our Ground," *The Guardian*, October 8, 2022, https://tinyurl.com/2f6rakrm.

41 In South America, 200 times more land is used to grow soy today than in 1961. See Walter Fraanje and Tara Garnett, "Soy: Food, Feed, and Land Use Change," Food Climate Research Network, University of Oxford (TABLE Debates), January 30, 2020, https://tinyurl.com/5c5n9ycy.

42 Johnny Hughes and Neil Burgess, "Rare Wildlife in Brazil's Savannah Is Under Threat—We Are All Responsible," United Nations Environment Programme World Conservation Monitoring Centre (UNEP-WCMC), October 29, 2019, https://tinyurl.com/4pz2cpjd.

43 Monbiot, *Regenesis*, 69–70.

44 Jonathan Watts, "'No Doubt' Left about Scientific Consensus on Global Warming, Experts Say," *The Guardian*, July 24, 2019, https://tinyurl.com/4k9n7abb.

45 Wildfires are ravaging forests set aside to soak up greenhouse gases. https://tinyurl.com/ycxneeay.

46 Fred Pearce, *With Speed and Violence: Why Scientists Fear Tipping Points in Climate Change* (Boston, MA: Beacon Press, 2008).

47 See Chris A. Boulton, Timothy M. Lenton, and Niklas Boers, "Pronounced Loss of Amazon Rainforest Since the Early 2000s," *National Climate Change*, March 7, 2022, https://doi.org/10.1038/s41558-022-01287-8.

48 "IPCC, 2021: Summary for Policymakers," in *Climate Change 2021: The Physical Science Basis. Contribution of Working Group I to the Sixth Assessment Report of the Intergovernmental Panel on Climate Change*, ed. V. Masson-Delmotte, P. Zhai, A. Pirani, S. L. Connors, C. Péan, S. Berger, N. Caud, Y. Chen, L. Goldfarb, M. I. Gomis, M. Huang, K. Leitzell, E. Lonnoy, J. B. R. Matthews, T. K. Maycock, T. Waterfield, O. Yelekçi, R. Yu, and B. Zhou (Cambridge: Cambridge University Press, 2021), https://tinyurl.com/29h7un2f.

49 Oliver Milman, "Severe Drought Threatens Hoover Dam Reservoir—and Water for US West," *The Guardian*, July 13, 2021, https://tinyurl.com/5xn4jebu.

50 This is according to the latest Living Planet Report of the World Wildlife Federation and Zoological Society of London (ZSL), compiled by eighty-nine authors: "Living Planet Report 2022: Building a Nature-Positive Society," accessed October 16, 2022, https://tinyurl.com/3sbsbxex.

51 The most severe extinction so far in the three-and-a-half-billion-year history of life on earth, and "the most severe biodiversity crisis in Earth history," was most likely caused by global warming. See Shu-zong Shen et al., "Calibrating the End-Permian Mass Extinction," *Science* 334 (6061): 1367–72, https://tinyurl.com/4vs2y9wa.

52 Kolbert, *The Sixth Extinction*, 17–18.

53 Robin McKie, "'Soon the World Will be Unrecognisable': Is It Still Possible to Prevent Total Meltdown?," *The Guardian*, July 30, 2022, https://tinyurl.com/27us5wbb.

54 Bill McGuire, as reported by Robin McKie. See Bill McGuire, *Hothouse Earth: An Inhabitant's Guide* (London: Icon Books, 2022).

55 Bruno Latour, *Facing Gaia: Eight Lectures on the New Climatic Regime*, trans. Catherine Porter (London: Polity, 2017), 7–8. Had the world paid attention to the first global warming evidence, published in 1955, this could have been just a crisis. See Gilbert N. Plass, "The Carbon Dioxide Theory of Climate Change," *Tellus* 8, no. 2 (1956): 140–54.

56 Latour, *Facing Gaia*, 9.

57 Latour, *Facing Gaia*, 8, 9.

58 Bruno Latour, *Politiques de la nature. Comment faire entrer les sciences en démocratie* (1999; Paris: La Découverte, 2004), 32–42, 93–100. On this point, Latour is indebted

to Beck. See Ulrich Beck, *Risk Society: Towards a New Modernity* (London: Sage, 1992) and *Ecological Politics in an Age of Risk* (Cambridge: Polity, 1995).

59 James Lovelock, *The Revenge of Gaia: Why the Earth is Fighting Back—and How We Can Still Save Humanity* (2006; London: Penguin Books, 2007), 66.

60 Lovelock, *The Revenge of Gaia*, 32.

61 Lovelock, *The Revenge of Gaia*, 58–9.

62 Lovelock, *The Vanishing Face of Gaia* (London: Penguin Books, 2009), 46.

63 Lovelock, *The Vanishing Face of Gaia*, 163.

64 G. Gao, X. Zhao, M. Jiang, and L. Gao, "Impacts of Marine Heatwaves on Algal Structure and Carbon Sequestration in Conjunction with Ocean Warming and Acidification," *Frontiers in Marine Science* 8 (2021): 758651, https://tinyurl.com/3scenc9k.

65 Damian Carrington, "Amazon Rainforest Now Emitting More CO_2 Than It Absorbs," *The Guardian*, July 14, 2021, https://tinyurl.com/4kb7tpvs.

66 Lovelock, *The Vanishing Face of Gaia*, 34.

67 Stuart Kauffman, *At Home in the Universe: The Search for Laws of Complexity* (London: Penguin Books, 1996), 91.

68 For further details, see Lovelock, *The Vanishing Face of Gaia*, 34.

69 Lovelock, *The Vanishing Face of Gaia*, 35.

70 Kauffman, *At Home in the Universe*, 9.

71 Kauffman, *At Home in the Universe*, 9.

72 See Stuart Kauffman, *At Home in the Universe*. Not every critical threshold is negative; in fact, Kauffman argues that what he calls "supracritical behavior"—or the explosion of molecular species resulting from chemical chain reactions, in which chemicals act not only as chemical substrates, but as catalysts for the creation of further chemical products—accounts for the complexity and creativity that lies everywhere in the biosphere: "supracriticality . . . is the ultimate wellspring of molecular diversity in the biosphere" (p. 122). Similarly, not every critical threshold is irreversible.

73 Lovelock, *The Revenge of Gaia*, 21.

74 James Lovelock, *Gaia: A New Look at Life on Earth* (1979; Oxford: Oxford University Press, 2016), xxi and xviii. The quotes are from the preface to the 2000 edition.

75 Lovelock, *The Vanishing Face of Gaia*, 155.

76 Manuele Coccia, *Metamorphoses*, trans. Robin Mackay (London: Polity, 2021), 159.

77 Paul-Antoine Miquel, *Vénus et Prométhée. Essai sur la relation entre l'humain et la biosphère* (Paris: Kimé, 2019), 9.

78 Miquel, *Vénus et Prométhée*, 52.

79 Miquel, *Vénus et Prométhée*, 64–5.

80 Kauffmann, *At Home in the Universe*, 87.

81 Kauffmann, *At Home in the Universe*, 90.

82 Coccia, *Metamorphoses*, 68.

83 Cited in Coccia, *Metamorphoses*, 68.

84 Coccia, *Metamorphoses*, 68.

85 Coccia, *Metamorphoses*, 69.

86 Coccia, *Metamorphoses*, 70.

87 Autocatalytic reactions are chemical reactions in which one of the reaction products is also a catalyst for the same or a coupled reaction. Stuart Kauffmann proposes that life initially arose as autocatalytic chemical "sets"—that is, self-sustaining chemical reaction networks in which all the molecules mutually catalyze each other's formation from a basic food source. As Hordijk explains, his theory, originally formulated in 1971, was further developed by him and others, with computational and experimental studies looking to investigate and identify the chemical compounds necessary to form autocatalytic sets for the creation of RNA, DNA, and other complex cellular life. See Wim Hordijk, "A History of Autocatalytic Sets," *Biological Theory* 14 (2019): 224–46, https://tinyurl.com/cbpy6a22. See also Wim Hordijk and Mike Steel, "Chasing the Tail: The Emergence of Autocatalytic Networks," *BioSystems* 152 (2017): 1–10, published online December 25, 2016, https://tinyurl.com/5n8cuzxy.

88 Thom van Dooren and Vinciane Despret, "Evolution: Lessons from Some Cooperative Ravens," in *The Edinburgh Companion to Animal Studies*, ed. Lynn Turner, Ron Broglio, and Undine Sellbach (Edinburgh: Edinburgh University Press, 2019).

89 A. Frank, "Über die biologischen Verhältnisse des Thallus einer Krustflechten," *Beiträge zur Biologie der Pflanzen* 2 (1877): 123–200. It should be noted that Frank speaks of *Symbiotismus*, not *Symbiose*, a term that was coined by Heinrich Anton de Bary in *Die Erscheinung der Symbiose* (Strasbourg: Tübner, 1879).

90 See Sheldrake, *Entangled Life*, 81–2. For Albert Frank and symbiosis, see Jan Sapp, *Evolution by Association* (Oxford: Oxford University Press, 1994), chapter 1, and "The Dynamics of Symbiosis: An Historical Overview," *Canadian Journal of Botany* 82 (2004): 1046–56. See also Rosemarie Honegger, "Simon Schwendener (1829–1919), and the Dual Hypothesis of Lichens," *The Bryologist* 103 (2000): 307–13, https://tinyurl.com/mr3588mh.

91 Sheldrake, *Entangled Life*, 82.

92 Sheldrake, *Entangled Life*, 82.

93 Sheldrake, *Entangled Life*, 90–1. Margulis's paper was published under the name of Lynn Sagan. Whilst already divorced from astronomer Carl Sagan when she wrote the paper, she kept his name for a while. See Lynn Sagan, "On the Origins of Mitosing Cells," *Journal of Theoretical Biology* 14 (1967): 225–74.

94 Sheldrake, *Entangled Life*, 91.

95 Norton D. Zinder and Joshua Lederberg, "Genetic Exchange in *Salmonella*," *Journal of Bacteriology* 64 (1952): 679–99. See also N. D. Zinder, "Forty Years Ago: The Discovery of Bacterial Transduction," *Genetics* 132 (1992): 291–4; Rosanna Alegado and Nicole King, "Bacterial Influences on Animal Origins," *Cold Spring Harbor Perspectives in Biology* 6, no. 11 (October 3, 2014): a016162, https://tinyurl.com/2vy6b6nv.

96 Lynn Margulis, *The Symbiotic Planet: A New Look at Evolution* (London: Phoenix, 1999).

97 Sapp, *Evolution by Association*, 179.

98 Richard Dawkins and Daniel Dennett, respectively. Cited in Sheldrake, *Entangled Life*, 92.

99 Lynn Margulis and Dorian Sagan, "The Beast with Five Genomes," *Natural History*, June 2011; Haraway, *Staying with the Trouble*, 61–2.

100 Purificación López García, Laura Eme, and David Moreira, "Symbiosis in Eukaryotic Evolution," *Journal of Theoretical Biology* 434 (December 2017): 20–33.

101 Haraway, *Staying with the Trouble*, 66.

102 See Scott F. Gilbert, Jan Sapp, and Alfred Tauber, "A Symbiotic View of Life: We Have Never Been Individuals," *Quarterly Review of Biology* 87, no. 4 (December 2012): 325–41.

103 Gilbert, Sapp, and Tauber, "A Symbiotic View of Life," 327–8.

104 Gilbert, Sapp, and Tauber, "A Symbiotic View of Life," 328.

105 Gilbert, Sapp, and Tauber, "A Symbiotic View of Life," 328.

106 Gilbert, Sapp, and Tauber, "A Symbiotic View of Life," 330.

107 Gilbert, Sapp, and Tauber, "A Symbiotic View of Life," 331.

108 Gilbert, Sapp, and Tauber, "A Symbiotic View of Life," 331.

109 Gilbert, Sapp, and Tauber, "A Symbiotic View of Life," 331.

110 Gilbert, Sapp, and Tauber, "A Symbiotic View of Life," 333.

111 Sheldrake, *Entangled Life*, 12.

112 Sheldrake, *Entangled Life*, 147.

113 Sheldrake, *Entangled Life*, 151.

114 See Paul Stamets, *Mycelium Running: How Mushrooms Can Help Save the World* (Berkeley, CA: Ten Speed Press, 2005); Peter Wohlleben, *The Hidden Life of Trees: What They Feel, How They Communicate*, trans. Jane Billinghurst (Vancouver: Greystone Books, 2016). The phrase "Wood Wide Web" first appeared on the cover of an issue of *Nature* devoted to mycorrhizal networks. See David Read, "Mycorrhizal Fungi: The Ties That Bind," *Nature* 338 (1997): 517–18; Suzanne Simard, "Net Transfer of Carbon Between Ectomycorrhizal Tree Species in the Field," *Nature* 388 (1997): 579–82; Sheldrake, *Entangled Life*, Chapter 6.

115 Sheldrake, *Entangled Life*, 52.

116 Sheldrake, *Entangled Life*, 161–2.

117 Sheldrake, *Entangled Life*, 205–6, 214–16.

118 Monbiot, *Regenesis*, 13.

119 Monbiot, *Regenesis*, 17.

120 Monbiot, *Regenesis*, 17; Shamayim T. Ramírez-Puebla et al., "Gut and Root Microbia Commonalities," *Applied and Environmental Microbiology* 79, no. 1 (2012): 2–9.

121 Monbiot, *Regenesis*, 21.

122 Monbiot, *Regenesis*, 22.

123 Monbiot, *Regenesis*, 23.

124 Monbiot, *Regenesis*, 23.

125 Monbiot, *Regenesis*, 24.

126 Monbiot, *Regenesis*, 24.

127 Morton, *Dark Ecology*, 125.

128 Morton, *Dark Ecology*, 130.

129 Elizabeth Marks et al., "Young People's Voices on Climate Anxiety, Government Betrayal and Moral Injury: A Global Phenomenon," Preprints with *The Lancet*, *SSRN*, September 7, 2021, https://tinyurl.com/msmberz3. See also Sarah Jaquette Ray, *A Field Guide to Climate Anxiety: How to Keep Your Cool on a Warming Planet* (Berkeley, CA: University of California Press, 2020); Anouchka Grose, *A Guide to Eco-Anxiety: How to Protect the Planet and Your Mental Health* (London: Watkins Publishing, 2020).

130 Cited in Stephen M. Gardiner, *A Perfect Moral Storm: The Ethical Tragedy of Climate Change* (Oxford: Oxford University Press, 2011), 195. For my view on Gardiner's perspective on the ecological crisis as an intergenerational conflict, see Chapter 1, endnote 119.

131 Cited in Gardiner, *A Perfect Moral Storm*, 194.

132 Günther Anders, *Die Antiquertheit des Menschen*, vol. 1, *Über die Seele im Zeitalter der zweiten industriellen Revolution* (Munich: C. H. Beck, 1956), 301–7, 346–52.

133 Anders, *Die Antiquertheit des Menschen*, 37.

134 See Joanna Many, "Working Through Environmental Despair," in *Ecopsychology: Restoring the Earth, Healing the Mind*, ed. Theodor Roszak, Mary E. Gomes, and Allen D. Kanner (San Francisco, CA: Sierra Club Books, 1995). As a psychotherapist, scholar of Buddhism, and activist in the civil rights, peace, anti-nuclear, and environmental movements, Macy suggests ways of "breaking through" sadness, rage, guilt, and despair. In the case of the ecological crisis, the affects of which are similar to those felt in the presence of nuclear apocalypse, it is a matter of "reconnecting us with the larger web of life" by "working through" and "unblocking" our feelings of pain for the world.

135 Anders, *Die Antiquertheit des Menschen*, 1.302.

136 Anders, *Die Antiquertheit des Menschen*, 303.

137 Anders, *Die Antiquertheit des Menschen*, 316.

138 Like Anders, Jonas does not cite Heidegger as a source of inspiration. This is not surprising, given his break with Heidegger following the latter's Nazism, his rectoral address, and his shameful treatment of Husserl in and after 1933. But it is very difficult to believe that the author of *The Principle of Responsibility* did not have in mind Heidegger's two seminal essays on technology—namely, "The Question Concerning Technology" and "Science and Meditation"—when writing his book. In his memoirs, published over twenty years after *The Imperative of Responsibility*, Jonas describes Heidegger as "the most important thinker of our century" and "the teacher from whom [he] learned more than from any other." See Hans Jonas, *Memoirs*, ed. and annotated Christian Wiese, trans. Krishna Winston (Waltham, MA: Brandeis University Press, 2008), 190. In an earlier chapter, he speaks of Heidegger as a "brilliant teacher" (p. 41), gifted with a "profoundly creative depth of thought" (p. 42), who was "striking out in a new direction" (p. 42).

139 Jonas, *The Imperative of Responsibility*, preface to the English edition (1983).

140 In his *Memoirs*, Jonas praises Heidegger for raising the question of ethics in the age of technology, while rejecting Heidegger's "destinal" interpretation of that event, or the view that technology is the metaphysical *fate* of the West (p. 203). Yet, like Heidegger, he locates the origin of the technological project in modern scientific thought, as exemplified by Bacon and Descartes. He distinguishes clearly the modern, mechanical view of nature from the Greek vision of knowledge, oriented toward the comprehension of nature and the contemplation of eternal essences. Carolyn Merchant holds a similar view in *The Death of Nature: Women, Ecology and the Scientific Revolution* (San Francisco, CA: Harper and Row, 1980). The ecofeminist historian attributes the nature/culture dualism to the scientific revolution, and

especially to Bacon's rhetoric of the domination and control of nature (pp. 168–72). See also C. Merchant, *Reinventing Eden: The Fate of Nature in Western Culture* (London: Routledge, 2003), 1–8. In a more recent article, and in response to some of her critics, Merchant provides ample evidence in support of the view according to which Bacon, and various other scientists and philosophers of his time, saw torture and other coercive interrogation techniques as necessary measures in the extraction of nature's secrets and truths. See C. Merchant, "The Scientific Revolution and *The Death of Nature*," *Isis* 97 (2006): 513–33. See also James Spedding, Robert L. Ellis, and Douglas D. Heath, eds., *The Works of Francis Bacon*, vol. 4, *Translations of the Philosophical Works 1* (Cambridge: Cambridge University Press, 2011), 20, 287, 294.

141 Jonas, *The Imperative of Responsibility*, 139.

142 In this, Jonas disagrees with, and responds to, Ernst Bloch's Marxist utopianism in *The Principle of Hope*, published in three volumes in 1954, 1955, and 1959. We should, Jonas claims, be less concerned with the "not-yet" of our dreams and aspirations, so dear to Bloch, and more concerned with the "too much" of technological production. See *The Imperative of Responsibility*, 202, and more generally chapter 6. This brings Jonas closer to Anders.

143 Jonas, *The Imperative of Responsibility*, 202.

144 Jonas, *The Imperative of Responsibility*, 202.

145 Jonas, *The Imperative of Responsibility*, 27.

146 Jonas, *The Imperative of Responsibility*, 28, emphasis added.

147 Haraway, *Staying with the Trouble*, 1–3.

148 Lovelock, *The Revenge of Gaia*, 3. I return to the crucial issue (and eco-ethics) of care in the next section of this chapter.

149 See Achille Mbembe, *La communauté terrestre* (Paris: La Découverte, 2023).

150 Monbiot, *Regenesis*, 199.

151 See "Duarte Agostinho and Others vs Portugal and 32 Other States," Sabin Center for Climate Change Law, Columbia Law School, https://tinyurl.com/2nmr3t8a/.

152 Convención constitucional, Oficio No. 659, accessed August 24, 2022, https://tinyurl.com/yc8m75xk.

153 Ricardo Rozzi, "Biocultural Conservation and Biocultural Ethics," in *Ecology and Ethics, Volume 3: From Biocultural Homogenization to Biological Conservation*, ed. Ricardo Rozzi, Roy H. May Jr., F. Stuart Chapin III, Francisca Massardo, Michael C. Gavin, Irene J. Klaver, Aníbal Pauchard, Martin A. Nuñez, and Daniel Simberloff (Cham: Springer, 2018), 305.

154 See Philip Altmann, "Sumak Kawsay as an Element of Local Decolonization in Ecuador," *Latin American Research Review* 52, no. 5 (2017): 749–59, https://tinyurl

.com/5ye859vf. See also the new constitution of Bolivia (2009), Constitución Política del Estado, La Paz, accessed August 29, 2022, https://tinyurl.com/2rsmm5a3.

155 LXIV Legislatura, H. Congreso del Estado de Oaxaca, Comisión permanente de estudios constitucionales, Expediente Número 413, accessed August 24, 2022, https://tinyurl.com/mpc8ujc3.

156 Karen Maessen, "Landmark Ruling Upholds Mar Menor's Legal Rights in Spain," accessed May 21, 2025, https://www.earthlawcenter.org/blog-entries/2025/1/in-a-european-first-landmark-verdict-upholds-constitutionality-of-mar-menors-legal-rights.

157 Environmental Law Foundation, "Historic Decision Sees River Ouse Set to Become First in England with Legal Rights," accessed May 21, 2025, https://elflaw.org/news/historic-decision-sees-river-ouse-set-to-become-first-in-england-with-legal-rights/.

158 "L'Appel du Rhône," accessed December 19, 2024, https://en.appeldurhone.org/la-demarche.

159 "Snake River," Earth Law Center, accessed July 18, 2022, https://tinyurl.com/5brkvs4v.

160 Victor David, "'One Ocean' Symposium: Toward a Regional Convention on the Rights of the Pacific Ocean as a Legal Entity," PowerPoint Presentation, August 24, 2019, https://tinyurl.com/5fdsu93r.

161 Carolyn Merchant, "Mining the Earth's Womb," in *Machina Ex Dea: Feminist Perspectives on Technology*, ed. Joan Rothschild (Oxford: Pergamon Press, 1983), 97–119. See also Merchant, *The Death of Nature: Women, Ecology, and the Scientific Revolution* (New York: HarperCollins, 1980).

162 María Puig de la Bellacasa, *Matters of Care: Speculative Ethics in More Than Human Worlds* (Minneapolis, MN and London: University of Minnesota Press, 2017), 150–1.

163 Puig de la Bellacasa, *Matters of Care*, 210; Vicky Singleton and John Law, "Devices as Rituals: Notes on Enacting Resistance," *Journal of Cultural Economy* 6, no. 3 (2013): 259–77.

164 See Monbiot, *Regenesis*, chapter 7.

165 Benjamin C. Bromley, Sameer H. Khan, and Scott J. Kenyon, "Dust as a Solar Shield," *PLOS Climate* 2, no. 2 (February 8, 2023), https://tinyurl.com/4rn8hwhb.

166 See Sam Uden, Paul Dargusch, and Chris Greig, "Cutting Through the Noise on Negative Emissions," *Joule* 5, no. 8 (2021): 1956–70, https://tinyurl.com/ysenadnt.

167 Uden, Dargusch, and Greig, "Cutting Through the Noise on Negative Emissions."

168 Arne Naess, "Ecosophy and Gestalt Ontology," in *Deep Ecology for the 21st Century*, ed. George Sessions (Boston, MA: Shambhala, 1995), 240. See also A. Naess, "The Shallow and the Deep, Long-Range Ecology Movements: A Summary," *Inquiry* 16 (1973): 95–100; A. Naess, *Ecology, Community and Lifestyle: Outline of an Ecosophy*

(Cambridge: Cambridge University Press, 1989). Naess's intuition, some have argued, applies not only to those beings deemed natural and wild, but to all beings and relations, including the relations we find and experience in the built (especially the urban) environment. See Kate Booth, "Holism with a Hole? Exploring Deep Ecology Within the Built Environment," *The Trumpeter* 24 (2008): 68–86.

169 Aldo Leopold, "Land Ethic," in *A Sand County Almanac and Sketches Here and There* (Oxford: Oxford University Press, 1949). Many environmental philosophers consider Leopold's land ethic the first *environmental* ethics (not just *animal* ethics).

170 Historically, the emergence of ecofeminist philosophy was intimately related to deep ecology. As already indicated (see note 15), many ecofeminists began to question this connection in the 1980s and 1990s, in what came to be known as the "deep ecology-ecofeminism debate." But they retained and developed further deep ecology's emphasis on relationality. See Karen J. Warren: "Toward an Ecofeminist Ethic," *Studies in the Humanities* 15, no. 2 (1988): 140–56; "The Power and Promise of Ecological Feminism," *Environmental Ethics* 12 (1990): 125–46; and her main work, *Ecofeminist Philosophy: A Western Perspective on What It Is and Why It Matters* (New York: Rowman and Littlefield, 2000). See also Karen J. Warren and Jim Cheney, "Ecological Feminism and Ecosystem Ecology," *Hypatia* 6, no. 1 (March 1991): 179–97; Carol Christ, "Ecofeminism and Process Philosophy," *Feminist Theology* 14, no. 3 (2006): 289–310; Chris J. Cuomo, *Feminism and Ecological Communities: An Ethic of Flourishing* (London: Routledge, 1998); and Marti Kheel, *Nature Ethics: An Ecofeminist Perspective* (Lanham, MD: Rowman and Littlefield, 2007). The following three articles from *Reweaving the World: The Emergence of Ecofeminism*, ed. Irene Diamond and Gloria Feman Orenstein (San Francisco, CA: Sierra Club Books, 1990), are also relevant: Riane Eisler, "The Gaia Tradition and the Partnership Future: An Ecofeminist Manifesto"; Carolyn Merchant, "Ecofeminism and Feminist Theory"; and Marti Kheel, "Ecofeminism and Deep Ecology: Reflections on Identity and Difference."

171 Unsurprisingly, ecofeminist readings of Heidegger have multiplied in the last two decades. See Nancy Holland and Patricia Huntington, eds., *Feminist Interpretations of Martin Heidegger* (University Park, PA: Pennsylvania State University Press, 2001). From that volume, Trish Glazebrook's "Heidegger and Ecofeminism" is particularly helpful.

172 Walther Schoenichen, *Naturschutz als völkische und internationale Kulturaufgabe* (Jena: Gustav Fischer Verlag, 1942), 1. For a historical account of fascistic ecology, see Clifford R. Lovin, "*Blut und Boden*: The Ideological Basis of the Nazi Agricultural Progam," *Journal of the History of Ideas* 28, no. 2 (April–June 1967): 279–88; and Michael Zimmerman, "The Threat of Ecofascism," *Social Theory and Practice* 21, no. 2 (1995): 207–38.

173 For a conception of soil as a living system, see David C. Coleman, D. A. Crossley, and Paul F. Hendrix, *Fundamentals of Soil Ecology* (Amsterdam: Elsevier, 2004); David Wardle, *Communities and Ecosystems: Linking the Aboveground and Belowground*

Components (Princeton, NJ: Princeton University Press, 2002); María Puig de la Bellacasa, "Encountering Bioinfrastructure: Ecological Struggles and the Sciences of Soil," *Social Epistemology* 28, no. 1 (2014): 26–40; and Puig de la Bellacasa, *Matters of Care*, 188–91.

174 Sheldrake, *Entangled Life*, 18.

175 Gilbert, Sapp, and Tauber, "A Symbiotic View of Life," 336.

176 See Ethan Siegel, "How Many Atoms Do We Have in Common with One Another?," *Forbes*, April 30, 2020, https://tinyurl.com/29faff85.

177 Coccia, *Metamorphoses*, 154.

178 Coccia, *Metamorphoses*, 4.

179 Coccia, *Metamorphoses*, 90.

180 María Puig de la Bellacasa devotes an entire chapter ("Soil Times") to that question in *Matters of Care*.

181 Puig de la Bellacasa, *Matters of Care*, 176.

182 Food and Agriculture Organization of the United Nations, *Building on Gender, Agrobiodiversity and Local Knowledge—A Training Manual* (Rome: FAO-UN, 2006), https://tinyurl.com/37wubc2t.

183 See Daniel Hillel, *Out of the Earth: Civilization and the Life of the Soil* (Berkeley, CA: University of California Press, 1992).

184 Stephen Leahy, "Peak Soil: The Silent Global Crisis," *Earth Island Journal*, April 2008, https://tinyurl.com/2ut968xm. See also Nafeez Ahmed, "Peak Soil: Industrial Civilisation Is on the Verge of Eating Itself," *The Guardian*, June 7, 2013, https://tinyurl.com/59nck232.

185 Puig de la Bellacasa, *Matters of Care*, 173.

186 Cited in Alfred E. Hartemink, *The Future of Soil Science, CIP-Gegevens Koninklijke Bibliotheek, Den Haag* (Wageningen: IUSS Union of Social Sciences, 2006), 7.

187 Jonas, *The Imperative of Responsibility*, 8, emphasis added.

188 Jonas, *The Imperative of Responsibility*, 11.

189 Jonas, *The Imperative of Responsibility*, 11.

190 Jonas, *The Imperative of Responsibility*, 43.

191 Jonas, *The Imperative of Responsibility*, 136.

192 Lukas H. Meyer, "Intergenerational Justice" (3.2), *Stanford Encyclopedia of Philosophy*, April 3, 2003, substantive revision May 4, 2021, https://tinyurl.com/46bhsnfh.

193 See Amartya K. Sen, *Resources, Values, and Development* (Cambridge, MA: Harvard University Press, 1984); David Braybrooke, *Meeting Needs* (Princeton, NJ: Princeton University Press, 1987); David Wiggin, "Claims of Need," in *Needs, Values, Truth: Essays in the Philosophy of Value*, ed. David Wiggins, 3rd ed. (Oxford: Oxford University Press, 1998); Edward A. Page, *Climate Change, Justice and Future Generations* (Cheltenham: Edward Elgar, 2006), 71–5.

194 Martha Nussbaum, *Frontiers of Justice: Disability, Nationality, Species Membership* (Cambridge, MA: Harvard University Press, 2006).

195 Peter Singer, *Practical Ethics*, 2nd ed. (1979; Cambridge: Cambridge University Press, 1993), chapter 10 ("The Environment"), esp. 269–74 ("Future Generations"). See also Peter Singer, "Possible Preferences," in *Preferences*, ed. Christoph Fehige and Ulla Wessels (Berlin: de Gruyter, 1998), 383–98, https://tinyurl.com/5n7wyusw.

196 John Rawls, *A Theory of Justice* (Cambridge, MA: Harvard University Press, 1971), 289, and section 44 more broadly. See also his *Political Liberalism* (New York: Columbia University Press, 1993), 274; and *Justice as Fairness: A Restatement* (Cambridge, MA: Harvard University Press, 2001), esp. sections 49.2 and 49.3.

197 See Meyer, "Intergenerational Justice," 5.2; see also his "More Than They Have a Right To: Future People and Our Future-Oriented Projects," in *Contingent Futures: On the Ethics of Deciding Who Will Live, Or Not, In the Future*, ed. Nick Fotion and Jan C. Heller (Dordrecht and Boston, MA: Kluwer Academic, 1997), 137–56; and *Historische Gerechtigkeit* (Berlin and New York: de Gruyter, 2005), chapters 4 and 5.

198 Donna Haraway, "Situated Knowledges: The Science Question in Feminism as a Site of Discourse on the Privilege of Partial Perspective," *Feminist Studies* 14, no. 3 (1988): 585.

199 Janet Biehl, *Rethinking Ecofeminist Politics* (Boston, MA: South End Press, 1991), 2–4; Baird Callicot, "The Search for an Environmental Ethic," in *Matters of Life and Death*, ed. Tom Regan (New York: McGraw-Hill, 1993), 335–7.

200 Trish Glazebrook, "Karen Warren's Ecofeminism," *Ethics and the Environment* 7, no. 2 (Autumn 2002): 20.

201 Puig de la Bellacasa, *Matters of Care*, 126.

202 Puig de la Bellacasa, *Matters of Care*, 127.

203 Puig de la Bellacasa, *Matters of Care*, 129.

204 Puig de la Bellacasa, *Matters of Care*, 203.

205 Chris J. Cuomo, *Feminism and Ecological Communities: An Ethic of Flourishing* (New York: Routledge, 1997), 126.

206 See Eileen Boris and Rhacel Salazar Parreñas, eds., *Intimate Labors: Cultures, Technologies, and the Politics of Care* (Stanford, CA: Stanford University Press, 2010).

See also Emma Dowling, "The Waitress: On Affect, Method, and Representation(s)," *Cultural Studies-Critical Methodologies* 12, no. 2 (2012): 109–17. In Chapter 4, I also discussed Fraser's critique of women's emotional and physical labor as crucial to the reproduction of capital, yet never valued or recognized as such.

207 Alice Schwarzer, ed., *After the Second Sex: Interviews with Simone de Beauvoir* (New York: Pantheon Books, 1984), 103.

208 The Overman, through whom European nihilism will be overcome, is "the meaning of the earth." The goal and ethical task, at this stage, is to *"remain true to the earth."* See Friedrich Nietzsche, *Thus Spoke Zarathustra*, trans. R. J. Hollingdale (London: Penguin Classics, 1961), prologue, 3.

209 Puig de la Bellacasa, *Matters of Care*, 163.

210 Joan C. Tronto, *Moral Boundaries: A Political Argument for an Ethic of Care* (New York: Routledge, 1993), 103.

211 Puig de la Bellacasa, *Matters of Care*, 161.

212 See also Carol J. Adams and Josephine Donovan, eds., *Beyond Animal Rights: A Feminist Caring Ethic for the Treatment of Animals* (London and New York: Continuum, 1996) and *The Feminist Care Tradition in Animal Ethics: A Reader* (New York: Columbia University Press, 2008).

213 Xavier Albó, *"Suma Qamaña* or Living Well Together: A Contribution to Biocultural Conversation," in *From Biocultural Homogenization to Biocultural Conservation*, ed. Riccardo Rozzi et al. (Dordrecht: Springer, 2018), 339.

214 Peter Vitousek and Kamanamaikalani Beamer, "Traditional Ecological Values, Knowledge and Practices in Twentieth-Century Hawai'i," in *Linking Ecology and Ethics for a Changing World: Values, Philosophy, and Action*, ed. Riccardo Rozzi, S. T. A. Pickett, Clare Palmer, Juan J. Armesto, and J. Baird Callicott (Dordrecht: Springer, 2013), 63–70.

215 Riccardo Rozzi, "Biocultural Conservation and Biocultural Ethics," in Rozzi et al., eds., *From Biocultural Homogenization to Biocultural Conservation*, 306.

216 See the three-volume *summa* by the French anthropologist Dominique Temple, *Teoría de la reciprocidad* (La Paz: PADEP-GTZ, 2003). In his exploration of the idea and practice of reciprocity in Aymara culture, Temple builds on Marcel Mauss's 1923–1924 *Essai sur le don*. I leave aside the question of whether the relation in question is best described as one of reciprocity, as argued by Temple, or as sharing, as described by David Graeber in *Debt: The First 5,000 Years* (New York: MelvilleHouse, 2011). In the end, I don't think the difference is significant. What matters is to see the relationship in question as one of "basic communism," and even as the most basic form of communism, since all other relations depend on it.

217 Albó, "*Suma Qamaña* or Living Well Together," 334. Albó's article is largely indebted to F. Layme's *Diccionario bilingüe aymara castellano* (La Paz: Consejo Educativo Aymara, 2004), which I also consulted.

218 Albó, "*Suma Qamaña* or Living Well Together," 334.

219 Rexroth, "Facing Extinction," 185.

Index

9/11   6, 13, 75, 88

absolute   21, 49–53, 55, 63, 74, 77, 78, 80, 83, 140, 168, 174, 216, 229
affect   16, 27, 43, 85, 91, 152, 178, 186, 203, 219, 234, 238, 242, 249, 267 n.83
affective   16, 49, 214, 215, 241, 242, 256 n.8
affectivity   17, 181, 216, 221, 234, 248, 251
Agamben, Giorgio   73, 76, 88, 115–17
Albó, Xavier, 243, 244
Anders, Günther   190, 216–20, 308 n.34, 314 n.138
androcentrism   302 n.46, 306 n.19
anomaly   61–3, 139, 165
anomie   13, 77, 88, 96, 165
Anthropocene   10, 187, 188, 221, 305 n.11, 306 n.18
anthropocentric   207, 234, 235
anthropocentrism   306 n.19
antinomy   14, 97, 139, 165, 180
anxiety   16, 57, 80, 214–16, 220, 240, 248
aporia   7, 14, 157, 164, 165, 175, 177, 180, 274 n.186
Arendt, Hannah   59–60
Argenson, Marquis d'   26
Aristotle   79
Aristotelian   21, 45, 51, 65
arkhè   153
Arnold, Dick   233
Aufhebung   55, 102, 104, 106, 132
autocatalysis   206
autocatalytic reactions   311 n.87

Avicenna   25
Aymara culture   243, 244, 320 n.216

bare life   88, 89, 92, 241
Bary, Heinrich Anton de   207
Beinhocker, Eric   27
Benjamin, Walter   77, 78, 81, 82, 109, 111, 113, 115–17, 119, 152, 158, 189, 279 n.55
biopower   30, 32, 33, 74, 92, 96
biosphere   3, 14, 15, 55, 184, 185, 188, 191–3, 196, 201–6, 213, 219, 229, 232–6, 238, 244, 251–3, 310 n.72
Bloch, Ernst   315 n.142
Bodin, Jean   21
body without organs   187, 202
Bolshevik   144, 147
boredom   79, 214, 215, 240, 248
Brown, Gordon   26
Burckhardt, Jacob   47, 286 n.2
Bush, George W. administration   88

capitalism   27, 29, 55, 69, 70, 101–5, 107–10, 120, 121, 124–6, 133, 138, 152, 153, 166, 172, 173, 178, 187–9, 252, 270 n.126, 287 n.11, 293–4 n.120
capitalist mode of production   13, 26, 28, 55, 100, 109, 178, 294 n.120
Capitalocene   10, 187, 221, 306 n.18
care   58, 92, 185, 218, 220, 221, 226, 232–43, 287 n.8
Carnegie, Andrew   189
centralism
   bureaucratic   130, 131

democratic 130
   organic 130
Cézanne, Paul 68
chinampas 242, 243
chronology of crisis 161
chronos 15
Clarke, Simon 26, 100
class
   alliance 121
   concept of 117
   consciousness 146, 294 n.120
   determinations 134
   dominant 121, 127, 133
   domination 126
   hegemoni 121
   identity 134
   intellectual 129
   interest 121, 134
   leading 130
   political 108, 216, 247
   relationship 125
   revolutionary 117
   ruling 110, 117, 129, 130
   struggle 116, 125, 172
   subaltern 111, 121, 123, 127, 133
   universal 111, 118, 120, 134, 144
   upper 123
   working 101, 119, 120, 129, 131, 132, 134, 147, 189
classical clinical paradigm 31
classical medicine 23, 24, 31, 33, 41
classless society 117, 144
climate change 92, 187-9, 193, 196, 198, 209, 215, 222, 225, 232, 233
Clover, Joshua 152, 153
Coccia 202, 204, 231
Comintern 131
commodity fetishism 172, 175
Communist Party of the Soviet Union 131
community
   African-American 147
   biotic 228
   of the earth 222, 246
   of interest 122

   scientific 250
contradiction 13-15, 29, 41, 47-9, 51, 53-5, 60, 70, 71, 77-8, 96, 101, 104, 106, 108, 110, 112, 123, 124, 127-9, 132, 133, 136, 139, 151, 163-5, 167, 171, 177, 180, 183-5, 191, 249, 250, 281 n.92, *see also* crises
   concept of 46
conversion 11, 68, 185, 252
cooperation 148, 149, 206, 207, 209, 212, 213, 252, 297 n.176
cooperatives 149, 150, 207, 297 n.176
Cordero, Rodrigo 7, 12, 34
COVID-19 109
crisis: as collapse 14, 185
   as aporia 14, 180
   as contradiction 14, 29, 151, 167, 180
   critical history of 70
   critique of 19, 20, 53, 247, 248
   as deviation 11, 12, 44, 73, 77, 249
   as exception 73, 77, 95
   as extinction 95, 184, 185, 191
   of legitimation 126
   management 12, 32, 124, 227, 233
   regimes of 5, 10, 11, 14-17, 19, 180, 183, 249
   of representation 128
   of sovereignty 6, 13
critical theory 28, 99
critique 9, 10, 17, 19, 20, 28, 29, 35-7, 48, 50, 53, 55, 71, 77, 99, 106, 111, 112, 116, 117, 122, 132, 135, 137-9, 145, 151, 157, 166, 171, 172, 174, 176, 177, 186, 216, 247-9, 264 n.40, 271 n.141, 287 n.11, 293-4 n.120, 306 n.18, 308 n.34

d'Eaubonne, Françoise 191
Dalton, John 274 n.186
Deleuze, Gilles 135-7, 204, 239
Deleuze and Guattari 135, 136
Del Lucchese, Filippo 43, 45
Derrida, Jacques 7, 14, 56, 77, 86, 111, 137, 138, 157-63, 165-77, 179-82, 249

deviation   5, 11–14, 26–7, 29, 31–2, 44, 62, 70, 71, 73, 77, 88, 96, 100, 183, 249, 250, *see also* crises
dictatorship   5, 45, 75–6, 83, 86, 87, 113–17, 120–1, 146, 276 n.11
Dietzgen, Josef   189, 190
différance   14, 170, 176–8, 180
discursive event   12, 33, 94
domination
   class   126
   of nature   306 n.19
   planetary   58
   white   145
   of women   306 n.19
Doyle, Conan   186, 187
Du Bois, W. E. B.   111, 138–49

earth   11, 16, 22, 24, 27, 55, 58, 104, 128, 142, 184–9, 191–3, 197, 199, 201–3, 211, 215, 219–37, 239–43, 245, 246, 251–3, 270 n.126, 305 n.11, 309 n.51
earthworms   212, 229
earthworm zone   212
eco-anxiety   215, 216, 256 n.5
eco-depression   216
ecofeminism   191, 239
   debate   306 n.19, 317 n.170
ecofeminist
   historian   314 n.140
   philosophers   228
   philosophy   239, 317 n.170
   spiritualities   241
ecofeminists   188, 306 n.19, 317 n.170
ecological crisis   2, 11, 14–17, 126, 149, 154, 157, 184, 185, 191, 194, 197, 213, 218, 220, 227, 232, 234, 235, 237, 238, 251, 252, 270 n.126, 306 n.18, 314 n.134
economics   10, 26, 27, 33, 100, 105, 124, 154, 233, 294 n.120
eco-solidarity   246
end of history   1, 4, 15, 166, 171, 174
English revolution   286 n.2
Enlightenment   37, 61, 140, 161, 219

eschatology   1, 5, 166, 171, 179, 180
exception, *see also* crises
   regimes of   70, 87
   techniques of   14
   zones of   91, 285 n.133
exchange value   101, 175, 176, 178, 179
extinction, *see also* crises
   of the biosphere   14
   human   304 n.3
   of species   184, 187, 197

fear   1, 16–18, 51, 91, 116, 131, 140, 147, 191, 219, 220, 248, 252
   spiritual   240
   of war   216
Foucault, Michel   7, 12, 30–2, 34–41, 74, 137, 256 n.6
Fourier, Charles   149, 190
Frank, Albert   37, 38, 206, 207
Fraser, Nancy   99, 109, 110, 124, 126
French revolution   47, 48, 115, 127, 286 n.2
Freud, Sigmund   145, 229
Freudian metapsychology   145
Fukuyama, Francis   1, 2, 15, 173, 257 n.14

Gaia   201–6, 221, 223, 229, 234, 317 n.170
gaiapolitanism   222, 252
Galen   23, 24, 41, 262 n.17, 263 n.22
Gerbier, Laurent   41, 267 n.85
German ordoliberalism   30, 124
German Reformation   286 n.2
German revolution   114
Gilbert, Scott F.   209, 210
Graeber, David   150, 151, 320 n.216
Gramsci, Antonio   99, 101, 111, 121–3, 127–36, 138, 143, 291 n.69
Great Depression   30, 92, 131, 145, 147, 148
Guattari, Felix   2, 3, 15, 135, 136, 239, 244, 253, 256 n.6, 257 n.10

Habermas, Jürgen   99, 123, 124, 126
habitability   187, 199, 227, 229, 245

Hamlet   22, 23, 77–9, 82–6, 157, 160,
   167, 168, 170, 261 n.15, 269 n.108,
   277 n.24, 280 n.63, 302 nn.45–46
Haraway, Donna   209, 221, 239, 241,
   242
Harcourt, Bernard   148–50, 229, 297
   nn.174–175
hauntology   159, 170, 173, 176, 180
Hecuba   78, 79, 84, 85, 168, 277 n.24
Hegel, Georg Wilhelm Friedrich   47,
   50–5, 57, 71, 99, 106, 127, 165, 167,
   171
hegemony   69, 99, 120–3, 127, 129–36,
   138, 151–2, 163, 173, 179, 218, 248,
   257 n.10, 293 n.117
Heidegger, Martin   57, 58, 60, 117, 158,
   159, 163, 215, 216, 228, 229, 245,
   271 n.141, 287 n.11, 299 n.8, 308
   n.34, 314 nn.138, 140
   ecofeminist readings of   317 n.171
Hicks, John   26
Hippocrates   24, 262 n.18
Hölderlin, Friedrich   47, 49, 50, 171, 269
   n.105
holobiont   208–10
Horkheimer, Max   28, 99
Hugo, Victor   259 n.36
Hume, David   36
Husserl, Edmund   56, 57, 60, 159, 271
   n.136, 308 n.34, 314 n.138

ideology   109, 111, 121, 127, 133, 146,
   172, 176
   nonorganic   123, 127
   organic   122, 127
idleness   154, 298 n.194
Iselin, Isaak   1, 255 n.3
Israel   5, 13, 94, 95, 285 n.130, 304 n.4
Italian Communist Party   131
iustitium   73, 74

James, William   80, 82, 83, 141, 145
Jonas, Hans   191, 192, 218–20, 235, 307
   n.30, 30 n.34, 314 nn.138, 140, 315
   n.142

Kahn, Victoria   78, 80, 85
Kant, Immanuel   48, 49, 162, 167, 217,
   235–7, 253, 266 n.63
Kantian   17, 20, 35, 47, 48, 77, 165, 237,
   253
   critique   50, 55
Kauffman, Stuart   200, 310 n.72
Kehre   58, 159
Keynes, Keynesian   26, 27, 30, 124, 264
   n.40
Kierkegaard, Søren   79, 80, 278 n.40
Kolbert, Elizabeth   197
Koselleck, Reinhart   7, 19, 20, 26, 41, 47
Kropotkin, Peter
Kuhn, Thomas   61–3, 65, 68, 69, 151,
   250, 274 n.186

Lacan, Jacques   296 n.158
Laclau and Mouffe   99, 121, 134–6, 138,
   293 nn.117, 120
Lakatos, Imre   60, 61, 63, 69
Lassalle, Ferdinand   189
Latour, Bruno   7, 198, 214
law   10, 11, 20–2, 43, 63, 71, 84, 87, 90,
   93, 96, 97, 101, 105, 106, 113–15,
   125, 144, 158, 161, 162, 165, 168,
   174, 175, 178, 201, 218, 222, 223,
   274 n.186, 282 n.100, 288 n.20
   constitutional   75, 76, 116
   earth   224
   international   90, 165, 174
   martial   73, 75, 120
   natural   21, 51
   rule of   6, 73, 74, 88, 95, 116, 121,
      158, 250
Lenin   121, 142
Leninist Polish United Worker's
   Party   119, 120
Leopold, Aldo   228, 310 n.169
liberal democracy   1, 2, 5, 30, 86, 153,
   257 n.14
liberalism   1, 4, 12, 30, 34, 38, 56, 120,
   145, 173
Liebknecht, Wilhelm   189
Lincoln, Abraham   87, 88

Lovelock, James 198–202, 221
Lowell, James Russell 141
Löwith, Karl 85

Machiavelli, Niccolò 39, 41–7, 53, 268 n.100
Mallarmé, Stéphane 68, 69, 259 n.36
Mandela, Nelson 144, 301 n.31
Marcuse, Herbert 146
Margulis, Lynn 207, 208
Marsilius of Padua 41, 267 n.84
martial: language 92
  law 73, 75, 120
Marx, Karl 28, 29, 55, 69, 71, 78, 99, 101–7, 109, 122, 132, 143, 144, 149, 158, 166
Marxism 28, 62, 99, 105, 129, 131, 134, 146, 166, 170, 172–4, 181
Marxism-Leninism 146
Marxist 28, 29, 53, 60, 86, 100, 101, 105, 129, 134, 138, 144, 146, 165–7, 174, 181, 189, 282 n.92, 287 n.11, 307 n.30
  discourse 7
  thought 101, 286 n.2
  tradition 46
Mary Queen of Scots 82, 85
Mbeki, Thabo 144, 145
Mbembe, Achille 89, 285 n.133
McGuire, Bill 197, 198
medicine 8, 11, 20, 23–6, 31–3, 37, 39, 41–3, 47, 53, 71, 261 n.13, 262 n.18, 276 n.7
Meinel, Fabian 22
Mendelssohn, Moses 266 n.63
mental health crisis 4, 255 n.5
messianism 158, 180
Meyer, Lukas 237
migrant camps 89
minority-becoming 135
minority politics 134, 135
Minsky, Hyman 27
Monbiot, George 192, 194, 212, 305 n.9
Moore, Jason W. 189
Morin, Edgar 6

Morton, Timothy 188, 215
The Mousetrap 84
Mussolini 128
mycelium 211, 231

Naess, Arne 228
necropolitics 92, 96
neo-capitalism 173
neoliberalism 12, 30, 34, 38, 264 n.40
New Economic Policy (NEP) 131
Newman 154
nomos 13, 21–3, 34, 88, 96, 158, 165, 169, 170
normativity
  of the biosphere
  of life
norms 2, 5, 8, 11–15, 38, 42, 44, 47, 57, 61, 63, 64, 76, 77, 88, 96, 97, 100, 108, 116, 133, 135, 139, 142, 145, 151, 155, 162, 163, 183, 184, 186, 191–3, 203, 206, 213, 214, 235, 242, 249, 250, 252, 289 n.20, 296 n.158

Oedipus 21, 49, 50, 198
ontological conversion 11, 227, 252
ontology 173, 227–9, 231, 232, 239
  imperialistic 228
  of interconnectedness 228, 229
  of spectrality 172, 176
Orestes 21, 52

Pachamama 223, 243
Palestine 184, 185
Palestinian sovereignty 95
parrhēsía 37, 38, 40
plasticity 10, 199, 203–6, 213
Plato 38, 39, 175
political economy 11, 20, 26, 30, 32, 55, 70, 105, 166, 172, 176, 181
pono 243
post-coloniality 129
post-kantian 20, 47
  critical edifice 47
  German philosophy 47, 48
Preciado, Paul 257 n.10

Professor Challenger 186, 187, 201
proletariat 3, 115, 117, 120, 121, 131, 134, 136, 144, 146, 190, 293 n.120
   industrial 46
Pufendorf, Samuel von 21
Puig de la Bellacasa, Maria 226, 232, 233, 240, 241

Quichua 243

race 64, 129, 256 n.5
   consciousness 140
   crisis 4
   hate 143, 146
   human 305 n.13
   prejudice 54, 103, 127, 139, 140, 143–8
   problem 138, 142, 147
racism
   institutional 144
   state 96, 144
   systemic 143
Rancière, Jacques 153
reform 29, 44, 45, 100, 110, 143, 252, 266 n.72, 297 n.175, 302 n.46
   economic 121
   policy 26
Reformation 82, 106, 286 n.2
reformism 105
regimes
   of accumulation 71, 109, 110
   of apartheid 285 n.133
   of crisis 5, 10, 11, 14–17, 19, 180, 183, 249 (*see also* crisis)
   of power 2, 19, 96
Reich, Wilhelm 6, 116, 146
responsibility 14, 80, 159, 160, 162–8, 180, 195, 196, 217, 222–4, 234, 236–9
   ethical 219
   moral 218
revolution
   of 1848 190
   of history 36
   idea of 99

   industrial 188, 190, 233, 308 n.34
   Nazi 97
   neoliberal 3
   ontological 232, 234
   peaceful 142
   scientific 61, 63, 65, 66, 68, 151
   technological 226
   technoscientific 225
revolutionary
   action 154
   becoming 136, 138
   classes 117
   communist 62
   conflict 69
   dictatorship 114, 117
   dynamic 110
   force 136
   logic 96
   Marxism 105
   means 153
   moment 113, 117, 181, 259 n.36
   paradigm 145
   position 138
   potential 136
   process 286 n.2
   regime 46
   science 61, 63
   strike 109–12, 119
   violence 113, 115
rhizosphere 212
Ricardo, David 27
Roitman, Janet 6, 9
Röpke, Wilhelm 30, 40, 264 n.40
Rossiter, Clintin L. 87
Rozzi, Ricardo 223
Rudyerd, Sir Benjamin 26
Russell, Bertrand 154
Russian Revolution 143

Sapp, Jan 209, 210
Say, Jean-Baptiste 27
Schelling, Friedrich Wilhelm Joseph 47, 49, 171
Schmitt, Carl 53, 73–87, 89, 111, 113–18, 157, 168–70, 175

Schwendener, Simon   207
Shakespeare, William   78, 79, 83, 261 n.13
Sheldrake, Merli   192, 207, 211, 230
Shelley, Percy Byshe   186
Simondon, Gilbert   204
simulacra   175, 176
singularities   135, 136
Smith, Adam   27
soil   104, 211–13, 220, 226, 228, 229, 232–4, 243, 246
    degradation   188, 189, 195, 307 n.24
    erosion   188, 212
    science   233
soil-caring   240
Solidarity (movement in Poland)   16, 122, 216, 223, 227, 238, 239, 244, 246, 252, 256 n.8
Sorel, Georges   110, 112
spectrality   77, 170, 172–7, 180
Spirit   59, 158, 159, 169, 176
Spivak, Gayatri Chakravorty   136, 138, 294 n.127, 301 n.40
Stakhanov   189
state of exception   6, 13, 21, 73–7, 81, 87–9, 93, 94, 111, 113–19, 129, 158, 162, 168–70, 183, 250, 276 n.10, 278 n.40, 283 n.114
subaltern   118, 136
    groups   121, 123, 127, 139
    position   138
    strata   110
    strategy   109, 111, 131, 133, 139
    voice of the   157
sublime   217, 236, 253
Sumak Kawsay   224, 243
superstructure   122, 123

Swann-Morton, worker cooperative   297 n.181
symbiosis   186, 199, 206–8, 211, 212

Tauber, Alfred   209, 210
Technocene   10, 188, 190, 191, 219, 227, 234, 235, 238, 252
teleology   106, 174, 180, 227
tendency of the rate of profit to fall (TRPF)   101, 105
Thatcher, Margaret   124, 264 n.40
Thunberg, Greta   193
tragedy   11, 15, 20–2, 47–53, 71, 77–81, 84–6, 158, 171, 175, 260 n.36, 261 n.15, 270 n.126, 277 n.24, 278 n.34, 279 n.49, 302 n.45
trauma   50, 91
traumatic   59
Trump, Donald   3, 4, 90

use value   101, 175, 177, 179, *see also* exchange value

Valéry, Paul   56, 161, 271 n.135
violence   15, 18, 46, 58, 74, 76, 77, 80, 91, 96, 97, 106, 111–13, 115–17, 132, 137, 138, 143, 146, 181, 185, 250, 252
    to norms   88
virtual   2, 118, 204–6, 213, 257 n.11

Warren, Karen   239, 241, 317 n.170
Weber, Elke   215, 271 n.141, 280 n.65
Werner, Brad   189
Wilson, Woodrow   139, 140

Yoo, John   88, 89, 282 nn.99–100